Exploring IBM @server zSeries and S/390 Servers

D1558329

Other Titles of Interest From Maximum Press

Exploring IBM Technology, Products & Services, Fourth Edition: Hoskins, 1-885068-62-X

Exploring IBM RS/6000 Computers, Tenth Edition, Davies, 1-885068-42-5

Exploring IBM @server iSeries and AS/400 Computers, Tenth Edition: Hoskins, Dimmick, 1-885068-43-3

Exploring IBM @server xSeries and PCs, Eleventh Edition: Hoskins, Wilson, 1-885068-39-5

Exploring IBM e-Business Software, Young, 1-885068-58-1

Building Intranets With Lotus Notes and Domino 5.0: Krantz, 1-885068-41-7

Exploring IBM Network Stations: Ho, Lloyd, & Heracleous, 1-885068-32-8

Internet Marketing for Your Tourism Business: Sweeney, 1-885068-47-6

Marketing With E-Mail, Second Edition: Kinnard, 1-885068-51-4

Business-to-Business Internet Marketing, Third Edition: Silverstein, 1-885068-50-6

Marketing on the Internet, Fifth Edition: Zimmerman, 1-885068-49-2

101 Internet Businesses You Can Start From Home: Sweeney, 1-885068-59-X

The e-Business Formula for Success: Sweeney, 1-885068-60-3

101 Ways to Promote Your Web Site, Third Edition: Sweeney, 1-885068-57-3

Internet Marketing for Information Technology Companies, Second Edition: Silverstein, 1-885068-67-0

Internet Marketing for Less Than $500/Year, Second Edition: Yudkin, 1-885068-69-7

The Business Guide to Selling Through Internet Auctions: Hix, 1-885068-73-5

For more information, visit our Web site at *www.maxpress.com* or e-mail us at *moreinfo@maxpress.com*

Exploring IBM @server zSeries and S/390 Servers

Seventh Edition

See why IBM's redesigned mainframe server family has become more popular than ever!

Jim Hoskins and

Bob Frank

MAXIMUM PRESS
605 Silverthorn Road
Gulf Breeze, FL 32561
(850) 934-0819
www.maxpress.com

Publisher: Jim Hoskins

Manager of Finance/Administration: Joyce Reedy

Production Manager: ReNae Grant

Cover Designer: Lauren Smith Designs

Compositor: PageCrafters Inc.

Copyeditor: Andrew Potter

Proofreader: Kim Stefansson

Indexer: Susan Olason

Printer: P.A. Hutchison

This publication is designed to provide accurate and authoritative information in regard to the subject matter covered. It is sold with the understanding that the publisher is not engaged in rendering professional services. If legal, accounting, medical, psychological, or any other expert assistance is required, the services of a competent professional person should be sought. ADAPTED FROM A DECLARATION OF PRINCIPLES OF A JOINT COMMITTEE OF THE AMERICAN BAR ASSOCIATION AND PUBLISHERS.

Library of Congress Cataloging-in-Publication Data

Hoskins, Jim.
    Exploring IBM eServer zSeries and S/390 servers : see why IBM's
redesigned mainframe server family has become more popular than ever! /
Jim Hoskins and Bob Frank.— 7th ed.
        p. cm.
Includes index.
ISBN 1-885068-70-0
1. IBM computers. 2. IBM System/390 (Computer) I. Frank, Bob, 1937-
II. Title.
QA76.8.I1015 H669 2001
004.1'25—dc21
                        2001003706

Acknowledgments

I would like to thank the many members of the IBM team who were willing to take time out from their busy schedules to provide technical support and answer my unending list of questions. There were several of those that committed considerable efforts to advise and counsel me such as Marcy Nechemias, zSeries Platform Marketing Pricing Strategy, who was integral in assisting with the software and Linux pricing examples, Jim Goethals, z900 and S/390 Networking Offering Manager, for the networking and communications technical support. George Katopis, z900 Processor Design Team, was so enthusiastic in his help and advice on the z900 packaging technology. Robert Rogers, z/OS Design Team, was supportive and patient with my many questions regarding the z/Architecture. Thanks also to Steven Curtis, Sales and Marketing High-end DASD, and George Bate, High-end Printers, who were so helpful in getting me up to speed with the new DASD and Printers.

A very special thanks to Bill Smith, eServer zSeries and S/390 Marketing Communications, who, throughout this endeavor, enthusiastically acted as my IBM Technical Community contact. His knowledge, guidance and effective rapport with the multiple staffs and Management teams in IBM made my efforts productive and satisfying. Finally, I would like to thank my old IBM colleague, Bernhard Fuhrer now living in Germany who was so willing to share his knowledge and expertise and it was such a pleasure and honor to work with him again.

I would like to acknowledge the willingness of IBM for permitting me to use their images and tables related to the zSeries that are reproduced in this book which are from their IBM eServer zSeries 900 Technical Guide (SG24-5975-00) and IBM eServer zSeries 900 and z/OS Reference Guide (G326-3092-00).

Most importantly I would like to thank my wife, Pat, for her support and patience with all the days and evenings I toiled.

Disclaimer

The purchase of computer software or hardware is an important and costly business decision. While the author and publisher of this book have made reasonable efforts to ensure the accuracy and timeliness of the information contained herein, the author and publisher assume no liability with respect to loss or damage caused or alleged to be caused by reliance on any information contained herein and disclaim any and all warranties, expressed or implied, as to the accuracy or reliability of said information.

This book is not intended to replace the manufacturer's product documentation or personnel in determining the specifications and capabilities of the products mentioned in this book. The manufacturer's product documentation should always be consulted, as the specifications and capabilities of computer hardware and software products are subject to frequent modification. The reader is solely responsible for the choice of computer hardware and software. All configurations and applications of computer hardware and software should be reviewed with the manufacturer's representatives prior to choosing or using any computer hardware and software.

Trademarks

The words contained in this text which are believed to be trademarked, service marked, or otherwise to hold proprietary rights have been designated as such by use of initial capitalization. No attempt has been made to designate as trademarked or service marked any personal computer words or terms in which proprietary rights might exist. Inclusion, exclusion, or definition of a word or term is not intended to affect, or to express judgment upon, the validity of legal status of any proprietary right which may be claimed for a specific word or term.

Table of Contents

Introduction xiv
  What This Book Is xiv
  What This Book Is Not xiv
  Some Historical Background xv
  Your "Members Only" Web Site xx

Chapter 1:
zSeries—Forty Years of Evolution   1

  Do I Need to Worry? 1
  e-Business Evolution 2
    The Next Generation e-Business 4
  What Should I Do? 5
  IBM @server Advantages 6
    Capacity 6
    Availability 7
    Customer Care 7
    Solution Assurance 7
    Financial 7
    System Management 7
    The IBM @server Family of Products 10
      zSeries 10
      pSeries 10
      iSeries 11
      xSeries 11
  Summary 12

Chapter 2:
The Evolution of the S/390 and zSeries 900 Servers   13

  1950s to 1990—The Real Beginning 14
  S/390 1990–2000 20
  zSeries 2000 and Beyond 25

Model Structure 27
Linux Operating System Support 28
I/O Subsystem—Channels and Adapters 29
Bulletproof Security 33
z/Architecture 34
Operating Modes 35
Processor Technology 36
CMOS—The Technology of Preference 41
Processor Elements—Partitions 47
Storage Hierarchy 49
Registers and Cache 49
Central Storage 51
Expanded Storage 51
External Storage—Peripherals 52
Processor Controller 56
Parallel Processing 57
Parallel Sysplex 59
Coupling 64
Coupling Links 69
Geographically Dispersed Parallel Sysplex 70
IBM Sysplex Timer (9037) 71
IBM Fiber Saver (2029) 72
Availability and Fault Tolerance 72
Software—Supporting Business Objectives 77
System Concepts—Bringing the System to Life 80
Batch versus Interactive Processing 82
Multiuser Support 83
Multiprogramming 83
Communications—Connecting the Business 84
Interfaces and Protocols 88
Additional Integrated Function 94
UNIX Services 94
Object Technology 95
Data Management Alternatives 96
Enterprise Multimedia Servers 97
Performance Overview 98
Large System Performance Reference (LSPR) 100
Using the Transaction Processing
Performance Council (TPC) 102
Summary 102

Chapter 3:
Peripherals—Fueling a Revolution   104

Input/Output (I/O) Channel Architecture 106
   Parallel Channels 108
   ESCON Channels 109
      ESCON Directors 113
      ESCON Converters 116
   FICON Channels 118
9729 Optical Wavelength Division
Multiplexor (Muxmaster) 119
Disk Storage 120
   DASD Performance 120
   RAID Technology 121
   RAMAC Array Architecture 123
      Performance Features 125
      Availability Features 127
   Direct Access Storage Device (DASD) Characteristics 128
      RAMAC 2 Array 128
      RAMAC 3 Storage Frame and Drawer 130
      RAMAC Virtual Array 2 (RVA 2) Turbo and Turbo X83 130
      3990 Storage Control 131
   Enterprise Storage Server (ESS) (a.k.a. "Shark") 135
Optical Storage 136
Tape Storage 139
   3590 High-Performance Tape Subsystem 140
   3494 Automated Tape Library (ATL) Dataserver 144
   3490 Magnetic Tape Subsystems 146
Display Stations 147
Printers 148
   Character Printers 149
   Line Printers 150
   Page Printers 151
Serial Storage Architecture 155
   Business Benefits of SSA 155
   Features of SSA 158
      Network Characteristics 158
      Frame Routing 159
      Spatial Reuse 160
Summary 160

Chapter 4:
S/390—zSeries Software   161

Software Compatibility 162
Application Program Compatibility 162
Software Frameworks 163
   The Network Computing Framework 165
Application Programs on the S/390 167
   Prewritten Programs 169
   Cross-Industry Application Programs 169
      IBM WebSphere Software Platform 170
         WebSphere Application Server for OS/390 and z/OS .. 170
         Query Management Facility 173
         Application System 176
         ImagePlus 177
   Industry-Specific Application Programs 179
      SAP R/3 180
      IBM – Siebel Global Strategic Alliance 181
   Custom Application Programs 182
   Custom Application Program Development 183
   Front-Ending Existing Applications 183
   Procedural Application Development Tools 186
   Advanced Application Generator Tools 188
      Object-Oriented Application Development 188
      Support Services for S/390 and
         z900 Application Development 189
      Application Enablers—Extending the API 190
      Transaction-Processing Application Enablers 190
      Database Application Enablers 195
         Relational Database Enablers: DB2 and SQL 195
         Hierarchical Database Enablers 197
      Developing Usable Business Information 200
      Data Mining 204
      Special-Purpose Application Enablers 205
Operating System Alternatives 207
   Evolution of OS/390 208
      MVS/ESA 208
         *Operating System/Multiprogramming
            with Variable Tasks (OS/MVT)* 208
         Operating System/Virtual Storage 2 (OS/VS2) 209
         Multiple Virtual Storage/370 (MVS/370) 209

Multiple Virtual Storage/eXtended
Architecture (MVS/XA) 211
Multiple Virtual Storage/Enterprise
Systems Architecture (MVS/ESA) 213
Multiple Virtual Storage/Enterprise
Systems Architecture, System Product
Version 4 (MVS/ESA SP Version 4) 216
MVS/ESA Version 5 219
UNIX Services 227
SOMobjects for MVS 232
OS/390 233
z/OS Version 1, Release 1 and OS/390 Version 2, Release 10 .. 238
TCP/IP Networking Enhancements 241
Some Exploiters of z/Architecture 242
Migration Considerations 242
OS/390 and z/OS Example 242
VM/ESA and z/VM example 243
LPAR Coexistence 244
OS Release Coexistence 244
Evolution of VM 246
VM/ESA 246
Origins of VM/ESA 248
VM/ESA Version 1 251
VM/ESA Version 2 256
VM/ESA in an Open Systems Environment
(OpenEdition for VM/ESA) 259
VM/ESA Version 2, Release 3.0 262
z/VM Version 3, Release 1 263
Evolution of VSE 264
VSE/ESA 264
Disk Operating System (DOS) 264
Disk Operating System/Virtual Storage (DOS/VS) 265
Virtual Storage Extended/System Package (VSE/SP) .. 267
Virtual Storage Extended/Enterprise System
Architecture (VSE/ESA) Version 1 269
Virtual Storage Extended/Enterprise System
Architecture (VSE/ESA) Version 2 275
Other VSE/ESA Components 277
Other Operating Systems 278
Advanced Interactive eXecutive/Enterprise
Systems Architecture (AIX/ESA) 278

Linux Operating System 278
Transaction Processing Facility (TPF) 280
Distributed Processing Programming
    eXecutive/370 (DPPX/370) 281
Summary 281

Chapter 5:
Communications—Accessing the Data   283

Local Area Networks 284
Distributed Computer Communications 291
    Distributed Networks 292
    S/390 and z900 with Distributed Networks 295
    Open Blueprint Network Services 296
        Communication Services 298
        Network Services 302
        Common Transport Semantics 302
    Transport Services 306
        Subnetworking 306
        Signaling and Control Plane 308
        Systems Management 309
    Communications Options 309
        I/O Channel Controllers and Connectivity 310
            3745 Communications Controller 311
            3746 Model 900 Extension Unit 314
            3746 N-way Multinetwork Controller Model 950 316
            Open Systems Adapter—Express (OSA-Express) 317
            HiperSockets on the zSeries 900 319
        eNetwork Communications Servers 319
            eNetwork Host on Demand 320
        Modems 320
    Summary 321

Chapter 6:
Applying z900 and S/390 to Your Business   322

Choosing Server Configurations 323
Managing Complexity 323
    TME 10 NetView 324
    System Automation 327
    Automated Operations Network/MVS (AON/MVS) 328
    OS/390 and z/OS Network File System (NFS) 328

Tivoli Storage Manager 328
InfoPrint Manager 330
Performance Management 330
Problem Management 331
Business and Security Management 332
Operations Planning and Control/ESA (OPC/ESA) 333
System Display and Search Facility (SDSF)
for OS/390 and z/OS 334
Resource Measurement Facility (RMF) for OS/390 and z/OS .. 336
Global Enterprise Management (GEM) 337
The "Open Business" Policy—Protecting Your Assets 338
Data Preservation Options 339
Backup and Restore 339
Archiving 340
Disaster Recovery 341
Ensuring Real-Time Data Recovery 342
Access Control Options 344
Securing Data in a Distributed Environment 345
Building Your Total Security Solution 347
Evaluating Vendor Offerings 349
Cost Justification 349
Hardware—Lease or Buy? 353
Software Licensing 355
Parallel Sysplex License Charge (PLSC) 357
Indexed Monthly License Charge (IMLC) 359
Workload License Charges 359
Example of Software Pricing Offerings 360
Linux Integrated Facility Example 362
IBM License Manager (ILM) for z/OS 362
IBM Global Finance 363
Integrated Offerings 363
Parallel Server Offerings 363
IBM e-Business Start Now Program 364
Configuration Options—S/390 Multiprise 3000 366
IBM Global Services 367
Education 368
Servicing A System 369
Summary 371

Appendix A: Upgrade Paths 373
Appendix B: S/390 G5/G6 and z900 Relative Performance 377

Introduction

The Internet has suddenly changed the way business strategies and models are implemented. The Customer rules, and the e-business infrastructure must provide dynamic levels of performance, real-time responsiveness, total reliability, application flexibility, and simplified management. With the outlook for growth reaching annual electronic transaction rates of $7 trillion in the next three to four years, with 300 petabytes of information on-line and an increase of half a million new internet users a day, a business must have its server infrastructure in place now in order to participate.

What This Book Is

In early October 2000, IBM announced their new brand of enterprise-class server to address the unique demands of the fast growing e-business with new tools and application flexibility for the next generation of e-business. The IBM eServer zSeries 900, one of the four new IBM eServer platforms, is an advanced technology platform preserving a business's investment in S/390 and ESA/390 while providing, through design, high-performance data and transaction serving in a nonstop e-business environment running mission-critical applications. This book will guide you through the basic technical and functional attributes leading up to and including the S/390 platform. Learning about this evolution will provide a foundation to better understand the value of the new architecture and added functions in the IBM zSeries and z/Architecture. This book will provide an understanding of the hardware, architecture exploiters, peripherals, operating systems, and communications.

What This Book Is Not

This book is not intended to be all things to all people. It is specific to the zSeries Servers but is not a technical reference manual. The book will not devote any time to the 1990s discussion of the pros and cons of a mainframe because those debates have been had and are no longer pertinent. It isn't intended to cover application programs for this platform, although some partner perspectives will be mentioned. Finally, the book will not assume you are a computer professional but will assume that you possess some basic computer knowledge.

Some Historical Background

The notion of the mainframe was introduced very early in the history of computing to differentiate the primary computing system, which supported the most business-critical applications, from those systems performing less critical functions. The term implied a computer system that provided the characteristics most crucial to business operations, independent of vendor and technology. As these computing systems evolved into increasingly large general-purpose systems, they also evolved toward centralized support by Information Technology (IT) organizations with the technical expertise to support and maintain them and the operating systems and applications that ran on them.

As small, personal computers evolved into powerful, interconnected workstations, more and more business-critical applications were supported on distributed networks of workstations from different vendors. With this change, the term "mainframe" became associated more narrowly with the large centralized aspect of its early definition. The concept of being the platform providing business-critical support was overlooked.

In the context of the original intent, powerful System/390 servers continue as business-critical server platforms for many businesses. In that same context, it is also accurate to speak of networks and workstations as part of the server system environment for a growing number of businesses in the 1990s. For these businesses, the mainframe environment is a mix of computing elements that range from powerful workstations, interconnected on local area networks that are in turn interconnected through wide area networks, to powerful centralized servers running new and legacy applications on traditional operating systems.

The demand for powerful servers is increasing, driven by radical changes that are occurring in the way our global society functions. Scientists have evolved their knowledge base at unprecedented rates; industrial capacity has exploded, so far fewer resources are needed to satisfy the needs of far more people; financial institutions operate regularly on a global basis; and now more businesses have moved rapidly to international operations requiring nondisruptive access to corporate data 24 hours a day, 7 days a week. Now the basic unit of society, the family, is dynamically and directly influenced by the same computer literacy factor that has supported the rapid changes in the rest of our society and fueled by the Internet. The price/performance curves of computers—and more important, the access that home-to-business, families, and business-to-business consumers now have via the Internet—are unprecedented. In this global electronically interconnected society the security of personal information and business data is challenged with each transaction. Cryptography, a technology restricted in use by governments and military alliances, has recently been declassified for most of the free world to utilize.

Beginning in the late nineteenth and early twentieth centuries, mechanical invention and innovation laid the groundwork for electronic computers. From the 1940s to the present, ongoing invention and practical application transformed the computing industry from a contributor to science and large business to an essential participant in every dimension of late-twentieth-century life. It is the radical nature of these changes, changes that cut to the root of every aspect of our society, that merits the designation of a New Age.

The extent of the transition that has occurred is perhaps best represented by views expressed by two figures central to the beginning and current states of computing. In the 1950s, as the potential for computing became apparent, IBM's Thomas J. Watson, Sr., expressed his view that there would be a need for no more than a dozen or so large computers to handle the world's needs. In 1995, as Microsoft Corp. launched its Windows 95 product, Bill Gates expressed his expectation of shipping over 100 million copies of the system within the first several months. Today systems operating under Windows potentially have more power than one of IBM's large computers built in the 1950s.

More important than the comparison of today's computing power with yesterday's, however, is the use of that power. Already computing is pervasive. Schools, businesses, and services of all sizes have either installed computers or are quickly looking for ways in which to gain access to them. The home and individuals on the move are the current target of the communication industry with the explosion of connectable wire and wireless, devices, and there is no end in sight for new devices doing new functions. Whether used for home shopping, access to information, or pure entertainment, computers will become an even more dominant aspect of home life in the future. With the demand that these home, personal, and business devices will bring for access to data, the S/390 and especially the new zSeries 900 server, with its new architecturally unprecedented scalability and processing power, will be the natural provider. Technology's ability to bring the power of computers to individuals has broadened total demand and transformed the industry.

Because we are only in the beginning stages of this new emerging age of a globally connected society, it is virtually impossible to determine in what new direction it will lead. It is apparent, however, that computing in one form or another will continue to enable rapid change. Those changes, in turn, will demand flexible, open, and adaptable computing infrastructures that will support users' evolving business needs. In the context of this evolving new age, this book has both a general and a specific purpose. The general purpose is to explore briefly the early days of computing and its early technology. The specific purpose is to look closely at the technology used in the large commercial server environment, popularized by IBM as the System/360 architecture and known today, after more than 40 years of evolution, as the IBM z/Architecture.

It is particularly appropriate to review the evolution of the IBM's eServer zSeries 900 and S/390 servers now, in the context of an industry and technology that is emerging from its adolescence. The z/Architecture now provides the technical capacity to addresses the long-term need for lower overall costs that drives decision making across all layers of the business. The zSeries architecture's flexibility and adaptability, having evolved over four decades, delivers the business benefits of a server platform that fits into a decentralized, open, architecturally mixed, network computing environment.

If there is a single bylaw for businesses IT infrastructure today, a bylaw that affects both the drive for lower costs and the drive for more business value, it is this: Information, not technology, solves business problems. Implicit in that simple statement are two broad issues driving the computing industry in general and IBM's z900Series and S/390 in particular: There is a distinction between data and information; it is information that must drive business goals and objectives. The derivative of this bylaw is that technology is no longer the master driving business decision processes, it is the servant responding to business needs.

The first issue, distinguishing between data and information, is now driving much of the business and management change within IT organizations. In the past, senior executives in many businesses failed to view IT as a strategic asset because it did not provide the business information they needed in a timely fashion, but with the changes that are now occurring in the industry, reaction time is crucial. New applications have to be rolled out in weeks or even days, not months as was previously the case. Network computing, specifically e-business, is a core requirement of today's businesses and will only continue to grow in importance. Many of the technology developments of the last decade, both in software applications and in hardware, are focused on enabling this move from data orientation to the information age.

The second issue, applying the information to business goals, takes the use of information one step further by making it available to the appropriate business users in a form that they can comprehend. This drives much of the business and process change reengineering throughout business functions. Many businesses view managing the flow of information and the flow of cash as the two most critical business processes in the twenty-first century.

As vendors and end users have become more aware of the new age bylaw that information, not technology, solves business problems, the focus has moved from debating the merits of technology to applying them in a cost-efficient manner to meet users' needs.

The emerging new e-business places new demands on all components of server systems. Perhaps the single greatest demand is that of "scalability," allowing incremental growth that meets business needs when and where they exist. In the past, scalability was restricted to growing installed hardware by upgrading to larger and more expensive server models that provided more capacity than needed. Today, there are far more options for individual server families and, more significant, for total business solutions. We have attempted to highlight these practical business options throughout our discussion of the evolution to the IBM eServer zSeries.

Chapter 1 provides an overview of the emerging new e-business issues and the new challenges a business must address in determining the most appropriate server to meet the immediate and future business goals.

Chapter 2 first introduces S/390 by looking at its origin and evolution. Then the relationship of the S/390 to the new zSeries will be described. Although there is significant new function in the zSeries, compatibility with S/390 has been protected, because these two families must coexist in many businesses IT infrastructure for a period of time. We introduce the basic technology and business concepts applicable to this class of server and discuss the latest feature and functional enhancements that make it an excellent business solution for the next decade and beyond.

Chapter 3 covers the peripherals and the connectivity that have emerged and are evolving to support the new server strategy. We include a discussion of some of the newer technologies including Storage System Architecture (SSA), Enterprise Storage Server (ESS) (a.k.a. "Shark"), enhanced Magstar Tape Systems, and new additions to the InfoPrint printing systems.

Chapter 4 introduces these new and enhanced operating systems based on the z/Architecture and the Linux operating system, which is an integral part of the S/390 and zSeries platform. We will describe the coexistence of S/390 with OS/390, VM/ESA or VSE/ESA and z900, and z/OS and z/VM. As always, availability and capacity scalability are required to participate in the new e-business arena and we will discuss new function introduced to manage and control your server infrastructure including costs. We introduce IBM's Network Computing Framework (NCF) as a guide for businesses that will want to integrate traditional applications with their e-business platform to take advantage of their enterprise database.

In today's expanding server environment, a renewed emphasis has been placed on better technologies for providing businesses with faster, more secure, and less expensive communications capability, which includes networks. TCP/IP (Transmission Control Protocol/Internet Protocol) and System Network Architecture (SNA) evolved to Advanced Peer-to-Peer Networking (APPN) and High-Performance Routing (HPR) as a means of interconnecting IBM's server infrastructures. Chapter 5 explores the variety of new network and communications alternatives available for the zSeries and System/390 server.

Choosing and managing these infrastructures is our focus in Chapter 6. Integration of the proliferation of types of servers, ranging from PCs as servers to very large zSeries servers, the large number and types of peripherals required to support very large business computing environments, the diversity of applications and operating systems, and the geographic expanse of networks make this a tremendously complex undertaking, but cost and efficiency pressures make it a critical need. In Chapter 6 we present other business considerations to weigh when evaluating the zSeries 900 and S/390 environment for meeting business needs.

Because this book focuses on the most recent announcement of a new family, the zSeries 900, and the consequent generation-backward enhancements for the S/390 server family, it provides an overview of the relative performance of the models in these families and their upgrade capability for investment protection in an appendix.

The eServer zSeries 900 family and the S/390 family preserve investments made by businesses over the past forty years and position businesses for reaping value for the next decade and beyond. The z900 and S/390 has successfully integrated its forty years of experience with the latest technologies emerging in the new and demanding e-business environment. It represents the means for you to make your business all that you want it to be.

Your "Members Only" Web Site

The S/390 and eServer zSeries knowledge base and offerings change frequently. That's why a companion Web site is associated with this book. On this site you will find the latest news, book updates, expanded information and other related resources. However, you have to be a member of the "S/390 or zSeries Insider's Club" to gain access to this site.

When you purchased this book, you automatically became a member (in fact that's the only way to join). To access the companion Web site, go to the Maximum Press Web site located at *http://www.maxpress.com* and follow the links to the "S/390 or zSeries companion Web site." When you try to enter the companion Web site, you will be prompted to enter a user ID and password. Type in the following:

- For User ID: *zseries7e*

- For Password: *longboard*

You will then be granted full access to the "Members Only" area. Once you arrive, bookmark the page in your browser and you will never have to enter the user ID and password again. Visit the site often and enjoy the news and information with our compliments—and thanks for buying the book. We ask that you not share the user ID and password for this site with anyone else.

1

zSeries—Forty Years of Evolution

The sudden emergence of the Internet has caused businesses to look at their infrastructure and determine what they need to do to be a serious player in this new world where the end user is in command. The new Internet users will very likely reside in a different geography, be it a business office or a personal residence, and will be willing to look nationally if not globally for what they need. They will most likely find more than one source for the goods or services desired, and it is becoming more common that they will have little or no allegiance to any vendor or supplier. If your Web site is not easy to navigate, is slow, or is not available, then with a mere click of the mouse they can move on to a competitor's Web site and in all likelihood you just lost a client—a simple little example, but maybe not so simple or so little.

Do I Need to Worry?

Let's try to put this new business segment into perspective. We have heard a lot of talk about the Web creating an information explosion. You've probably heard some of the numbers: Web usage is growing by half a million users a day, yet less than 3% of the world's population is Web enabled, and only 1% of those are on at any given time. There is purported to be 300 petabytes of information already on-line today and no end in sight. There are forecasts that predict that by the year 2004 electronic transactions will be in the range of $7 trillion. So, is this forecasted $10 trillion Internet economy with 1 billion Internet users destined to suffer the fate the dot-com industry has suffered in the last year? Most assuredly not! The size of this segment may be larger or smaller than the projections, but whatever the actual size turns out to be it will be huge.

It appears that we are in fact faced with managing our business in this chaos. Maybe a better way to describe what we are seeing is a tidal wave: We can see it coming; it's not yet here, but when it hits us we had better be seriously prepared. The only other alternative is to run for cover and not be a player, and that strategy should be considered unacceptable. The important point is, now is decision time and you need to know what your options are to be a serious world-class participant in whatever is behind that tidal wave. There are those who say that we have only seen 3% of the changes that will ultimately result from this e-business revolution. Fortunately, technology is moving rapidly and is expected to be there ready to solve requirements that have not yet even been defined. How big is your investment, and how will you have confidence that what you invest in now will be capable of growing to meet the challenge in a timely fashion? IBM has recognized the demands that will impact IT infrastructure and has marshaled its resources to address emerging new business models and new business segments in support of the customer's challenges. In October of 2000, IBM announced their comprehensive approach to building a flexible e-business infrastructure called IBM eServer, including servers, storage, software, services, and financing.

This book will provide an overview of the new IBM eServer family of products, with a detailed focus on the S/390 and the new IBM eServer zSeries 900.

e-Business Evolution

It is important to understand some of the thinking within IBM that led them to bring their offering forward. In the early to mid-1970s IBM introduced their own intranet system, called VNET, which eventually served upward of 300,000 IBM'ers worldwide as well as many IBM

Vendors. This was probably the first such corporate-wide system to be implemented in any corporation anywhere. It provided any employee with quick access to corporate data, including the phone directory and the organization structure—including names, titles, reporting structure, location, and all contact information. The ability to send a note to any employee became a major time saver because it virtually eliminated typed letters and secretary typing pools.

For a global corporation like IBM, it was a way to avoid the inconveniences of communication across virtually all time zones with the inadequacies of the various national postal systems and the many unreliable national phone systems. Hardcopy internal IBM facility phone books were phased out in favor of the electronic version. It was now easier to reserve conference rooms electronically, and many travel arrangements could be accomplished by VNET. Over a period of time home terminals were introduced, which highlighted a whole new set of opportunities and management challenges. In the late 1980s employees began to have desktop PCs replace their "dumb" terminals, allowing them to access VNET as well as work with applications such as Lotus Spreadsheet. Employees began installing desktop PCs in their home, connecting to the IBM site computer over their phone line, and continuing their work at home in the evenings or when weather conditions prevented them from commuting to their office. Then, in 1995, IBM acquired Lotus Corp. and in 1996 and 1997 began a major conversion effort from their homegrown VM-based VNET system to Lotus Notes Domino.

In the 1994 to early 1997 time frame, IBM took notice of the growing interest in the Internet both in home use and in business. They watched worldwide interest in the Net growing quickly and described this period as one of user novelty with a new, cool technology, enabling them to get connected and surf the Net. Sending e-mail and joining chat rooms was new and exciting. Visiting a Web site meant looking at a static Web page and finding the fax or phone number. Users could then make a phone call or send a fax for more information or to place an order. At this time IBM realized the Internet was about business and decided to view network computing and business strategy as "e-business." This was considered a new business opportunity, and IBM formed a fledgling organization outside of the existing service organizations and allowed it to report directly to the Corporate Office. A general manager was appointed to nurture the endeavor into a contributing mature business unit. Their objective was to establish IBM visibility in this emerging segment of the marketplace. More important, focusing on e-business provided the opportunity to begin to understand clients' infrastructure change requirements in this new market segment and help solve their implementation problems.

The process tried to unite the world of transactions and databases utilizing IBM's industrial-strength systems with the interconnectivity of the Internet. When maturation was deemed to be accomplished, the unit would be moved elsewhere in the organization. During this period the number of companies born on the Web grew quickly. Venture capital was readily available. Web sites were expanded to be interactive— for example, American Airlines allowed their frequent flyer members access to their accounts from their home or office and permitted them to plan and make travel arrangements on-line. UPS offered their clients the opportunity to track their own shipments. FedEx and the U.S. Postal Service soon followed the UPS lead.

Then the phase of just being cool was not enough. Businesses had to be known as reliable and could not afford to be unavailable. There was no room for scheduled down time, there would be no batch window, and the stakeholders began to demand profitability.

The Next Generation e-Business

IBM realized that the changing world required them to alter the way they viewed themselves and their markets. They needed to rethink what the e-infrastructure required for the future. The process had to be fast to design, fast to build, fast to deploy, and fast to scale. It had to be always available, always reliable, and capable of withstanding any level of usage spike. It had to be intelligent, completely secure, flexible, and based on open standards. It had to be real-time, which meant it had to continue running if it needed to be fixed or upgraded. Finally, the infrastructure had to be real-world, which was a recognition that no single product or system would be the answer to all the requirements. The conclusion was that it would take an open, flexible, real-world infrastructure to build, expand, integrate, and scale for this new business environment while still protecting a company's investments in its existing IT infrastructure. Clearly, serious e-business is about an entirely new generation of devices such as smart phones, palm handheld devices, two-way pagers, in-car systems like GM's OnStar system, mobile machines, and appliances with embedded wireless devices. All these devices will have the capability of putting data into and extracting data out of an e-business infrastructure. So now we are back to an earlier realization of a million businesses, a billion people, connected by a trillion devices, all taxing the enterprise. Will your enterprise be ready?

What Should I Do?

In simple terms there are three e-business infrastructure workload categories for which an individual cross section of these workloads will determine the appropriate servers and platforms that will be needed to handle the business requirement.

1. *Data transaction* workloads include complex, integrated transactions and data handling that generate heavy computer loads. The database transaction rates are high, and the databases are expected to be complex. The systems need bulletproof security and absolute reliability because they're responsible for managing core business processes. This is the workload that typifies large banks, insurance companies, airlines, brokerages, and retail companies. The servers that are normally required to satisfy these requirements and offer the highest qualities of service, and tend to be scaled vertically.

2. *Web application* workloads would be expected to perform repetitive, similar transactions such as Web application and content hosting, but must be capable of withstanding unexpected spikes. Web application computing requirements often require a flexible infrastructure that is capable of supporting multiple individual servers that are optimized to specific applications. Servers scaled horizontally typically solve this requirement.

3. *Appliance* workloads are normally composed of an extremely high volume of similar transactions as experienced in managing the network, such as caching, firewalls, load balancing, and network storage. The servers that would be expected to satisfy these requirements would normally be simple to install, simple to run, and simple to manage while being optimized for their individual workload.

In the real world of e-business it must be understood that different users need different solutions. One business may desire to have the flexibility of multiple horizontally scaled servers in a Web application whereas another may prefer to simplify management by consolidating a server farm onto a single data/transaction server system. Some businesses will desire a combination of platforms and systems to handle their varied workloads. In keeping with this conclusion, IBM responded in October 2000 with their IBM eServer strategy, which is a combination of hardware, software, services, and financing that engages the full resources of IBM to meet the challenges of the next generation of e-business.

IBM @server **Advantages**

IBM will assist a business in determining server and platform alternatives in order to satisfy its workload requirements. This service is called the IBM eServer Advantage and is based on helping to fulfill three critical business requirements.

First, new tools for managing a business must be able to manage end-to-end growth while keeping risk and cost in check. To grow an IT infrastructure quickly, but limit the rate of growth of the IT staff and budget, IBM offers tools to assist.

Capacity

To manage unpredictable growth in processing power with minimal risk, IBM offers the ability to pay only for the capacity used. Inactive processor capacity in selected models affords the user the ability to turn on, when unusual peak loads occur, the extra processors already built into the system through Capacity Upgrade on Demand (CUoD) or through Horizontal Capacity Upgrade on Demand, which provides clustered auxiliary servers at a user's site. There are also attractive CUoD offerings for storage. Finally, there is workload pricing (workload license charges) for software on the z900, allowing users to pay for only the software that they use when they use it rather than based on the total system capacity. CUoD and Workload License Charges will be discussed in Chapters 2 and Chapter 6, respectively.

Availability

All IBM eServer products are inherently designed to be highly available. IBM High Availability Services can help ensure that an entire IT system, including middleware, applications, network and some non-IBM hardware and software is running when needed.

Customer Care

IBM provides an industry-leading remote service delivery capability. With permission, IBM can establish a link to the user's system, enabling Web-based capacity and performance monitoring of selected models of the zSeries. The intention is to extend this capability to the whole zSeries family. IBM has enhanced its on-line technical support access and learning services to better serve the users needs.

Solution Assurance

IBM offers their vast industry experience in system and solution testing through a range of free and fee-based packages, services, and offerings for businesses and business partners. These services, coupled with IBM's eServer products, are intended to provide minimum risk and successful implementation of a user e-business solution in the areas of B2B, B2C, e-commerce, and Customer Resource Management (CRM).

Financial

A wide range of financing options, technology upgrades, total solution financing, trade-ins and other financing programs are offered to help the user manage costs. Their financing service covers IBM and non-IBM hardware, software, and services.

System Management

Tivoli e-business systems management solutions for IBM eServer products are designed to manage all of the critical components of an e-business infrastructure such as security, storage area networks, servers, and wireless devices.

The second pillar of the IBM eServer Advantage is application flexibility. This initiative addresses the explosion of attached devices and transactions, and the necessity that those devices and the servers and applications that run them can interoperate.

IBM has fully embraced the open industry standards such as Java, eXtensible Mark-Up Language (XML), and Linux that are at the heart of the e-business evolution. This approach starts with the application framework for e-business, an architectural model based on open standards and proven development and deployment practices that are supported by a portfolio of leadership products such as development tools and middleware, now enhanced with support for Linux and new wireless protocols. This framework has gained wide support from systems integrators and software developers who are delivering applications that run across the IBM eServer family.

The IBM eServer family was chosen to be the IBM vehicle to offer the industry's broadest support for Linux. It is believed that Linux has the potential to be to business applications what the Internet was to networking. As the industry moves to a standards-based applications environment, Linux and open source computing are having a profound impact on software developers worldwide. Since IBM believes that over time, more and more applications will be written in Linux, it is working with the open source community to help build a better Linux that will be capable of supporting more robust, industrial-strength applications. In support of their expectations of Linux importance, IBM is offering a comprehensive tool kit for developing Linux applications on Intel and is deploying them across a full line of IBM eServer products. IBM has 10 worldwide Linux porting centers for prototyping real-world IT environments and pretesting Linux applications.

Additionally, each IBM eServer has the option of shipping with IBM WebSphere Application Server preinstalled and tested. WebSphere is a comprehensive, award-winning, flexible e-business platform based on the application framework that allows one to build, integrate and deploy e-business solutions that are based on business needs, not platform restrictions.

IBM also offers pretested, integrated solutions from industry-leading developers such as Siebel, Ariba, Logility, SAP, Chilisoft, and Hyperion, and more are being added. An example of the recent IBM - Siebel relationship will be described in Chapter 6.

The third and last pillar is the use of innovative technology, which drives leading server performance. The evolution of e-business is predicated on the need for optimized performance to ensure higher user value as with traditional back-office applications, new front-office applications, Web applications, and network management applications.

IBM's answer to this requirement is clearly seen in the eServer family of products. IBM offers the world's most scalable servers, which are capable of enormous growth within each series. One can scale from a 1-way to a 640-way using the world's most advanced clustering technology; another offers a multiple of 330 times in scalability. Leading-edge microprocessor design delivers industry-leading performance and price/performance. IBM's copper interconnects and Silicon-On-Insulator (SOI) processors set records in four different benchmarks. IBM reliability technology includes features such as "phone home," made possible by built-in service processors able to diagnose developing problems and then "phone home" for corrective actions, thus avoiding any business impact. Their cryptographic coprocessor exclusively holds the highest U.S. Government certification for commercial security ever awarded. Pioneering software technology is incorporated for wireless and embedded devices—such as advanced transcoding capabilities to simplify and accelerate the process of translating Web and other data formats for cell phones, PDAs, and pagers, and an XML parser that allows the interchange and analysis of Web data in an open, standard manner.

Let's summarize what we have covered so far. There should be no uncertainty that the Internet growth wave is upon us and the challenge for a business is to be well positioned to participate. IBM has been actively involved in the evolution of the e-business from the beginning. It recognized the opportunity, and over the years has invested heavily ($5.5 billion in research and development) in building experience, skills, and product, financial, and service offerings. The IBM eServer family was unveiled in October 2000 and represented their statement to the industry that having already had experience in more than 20,000 e-business engagements, they recognize the difficulty businesses face in finding the right solution for their enterprise. The most practical solution may well be a combination of these platforms, depending on many factors including the technology platform presently installed, the long-range plans, and budget considerations. IBM has built its offerings around four proven technology platforms that can be deployed individually or in combinations to accommodate any businesses requirements and priorities.

The IBM @server **Family of Products**

zSeries

The zSeries is the first e-business Enterprise Server designed for the high-performance data and transaction requirements of the next generation of e-business. It brings many new features to the industry including Capacity Upgrade On Demand (CUoD) for processors, memory, and I/O. The new zSeries Intelligent Resource Director (IRD) can automatically and continuously reallocate processor, memory, and I/O channel resources in response to user requirements as defined by business priorities. This means that the server is truly a self-managed system. The zSeries offers an awesome range of performance of the z900 processors from a 1-way to a 16-way and up to a 32-way in a z900 parallel sysplex, which provides 640 processors, with 512 processors performing customer workloads and up to 128 processors performing system and backup functions.

The zSeries offers 64-bit architecture for the first time, as well as industry-leading security features. With Linux on the zSeries, it is enabled for a truly open application environment. Mean time between failure on the zSeries is measured in decades.

The major operating systems for the zSeries are OS/390 Version 2, Release 10, VM/VSE, and the new z/OS and z/VM, which fully support the 64-bit architecture. Linux in 31-bit and 64-bit modes runs on the S/390 and the zSeries.

A business's investments in the S/390 G5/G6 servers is protected because they are upgradable to the new z900 and operating system coexistence is preserved. We will discuss these topics in Chapter 2 and Chapter 4.

pSeries

The pSeries offers the world's leading RISC/UNIX performance with large Symmetric MultiProcessor (SMP) scalability, industry-leading clustering advantages, industry-leading Storage Area Network (SAN) solutions, and NT/UNIX workload interoperability. The pSeries 680 is the world's fastest Web server, and its High Availability Cluster

MultiProcessing (HACMP) has been rated the highest availability solution in the UNIX market as well as the fastest UNIX system on earth. The pSeries 680 24-way will outperform a 64-way SUN E1000 by nearly 30% and at a lower cost.

The pSeries 640 and 680 feature IBM's award-winning UNIX operating system, AIX. The pSeries servers will support POWER and PowerPC Linux distributions when they become available.

iSeries

The iSeries is the industry's leading integrated business server for midmarket companies. The "i" in iSeries stands for "integration" and features the series integrated open system functions built into the operating system and pretested for reliable turnkey functionality. Some integrated examples are Web servers (IBM HTTP and the Apache server), Web application server (Web Sphere Standard Edition), Java Virtual Machine (JVM), database (IBM DB2 Universal DataBase for OS/400), communications (TCP/IP), and UNIX (AIX) Runtime Environment (OS/400 PASE).

The iSeries demonstrated outstanding collaborative performance supporting 75,000 concurrent Notes Bench Domino R5 mail users with an average response time of 276 milliseconds. Additionally, the iSeries achieved exceptional Java scalability by exceeding 80,000 operations per second based on the industry standard SPECjbb2000.

The iSeries runs any combination of OS/400, Windows NT or 2000, Domino, or Java applications concurrently, utilizing logical partitioning and the integrated IBM eServer for iSeries.

xSeries

The xSeries offers affordable, industry-standard servers running Windows 2000/NT, Linux, Novell, and other operating systems. The xSeries is a reliable solution for businesses of all sizes. It provides industry-leading single-system reliability, supports mixed operating system workloads, and is the industry's leading turnkey environment.

The xSeries models are available as point solution servers, universal servers, and rack-optimized servers. The point solution servers are targeted for demanding application environments such as Web serving, Web caching, and Network Attached Storage (NAS). The universal servers are designed for scalability to enable maximum internal expansion to meet increasing and varied IT demands. The rack-optimized servers deliver powerful performance in a small package for space-constrained data centers.

Summary

Businesses must be positioned to take advantage of the opportunities and challenges the emerging new e-business presents. The solutions associated with the IBM eServer family of platforms represents decades of proven value and billions of dollars of product and skill development.

This book will focus now only on the IBM eServer zSeries and S/390 families, but it must be understood that a business's server choices are, in some cases, best satisfied with a combination of IBM server platforms, depending on what is currently installed and where the business wants to be in the next few years.

2

The Evolution of the S/390 and zSeries 900 Servers

The evolution of S/390 hardware technology over a period of nearly 40 years and now the new z900 servers demonstrates IBM's commitment to finding solutions to technical problems only now being explored by newer business computing systems. With all of this history, S/390 and the new zSeries continue to demonstrate flexibility and adaptability in supporting the emerging e-business environments.

Beginning with a look back at the evolution of IBM's large computer system architecture, this chapter introduces you to the key elements of the server system environment—processors, peripherals, software, and communications—which are explored in detail in the three chapters that follow. You will also become acquainted with the new architecture and functions that keep these servers the most powerful commercial business systems available.

It is in this context that we look back over 40 years of history, tracing the evolution of System/360, System/370 through the S/390 and now the zSeries, demonstrating that it is still the industry-leading solution for your business. The use of the OS/390 Operating System terminology will be found throughout this book. z/OS Version 1 Release 1 and OS/390 Version 2 Release 10 should be considered functionally equivalent. Where only OS/390 is mentioned it should be understood that the functionality comments apply equally to z/OS and vice-versa unless specifically stated otherwise.

1950s to 1990—The Real Beginning

In the 1950s, IBM helped shape the fledgling computer industry with a line of computers—with names like the 650, the 701, and the 305 RAMAC—based on vacuum tubes (Figure 2.1). (The 305 RAMAC, shown in Figure 2.2, provided the first disk storage in the industry.) During the decade of the 1950s, IBM enhanced these products and continued development of other computer systems—each uniquely designed to address specific applications and to fit within narrow price ranges.

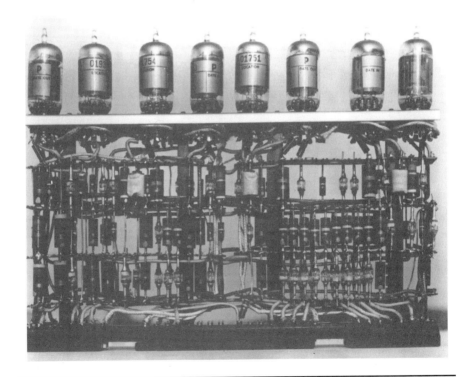

Figure 2.1.   Vacuum tube rack used in Model 701.

Figure 2.2. IBM 305 RAMAC computer system.

This undisciplined proliferation of unique and incompatible computer systems caused confusion, even within IBM's own marketing, service, and software development organizations. The lack of "compatibility" among these systems also made it difficult for users to migrate to new generations of IBM computers.

In 1961 a corporate task force (code-named "SPREAD" to indicate a wide scope) assembled at a Connecticut motel to define a new family of mutually compatible, general-purpose computers. The task force's final report recommended building a new series of computer systems spanning a wide range of price and performance. IBM's senior management accepted the recommendation just a week later, and a new development project was launched.

The first task undertaken by the development team was to define a set of rules—termed an architecture—to which a group of five computers would conform. This architectural definition step was the key to ensuring that all five computer systems would be compatible with one another—a first for IBM. The architecture was completed and documented by the fall of 1962. During this highly confidential development project, the code names for the individual computers in the new family (101, 250, 315, 400, and 501) were the same as those of some computer systems marketed by competitors at that time. Thus, if careless conversation or correspondence were intercepted outside of IBM, the listener/reader would likely think the reference (for example, to a 101 computer) was to one of the competitive products rather than to a secret IBM product.

After defining the architecture, the development team turned to the task of simultaneously designing the five different models that made up the family. Enhanced core memory and a new Solid Logic Technology (SLT) improved performance and reliability. Finally, on April 7, 1964, IBM held a press conference, with over 200 editors and writers in attendance, to announce the IBM System/360 family of computers (Figure 2.3). The "360" in the name referred to all points of a compass to denote universal applicability, a wide range of performance and prices, and the "whole-company" scope of the development effort. A wall-sized compass rose was displayed on the stage backdrop during the press conference.

The work started by the SPREAD task force came to fruition in the System/360. Although the System/360 architecture remained unchanged for six years, just six months after its introduction, IBM executives began to plan for systems that would exploit the emerging MonoLithic Circuit (MLC) technology. By the end of 1965, a draft document defining a new family of computer systems, called "NS" for "new systems," was complete. The new systems were to be based on monolithic circuit technology and an extended System/360 architecture to be called System/370.

In June 1970, IBM announced the System/370 Models 155 and 165. The System/370 architecture preserved upward compatibility with appli-

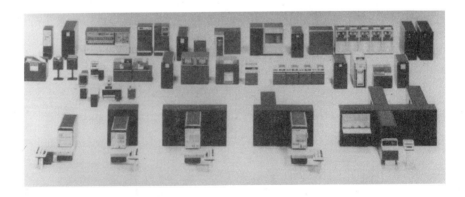

Figure 2.3.   The IBM System/360 family of computers (mainframes in foreground).

cation programs written for the System/360 architecture (that is, applications written to run on System/360 could also run on System/370 systems, but those written for System/370 would not execute on the older systems) and added new capability (an additional mode of operation called Extended Control, or EC, mode). Additional System/370 models were announced in September 1970 (Model 145) and March 1971 (Model 135), rounding out IBM's first wave of System/370 computers.

During the development of the System/370 family, IBM recognized the need to expand the amount of main storage (often referred to as memory) available to application programs. This need led to the development of a second wave of System/370 computers, which implemented a new concept called virtual memory. The virtual memory concept used a level of storage address translation to increase the amount of storage perceived available by application programs. That is, virtual memory made computer systems seem to have much more main storage than they actually did. Virtual memory was publicly announced in August 1972 along with the System/370 Models 158 and 168 (Figure 2.4), replacing the original System/370 Models 155 and 165.

Figure 2.4. IBM System/370 Model 168 computer complex.

The Models 158 and 168 brought the multiprocessing configuration to the System/370 family. With multiprocessing, two or more processors housed in a single computer system cooperate to execute available work. Also announced at the same time were virtual memory options for the Models 155/165 and the disclosure that previously announced System/370 Models 135 and 145 had built-in virtual memory capabilities. By the end of 1976, the addition of the Models 125 and 115 brought the number of announced System/370 models to 17.

Prompted by the still growing need of users for main storage fueled by the increase in interactive processing (in which users hold a dialog with the computer), the System/370 product line was split into two compatible lines: the 30XX series of large systems and the 43XX series of midrange systems (Figure 2.5).

In 1981, the main storage addressability of the 30XX series was quadrupled (up to 64 MB) by exploiting some extra addressing bits available, but not used, in the System/370 architecture. Additional main storage support came with the System/370 Extended Architecture (370-XA), announced in 1981 and first shipped in 1983. The 370-XA increased the main storage addressing capability by 128 times by extending

Figure 2.5.   IBM 4331 computer complex.

the address field from 24 to 31 bits. At the same time, it maintained a 24-bit compatibility mode (upward compatibility), allowing application programs written for systems without this new option to run unchanged.

In February 1985, IBM extended the 30XX series with the addition of the IBM 3090 (Figure 2.6). This series, originally announced with the Models 200 and 400, extended the performance range of the System/370 architecture beyond that of the preceding members of the 30XX series. The 3090 series was later extended and became IBM's large-system flagship. The 370-XA added expanded storage to the 3090. Expanded storage was a new form of processor storage, separate from main storage, used to hold much more information inside the computer. This additional storage resulted in an overall system performance improvement.

In October 1986, IBM extended downward the range of the System/370 architecture with the introduction of the IBM 9370 series of computers. These rack-mounted systems were designed to work as distributed processors in a network of System/370 computers or as standalone computers for smaller businesses or departments. The rack-mounted design of the 9370 systems became a part of the ES/9000 family.

Figure 2.6. IBM 3090 Model 200 computer complex.

The next advance in the architecture came in 1988 with the introduction of the Enterprise Systems Architecture/370 (ESA/370). This architecture again improved virtual storage addressing by adding access registers, which allowed access to another form of virtual storage called data spaces. Data spaces allow more data to reside in main and expanded storage, reducing input/output (I/O) and improving throughput. Other capabilities of the ESA/370 architecture made it easier for information to be shared among the users of the system.

The true test of a computer architecture is in the marketplace. Only by the life or death of the architecture do computer designers really know whether they hit the mark. The longevity and extendibility of the System/360 and System/370 architectures speak highly of their original designers. Bob Evans, Fred Brooks, and Erich Block received the National Medal of Technology at a White House ceremony in 1985 for their part in developing the System/360.

S/390 1990–2000

In September 1990, IBM introduced the Enterprise System Architecture/390 (ESA/390) and the ES/9000 S/390 (now referred to as S/390) family of computers, covering the range of price and performance previously covered by the System/370 9370, 43XX, and 3090 computers. The ESA/390 architecture and the 18 original models of the ES/9000 line again maintained application program compatibility all the way back to the first System/360 computers while enhancing performance and increasing functionality. Like the IBM System/370 family, the S/390 is a family of multiuser systems, meaning that a single server interacts with more than one user at a time (from two users to thousands of users). ESA/390 today includes many newer features, such as ESCON and parallel sysplex (defined later), continuing IBM's evolution of its large business server architecture.

In 1994 IBM announced extensions to the S/390 family, including additions to the ES/9000 line, and introduced new, scalable S/390 parallel processing systems in a parallel sysplex environment. These new processors, known as the S/390 Parallel Enterprise Server, established the parallel sysplex technology in the marketplace. For IBM, two new system directions were set with this announcement. CMOS technology was introduced as a building block for very large servers, complementing bipolar technology, and systems targeting specific application environments, such as transaction and database serving, rather than the full general-purpose environment were introduced. Later announcements extended the CMOS technology to low-end, standalone servers and then to a broad range of servers providing performance that now approaches the older bipolar technology processors, but with the ability to be coupled into parallel sysplexes in which total MIPS (Millions of Instructions per Second) can far exceed those of a bipolar processor. These new models reduced the overall cost of computing for businesses while providing them with greater flexibility.

In April 1994, IBM added three configurations to the S/390 family, moving the S/390 into the world of parallel processing. In these configurations, S/390 microprocessors were installed in Central Electronic Complexes (CECs) that were clustered in frames designed to hold from one to eight CECs. Each CEC supported two to six S/390 microprocessors. The new configurations were the S/390 Parallel Transaction Server (9672), the Coupling Facility (9674), and the S/390 Parallel Query Server (9673).

In late 1996, IBM shipped 13 new S/390 Parallel Enterprise Server models, known as Generation 3. The machines were targeted as replacements for older bipolar machines or for users needing more memory or channel connections. Improvements were also made to the number of processors supported, raising the processor speed and the limit to 10 processors or a 10-way multiprocessor system. At that time, IBM also shipped a new model of the Coupling Facility, the Model C04. The prior Enterprise server models and Coupling Facility were upgradable to the new models.

The G3 machines were the first to include an optional CMOS cryptographic processor, providing more capability than any previous offering, all on a single S/390 chip. The Model RY4 also included one Open System Adapter (OSA 2) on every machine shipped, providing an integrated communications adaptor for the S/390.

For the smaller business environments, IBM introduced the S/390 Multiprise 2000 system and delivered it as a package of both software and hardware. Then in late 1996 IBM announced 13 new models of the Multiprise 2000 systems, with an internal disk feature, OSA 2, and an optional cryptographic processor. These Enterprise Server Offering (ESO) solutions provided users robust S/390 advantages and substantial cost-of-computing savings. They included fully operational, prepackaged solutions aimed at the smaller S/390 enterprise.

In June 1997, IBM announced 14 new Enterprise Server models, known as Generation 4, which were positioned as replacements for most bipolar machines. IBM also announced a new Coupling Facility model, the Model C05, providing improved processor performance and speed on the Coupling Facility links in a parallel sysplex environment. Once again, the prior 9672 and 9674 models were generally field upgradable to the new models. The new models supported more memory and included the cryptographic processor as a standard feature.

In October 1997, IBM announced 15 new models of its Multiprise 2000 systems, increasing capacities over those of the prior models. In May 1998, IBM began shipping the Generation 5 or G5 processors, which represented at least a doubling in processor power over the G4 models. The largest of the 18 new models, a 10-way G5 processor, could sit on just a single square meter. The key to this dramatic reduction in size was a new advance in CMOS technology that permitted up to 10 CPs to reside on a single MultiChip Module (MCM). Basically, all the computing power resided in a single board. (See Figure 2.13.) The G5 MCM contained 29 chips, but its capability was equivalent to over 12,000 chips on 28 boards in the 9021 models.

In May 1999, IBM began shipping the Generation 6 or G6 processors, the last enhancement to the S/390 server series. In relation to the G5 generation, the new G6 models provided a number of improvements. The performance was increased, with a cycle time reduction over the G5 from 2.0 ns to 1.57 ns on the Turbo models and 2.6 ns or 2.4 ns to 1.8 ns on the standard models, and the G6 was now able to scale from a 1-way to a 12-way. The G6 models contained two versions of the MCM, which reflected different cycle times and SAP content. Both the standard and turbo models contained 14-PU MCMs, permitting up to 12 PUs to be utilized as Central Processors (CPs) and therefore function as a 12-way. With Capacity Upgrade on Demand (CUoD) combined with S/390 Parallel Sysplex, the G6 is capable of nondisruptive growth from 1 to 384 engines. More details on CUoD will follow in this chapter. The G6 Turbo models contained the advanced Modular Cooling Unit (MCU).

The models at the top of both the standard and turbo model tower did not contain a spare CP and as a result Capacity BackUp (CBU) was only available through "emergency" target models or through temporary fast upgrades, all of which are disruptive. New high-bandwidth fiber FICON (FIber CONnection) channels were introduced on the G5/G6 servers. They supported up to 24 FICON channels. A detailed description of FICON appears later in this chapter. Finally, the maximum main memory was increased from 24 GB to 32 GB. The G5 R and Y models were selectively upgradable to the G6 X and Z models. You can see the upgrade paths within the S/390 family and out of the family in the appendix.

IBM positioned the S/390 family in roles never before envisioned, such as the server for applications such as Lotus Notes and database server for SAP R/3. The S/390 would also be the centerpiece of Internet access to enterprise data via the World Wide Web using Lotus Domino, supporting thousands of concurrent connections with its initial release. The S/390 fully supported UNIX and LANs, and subsequently print server functions would support Windows NT applications. IBM viewed systems management, network management, security, balancing of heterogeneous workloads, and data management as strengths of the S/390 family in the server environment.

What characteristics make the IBM S/390 family different from the System/370 family of computers? Initially, the major differences were in the performance range offered and in the architectural enhancements, such as the Enterprise Systems CONnection (ESCON) Architecture, the Cryptographic Architecture Facility, subsystem storage protection, VM Data Spaces, S/390 Data Compression, DB2 Sort Enhancement, and the ESCON Multiple Image Facility (EMIF)—all introduced with the ESA/390 architecture and implemented in the S/390 family. Since then, major architectural changes—including coupling, parallel sysplex, integrated cryptography, and FICON channels—have carried System/390 processors into the new age of network computing.

The Enterprise Systems CONnection (ESCON) Architecture, first introduced on S/390 servers, set them apart from their predecessors. ESCON is a set of rules that define how I/O devices, such as storage subsystems, control units, or communications controllers, are attached to processors in the ESA/390 architecture. ESCON employs fiber-optic cables, which carry light waves (photonics) rather than the traditional electrical signals (electronics) used in System/370 channels. The use of photonics allows for higher-speed information flow between I/O devices and the channel subsystem. Further, the use of photonics allows I/O devices to reside from 3 km to 60 km away from the processor unit, depending on the I/O device, the ESCON channel type, and the cabling configuration. FICON (FIber CONnection) was a major improvement on ESCON. It utilizes the same fiber-optic cables but is capable of handling up to eight times as many I/O operations as ESCON, up to 4,000 per channel per second. Also, it extends the connectivity distance to 43 km without a repeater. There is a more detailed description of FICON channels, including the most recent enhancements, later in this chapter.

The S/390 Cryptographic Facility is implemented in S/390 servers with one chip in the MCM as the Integrated CRyptographic Feature (ICRF). This feature is used to encrypt and decrypt information in the S/390 computer. Users can store, access, and transmit scrambled information to prevent its unauthorized access. There is a more detailed description of cryptography in the section on the z900 Series in this chapter.

The S/390 family has an electronic version (CD-ROM) of manuals that allows the user with a properly equipped personal computer to look up information with the help of computer-based keyword searches. Also, the PR/SM facility, which allows the system operator to divide a single S/390 computer into what appear to be several independently operating computer systems, is standard with all models.

- *Subsystem storage protection* helps prevent storage violations of subsystems such as CICS. It is standard on all S/390 processor models that support parallel sysplex. Software support is provided by OS/390 and the CICS/ESA subsystem.

- *VM Data Spaces architecture* provides for data space implementation in a VM environment. VM Data Spaces architecture is standard on all S/390 processors.

- *S/390 Data Compression*, standard on all processors supporting parallel sysplex, provides for hardware compression, executed in microcode, which requires about one-fifth the number of processor cycles of software-only compression.

- *The Asynchronous Data Mover Facility (ADMF)* uses the I/O processor to move large amounts of data between central and expanded storage more efficiently, freeing the central processor for other work. Up to a 20% reduction in elapsed time for selected DB2 query applications is realized by using ADMF rather than Direct Access Storage Devices (DASDs).

- *DB2 Sort Enhancement* allows for implementation of DB2 Sort algorithms in hardware. It provides improved DB2 performance and is standard on all processors supporting parallel sysplex.

- *The ESCON Multiple Image Facility (EMIF)*, also standard on all processors supporting parallel sysplex, reduces cost, and simplifies Logical PARtition (LPAR) configurations. It allows sharing of ESCON channels and a coupling link (needed for parallel sysplex environments, described later) among multiple PR/SM logical partitions, reducing the configuration connection requirements.

IBM evolved the S/390 family to be a more open computing environment, one in which it operated with other computing platforms using industry standards adopted by the Open Software Foundation (OSF). IBM later positioned the S/390 family as servers, based on the strengths of the S/390 architecture, and continued to improve its price and performance. The final additions to this family, based on new technology and targeted application environments, launched the S/390 family into these new roles. The installed base of S/390 servers will continue to provide outstanding solutions to existing business requirements and is the platform most businesses will move from when upgrading to the new IBM eServer zSeries.

zSeries 2000 and Beyond

In October 2000, IBM announced and began delivery of the new zSeries servers based on the new 64-bit z/Architecture. The new line of servers is made up of 26 air-cooled CMOS 8S models from 1-way to 16-way. In a z900 Parallel Sysplex up to 32 z900s can be coupled, resulting in as many as 640 processors employed, with 512 of them able to perform user workload and the remaining 128 processors available to perform system and backup functions. The z900 Processor Unit (PU) MCM can contain either a 12-PU or a 20-PU version (Figure 2.7) with a cycle time reduced to 1.3 ns on all models. As a result, a dramatic increase in available performance over the S/390 G6 servers is obtained through cycle time improvements and the increased MP configuration to 16-way. The z900 performance, in terms of Millions of Instructions Per Second (MIPS), ranges from 250 for a 1-way up to over 2,800 for a 16-way system. Although it is commonly used as an indication of performance, MIPS is not a good indicator of any given user's work throughput. It is, at best, a means of performance capability comparison for one

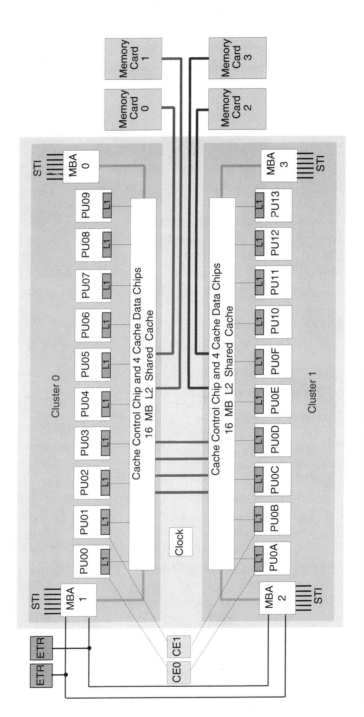

Figure 2.7. z900 20-PU MCM structure.

computer relative to another. Large System Performance Reference (LSPR) performance comparisons, covered later, should be used for real work throughput comparisons.

Model Structure

The z900 is made up of 16 general-purpose server models (Figure 2.8), Models 101 to 116, 9 Capacity server models, Models 1C1 to 1C9, and one standalone Coupling Facility (CF), Model 100. All multiway models are Symmetrical MultiProcessors (SMPs). The z900 general-purpose servers, Models 101 to 109, utilize the 12-PU MCM and two memory cards, and up to 32 GB of storage with entry storage of 5 GB. The remaining general-purpose servers, Models 110 to 116, and the Capac-

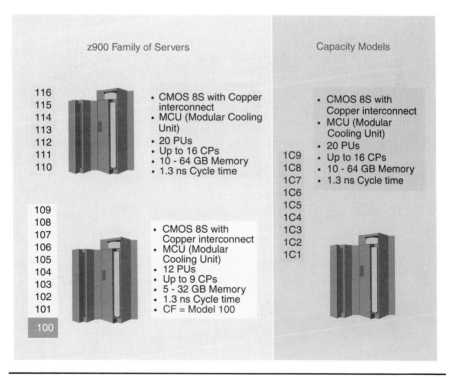

Figure 2.8. Models in the z900 family of servers.

ity servers, Models 1C1 to 1C9, all utilize the 20-PU MCM and four memory cards, 3 SAPs (System Assist Processors), up to 64 GB of storage with entry storage at 10 GB, and up to 24 STI links for I/O attachment. Any of the spare PUs on the MCM can be assigned as a CP (Central Processor), SAP, Integrated Coupling Facility (ICF) or Integrated Facility for Linux (IFL).

The general-purpose Models 101 to 109 can easily upgrade from one model to the next through Capacity Upgrade on Demand (CUoD), but the available upgrade paths to the Models 110 to 116 require a system outage. The Models 110 to 116 can easily upgrade from one model to the next through CUoD and support Capacity BackUp (CBU) with several exceptions. In the case of the Models 109 and 116, should a PU fail, it cannot support CBU, because this would result in the last spare PU being utilized breaking the minimum configuration requirement. The Capacity models are upgradable one to the next through CUoD and CBU or can be upgraded to a 16-way z900 without a system outage. The advantage of the Capacity models is to provide a business expecting to eventually exceed the capacity of the Model 101 to 109 range to easily upgrade to the bigger models. This explains why they were built with the 20-PU MCM technology. The standalone CF, Model 100, uses the 12-PU MCM, permitting up to 9 CF engines. The new zSeries standalone CF offers improved efficiency over the S/390 9672 R06 and in addition provides significant memory capacity. The z900 CF Model 100 can be upgraded to the z900 general-purpose models. The 9672 R06 can be upgraded to the z900 CF Model 100.

Linux Operating System Support

In December 1999 IBM declared its intent to support in an industry-leading way the Linux operating system through the release of special source code for the G5/G6, and the S/390 Virtual Image Facility for Linux (VIF)became a reality. It will also operate in conjunction with the S/390 Integrated Facility for Linux (IFL). This feature provides additional capacity to run Linux workload without increasing the G5/G6 model designation. The importance of maintaining the same model designation is the savings in software charges associated with the model type. In the case of S/390, the installation required a simple restore from a 3480 tape medium to a 3390-3 disk device. After installation an initial Linux image must be obtained from a Linux for S/390 distribution such as those provided by SuSE or TurboLinux, then installed and booted.

The VIF can help the business consolidate Linux and/or UNIX workloads currently deployed on multiple servers onto a single S/390 server while maintaining the same number of distinct server images. VIF interacts with all existing S/390 servers or when data and applications are located on the same S/390 server, and can utilize all the management, communication, storage, and channels that server offers. The z900 support for Linux enhances what is available on the S/390. The IFL on a z900 is a PU used to run Linux or Virtual Image Facility (VIF) for Linux images. Up to 15 optional orderable IFLs are available, depending on the z900 model. The model limitation is the number of available PUs (12 or 20) and their use by subtracting model defined CPs, standard SAPs, a minimum of one spare PU, and defined optional SAPs, ICFs, and CBUs. Using this algorithm the Models 109, 116 and 100 provide no IFL option. All IFL processors within a configuration are grouped into the ICF/IFL processor pool where no ESA/390, z/Architecture, or TPF operating systems can run. Because only Linux or VIF for Linux can run on these PUs, the server model number is not affected and software licensing charges are also not affected by the addition of IFLs. Running Linux as a guest of z/VM enables the user to run nearly unlimited number of Linux images and get the benefit of the zSeries reliability, availability, and serviceability. There will be further discussion of the Linux operating system in Chapter 4.

I/O Subsystem—Channels and Adapters

A channel subsystem provides a versatile way to attach optional devices—providing the server access to the communications network or DASD, using devices such as a 3745 Communications Controller, OSA-Express, or a 3990 Storage Control. It is necessary to attach external devices to a server to make a complete computer system, but the choice of devices depends on the user's needs.

Support for attaching I/O subsystems is housed in the S/390 processor unit or in the bottom of the A-Frame in the z900, under the Modular Cooling Units (MCUs), which contain the Central Processor Complex (Figure 2.9). More technical descriptions of MCMs and MCUs will follow in the technology discussions. The z900 has a new and improved

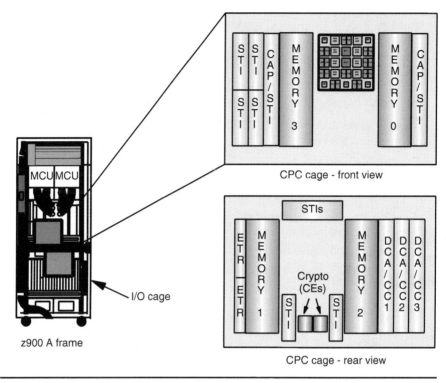

Figure 2.9. z900 A-Frame.

I/O subsystem infrastructure utilizing a new I/O cage (feature code 2023) containing 28 I/O slots compared to the 22 slots in the G5/G6 style cage. All new FICON (up to 32 channels on 16 cards, maximum of 96 supported), ESCON (256 ESCON channels using new 16-port ESCON cards), and OSA-Express cards plug into the new nI/O cage, standard in the new A-frame, provide a subsystem with about seven times higher bandwidth than the G5/G6 I/O cage. The new z900 HiperSockets feature provides "Network in the Box" functionality that allows high-speed any-to-any connectivity among OS images without requiring any physical cabling. The TCP/IP traffic travels between images at memory speed rather than network speed. This concept minimizes network latency and maximizes bandwidth capability between or among z/VM, Linux, and z/OS images. HiperSocket performance improvements are estimated to be up to four times that of OSA-Express Gigabit LPAR to LPAR latency. The z900's new I/O cage offers an enhanced OSA-Express design with dual-port density occupying only a single I/O slot.

The new Open Systems Adapter–Express Gigabit Ethernet, Fast Ethernet, and 155 ATM features deliver a balanced system solution, maximizing throughput and minimizing host interrupts. In addition to the increased port density, the new OSA-Express Gigabit Ethernet feature has the performance-enhanced 66 MHz, 64-bit PCI infrastructure for significantly improved interactive workload performance. The OSA-Express Fast Ethernet and 155 ATM features are capable of achieving line speed with their 33 MHz 32-bit PCI infrastructure. It should be noted that the previous G5/G6 OSA-Express features are not supported on the zSeries 900. In addition, there is a 22-slot compatibility I/O (cI/O) cage for parallel channel (the 4-port card is the same as in G5/G6 and allows a maximum of 88 parallel channels), OSA-2 Token-Ring and FDDI, and ESCON 4-port cards. When upgrading from a G5/G6 model, only ESCON 4-port cards are used.

All I/O cards and their support cards can be hot-plugged in the nI/O cage, but installation of an I/O cage remains a disruptive MES, so the business should consider using the Plan Ahead feature when ordering a z900 server. An optional I/O Frame, Z-Frame, is attached to the A-Frame and can accommodate up to two of the new nI/O cages, up to two cI/O cages, or a mixture of both. The Z-Frame can be configured in several ways, depending on whether the z900 was a new build or upgraded from an S/390 G5 or G6. The details are not required for the purposes of this book, but it is important to understand that the use of cards from a G5 or G6 in combination with new cards can be accommodated and will determine the feature code number and quantity of Z-Frames, either feature code 2023, 2022 or a combination of the two. Figure 2.10 is an example of a two-I/O-cage (A- and Z-frame) configuration for ESCON and FICON channels.

There is a new 4-port ISC-3 card consisting of a mother card and two daughter cards, each having two ports. Each of these ports is capable of operating at 1 Gbit/s in Compatibility mode or twice that speed in native mode up to a distance of 10 km. ISC-3 distances can be extended to 20 km by an RPQ card, and ISC-3 runs in Peer mode at 1 Gbit/s.

The FICON I/O architecture was announced in May 1998 along with the introduction of the S/390 Generation 5 models and was delivered on G5, along with the G6 models, a year later. It was determined that a better I/O channel architecture than ESCON architecture was required to support data-intensive applications and to keep pace with technological advances made in other areas such as faster servers and greater server capacity, disk capacity, and communications bandwidth

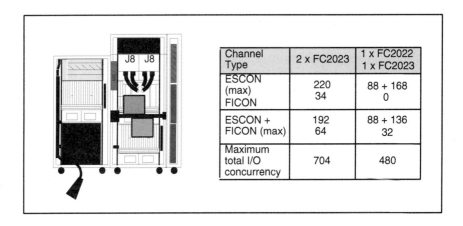

Channel Type	2 x FC2023	1 x FC2022 1 x FC2023
ESCON (max) FICON	220 34	88 + 168 0
ESCON + FICON (max)	192 64	88 + 136 32
Maximum total I/O concurrency	704	480

Figure 2.10. z900 two-I/O cage configuration.

as with Gigabit Ethernet. Business Intelligence (BI) applications with vast amounts of data required fast data transfer. Separate databases for decision support and Online Transaction Processing (OLTP) existed, and to accommodate BI applications the databases needed to be combined to offer excellent response times for Internet commerce dealing with large data types as in audio, video, and imaging. It was helpful to offer clients CD music sampling before they made a purchase, to show images of available parts, or to use videos in marketing. Businesses were also going through a period of recentralization of IT servers and were realizing the ESCON addressability limitations. FICON architecture was an important solution to the evolving channel requirements, and FICON channels are considered the channels of choice for the new zSeries.

Fiber cable has been mentioned many times in this chapter, and now would be a good time to discuss the types of fiber that most businesses already have or will have installed and in use. We will use the FICON channel as the format, but the concepts apply wherever fiber cable is utilized. There are two FICON channel card types available on a z900. The first is a Long Wave card (1300 nm) Fiber Optic Sub Assembly (FOSA) technology, which can achieve an unrepeated distance of 10 km (20 km with an RPQ) using single-mode 9-micron (mm) fiber-optic cabling. Alternatively, 62.5-mm or 50-mm fiber-optic cable can be accommodated by use of a Mode Conditioner Patch (MCP) cable. In this environment the maximum unrepeatable distance is 550 meters.

The second choice is a Short Wave card (850 nm) Fiber Optic Sub Assembly (FOSA) technology having an unrepeated distance of 550 meters using multimode 50-mm fiber-optic cable or 250 meters using multimode 62.5-mm fiber-optic cable. It must be remembered that a 9-micron fiber-optic cable is single mode. To get duplex mode with 9-mm fiber requires a pair of 9-mm fiber cables, one for outgoing data transfer and one for incoming. For performance reasons the fiber cable installation should include more than one pair of 9-mm cables and at least a pair of 50-mm or 62.5-mm cables. You may encounter a reference to 125-mm fiber cables, which are actually 62.5 mm cables with an outside cladding diameter of 125 m. This type of fiber cable is armored sheath multimode used as backbone cable operating in short-wave (minimum bandwidth of 160 MHz-km) or long-wave (minimum bandwidth of 500 MHz-km) modes. Normally there is a limit of one splice per 500 meters.

Data transfer in the ESCON environment is half-duplex, which allows the data to travel in only one direction at a time. In the ESCON environment only one controller can perform an I/O at a time. In a FICON environment with multiple control units connected to a single channel there can be multiple concurrent I/Os and they can travel in both directions, so FICON is full-duplex capable.

The 9032 Model 5 ESCON Director will support FICON channels with the installation of a FICON Bridge card on the Director. Native FICON implementation is enabled on the new FICON Tape Controller 3590 A60 (MAGSTAR) and on Shark, the new Enterprise Storage System (ESS). New FICON directors will be made available through resellers, McDATA and INRANGE.

Bulletproof Security

E-business applications increasingly rely on cryptographic techniques to provide the confidentiality and authentication required in this demanding environment. IBM invented the Data Encryption Standard (DES) in the 1970s and now deliver the only integrated cryptographic hardware in a server to achieve the U.S. Government's highest Federal Information Processing Standard (FIPS) 140-1 Level 4 rating for secure cryptographic hardware. IBM's industry-leading high-availability CMOS Cryptographic Coprocessors feature for the z900 general-purpose models, other than the Models 101 and 1C1, are delivered as a pair of Single

Chip Modules (SCMs), removed from the MCM where it was located in G6, and plugged directly into the rear of the new Central Processor Complex (CPC) backplane. This approach allows them to be individually serviceable, which avoids the potential for system outage.

The Models 101 and 1C1 use only one cryptographic coprocessor. Sixteen additional cryptographic coprocessors can be accommodated with the eight optional Dual Peripheral Component Interconnect Cryptographic Coprocessor (Dual PCICC) features. With these features installed, the server is capable of supporting 2,000 SSL transactions a second. As an example of this level of throughput, it would require 39 S/390 G6 engines running SSL clients to equal this rate of requests over an intranet network. The CMOS cryptographic coprocessors are physically secure because they are designed for a tamper-sensing and tamper-responding environment to fit the requirements of sensitive applications. Upon detection of physical attack, including penetration, radiation, voltage, or excessive cold or heat, the device is "zeroized" and the sensitive information erased. Each cryptographic coprocessor has a primary path to a PU and an alternate path to a second PU, with only one path active at a given time. The two PUs assigned as paths are the last to be configured as CPs, SAPs, ICFs, or IFLs, which increases the likelihood that these PUs will be available as spares.

z/Architecture

The new z/Architecture may well be considered the largest architecture change since the introduction of the IBM S/360 nearly 40 years ago. z/Architecture allows a zSeries 900 server to achieve unprecedented scale in memory addressing, which results in the elimination of the central storage to expanded storage page movement overhead associated with a large single system image. The user need not understand the design intricacies at this time, but some understanding of the functional differences and the inherent ease of migration, hardware, and software is important for a business's consolidation and investment plan for servers.

Full LPAR and VM support for 64-bit guest operating systems is integrated, and the combination of multiple 64-bit guests or data spaces allows the architecture to satisfy any imaginable main memory growth for the coming decade and beyond. z/Architecture allows independent exploitation of 64-bit real or virtual storage. As noted earlier in this chapter, addressing is trimodal, accommodating 24-, 32-, and 64-bit addressing coexistence. All general registers are expanded from 32 to

64 bits, enabling full upward compatibility. Newer 64-bit programs can invoke older S/390 programs without changing program linkage. Operating system support (31-bit and 64-bit) and operating system and hardware migration considerations will be discussed further in Chapter 4.

Operating Modes

In ESA/390 Architecture mode, storage addressing is 31 bits, allowing an addressing range up to 2 GB. That permits a maximum of 2 GB for central storage usage. Because processor storage can be configured as central and expanded storage, the processor storage above 2 GB would normally be configured and used as expanded storage. In this mode both 24-bit and 31-bit addressing are permitted under program control, which allows existing applications to run on a z900 server.

In z/Architecture mode the storage addressing is 64 bits, allowing for addressing up to 16 exabytes (16 EX), and all can be used as central storage. The current available z900 implementation is limited to 64 GB of storage, and you should expect this to incrementally increase up to the architectural maximum in the future. Only z/VM is able to use expanded storage in z/Architecture mode. z/OS will not address the configured expanded storage if so configured.

In Coupling Facility mode, storage addressing is 31 bits, which permits addressing up to 2 GB, and storage above 2 GB can be configured and used as expanded storage as in ESA/390 mode.

In LPAR mode the storage is not split into central and expanded storage at Power-On-Reset (POR) time. At this time storage is considered a single central storage pool that is dynamically assigned to Expanded Storage (ES) and back to Central Storage (CS) as needed. Logical partitions are defined to have CS and optional ES as before, while partition activation as well as dynamic storage reconfigurations will cause LPAR to convert storage to the type needed without POR. LPAR Dynamic Storage Reconfiguration (DSR) on general-purpose models of the z900 can occur, allowing nondisruptive add or removal to any partition with a cooperating partition. This new capability removes the restriction that storage reconfigurations are only possible from an adjacent and above logical partition.

In summary, the S/390 Generation 5 and Generation 6 server's usefulness has been maintained because they can, when running OS/390 R10, coexist alongside the zSeries and there are upgradable paths to a z900 server. The zSeries offers new levels of flexibility to the enterprise to speed deployment of e-business solutions while offering best-of-breed security options and new levels of automated management. The new 64-bit z/Architecture affords traditional partitioning and guest support capabilities while eliminating the system overhead experienced in 31-bit architecture, caused by the 2 GB addressing ceiling and high rates of paging. The improved I/O subsystem design from 8 to 24 GB/s is capable of minimizing potential I/O constraints and supports high-speed storage and communications networking devices. The increased bandwidth, coupled with more FICON channel capacity, allows for faster data transfer in and out of the server. The z900 coupling link bandwidth can now support requirements up to 100 MB/s for shorter distance Integrated Cluster Bus (ICB) links and as high as 200 MB/s for ISC links, continuing to offer the industry-leading clustering solution in the parallel sysplex implementation.

The balance of this chapter provides an overview of IBM S/390 and eServer z900 technology, design concepts, and functionality. Equally important to a fully functioning server system are the peripherals and software, operating systems and software subsystems, and communications that make these systems work. These later subjects will be introduced as concepts in this chapter but will be covered in depth in Chapters 3 through 5.

Processor Technology

Fortunately, knowing the details of what makes up the computer system you use daily is no more necessary than understanding the inner workings of your car's carburetor. However, it will help you to have a fundamental understanding of the general elements that comprise a system in the S/390 or z900 family, because the S/390 will be an active part and reside alongside the z900 in many businesses' IT infrastructure for years to come, and many of the S/390 design concepts will be employed for years.

The basic building blocks of computers are computer chips. Chips house thousands of small circuits, which are created and connected together using lithographic techniques. Figure 2.11 shows a silicon wafer consisting of many small chips (seen as small square areas on the wafer). Many different types of chip technology have been used in the

Figure 2.11. Silicon wafer with chips visible on the surface. Each chip is cut out separately and mounted on a ceramic substrate.

S/390 family. Rack-mounted ES/9000 processors employed IBM's Complementary Metal Oxide Semiconductor II (CMOS II) to implement the ESA/390 architecture in just nine chips. The larger ES/9000 processors used a new generation of IBM's Advanced Transistor Technology (ATX), based on the Emitter-Coupled Logic (ECL) transistor configuration. This version of ATX houses nearly 6,000 ECL circuits, four layers of metals, and 1-micron lithography, with more than 600 pad connections—a chip density twice that of predecessor chips. This higher density reduced the capacitance of connections, providing for a 30% improvement in circuit speed.

Another type of memory chip technology, called Static Random Access Memory (SRAM), was used in high-speed buffer areas of ES/9000 processors. The SRAM chips stored over 64,000 bits of information and were fabricated using lithographic techniques that created circuit elements 1 micron in size. These high-speed memory circuits stored or recalled information in 2.5 ns (2.5 billionths of a second). Some chips used in ES/9000 processors combined different technologies such as ECL and Differential Current Switch (DCS) to best meet the performance needs of the design and to keep power requirements, and thus cooling requirements, to a minimum. Other storage areas, including central storage, were built using IBM's 4 MB memory chip. This chip employed a combination of CMOS II technology, advanced lithography, and a trench capacitor memory cell to create an extremely dense memory chip. This chip was able to store or recall information from any one of its over 4 million storage locations within 65 ns.

The chips were then mounted in modules and packaged on a circuit card in rack-mounted ES/9000 processors or mounted on a ceramic square called a substrate in frame-mounted ES/9000 processors. Built within this substrate were the copper wires that made the necessary electrical connections between chips.

Once the ceramic substrate was populated with chips, the substrate was encapsulated into a structure called a Thermal Conduction Module (TCM), shown in Figure 2.12. The TCM carried the heat generated by the many chips on the ceramic substrate away from the chips and disposed of it outside the computer system. The TCM did this by pressing a spring-loaded metal piston against the top of each chip on the ceramic substrate. These pistons absorbed the heat and pulled it up to the cold plate, where it is dissipated into either circulating air in air-cooled-frame ES/9000 processors or circulating chilled water in water-cooled-frame ES/9000 processors. In ES/9000 processors, four TCMs housed more circuitry than six of the TCMs used in IBM 3090 systems.

The combination of these technologies was formerly used by IBM to build its largest computers. The technology is often referred to as bipolar technology. During its last years, many improvements enabled bipolar technology to decrease the processor's cycle time. Simply put, at the heart of every processor is a system clock that provides the time reference, or heartbeat, setting the pace for all processor activities, including each step in the execution of a program. One pulse or beat of the system clock is called a machine cycle, and the time duration of one machine cycle is called the system's cycle time. Consequently, a lower cycle time means it takes less time for the processor to execute a cycle. The amount of work a processor can accomplish is directly related to that processor's cycle time. The fastest bipolar large processor was ultimately the 9021 711 models at 7.1 ns.

Figure 2.12. Thermal conduction module (TCM) used in ES/9000 processors. A portion has been cut away to provide a view inside.

Thirty years of experience with bipolar technology significantly improved the performance of these systems. However, bipolar technology matured and was no longer used in IBM's S/390 computers. Further cycle time improvement had reached the point where the investment required was out of line with the result. Another major factor in the maturing of bipolar technology was the cost associated with removing the heat produced by high-speed, densely packed circuits. In bipolar technology, power is permanently applied to save time in executing a logical operation. Each logical operation (executing a Add, Compare, or Decode instruction, for example) uses a set of cells (a circuit) on a chip.

The combination of continually applying power and the dense packaging of many chips generates large quantities of heat. Too much heat causes the circuitry within the chip to fail. This problem led to two design limitations, which contributed to the eventual move away from bipolar technology. First, the heat restricted the density of circuits designed into bipolar chips, reducing both the maximum chip size and the number of useful circuits in a chip. Second, cool air, even forced through the processor at high speeds, was not adequate for removing the heat. Chilled water, with all of the associated plumbing, was required to maintain the heat on the chip at the appropriate level. The invention and subsequent evolution of TCMs (discussed earlier) as heat sinks used to carry the heat away from the chips was a major investment (both for IBM and the users), necessary for making bipolar technology practical for the ES/9000 generation.

The growing cost and complexity of continued use of bipolar technology coincided with the gradual evolution of a new technology—CMOS. Already in 1982, IBM was actively redesigning the System/370 processor to use industry-standard Very Large Scale Integration (VLSI) CMOS technology. This technology supported chips containing up to 450,000 circuits, more than needed to implement an entire S/390 processor. In CMOS technology, power is only applied during an actual logical operation, saving energy, lowering heat, and removing the need for artificial forms of cooling (forced cold air or water cooling).

The circuitry of a single bipolar processor requiring over 400 bipolar chips with 4 water-cooled TCMs could now be replaced with 4 CMOS chips and one MultiChip Module (MCM). A system requiring 24 TCMs and 6 highly complex, very heavy boards supporting the TCMs could now be built on a single processor card in a single cage, built into half of a frame. An even more dramatic comparison is illustrated in Figure 2.13. The advantages of moving to CMOS packaging was readily apparent.

By the mid-1980s, CMOS was introduced into the lower range of large processors (several models of the 9370 family and the ES/9221 family used CMOS technology). Since the introduction of those processors, IBM has invested in reducing the cycle time associated with CMOS technology. Today, CMOS cycle times are far superior to those reached through bipolar technology. As a comparison, the 7.1-ns cycle time of the bipolar 9021 711 models wasn't surpassed in the S/390 CMOS processors until 1996 in the Generation 3 models, in which the cycle time ranged from 6.6 ns for the RA4-RC4 models to 5.9 ns for the RY4 model.

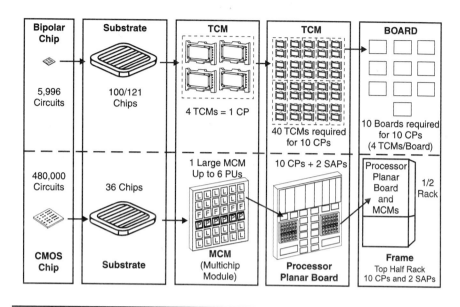

Bipolar Chip	Substrate	TCM	TCM	BOARD
5,996 Circuits	100/121 Chips	4 TCMs = 1 CP	40 TCMs required for 10 CPs	10 Boards required for 10 CPs (4 TCMs/Board)
480,000 Circuits	36 Chips	1 Large MCM Up to 6 PUs	10 CPs + 2 SAPs	Processor Planar Board and MCMs — 1/2 Rack
CMOS Chip	Substrate	MCM (Multichip Module)	Processor Planar Board	Frame Top Half Rack 10 CPs and 2 SAPs

Figure 2.13. 9672 Model R3 CMOS microprocessor packaging advantage.

CMOS—The Technology of Preference

The CMOS technology continued its evolution with increasing levels of compact, integrated, and sophisticated packages, often referred to as multichip modules. Where earlier packages contained 4 chips, subsequent packages evolved to 8 and then to as many as 31 chips in the G6 servers. In the earliest packages, only one of the four chips was a Processor Unit (PU), which acted as a Central Processor (CP) or as a System Assist Processor (SAP) dedicated to I/O processing. Later packages contained 2 PU chips, then 6, 8, 10, and growing to 12 or 20 on the same module. Each MCM, in addition to the actual processor, contained the Level 1 (L1) cache for temporarily storing data, the Control Store (CS) for storing microcoded hardware functions, and a Floating-Point (FP) assist processor (originally two chips). The floating-point processor provides significant performance improvements in floating-point instructions. In later models, the L1 cache and CS were included on the PU chip, and a Level 2 (L2) processor cache chip was added to improve the processor's performance.

This packaging represents only the base package, the first level of what evolved into "book and cage" packaging for some CMOS processors and board and frame packaging for the largest CMOS processors. Figure 2.14 illustrates the various packaging levels used in the early entry-level CMOS processors, the R1 models. In this design, up to 7 MCMs, containing 1 to 6 central processor PU chips and 1 PU chip dedicated to I/O processing (SAP), are placed on 1 processor card. Two memory cards, with up to 1 billion bytes (1 GB) of memory, are also placed on the card. The R2 models support up to 7 central processor PU chips on a card. The newest models support 20 central processor PU chips.

The cards (similar to a board found in a personal computer) are packaged in a booklike container that is plugged into the cage, referred

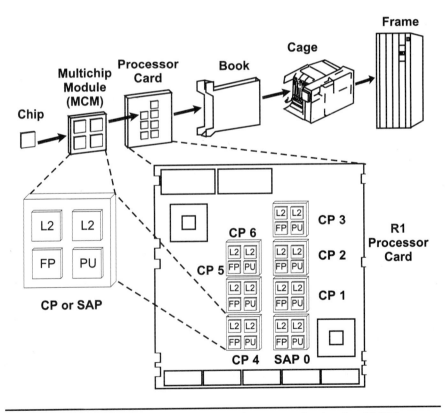

Figure 2.14. Example of 9672 "book and cage" packaging for CMOS processors.

to as a Central Electronic Complex (CEC), just as you would place a book on a shelf. The processor card together with equally compact channel and coupling cards (discussed in Chapter 3) and power regulators make up the building blocks in the cage.

Figures 2.15 and 2.16 illustrate in more detail the capability of the earlier levels of CMOS technology, introduced in IBM's largest CMOS processors in 1995. Both the 9672 R2 and R3 models used the same CMOS microprocessor, which fits on a single very dense but cool chip (labeled PU). On the same 14.5 × 14.5-mm PU chip are 16,000 bytes (16 KB) of level 1 cache, 32 KB of control store, and over 400 contact points (signals) for I/O handled through the SAP.

The chip is bonded to a standard ceramic substrate (approximately 7.45 mm thick) measuring 44 × 44 mm for the earliest R1 modules, 64 × 64 mm for R2 modules, and 127 × 127 mm for R3 modules. Chips are attached to the substrate using the Controlled Collapse Chip Connection (C4), which uses very small solder balls in a grid to provide a high number of signal paths into and out of the chip. This substrate, the base for the MCM, contains 42 layers of electronic circuitry used to connect

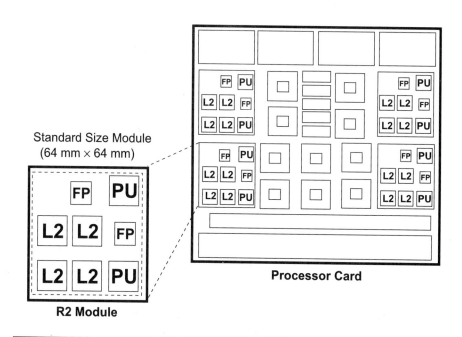

Figure 2.15. 9672 Model R2 CMOS microprocessor module and card.

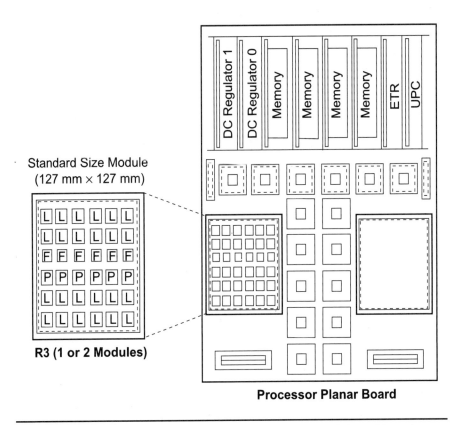

Figure 2.16. 9672 Model R2 CMOS microprocessor module and board.

the PU, L2, and Floating-Point (FP) chips. Although bipolar technology had evolved to glass substrate, which supports higher densities, IBM opted to use the more economical design until higher densities were required.

The R1 modules place both the PU chip and the processor storage (referred to as central storage or main memory) on the same module. R2 modules contain two Level 2 (L2) cache chips supporting each PU. The L2 cache resides between the standard L1 cache (located on the PU chip) and central storage (main memory). Two memory cards and I/O cards on the R2 models are plugged into the same cage as the processor card, which provides the path from the PUs to the memory cards. This integration allows the R2 models to operate with only one card cage. Located between the four processor MCMs on the processor card are single-chip modules providing communication and memory functions for the processors.

Four L2 chips support each PU on the larger R3 module. Again, the L2 cache resides between the standard L1 cache (on the PU chip) and main memory. Instead of sliding the processor card into a book, R3 models support one or two large processor MCMs plugged onto a planar board (a flat panel containing multiple levels of embedded electrical circuits used to connect modules), which provides a high-speed path to up to 4 memory cards from up to 10 CPs and 2 SAPs. The planar board also holds two DC power regulator cards, the External Time Reference (ETR) card (discussed later in this chapter), and the Universal Processor Controller (UPC).

In R3 models, the logic units are packaged in books and plugged into the Central Electronic Complex (CEC). A cage for holding I/O cards is located in the bottom half of the frame. These I/O cards are placed into the cage the way a book is placed on a shelf. You can remove and replace I/O cards "on the fly" without having to shut down the system. This is referred to as "hot plugging" cards.

The CMOS MCM technology has evolved through the multiple generations of S/390, ending with the CMOS 7S MCM on the S/390 G6 models, which has been extended over to the z900 as CMOS 8S, with improved cycle times and utilizing the same dual processor design as introduced on the 9672 G6 servers. As you have seen, the S/390 generation servers are at times referred to by their numerical model name, starting with 9674 and later changing to 9672 for the G5 and G6. Although not often used in the description of the z900, the models are named 2064. The explanation for the last two digits (64-bit architecture) is obvious. Each PU is the dual processor design and each processor contains one Instruction Unit (I-Unit) and one Execution Unit (E-Unit) and includes the floating-point function (Figure 2.17). The Compression Unit is now implemented on the PU chip, providing better hardware compression performance than the 9672 G5/G6, where it was implemented in microcode. The z900 MCM substrate is 127 mm × 127 mm and contains 12 or 20 PUs, CMOS 8S chips, each containing its own 512 KB Level 1 cache (split into 256 KB for data and 256 KB for instructions), the Storage Control Element (SCE) with 32 MB of L2 cache split into two clusters, a clock chip, and 4 Memory Bus Adapters (MBAs), which connect I/O through 24 Self-Timed Interconnects (STIs) (Figure 2.18). The 20-PU MCM contains 35 chips of which 30 are CMOS 8S, and the 12-PU MCM has 23 chips of which 18 are CMOS 8S.

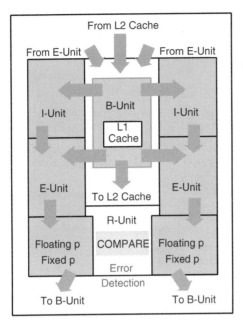

Figure 2.17. z900 dual processor design.

In the z900 the Cryptographic Element (CE) is implemented as a CMOS 7S Single Chip Module (SCM), external to the MCM, but mounted on the same board. The standard configuration provides two cryptographic coprocessor elements. The second acts as a spare, so that should there be a failure the spare is automatically recovered by the operating system avoiding any user disruption. The board, mounted in the Central Processor Complex cage, the upper half of the A-Frame (see Figure 2.19), contains one MCM, two Cryptographic SCMs, four Memory cards (two on the 12-PU MCM models), which are plugged two in the front and two in the back of the board, and Dual External Time Reference (ETR), two half-high cards plugged in the back. All of this is cooled by dual Modular Cooling Units (MCUs) mounted above the CPC. It may be helpful to summarize the comparison of the characteristics of the z900 and the S/390 G6 servers described so far (Figure 2.19).

The use of CMOS technology has provided the user with another important but often overlooked advantage. The physical footprint reduction consistent with the introduction of the G3 series to about one

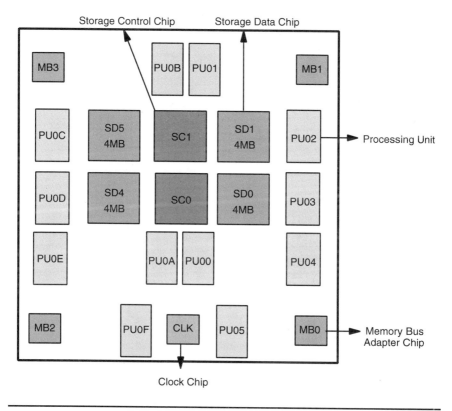

Figure 2.18. 12-PU MCM.

square meter has resulted from the designers' ability to maintain the MCM board at essentially the same physical dimension. This consistently small footprint should be expected to continue for the foreseeable future, allowing businesses to more easily do the physical planning and experience minimum data center disruption when upgrading from generation to generation.

Processor Elements—Partitions

Even when a single computer system employs multiple central processors, it appears to the system operator and users to be a single system (presents a single-system image). Conversely, any S/390 or z900 server,

	z900	G6 / G6 Turbo
Maximum number of PUs	20	14
Maximum number of CPs	16	12
Maximum number of ICFs	15	11
Maximum number of IFLs	15	11
Number of Standard SAPs	3 (2 on 12-PU MCM)	2
Minimum Number of Spare PUs	1	0
L1 Cache size	512 KB	
(256 KB Data + 256 KB Inst.)	256 KB	
Shared L2 Cache size	32 MB	
(16 MB on 12-PU MCM)	16 MB	
Cycle Time	1.3 ns	1.8 ns / 1.57 ns
Maximum Memory capacity	64 GB	32 GB
Number of STIs (bandwidth)	24 (1 GB/s)	24 (333 MB/s)
Maximum I/O throughput	24 GB/s	8 GB/s

Figure 2.19. Characteristics of z900 and S/390 G6 servers.

regardless of the number of central processors, can be divided logically into parts so that it gives the appearance of multiple computers to the users and to the system operator. This powerful feature makes it possible to provide multiple isolated images, all running on the same physical hardware. This is called logical partitioning, and it is facilitated by the Processor Resource/Systems Manager (PR/SM), provided as a standard feature. With PR/SM, a single G4/G5/G6 or z900 server can be divided into as many as 15 Logical PARtitions (LPARs) or 10 partitions with earlier S/390 generations.

Storage Hierarchy

As defined earlier, central processors actually manipulate the data as necessary to do work for the user. The rest of the computer system basically feeds information (programs and data) to the central processor or accepts information from it. If the rest of the computer system cannot keep pace with the central processors, the system is constrained and overall system performance is reduced. Thus, the rest of the computer system must be carefully balanced with the central processor(s) for maximum efficiency. To achieve balanced performance in a cost-effective manner, most computer systems employ several types of information storage devices with varying performance levels. In other words, they have a storage hierarchy. (Figure 2.20 illustrates an example of storage hierarchy)

The whole purpose of the storage hierarchy is to respond as quickly as possible to the central processor's relentless requests for the retrieval and storage of information. To achieve this, the system constantly adjusts and moves information among the different levels of the storage hierarchy, placing the information most likely to be needed next as high in the hierarchy as possible. The movement of information among the top four layers of the storage pyramid is primarily managed by the central processors and the central storage circuitry.

The computer system's full performance potential is realized only when information is kept as high in the storage hierarchy as possible. For this reason, each S/390 and zSeries server should be configured (or tuned) to provide the correct amount of each storage type for the environment in which it is used, something not always easy to predict. As the environment changes, it may become necessary to expand various lower levels of storage to keep the system running at its best.

Registers and Cache

The highest level in the storage hierarchy, registers and then cache, was described earlier as part of the CMOS MCM design description, but it is important to understand their importance in the storage hierarchy. At the top of the storage pyramid are the registers, which are very fast circuits inside the processor units that hold only the programming in-

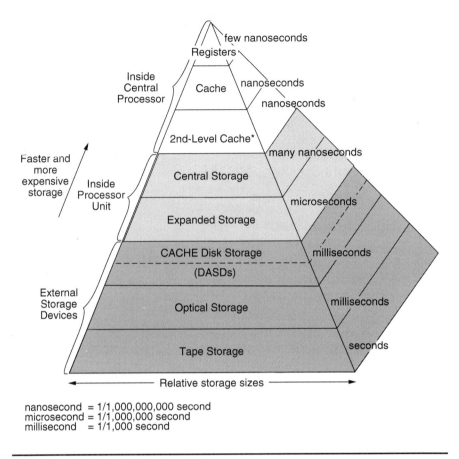

few nanoseconds

Registers

Inside
Central
Processor

Cache   nanoseconds

nanoseconds

2nd-Level Cache*

many nanoseconds

Faster and
more
expensive
storage

Inside
Processor
Unit

Central Storage

Expanded Storage   microseconds

CACHE Disk Storage   milliseconds

(DASDs)

External
Storage
Devices

Optical Storage   milliseconds

Tape Storage   seconds

←—————— Relative storage sizes ——————→

nanosecond = 1/1,000,000,000 second
microsecond = 1/1,000,000 second
millisecond = 1/1,000 second

Figure 2.20.   The anatomy of a direct access storage device (DASD).

structions and data on which the execution units (also within the central processor) are acting. Since the registers and Level 1 (L1) cache are extremely high-speed circuits (which switch in a few nanoseconds), they are very efficient at meeting the immediate storage needs of the central processor in executing work and are physically located near the CP to avoid loss in transfer speed.

Below the registers in the hierarchy is the Level 1 (L1) cache storage, an array of very high-speed electronic memory circuits that are also found in each z900 Processor Unit chip (see the MCM structure in Figure 2.7). As described earlier in the CMOS MCM design description the L1 cache in the z900 PU chip is split into two, one element for data and one for instructions, because the cache storage contains the next instruction and the initial data to be fed to the central processor's execution units.

Next in the storage pyramid is the second-level buffer, called Level 2 (L2) cache, which resides outside the PU but within the MCM. It automatically collects information from the next pyramid layer (central storage) and stages that information for the L1 cache. The whole purpose of the second-level buffer is to provide information to the cache more quickly than could the central storage. Like the L1 cache storage, the second-level buffer consists of an array of very high-speed electronic memory circuits.

Central Storage

The next level of the storage hierarchy is processor storage (often called *central storage* or *main memory*), which holds the programs and data acted upon by the processor units. In the S/390 31-bit design, central storage is made up of two different regions of memory: central storage and expanded storage. Central storage is the traditional type of memory found in most computers, from the smallest personal computers to supercomputers, and is a high-speed storage area used to hold information currently needed by the processor unit. This information is addressed a single byte at a time. Central storage, housed in the central processor complex, is the pivot point of the storage hierarchy. All information to be acted upon by any PU or I/O channel must reside, at some point, in central storage. It is much larger than the pyramid layers above it, but it still provides information to the PU very quickly and is made up of a large array of high-speed electronic circuits that reside on the CPC board. In the case of the z900 it can be as large as 64 GB in the current design.

Expanded Storage

The next layer in the storage pyramid, in ESA/390 architecture as in the S/390, is expanded storage, a cost-effective way to augment central storage without sacrificing too much in performance. It consists of a very large array of electronic memory circuits that act as an overflow area for central storage. In some S/390 computers, expanded storage is a region of central storage that is configured to behave like expanded storage. This allows those S/390 computers to comply with the requirement defined in the ESA/390 architecture to have expanded storage. In the larger S/390 computers, expanded storage actually is electronic circuits set apart from the central storage circuitry. Information that is still likely to be needed but cannot quite fit into central storage is moved automatically to expanded storage. All of the information stored in expanded storage, however, must be moved back to central storage before it can be accessed by the central processors. This transfer is managed by the S/390 computer hardware and operating system, which relieve the programmer from having to deal with the different memory subsystems. In fact, the processor units do not know that expanded storage exists. Together, central storage and expanded storage are referred to as processor storage.

With the introduction of the zSeries and z/Architecture, running 64-bit addressing, the need for expanded storage was eliminated. The new architecture is now capable of addressing up to 16 exabytes (EB), even though the current z900 implementation is limited to 64 GB of real storage. The z900 will operate in all three modes, 24-, 31-, or 64-bit addressing, but when operating in z/Architecture mode with z/OS, the expanded storage will not be addressed and all storage is considered main storage. Only z/VM is able to use expanded storage in z/Architecture mode. In Coupling Facility mode, the storage addressing is limited to 31 bits, which limits usage of central storage to a maximum of 2 GB although storage above 2 GB can be configured as expanded storage. This change to 64-bit addressing should be expected in the future.

External Storage—Peripherals

The next layer in the storage pyramid is disk storage, provided by Direct Access Storage Devices (DASDs), which are subdivided into DASDs with a high-speed cache for performance and DASDs without cache. DASDs are the first type of storage covered so far that physically resides outside the processor unit. They exist as I/O devices attached through one or more server I/O channels or system buses. DASDs are also the first type of storage covered so far that is able to retain information even when the power is turned off. Thus, disk storage is said to be permanent storage.

Issues related to external storage are no longer "peripheral." The speed with which organizations create new data and information, new applications that require a "data warehouse," the growing amounts of business-critical information on workstations, and the development of open system architectures all drive changes to the way data is managed. Capacity is no longer the primary issue. Rather, data availability, performance of the access method, data security and integrity, and data storage costs are driving rapid changes to computing environments. Nevertheless, the basic interactions between external storage and internal storage remain the same.

Like expanded storage, information stored on DASDs must be moved to central storage before it is available to a central processor. There is generally a delay (in the computer's time reference) from the time the central processor requests the information until the time that it is available inside the central processor. This delay results from the fact that DASDs are electromechanical devices, which are slower than electrical devices because they are constrained by mechanical motion. Further, since the DASDs are located outside the processor unit, the information is brought in through an I/O operation, which involves additional subsystems (I/O channels or system busses and control units) and the delays associated with them. However, if a DASD with cache memory is used and the data is within the cache, the mechanical motion and the reading from disk are eliminated. Data is transferred directly from the cache in response to the I/O operation. With a write-through cache, a write operation does not need to wait for the data to be written to disk before freeing the channel. When the data reaches the cache, the channel is freed for other operations, and the write then occurs synchronously from cache to disk.

The basic anatomy of a DASD is shown in Figure 2.21. It consists of a drive mechanism with permanently installed metallic disks, often called platters because their shape is like that of a dinner plate. These platters have a magnetic surface that can store information. A single DASD usually has multiple platters in order to store more information. The platters spin constantly at very high speeds while a built-in read/write head records or recalls information on the platter's surface. The arm that positions the read/write head is called the actuator. Although read/write heads in DASDs never actually touch the platter's magnetic surface, they are positioned extremely close to that surface. Together, the read/write heads and the platters compose a Head–Disk Assembly (HDA). The disk storage provided by DASDs acts as an extension to

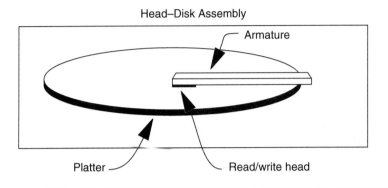

Figure 2.21. Software model of System/390 basic software structure.

expanded storage in that both are used as overflow areas for information unable to reside in central storage.

S/390 and zSeries servers support DASDs that store information in two formats: Count-Key-Data (CKD) or Fixed-Block Architecture (FBA). In either case, information is stored as small groups of data called blocks. With the CKD format, the byte count is stored in the first part of the block and defines the length of that block, so the size of a block matches exactly the amount of information that needs to be stored. With DASDs that use the FBA format, information written to the DASD is stored in blocks of fixed length. In this format, even if only 1 byte needs to be stored, a full block of DASD storage is consumed. Although wasteful of DASD space, the FBA format lends itself to higher performance than the CKD format.

More recently DASD technologies introduced include RAMAC devices and RAID. RAMAC (a name chosen by IBM to recall the earliest storage system) storage subsystems require far less physical resources (space and cooling, for example) while maintaining very high data densities, with scalable capacity of up to 1.368 terabytes of data per subsystem. A RAID, standing for Redundant Array of Independent Disks, assures the availability of data to the user by providing several techniques for mirroring and rebuilding data should a storage device become unavailable to the system. These topics are discussed in more detail in Chapter 3.

The next layer of the storage pyramid is optical storage. Rather than using magnetism as with DASDs, optical storage systems use optical techniques to achieve their extremely high recording density. Current optical storage technology, however, is significantly slower than DASDs, so it cannot replace them. Optical storage provides the capacity, random access, and volumetric efficiency needed to justify on-line access to the many documents that an enterprise now files on paper, microfiche, or microfilm. This is especially true of infrequently referenced information, as business value is gained from the speed and efficiency of on-line accessibility. Another advantage is the cost-effective retention of current on-line data for longer periods of time.

There are two types of optical storage technology: write-once and rewritable. Each uses a 5.25-inch optical cartridge. For permanent records, the write-once technology uses an ablative process (removing a portion of the surface) to record data permanently on the cartridge. Once data is written, it cannot be erased. A specialized microcoded file system allows the medium to appear as rewritable; however, previously recorded data remains on the disk, creating a permanent audit trail. For other storage uses, rewritable technology uses a reversible magneto-optic process. This recording technology is useful when stored data rapidly becomes obsolete and information archiving is not required. When the stored information is no longer needed, it is erased and the cartridge is reused.

Finally, the lowest level of the storage pyramid is tape storage. Tape consists of a long, flexible strip coated with magnetic material and rolled on a reel or into a cartridge. A tape drive reads and writes information on the tape much as a cassette recorder records and plays music on audio cassette tapes. The tape drive runs the tape across the read/write head. S/360 tapes had contact with the read/write head, but the newest tape drives do not; the tape rides over the head on a cushion of air. Electrical impulses in the read/write head transfer information to and from the tape's surface. One primary purpose of tape storage is to provide a backup storage medium for information in the computer's disk storage. With current compaction techniques and the enhanced capability recording format, cartridges (3590) can hold up to 10 GB of data. The low cost and high recording densities inherent in tape also make it ideal for archiving information. Tape is also commonly used in distributing programs and transferring information from one computer system to another. For general-purpose information archival and disk storage backup, tape is often used in preference to optical storage because of its lower cost. Tape continues to be the most frequently chosen medium for sequential processing applications because of its high data transfer rate over fiber channels.

Processor Controller

The function of the processor controller is to start up, configure, and maintain the server. It is the "cockpit" of the system and is used exclusively by the personnel who support the system, not by the business application users of the system. The processor controller consists of a small computer (actually, in some servers, it is a derivative of an IBM Personal Computer), a display, and a keyboard.

The processor controller for multiprocessor servers is a standalone duplexed unit. It provides the controlling mechanism for configuring the system, loading licensed internal code, and monitoring and supervising the processor. It assists the processors in error recovery and provides notification and automated problem analysis for certain processor conditions. In single-image mode, one side of the processor controller is actively controlling the computer system while the other side is serving as backup in case of failure of the active side. This allows for concurrent self-maintenance should one side require repair. When physically partitioned, the processor controller acts as two processors, one assigned to each physical processor partition.

Attached to the processor controller is a modem. The modem enables the processor controller, if authorized, to send and receive information over a telephone line; that is, the modem has the circuitry necessary to convert information encoded in the computer (digital information) to signals suitable for transmission over telephone lines (analog information) and vice versa. This modem link allows the server to automatically call an IBM Remote Support Facility and electronically report any problems detected with the system.

In the later S/390 generations and now the zSeries the processor controller function evolved to what is called the Hardware Management Console (HMC), but for the z900 it must be at Feature Code (FC) level 0061 or newer. The most significant difference to the S/390 G6 models is the connection method to the CPC. The S/390 connection is a single connection from the Support Element (SE) parallel port to the CPC's UPC card. To attain enhanced reliability with the z900 the SEs communicate with the CPC and each other through two independent and redundant internal Ethernet networks known as the Power Service and Control Network (PSCN). The z900 HMC can manage multiple systems via the user's Local Area Network (LAN), and as such it is recommended that the LAN be a private one planned and controlled by the user. The HMC supporting the z900 can also manage earlier generation S/390 servers including the 2003, 9672, 9674, and Multiprise 3000 (7060) as well as 9037 Sysplex Timer and 9032 ESCON director models. Limited function support is also available for the IBM Fiber Saver (2029). One HMC is capable of controlling as many as 100 systems. The HMC can control and monitor the z900 server via the Support Elements (SEs) to store configuration information, load Licensed Internal Code (LIC), and monitor and control the z900 server hardware. The z900 can be controlled by as many as 32 different HMCs.

The configuration would include two ThinkPad SEs mounted in the front of Frame A, where one acts as the primary active SE and the other is the alternate or spare and only used by IBM service personnel. Twice daily mirrored copies of critical configuration and log files are automatically placed on the alternate SE. Although the SE workplace is similar to previous S/390 servers, it has been enhanced to include several new tasks. It is recommended that at least two HMCs be installed for each installation site where one would be located in the same room as the z900 server and the other located in the operations area. More would be required where the user wanted to have the capability of manual remote operations. An example of a complex HMC to SE connectivity in a z900 and multiple earlier generation servers can be viewed in Figure 2.22. An alternate remote option would be to use a Web browser to monitor and control a local HMC and its configured SEs. A third option would be via a program product that supported remote control as in, for example, an emergency backup for a remote HMC via a SNA-switched connection, DCAF, or NetOp.

Parallel Processing

Stated in the simplest terms, parallel processing is accomplished through a collection of processing elements (computers of a variety of forms) that can communicate and cooperate to solve large to very large problems quickly. That definition is where simplicity ends. Parallel processing technology is not new. It has been used in scientific problem solving for many years. It is also not static. It has evolved into a variety of implementations over those decades. Today, with the lowering costs of technology and the increasing miniaturization of computing elements, both the options and the uses are increasing. No longer primarily a high-end tool for scientific and technical problem solving or commer-

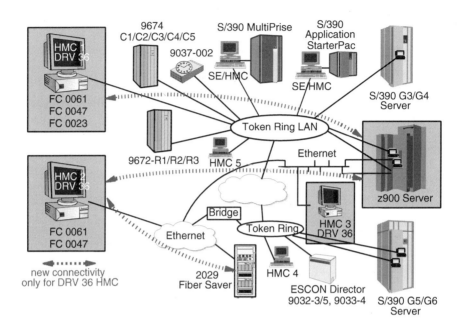

Figure 2.22. Complex HMC to SE connectivity.

cial transaction processing, it is evolving into a crucial tool for the demanding e-businesses.

Parallel processing appears essentially in three forms. Since the early years of computer development, multiprocessors have been designed as a means of increasing processor capacity. IBM has led the development of this technology and has been very effective in delivering a very high performance ratio in multiprocessing configurations. Now these configurations enable up to 16 processors to work together.

Highly parallel processing systems, sometimes referred to as Symmetric MultiProcessing (SMP) or simply parallel processing, also enable up a number of servers to work together. In most configurations, however, performance drops off quickly after adding a sixth or seventh processor. This is partially resolved through a process of clustering, interconnecting several groups of SMP processors.

Massively Parallel Processing (MPP) enables hundreds (and, theoretically, thousands) of processors to work together to solve problems. The primary factor enabling this number is a system design that "shares nothing." That is, no storage, devices, or operating systems are shared by a processor in solving a specific problem. This removes forms of contention for resources that occur in other types of "shared resource" configurations.

Implementing a parallel processing architecture requires more than changes to the processor. To work efficiently, the operating system must be designed to support multiple processors. Most important from the business perspective, the application must be designed to take advantage of access to multiple processors. In some cases, rewriting or redesigning an application will make it perform well in a parallel environment. In other cases, however, the nature of the application does not lend itself to better performance on multiple processors. Thus, crucial factors for your business to consider relative to parallel processing are the type of parallel architecture that best meets your business needs and the availability, through acquisition or reprogramming, of an application that meets your business needs.

In addition to many decades of work on multiprocessing configurations in the UNIX environment (including highly efficient multiprogramming through the MVS operating system, which is now a part of OS/390), the RS/6000 platform delivers scalability (the ability to retain performance levels when adding additional processors) and manageability (the process of managing a growing number of resources from a central point of control). In this environment, you can scale your system from 2 to over 512 nodes. Most popular databases are supported, and many vendors are designing software to work in this environment. In the S/390 and zSeries environment, IBM has developed the parallel sysplex technology. This technology, described next, builds on the S/390 generation processors and offers the potential for cost-efficient scalability well beyond current system limitations.

Parallel Sysplex

In today's business environment, applications frequently outgrow the capacity of the largest single machine. Running those applications on multiple software subsystems—for example, on multiple copies of the Information Management System (IMS) subsystem—can provide a pathway for continued, cost-effective growth. To do that without duplicating the data to run with each subsystem requires that each subsystem have concurrent access to the same data; that is, the system must support data sharing.

The term "parallel sysplex" defines two or more computing images operating under OS/390 or now z/OS in a system complex (sysplex), using a Coupling Facility as the means for sharing data. The net effect is a single-image, high-performance, data-sharing parallel system configuration. Parallel sysplex enables multiple processors to share data without distributing or partitioning the data, a critical factor in maintaining system availability and scalability. By using these new architectural facilities, the parallel sysplex harnesses the power of up to 32 computers, allowing them to access the same data concurrently. The sysplex enables the servers to cooperate as a single, logical computing facility by synchronizing their time references and enabling them to share data at the record level while preserving data integrity. While doing this, it keeps its underlying structure transparent to users, applications, and operations management. Benefits to a business include synergy with existing applications, continuous availability, single-image operations, dynamic workload balancing, and data sharing and integrity across multiple servers. Multisystem data sharing also supports a greater number of inquiries against a single database than previous single-image systems. This data sharing implementation removes the need to partition data or to repartition data when adding another system, removes the limitation of two systems accessing the database, and ensures that no single system creates a bottleneck.

Data sharing, as provided by the database managers and enabled by the parallel sysplex, provides substantial benefits compared to other system alternatives. The three primary alternatives for organizing data in a parallel environment are distributing data, partitioning data, and sharing data.

In distributed data systems, data is divided among multiple servers (processors), with each server connected via a network. The routing of requests for data across a network introduces overhead that significantly impacts response time for small transactions, making this implementation impractical for workloads consisting of many small units of work.

In partitioned data systems, the database is divided among the various servers in the system and the workload is distributed to those servers based on what data each needs to access and on the frequency of use for the data. That is, a server can directly access data that is directly attached to it and indirectly (through connection technology) access data directly attached to other connected servers. Each part of the data is accessed and updated by only one server, eliminating the possibility of data integrity problems introduced when multiple processors update the same data. This implementation requires splitting the database and continually managing it so that the workload remains evenly distributed among the processors. When the workload or processor configuration changes, the data must be reorganized.

By contrast, the shared data system provides each server direct and equal access (through data-sharing technology) to any data in the database. This provides the workload to be spread based on the server's utilization level rather than by data location. With shared data, workload and processor changes do not require a reorganization of the data.

One benefit of this form of data sharing is seen in the techniques used to distribute workload. In partitioned and distributed systems, as noted earlier, the data is preassigned to specific processors. To ensure equitable workload balancing, the data and workload are analyzed and matched accordingly. Since the work is routed to the server that has local access to the required data, hot spots (one server is overutilized while others are underutilized) occur. Workload is continuously monitored and data frequently redistributed to minimize this impact.

In an zSeries or S/390 shared data environment, the work is submitted to the server with the most available capacity, since every server has equal access to the data. This dynamic workload balancing provides more evenly balanced utilization of each server, resulting in more consistent and shorter response times for users. An operational benefit is also derived from eliminating server hot spots. Servers can be sized closer to the average workload across the system rather than having excess capacity installed on each server to handle large workloads. Compared to partitioning systems to achieve workload balance, dynamic balancing uses the installed processor capacity more efficiently.

Likewise, when a new server or storage is added to a system, partitioned and distributed systems must redistribute the database and rebalance work requests to optimize each server's performance. This requires analysis of the workload to determine the best split after new resources are added. Also, this often results in data being unavailable to users while the reorganization takes place.

Now in shared data environments, additional server and/or storage capacity is added to the sysplex without disrupting application workflow. The entire database is automatically rebalanced to use the new resources, and no lengthy analysis is needed to split the workload or data.

Similar benefits are derived in situations in which capacity is lost. In a partitioned environment, when a server fails, another server must take over the failed server's workload, usually by activating a backup data path to the failed server's data. Backup servers must be large enough to handle the current work plus the workload of a failed server, or a "reserve" server must be available to pick up that workload. The severity of the impact is determined by the amount of excess capacity on the remaining processors and the speed with which an alternative path to the lost processor's data is established. In distributed systems, by contrast, loss of a server results, at least for a period of time, in loss of access to data connected to that server.

In a shared data environment, loss of a server may result in diminished system capacity but minimal impact to the application in that all remaining servers continue to have access to all data. Workload continues to be balanced across the remaining processors in the sysplex. Because reserve capacity is spread across all servers, each server runs at a higher utilization rate and users should see minimal, if any (depending on available capacity), increase in response time during the failure of a server.

Through the use of the WorkLoad Manager (WLM) function, new work can be spread evenly across multiple sysplex images, assuring a balanced utilization. When an image is taken out of service, WLM realizes this and does not direct work to that failed image.

In a single system, growth is limited by the size of the system. Managing the system, however, is relatively easy because all of the resources are under the control of one copy of the operating system. Taking a large workload application (such as transaction processing) and permitting it to run on a large number of separate systems adds capacity for growth but significantly complicates managing the workload, which includes distributing the workload effectively across all of the systems.

A major business benefit is derived from maintaining the "single-system image" of the parallel sysplex. Transaction processing workloads are dynamically balanced across processors, and, with the introduction of high-performance coupling technology, data is also dynamically shared at a fine level of granularity with read and write access and full data integrity. The shared data model simplifies planning for new business applications, dynamic workload balancing manages changing patterns of use, and the parallel sysplex participates as an element of an open, client/server computing environment.

Many businesses require more than one processor within a data center to ensure sufficient capacity or to provide backup capability. Managing several of these large systems independently creates demand for resources and adds cost to operations. The System/390 design was the first IBM general-purpose system that made it possible to interconnect multiple systems and to view them as a single logical entity. The term for this configuration is "parallel sysplex" (sysplex is a shortened form of "system complex"). It provided businesses investment protection of their ES/9000 9121 511-based processors or 9021 711-based processors because it was possible to use those processors in a parallel sysplex along with newest S/390 family of 9672 Parallel Enterprise Server models to share workload among those older bipolar and the newer CMOS processors and thereby reduce capacity constraints.

The base sysplex environment, introduced by IBM in 1990, provided simplified multisystem management through a component of MVS/ESA (later renamed OS/390) called the Cross-System Coupling Facility (XCF). The XCF enabled authorized programs on one system to communicate with programs on the same system or other systems. In a base sysplex environment, processor images running OS/390 communicate using channel-to-channel connections and the shared dataset. When the OS/390 images are on different computers, a sysplex timer synchronizes the timing of the connected systems. These functions, along with the Coupling Facility and coupling links, discussed later, are critical to making data sharing work. Sharing data and providing processing redundancy between these systems are where businesses receive real value.

A parallel sysplex allows businesses to dynamically connect and disconnect systems into the sysplex without stopping system operations. It also allows incremental horizontal growth (adding new processors to the sysplex) while maintaining a single-image perspective. The parallel sysplex ensures data integrity in an environment of continuing change in which data is freely shared among processors and workloads.

When only one processor has access to data, traditional data management products apply cache (a form of temporary storage for data, also called a high-speed buffer) management and locking techniques (for controlling access to data). When users on more than one system require access to the same data, particularly if they need to change the data, keeping track of the status of the data across those systems is essential. This requires complex routines for managing and updating the cache and locks.

Traditionally, processors have passed messages to request and authorize access to data. The act of message passing required the participating systems to stop other work and process the message request. The complexity and delays associated with message passing increased exponentially with additional processors. If the most recent copy of the requested data was in an internal buffer, rather than on a DASD, even more time elapsed before the request could be completed.

To effectively manage data integrity in this shared environment and to manage the communication and serialization necessary for sharing data, IBM created a new structure, a combination of hardware, software, and licensed internal code called the Coupling Facility. Access to the Coupling Facility is through high-speed links called coupling links. These links connect each system involved in the parallel sysplex to the Coupling Facility, providing high performance with both high bandwidth and fast response time.

OS/390 and now z/OS provide the services enabling authorized applications, including components and subsystems, to use the Coupling Facility services to cache data, share queues and status, and access sysplex lock structures to implement high-performance data sharing and rapid recovery from failures. A parallel sysplex cluster consists of up to 32 z/OS and/or OS/390 images coupled to one or more Coupling Facilities using high-speed specialized links for communication.

Coupling

The S/390 Coupling Facility was the first to make high-performance, multisystem data sharing possible. It provided high-speed locking, caching, and message list services between coupling-capable S/390 processors running OS/390 that are connected by coupling links to the Coupling Facility in a parallel sysplex. To ensure fault tolerance and high-availability redundant characteristics for a production environment, more than one Coupling Facility is required. New licensed internal code in the Coupling Facility, the Coupling Facility Control Code (CFCC), provides the function that enables the parallel sysplex. The Coupling Facility is implemented in one of four ways.

- The Standalone Coupling Facility, which runs the Coupling Facility Control Code (licensed internal code)

- Coupling links (high-bandwidth connections) to connect the Coupling Facility to the servers.

- The Sysplex Timer to synchronize time-of-day (TOD) clocks across all participating systems

- Subsystems that exploit the Coupling Facility transparently to users and applications

The Standalone Coupling Facility has continually been improved as have the subsystem components, furthering the capability of the parallel sysplex investment. A standalone CF provides a physically isolated, totally independent CF environment with facilities dedicated to coupling function, and there are no software charges associated with a standalone CF.

The 9674 standalone CF models were introduced with each new early S/390 generation until the G5/G6 time frame, when the CF Model 9672-R06, based on G5 technology, was offered, and have remained the preferred CF for S/390. Now the 9672-R06 is upgradable to the z900 Model 100 Standalone Coupling Facility. The z900 Model 100 CF is capable of supporting a sysplex configured with both S/390 models and z900 servers (Figure 2.23). It is recommended, for purposes of

zSeries 900 Coupling Facility Options

★ Up to 32 GB of CS   z900 Model 100
   (z900 Model 100)

✓ Processor Assignments

★ z900 Peer-to-Peer Channels   — Dedicated or Shared
   z900 to z900   — Dedicated and/or Shared
   ▸ InterSystem Channels   — CPs and/or ICFs
   ▸ Integrated Cluster Bus
   ▸ Internal Coupling Channels   ✓ Dynamic CF Dispatch
              ✓ Dynamic CF (ICF) Expansion

★ z900 Compatibility Channels
   z900 to 9672
   ▸ InterSystem Channels
   ▸ Integrated Cluster Bus   9672 R06 > z900 Model 100 > z900 General Purpose

Figure 2.23. z900 Coupling Facility.

availability, that in addition to the standalone CF there be at least one other coupling link between OS/390 or z/OS and the CF images as well as at least two CF Images not running on the same machine.

Another option is to execute the Coupling Facility Control Code (CFCC) in an LPAR of a dedicated CP or shared CPs of a server or by running the CFCC in a PR/SM LPAR partition. However, it is not possible to have an OS/390 LP with dedicated and shared CPs at the same time.

Finally, an Integrated Coupling Facility (ICF) running in a dedicated PU can perform as a CF running CFCC always running on a logical partition. A CF image can use dedicated and/or shared ICFs as well as dedicated or shared CPs. The z900 Model 100 cannot have CPs, so it is an ICF-only machine to run CF images.

The G5/G6 models offered the capability to share ICFs among CF partitions providing those coupling workloads that did not require the full capacity of the ICF. Another new algorithm, Dynamic CF Dispatch, put the partition to "sleep" when there were no requests to service rather than be in "active wait" mode. This permitted the resources to be made available to other partitions sharing the resource to do work. Lastly, the new function of Dynamic ICF Expansion provided extra CF capacity for unexpected peak workloads or in the case of loss of CF capacity in the cluster due to failure.

Within the Coupling Facility, storage is managed as a set of objects called structures. Authorized users can manipulate data within the structures, each of which has a unique function:

- The *cache structure* provides a buffer invalidation list to ensure consistency of cached data. It also serves as a high-speed buffer for storing data that can be read or written from multiple systems.

- The *list structure* enables applications to share data—such as work queues, status information, or directories—that is organized in a set of lists.

- The *lock structure* provides shared and exclusive locking capability for serializing shared resources.

Enhanced reliability, availability, and serviceability for the Coupling Facility are achieved by

- Configuring both multiple Coupling Facilities and multiple coupling links with the processor, removing a single point of failure.

- Varying a single coupling link off-line and on-line for service.

- Utilizing an N + 1 power subsystem capable of supporting a processor complex for most power supply failures without interrupting system operation. With concurrent power maintenance capability, the failed power supply can be replaced without system interruption at a convenient time.

Achieving value from the Coupling Facility requires support from subsystems that interact with business and operations applications. The following subsystems use the Coupling Facility:

- *Information Management System Database Manager (IMS DB)* uses the IMS Resource Lock Manager (IRLM) Version 2, Release 1 to support up to 32-way data sharing. The configuration options include 1 system with 32 IMS subsystems; 8 systems, each with 4 IMS subsystems; or 32 systems, each with only 1 IMS subsystem. IMS takes advantage of Virtual Storage Access Method (VSAM) and Overflow Sequential Access Method (OSAM) database buffer invalidation notification and the IRLM lock table. This enhancement is applicable to IMS Transaction Manager/IMS Data Base Manager (IMS TM/IMS DB) and CICS/IMS DB N-way data-sharing environments.

  IMS offers dynamic workload balancing by placing a shared IMS queue (Shared Queue Support) in the Coupling Facility. With this support, the system that is ready for work pulls the transaction from the shared queue, which supports automatic workload balancing across all IMS systems in the parallel sysplex. Before IMS provided Shared Queue Support, the IMS MultiSystem Coupling (MSC) feature provided balanced workload for the IMS/TM among the systems in the parallel sysplex. In CICS, the equivalent support is provided through the OS/390 Work Load Manager (WLM) and CICSPlex System Manager (CPSM). CICS also enables the Terminal Owning Regions (TORs) and Application Owning Regions (AORs) to be located on different images within the sysplex, using the coupling facility for communications between the regions.

- *Database 2 (DB2) Version 4* allows multiple DB2 subsystems within a parallel sysplex to concurrently access and update shared databases. This subsystem serializes data access throughout a data sharing group via the IMS Resource Lock Manager (IRLM) and the Coupling Facility lock structure. DB2 also uses the coupling facility for stored Structured Query Language (SQL) procedures and to enable parallel queries with workload manager.

- The *Virtual Storage Access Method (VSAM)*, a component of Data Facility Storage Management System/MVS (DFSMS/MVS), supports record-level sharing in a later release. Using the Coupling Facility will enable sysplexwide data sharing of VSAM files in the CICS environment.

- The *Resource Access Control Facility (RACF)* uses the Coupling Facility to provide a large buffer, which it shares with other systems, for its database records. It also uses the locking capability of the Coupling Facility to improve its internal performance.

- The *Job Entry Subsystem 2 (JES2)* allows installations to define checkpoint data sets in the Coupling Facility as well as on DASDs. Placing this data in the Coupling Facility provides more rapid access to data and ensures equal access to the data by multiple JES2 subsystems.

- The *Virtual Telecommunications Access Method (VTAM)*, now an integral part of eNetwork Communications Server for OS/390, exploits the Coupling Facility to enable workload balancing for network access to applications within the parallel sysplex. VTAM Generic Resources exploits the Coupling Facility by maintaining the list of applications associated with a specific generic name. The generic name provides an alias name for a group of SNA applications, enabling VTAM to spread workload and recover failing workload across multiple images of an application providing improved end user availability. VTAM also retains information about individual sessions in the coupling facility when the MultiNode Persistent Sessions (MNPS) function is used.

- The TCP/IP communications support that is now part of eNetwork Communications Server for OS/390 uses the Coupling Facility for communications between TCP/IP images within the parallel sysplex. It also uses the Coupling Facility to maintain information for use by the Workload Manager/Domain Name Server support, which allows load sharing for TCP/IP workloads within the sysplex.

Coupling Links

The CFs and images in the parallel sysplex communicate over specialized high-speed connections called links. It is recommended that there be at least two links connecting each image to each CF for availability purposes. It is important to use the fastest links available to ensure that link speeds are not the bottleneck to performance.

The S/390 G5/G6 server has Internal Coupling (IC) channels, now referred to as the Integrated Cluster Bus (ICB), enabling high-speed, efficient communication between a CF PR/SM partition and one or more OS/390 logical partitions on the same G5/G6 server. The IC channel is a linkless connection, implemented in LIC, requiring no hardware or cables as would be required in external link alternatives. The Integrated Cluster Bus (ICB) is the next best alternative and has better performance and reliability characteristics than HiPerLinks, now referred to as ISC-2, which were first introduced in 1997 on the G3/G4 models. ICB uses a 333 Mbit/s Self-Timed Interconnect (STI) bus to perform coupling communication between the server and the standalone CF by a 10-meter cable, restricting the distance between them to about 7 meters. The HiPerLinks available on all S/390 servers starting with the G3 models and corresponding standalone CFs are fiber-optic links with transfer speeds up to 100 MB/s over distances of 10 km. That distance could be increased to 20 km via RPQ and up to 40 km in a geographically dispersed parallel sysplex configuration using the IBM 9729 Wave Division Multiplexors.

The z900 CF has many connectivity options. The links can use Peer or Compatibility mode support depending on the configuration and the type of connected servers. Compatibility mode is used to connect CF links to the z900 from S/390 models. The z900 maintains compatibility with these ISC and ICB channels by operating in Compatibility mode. The new enhanced links called Peer mode are used when connecting a z900 server to a standalone CF Model 100. In this mode the coupling link provides 200 Gbit/s capacity, the ICB link 1 GB/s peak capacity, and the IC link 1.25 GB/s capacity. When a coupling channel is operating in Peer mode, it may be used as both a sender and receiver at the same time, reducing the number of links required. InterSystem Coupling Facility-3 (ISC-3) channels provide the connectivity necessary for data sharing between the CF and the systems directly attached to it. They are point-to-point connections that require a unique channel definition at each end of the channel. In peer mode they connect z900 general-purpose models and z900 coupling facilities. In compatibility mode they provide connections between the z900 servers and HiPerLink (ISC) channels on S/390 servers. The z900 ISC-3 channels are capable of operation at 1 Gbit/s in Compatibility mode or 2 Gbits/s in Native mode up to a distance of 10 km. An RPQ is available to extend the distance up to 20 km running at 1 Gbit/s in both Peer and Compatibility mode.

HiPerLinks, single-mode links available on the S/390, were replaced by ISC-3 links on the z900 Series. For short distances (~7 meters) the Integrated Cluster Bus (ICB) is used for high-speed coupling of G5/G6 and/or z900 servers. The ICB-3 is used for short-distance (~7 meters) high-speed coupling communication between two z900 servers and ISC-3 links must be used for longer distances. The Internal Coupling-3 (IC-3) channel emulates the coupling links between images within a single server. No hardware is required with IC links, and they provide the fastest parallel sysplex connectivity.

Geographically Dispersed Parallel Sysplex

The Geographically Dispersed Parallel Sysplex (GDPS) complements a multisite parallel sysplex by providing a single, automated solution to dynamically manage storage subsystem mirroring, processors, and network resources. This will provide a business the ability to attain continuous availability and nearly transparent business continuity/disaster recovery without data loss. GDPS allows the business to perform a controlled site switch for both planned and unplanned site outages and at the same time maintain full data integrity across multiple storage subsystems.

GDPS requires Tivoli Netview for OS/390, System Automation for OS/390, and remote copy technologies. It supports both the Peer-to-

Peer Remote Copy (PPRC) and the asynchronous eXtended Remote Copy (XRC) forms of remote copy.

With GDPS a business can expect to meet a Recovery Time Objective (RTO) of less than one hour, a Recovery Point Objective (RPO) of no data loss, and protection against metropolitan area disasters up to 40 km between sites.

Because GDPS/XRC distance is not limited when using common communication links and channel extender technology or dark fiber between sites, it can also offer protection from metropolitan but regional disasters. A business can expect an RTO of one to two hours and an RPO of less than a minute.

Another important advantage a business may derive from GDPS is to enable automatic management of the reserved PUs through implementation of the Capacity BackUp (CBU) feature. When a site failure or processor failure is detected, GDPS will dynamically add PUs to the configuration in the takeover site to restore processing power for mission-critical workloads.

IBM Sysplex Timer (9037)

The Sysplex Timer Model 2 is a unit that synchronizes the Time-Of-Day (TOD) clocks of all attached central processing complexes within the parallel sysplex. It ensures a consistent time-stamp so that, for example, when multiple systems update the same database, all updates are time-stamped in sequence.

The Sysplex Timer Model 2 is a key element in the S/390 parallel sysplex. It ensures that multiple OS/390 systems can appear as a single system image, delivering the flexibility of running applications simultaneously on multiple systems. The connection between two Sysplex Timer Model 2 units can be up to 3 km (1.86 miles) of fiber-optic cable. This distance can be extended to 26 km (16.15 miles) using repeaters (RPQ 8K1919). If preferred, an external time source attaches to the sysplex timer to keep time. Multiple sysplex timers can keep correct time in the event of a failure of one sysplex timer.

A pair of 9729 Optical Wavelength Division Multiplexors (RPQ 8Q1488) can also be used to extend the distance between the Sysplex

Timer Model 2 units and the attached CPCs to 26 km (16.15 miles) over dark fiber.

IBM Fiber Saver (2029)

Broadband channels that enable enhanced data throughput have become necessary to businesses in the world of the Internet and extranets, or where they depend on geographically separated data centers. These businesses have moved to fiber-optic cable to allow such high-speed connectivity and therefore experience high monthly fees for each mile of cable. The IBM 2029 Fiber Saver provides relief because it is designed with advanced dense wavelength multiplexing technology. The Fiber Saver can transmit up to 32 channels over a single pair of fibers or up to 64 channels over two pairs. With a optional channel card a Fiber Saver system can support up to 128 channels over a single pair of fibers or up to 256 channels over two pairs, all at distances up to 50 km. The transmission rate is up to 1.25 Gbits/s for each channel card or an overall maximum of 80 Gbits/s for the system. That means a business using the 2029 for multiplexing up to 256 channels of data will replace 512 fibers with just 4.

A 2029 will support all commonly used server protocols such as ESCON, FICON, Fiber Channel, ISC, Sysplex Timer (ETR) FDDI, Fast Ethernet, Gigabit Ethernet, OC-3, or OC-12 channels. Not only are they supported, they are capable of being supported concurrently on the same fibers.

Availability and Fault Tolerance

The parallel sysplex provides enhanced availability by allowing nondisruptive incremental growth, by eliminating single points of failure, and by ensuring the integrity and consistency of data throughout the entire sysplex. With this technology, any level of availability—including full 24-hour-a-day, 7-day-a-week, 365-day-a-year operations—can be configured. Data sharing, as discussed earlier, is a critical component in ensuring availability and fault tolerance.

To ensure that software changes occur on a system-by-system basis within a sysplex without impacting the availability of the sysplex as a whole, IBM introduced software cloning. This permits different server systems that are part of the sysplex to share the same software libraries and definitions, allowing changes to be made on one system and replicated throughout the sysplex. Because parallel sysplex is designed to have a new level of software coexist with an old level, software changes can be made on one system, thoroughly tested, and replicated to the other systems without impacting the availability of the sysplex.

Multiple coupling links and/or Coupling Facilities can connect to each server, providing flexibility in configuring fault-tolerant shared data systems. This is particularly useful for mission-critical On-Line Transaction Processing (OLTP) application environments. Servers can be added to, or removed dynamically from, the parallel sysplex. The Coupling Facility can be configured at installation to allow coupling links (but not Coupling Facility channels, which can be installed at power-on reset and configured at a later time) to be installed while the system is operating. This supports horizontal growth without disruption. The impact of scheduled and unscheduled outages is reduced, if not eliminated.

The Coupling Facility also contains internal batteries to provide power to the Central Electronic Complex (CEC) for a short period of time during a power outage. The "power save state" keeps only the memory active but for up to 60 minutes. In addition, an external DC power connection minimizes the risk of extended power outages.

The power system in the G5/G6 and z900 has been enhanced with a power supply that offers dual primary power feeds. Each feed is electrically isolated and enables redundant power paths to each server, ensuring that a single power outage will not disrupt system operations. Also, a local Uninterruptible Power System (UPS) is available. This unit provides over five minutes of full-power hold-up in the event of extended customer power line disturbances.

In the event of a Central Processor (CP) failure on a G4 System or newer server, if a spare Processing Unit (PU) is available, the system will initialize the spare PU to take over as a CP. If the failure occurred in a Shared LPAR environment, the sparing is done dynamically, transparent to the customer. For multiprocessor systems, in basic or dedicated LPAR mode, the system will send a message to the operator to configure the new CP on-line, if the software supports reconfiguration of CPs. In these instances, sparing takes place concurrently with system operation. In most cases the application that was running on the failing CP will be preserved (application preservation) and will continue processing on another CP with no customer intervention. For Basic mode and for dedicated logical partitions in LPAR mode, application preservation capability eliminates the need for customer intervention in the recovery.

In the event of a System Assist Processor (SAP) failure, most S/390 servers will have a spare PU to take the place of the failed SAP to maintain continuity of processing without capacity degradation. In the event of a SAP failure with no spare PU, as may be the case for a fully configured S/390, a functioning CP is quiesced and dynamically reassigned as a SAP to maintain continuity of I/O processing. This capability may eliminate an outage and permits the repair to be deferred. Since the zSeries servers have at least two SAPs as standard, there is always a spare SAP PU in the unlikely case of one failing.

In the event of an Internal Coupling Facility (ICF) failure, most systems will have a spare PU to take the place of the failed ICF. For a Coupling Facility configured with two ICFs, the Coupling Facility will continue to operate with one ICF until the operator can vary the spare PU on-line. For a Coupling Facility with a single ICF, the spare PU will have to be activated and the Coupling Facility environment recovered. If there are plans to use the ICF capability, then always plan for a spare PU.

The Dynamic Coupling Facility (CF) Dispatching function helps enable continuous computing in the event of a coupling facility failure without requiring a standalone backup coupling facility. Enhanced dispatching algorithms enable customers to define a backup Coupling Facility in a Logical PARtition (LPAR) on their system. This backup facility shares CP resources with other logical partitions executing active workloads and only uses minimal CP resources until the primary CF fails.

Additional availability characteristics of the S/390 family and zSeries, not limited to coupled environments, assist in achieving continuous system operation (24 hours a day, 7 days a week, 365 days a year). A partial list includes

- *Subsystem storage protection*, which enables CICS/ESA to reduce system failures by protecting subsystem code, control blocks, and data areas from inadvertent modification or destruction. This prevents most failing applications from taking down the CICS subsystem.

- *Subspace Group Facilities* (available through CICS/ESA Version 4 and supported by OS/390), which increase CICS application program isolation through a function called transaction isolation. This function ensures that one transaction and/or application program cannot inadvertently damage the code or data belonging to other transactions and/or application programs. An application attempting to access storage outside of its own subspace is abnormally terminated, enabling users to quickly identify and resolve causes of data integrity problems.

- *Remote site recovery* for Information Management System (IMS) databases and transaction management resources, which is provided through IMS/ESA Version 5. This feature enables customers who maintain a remote secondary site for backup, in the event of an extended primary outage, to resume on-line operations within minutes of failure and to maintain data currency at that remote site. Also, shadowing (maintaining image copies of databases and critical data sets) is automatic.

- *Concurrent channel maintenance*, which allows the replacement of a failed channel card without powering down the system.

- *Concurrent patch maintenance*, which allows most updates to Licensed Internal Code (LIC), including those for the processor controller, central processor, and channel subsystem, to be applied and activated concurrent with operation. PR/SM LPAR LIC patches are also included. For 511-based and 711-based ES/9000 processors, a backup processor controller element is required to perform this maintenance.

- The *Fault Tolerant Dynamic Memory Arrays Facility,* which enables the hardware to detect a failure in central or expanded storage chips, flag and log it for future maintenance activity, and select a backup chip located on the same memory card.

- *Dynamic reconfiguration management*, which allows less disruptive I/O configuration changes for channel paths, control units, and devices by eliminating the need for a power-on reset and Initial Program Load (IPL) to define the new configuration. In an ESCON/FICON environment, this feature enables fiber-optic channel cables to be plugged into existing ESCON/FICON ports during system operation.

- The *Hardware Configuration Definition (HCD)*, a component of OS/390, which defines the channel and I/O equipment used by an S/390 computer. OS/390 uses the HCD to perform dynamic reconfiguration management (discussed earlier). VM/ESA permits the use of the HCD to define the I/O equipment once. The resulting definition can be used by both the hardware and the software.

- The *Hardware Configuration Manager (HCM)* for OS/390, which integrates logical and physical configuration data to provide accurate configuration reports in graphical and textual form. With the increasing complexity introduced into the System/390 environment (multiple-processor environments, logical partitions, ESCON, optical cables, distribution panels, and patch panels have all contributed), managing physical data has become increasingly important to the business and increasingly complex. HCM functions are designed to simplify this process.

  HCM provides a user-friendly Graphical User Interface (GUI) and is designed to work as a client/server application with the Hardware Configuration Definition (HCD) as the server on the S/390 host. It displays configurations as graphical diagrams, allowing users to quickly locate objects and to identify their connections within the total configuration. As changes are made, immediate visual feedback allows a rapid overview of planned changes. Easy navigation, including zooming, locating objects, and filtering capabilities, allows users to focus on critical parts of the configuration.

  The HCM GUI maintains the physical elements of configuration data and the logical configuration data controlled by HCD. Inconsistencies between the logical and physical elements of the configuration are highlighted. HCM guarantees correct and synchronized configuration data through the rigorous validation that HCD provides. HCM validates configuration data, when it is entered, for completeness, accuracy, and compliance with connectivity rules, and updates physical and logical configuration elements concurrently.

- *ESCON/FICON cables* eliminate the possibility of signal errors and bent pins, which cause outages in the bus and tag environment.

  Capacity Upgrade on Demand (CUoD) allows concurrent server upgrades, and memory upgrades if extra memory was shipped in advance. The CUoD upgrades are done by Licensed Internal Code

Configuration Control (LICCC). Fully configured models cannot use this capability, and any upgrades within a different MCM type (12-PU or 20-PU) are not concurrent.

Capacity BackUp (CBU) provides a designated system with the ability to concurrently add processing capacity via LICCC, to take over workload of a system lost to a disaster or via CUoD for unexpected workload spikes.

Software—Supporting Business Objectives

The previous sections of this chapter introduced the processor units and associated hardware options used to configure the servers. This section introduces the element that puts the hardware to work—namely, software. Software (a general term for the many programs that execute in computers) harnesses the server's computational power and allows users to perform many diverse and useful tasks.

The term "software" is analogous to the term "publication." Newspapers, annual reports, novels, and biographical directories are all categories of publications. These different categories fill different needs. The same situation exists with software. Each category of software has a unique role in enabling the hardware to perform useful work, but all must act together. The rest of this section takes a look at the roles played by each of the categories.

The basic categories of software used in S/390 and zSeries computers are illustrated in the simple software model shown in Figure 2.24. Three basic categories (or software layers) are commonly used: application program, operating system, and Licensed Internal Code (LIC). Each software layer performs a completely different job, but all three work closely together to perform useful work for the users. S/390 and zSeries application program alternatives and operating system alternatives are the focus of Chapter 4.

The top software layer in the software model is the application program layer (the top layer in Figure 2.24). Application programs perform the tasks (word processing or accounting, for example) for which the computer was purchased, but the other two layers play essential support roles. The "user's view" arrows in the figure indicate that the user most often interacts with an application program and less frequently

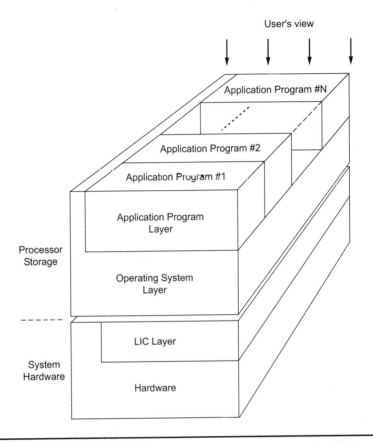

Figure 2.24.   Several alternatives provide network access to the S/390.

with the operating system. Working closely with the other software layers, the application program processes the various keystrokes made by the user and responds by displaying information on the computer's display or other output devices.

Programs written for System/370 computers can usually be executed directly on S/390 servers because S/390 programs can be ported on the zSeries. This compatibility allows users to bring forward their investment in application program development, database design, and user training when upgrading their system. Frequently, application programs in the business environment are used for such tasks as accounting, financial modeling, word processing, database management, electronic mail (e-mail), and computer graphics.

Application programs interact directly with the operating system to perform different tasks (such as reading and writing disk storage or sending information over a communications network). The interaction between the operating system and application programs takes place through the Application Programming Interface (API) presented by the operating system. Program products, called application enablers, extend the API presented by the operating system. Application enablers add function to the API, thus offering more services to application programs. As the figure shows, application enablers reside between the operating system and the application program layers of our software model, and they actively communicate with both layers.

By adding services to the API, application enablers make the job of application program development easier. This enables software development companies to develop prewritten application programs more easily, providing users with more prewritten application programs from which to choose. In the same way, the productivity of developing custom application programs is improved because the application enablers provide many functions that would otherwise have to be written from scratch by the developer during the custom application development project. Application enablers used with S/390 and zSeries servers are grouped into three categories:

- Transaction-processing application enablers

- Database application enablers

- Special-purpose application enablers

The next layer in our software model is the operating system. The operating system manages the hardware resources of the computer system and performs tasks under the control of application programs and keyboard commands typed by the users. Because the application program can rely on the operating system to perform many of the detailed housekeeping tasks associated with the internal workings of the computer, the operating system is said to provide the environment in which application programs execute. Since the application program interacts directly with the operating system, application programs are generally designed to work under a specific operating system. Operating systems also accept commands directly from the users to copy files, change passwords, and perform various other tasks.

The third and final layer of software in our model is the Licensed Internal Code (LIC). This is a set of highly specialized programs written by the manufacturer of a computer and rarely modified by either system operators or users. The set of LIC in S/390 and z900 servers is embedded deeply within the computer system and is therefore considered to be part of the computing machine itself rather than part of a program running on the machine. LIC exists only to help the hardware perform the more complex instructions in the ESA/390 or zSeries architecture. The LIC includes the programming executed by the many different microprocessors—for example, some LIC is executed by the microprocessors used to implement the I/O channels. The LIC approach helps shield the hardware details of the processor unit from the software's view of the processor unit. That is, it preserves compliance with the system architecture, and thus compatibility with operating systems and application programs, in the face of evolutionary system improvements.

When data is sent to a computer from an external source, such as a workstation, the software layers of our model come into play. First, the I/O channels and associated LIC verify that all went well in receiving the data; then the LIC notifies the operating system that the data is correct, ready, and waiting for use. The operating system makes the data available to the application program and then reactivates the application program, which was dormant waiting for the next keystroke(s). The application program processes the data as necessary and instructs the operating system to wait for the next keystrokes, and the whole cycle starts all over again.

Computers easily perform these steps in small fractions of a second. Similar but more complicated cooperation among the three software layers occurs for most functions performed by the computer such as reading or writing a file on a DASD and communicating with other computers.

System Concepts—Bringing the System to Life

Few areas in computer science create more confusion and apprehension than operating systems. Never before has the user had more alternatives in choosing an operating system. This section removes some of the mystery associated with the various S/390 and zSeries operating systems by familiarizing the reader with operating system concepts, such as multiuser and interactive processing, and with their application to the business environment.

Once devices for loading programs into the server and for interacting with the server have been installed, an operating system is loaded. The operating system is needed to perform any useful work because it provides the environment in which other programs execute. It is the program that manages the internal housekeeping associated with the computer system, and it provides the necessary interface between the users and application programs to control the server. The user can interact directly with the operating system's user interface to manage files on a disk, start application programs, print files, configure the server's various subsystems, and so on. The operating system also performs tasks directly under the control of application programs without any user assistance.

As noted earlier in this chapter (and discussed more fully in Chapter 4), the application program initiates tasks by interacting directly with the operating system through the Application Program Interface (API). The API is simply a set of operating system tasks that can be initiated directly by the application program. The API simplifies the job of application programmers by making it unnecessary for them to become involved with the details of hardware interaction. Further, when an application uses the API, it is shielded from changes in the computer hardware as new computers are developed. The operating system can be changed to support new computer hardware while preserving (or even extending) the API, allowing previously written application programs to run on the new computer system.

With technologies like IBM's MQSeries, applications are further isolated from change. Programs communicate using the MQSeries API, an easy-to-use, high-level program interface that shields programmers from the complexities of different operating systems and underlying networks.

To understand the role of the operating system, you need to understand these basic concepts:

- Batch versus interactive processing

- Multiuser

- Multiprogramming

Batch versus Interactive Processing

To grasp the concepts of batch processing and interactive processing, consider the analogy between the postal service and the telephone. If you wish to ask a distant friend some questions, you can either write a letter or phone. With the first option you gather all your thoughts, put them on paper, and put the letter in a mailbox. A few days later (assuming your friend is responsive), you go to your mailbox and get the responses to your questions in the form of a document. This is analogous to batch processing with a computer. First, you request the computer to answer some question(s) or perform some task(s), and some time later (from minutes to hours) you can go to the printer and get the computer's responses in the form of a report. In the early days of computing, batch processing was the only alternative for computer interaction. A user submitted a request (called a batch job) to the computer by placing a stack of computer punch cards into an electromechanical device called a card reader. The computer would read the cards, perform the requested task(s), and respond by generating a computer printout. Today, batch processing still has its place, but the batch jobs are usually submitted by typing commands into a computer terminal rather than by using punched cards. Card readers are rarely used today.

Moving back to our analogy, at times you cannot simply write down your list of questions in a letter because some of the questions depend on answers to one or more initial questions. In this case, you have to send several letters back and forth or call your friend to discuss the questions. Calling is preferable if you need answers in a hurry. Having a dialog with your friend over the phone is analogous to interactive processing on a computer. With interactive processing, you have a dialog with the computer system from a terminal: You type in questions or requests, and the computer immediately responds. The primary advantage of interactive processing is that the user gets an immediate response, which is required in many business applications (such as airline reservations, a retail checkout lane, or now e-business). Interactive processing was developed after batch processing and is now used in most business environments.

Some business applications of computers use a combination of batch and interactive processing. For example, a payroll clerk might enter information from time cards into a computer terminal in a dialog style (interactive processing). Once all time cards are entered and verified to be correct, the clerk may issue a command to the terminal that tells the computer to print all checks (a batch job). The clerk later gets the checks from the printer. The operating systems used with S/390 and zSeries servers support excel at both batch and interactive processing. System functions include using parallel processing to expand the capabilities of the batch processing environment.

Multiuser Support

A server is said to be a multiuser server system if the hardware and software enable a single computer system to be shared by two or more users simultaneously. By contrast, personal computers are single-user computer systems because they are primarily designed to interact with one user at a time.

A multiuser server has from two to even hundreds of thousands of terminals or workstations attached to it. Each workstation or terminal provides its user with a window into the computer system and allows the user to perform tasks independently. Although the single computer system is being used simultaneously by many users, users are typically unaware of and need not be concerned with the activities of other users, and can proceed as if it were their own computer system. However, a user may see the computer "slow down" (increase response time) as more and more users sign on to the computer and start doing work.

There are several advantages of a multiuser system over a single-user one. First, since the computer system hardware and programs can be simultaneously shared by many users, no one has to wait for a "turn on the computer." Everyone (assuming enough workstations are attached) has access to the server whenever it is needed to do a job. Other advantages offered by a multiuser system come in the areas of access to data, security, accounting, backup, recovery, and the like, but most important are the economies of scale. The operating systems used with S/390 and zSeries servers support a full multiuser environment. These servers also offer the advantage of being usable 24 hours a day, 7 days a week with diverse application support. Contrast this with a PC, which typically sits idle over 16 hours every day while its user is not at the job.

Multiprogramming

Many people confuse multiprogramming with the term "multiuser" (just discussed), which refers to the ability to have a single computer system shared among two or more users simultaneously. Multiprogramming means the ability of a server system to execute simultaneously two or more independent application programs. (We introduced the concept earlier in the discussion of parallel processing.)

Before multiprogramming, a computer had to finish processing one application program completely before another could be started. The operating systems used with these servers all support a multi-application environment. This means that multiple application programs are being processed at the same time, using a time-sharing technique. With time sharing, a computer system processes the first active application program for a period, or slice, of time; then it suspends that application program and spends another slice of time processing the next active application program; then it moves on to the next, and the next, until it comes back to the first application program and the cycle begins again. This round-robin approach to time sharing, also called time slicing, allows progress to be made on each of the active application programs. Because the computer system moves so quickly from one application program to another, it appears that all application programs are being executed simultaneously. A hierarchy of predetermined user-defined priority allows the server to spend more of its time on the most important application programs.

One of the biggest advantages to a multiprogramming environment is that it more effectively utilizes the processor unit. The majority of the time it takes to process a typical business application program is spent waiting for I/O activities (for example, reads and writes to disk storage) associated with that application program to complete. Before multiprogramming, the processor unit simply sat uselessly spinning in a high-speed programming loop while the I/O activity was in process. This wasted time. In a multiprogramming environment the processor simply goes on processing other application programs while one application program is waiting for an I/O operation to complete. Thus, multiprogramming makes for more effective utilization of the PU and allows more work to get done in a given period of time.

Communications—Connecting the Business

Once the operating system and application programs are loaded, the server is complete and the users can begin working with the system to perform the daily business activities. If one activity is most crucial to a business of any size, it is the act of communicating information to the proper decision maker. Based on the information available to the decision maker, important choices are made that can have far-reaching results on the success of the business. Improved communication in a business is likely to improve both productivity and profitability. Ironically, as a business grows, it becomes more important and more difficult to maintain efficient, accurate communications—the very thing that facilitated business growth in the first place. Communications difficulties grow geometrically with the size of the business.

Many businesses, especially large businesses, have personnel at more than one geographical location (be it across town or around the globe). In these cases, it becomes important to provide these distant (or remote) personnel with access to the central server. Figure 2.25 shows network attachment peripherals that allow remote users to interact with the server with all of the capabilities of local users.

The system pictured is that which was traditionally provided for Systems Network Architecture (SNA) networks. The system has a communications controller, which, like a local workstation control unit, handles the traffic between the remote users' workstations and the server. It attaches (through a modem) to one or more communications lines and manages communications lines and protocols (the language used to send information over the communications line). At the remote location, on the other end, a remote workstation controller does for remote workstations what a local workstation controller does for local workstations. It (along with a modem) sends and receives information over communications lines.

Finally, our example configuration also shows a second communications line that allows the system to communicate with a distant server system. Often it is desirable for a company to have two, three, or more server systems distributed at different locations to serve the needs of local communities of users, for disaster backup, or for balancing workload spikes. By allowing these distributed servers to communicate with one another, users of each server system have access to common system resources, such as information, printers, or programs, of all servers.

Even for the business that needs only one server, it is often desirable to communicate with servers belonging to other companies. Electronic Data Interchange (EDI) enables companies to electronically submit orders to suppliers; to receive delivery schedules, shipping notices, and invoices; and to effect an electronic transfer of funds—all through communications links between computers. EDI, like e-business, eliminates

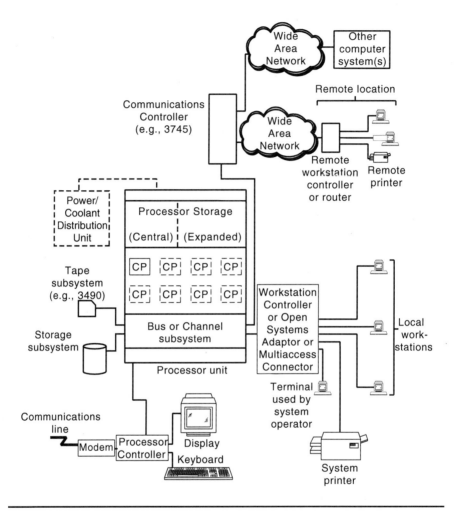

Figure 2.25. Example organization of information for Async communications.

the delay associated with mail and the logistical headache of dealing with thousands of documents circulating from in-basket to in-basket.

IBM recently announced e-business, and although it provides the same concept as EDI, e-business is much expanded to enable full business interactions across the Internet, coupling traditional IT with the World Wide Web.

In earlier times, computers were like islands, each performing very specific tasks independent of any other computer. As server systems became more popular, they grew in number and also spread over wide geographic distances. Almost as an afterthought, it became desirable to attach remote users to servers as well as to link distant server systems. For this reason, in 1974 IBM introduced a set of communications conventions called the Systems Network Architecture (SNA).

This set of published communications standards provided a direction for the evolution of flexible, cost-effective communications. SNA is a set of communications standards to which IBM committed support as a strategic direction for future products. It defines communications protocols, hardware specifications, and programming conventions that make for coherent growth of communications facilities. Since 1974, IBM and many other companies have provided servers and programming products that conform to SNA. SNA is now a predominant means for server communications in the business environment, although pressures of intranets and the Internet are driving TCP/IP demands for business.

IBM has evolved SNA to an open standard known as High-Performance Routing (HPR). HPR has many of the values of traditional subarea SNA, but with substantially improved ease of use and functionality, and with nondisruptive sessions providing protection from communications systems failures. HPR is a key part of the IBM server strategy.

Communications with the server do not have to be provided by SNA. The S/390 and zSeries communications functions have been expanded to permit communications using TCP/IP as well. TCP/IP, often associated with the Internet and the World Wide Web, is an open standard for communications, typically encompassing a router-based network that provides many of the functions envisioned by Figure 2.25 but using different underlying techniques.

Choices for connectivity to these servers have also expanded significantly. The network can consist of almost any combination of traditional subarea SNA, Advanced Peer-to-Peer Networking (APPN), High-Performance Routing (HPR), or TCP/IP devices and protocols. Many businesses use connectivity options such as the IBM 3746 Models 900 and 950 Controllers for attachment to the server. The Open Systems Adapter (OSA 2) or now the Open Systems Adapter– Express (OSA-Express) are the preferred means for direct access to the server, using standard LAN protocols without the need for a channel attachment using routers and switches from a variety of vendors. OSA-Express has become the technology of preference for network connection to the server as previously described in this chapter. More OSA-Express discussion will be found in the communications focus of Chapter 5. The client workstations can include personal communications or even exploit Web-browser-based access using IBM's Host on Demand.

Interfaces and Protocols

A communications line can be thought of as a cable between two or more servers. A single communications line can provide a connection to one other server across the room or to hundreds of other servers across global distances. By using multiple communications lines, a business can provide information from a single point (such as a single server system) to users or servers in many locations (that is, remote users or remote servers).

To be attached to a communications line, the server must first have the proper electrical interface. The term "interface" refers collectively to the connector, electrical voltage levels, connector pin functions, and so on that are provided for the attachment to a communications line. Some commonly used interfaces include RS-232/V.24, V.35, token-ring, Ethernet (802.3), X.21, and ISDN. It is not necessary to understand exactly what all these cryptic names mean, but it is important to know that different types of interfaces are necessary to support different types of communications. The interface may be provided by an integrated adapter card installed in rack-mounted S/390 servers or in a separate communications subsystem (for example, a 3745 Communications Controller).

In addition to the different interfaces, it is important to know about communications protocols. Just as there are different rules of grammar and punctuation in English, French, and other languages, there are different rules for various types of computer communications. In computer communications, a set of rules is called a communications protocol. Some commonly used communication link layer protocols include Async, Bisync, SDLC, X.25, ISDN, token-ring, Frame Relay, ATM, Ethernet, and Fast Ethernet. Each of these different protocols has the same basic goal of moving information from one place to another efficiently and reliably. Each has advantages and disadvantages. Selecting one depends on user requirements in the areas of transmission speed, cost, and compatibility with the other device(s) in the network. The options are discussed in greater detail in Chapter 5.

The Async (short for "asynchronous") protocol is a low-speed, low-cost communications method used by many devices. With Async, individual bytes of information are transmitted (one bit at a time) with no fixed relationship between bytes. Figure 2.26 shows one way a byte might be packaged before it is sent over an Async communications line. The start bit tells the receiving end that information is coming down the line. The user's data follow the start bit. The parity bit is used by the receiving end to check for transmission errors in the user's data. Finally, the stop bit signifies the end of the transmission of the character. The user can select other organizations, such as eight user-data bits, no parity bits, and two stop bits. These different organizations exist primarily because of the many types of equipment that have used this protocol over the years. The specific organization used must be established at both ends of the communications link before communications can begin.

In the Binary Synchronous Communications (BSC or Bisync) protocol, a special character preceding the information synchronizes the receiver with the incoming information. This synchronization allows many bytes of information to be sent as a single block, in contrast to the asynchronous protocol in which a single byte is sent at a time. The ability to send blocks of characters makes Bisync more efficient than the asynchronous protocol. Bisync is an older communications protocol used by terminals and other equipment to exchange information with many different types of servers, including IBM's System/360, Sys-

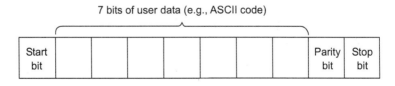

Figure 2.26. The token-ring network uses a token-passing communications protocol.

tem/370, and S/390servers. Because of its past popularity and simplicity, many of today's computer systems still offer this protocol.

The Synchronous Data Link Control (SDLC) protocol is basically an updated version of Bisync. As with Bisync, SDLC is a synchronous communications protocol. However, SDLC is a more flexible protocol that is included in IBM's Systems Network Architecture (SNA). Many SDLC connections are being replaced by frame relay connections as the performance, speed, and reliability of today's networks improve.

The X.25 protocol is an industry standard used in the packet-switched networks available to the public today. Although more traditional communications networks are based on analog or voice-type communications signals, packet-switched networks can use analog signals but are moving to use digital or computerlike communications signals. Since computer information is naturally in digital form, packet-switched networks are better able to carry computer information and can move the information more quickly. The X.25 protocol used on packet-switched networks splits the information into small groups (using, for example, the SDLC protocols as a packaging format) of digital data called packets. Each packet is then sent to its destination elsewhere in the network through the most economical and available route. Since each packet is routed in the most efficient way, overall information flow is improved over prior techniques. X.25 is fully supported in IBM's Systems Network Architecture and TCP/IP protocols.

The narrow-band Integrated Services Digital Network (ISDN) fits more naturally with computer communications than do the traditional analog signals used with telephone communications. Currently more popular in Europe and Japan, ISDN communications services are becoming more common in the United States. Computers attach to ISDN with a digital connection, which eliminates the need for the conversion to analog signals.

The token-ring network (Figure 2.27) is a communications configuration that allows for a collection of different computer systems within a small area (within the same building, for example) to communicate very efficiently. Token-ring networks use the token-ring protocol (known as IEEE 802.5). Basically, packets of information are passed around the ring (connected computer systems) from node to node in a continuous circle. These packets are called message frames. A unique frame called a token frame controls access to the ring.

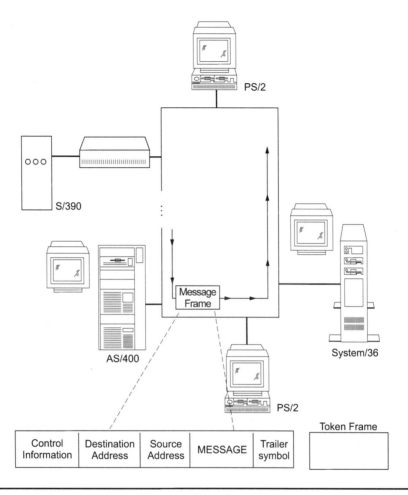

Figure 2.27. S/390 Microprocessor Complex (P/390).

When a node receives a frame, it checks to see whether it is a message or a token frame. If it is a message frame, the node examines the destination address to see if the message is intended for that node. If the message is not intended for that node, the message frame is passed on unchanged to the next node in the ring. If the frame received by a node is a token frame, the node knows that the network is idle and that it may send a message frame if it has information to transfer. After it sends a message frame, the node then sends a token frame to indicate that the ring is again inactive and ready to carry information.

Links in the ring can consist of any medium, such as coaxial, twisted-pair, or fiber-optic cable. Twisted-pair, used in millions of telephone lines connected to houses and businesses, is the most popular, even though it is limited in its capacity to carry large volumes of digital data. Coaxial cables have the capacity to transmit far higher volumes of data, including high-quality, interactive, digital data for multimedia applications. Fiber-optic links have an even greater capacity and can extend token-ring operations over longer distances. Communication takes place at 4 or 16 million bits per second. For proper operation, a token must circulate continuously, even if there is no activity on the ring. Each token contains 24 bits of information, and the ring must have enough delay built into the process to allow those bits to pass.

A 4-million-bit-per-second ring can be up to 240 meters long and can connect up to 96 devices. A 16-million-bit-per-second ring can be up to 1 km in length and connect up to 260 devices. Multiple rings can be bridged together for longer distances. Communication speed is expected to reach 100 million bits per second in the future.

Another type of local area network (LAN) popular today is the Ethernet LAN (IEEE 802.3). With Ethernet, each computer is attached as a tap off a common cable, or bus. For this reason, Ethernet is called a bus-wired network. Thus, an Ethernet LAN is basically a party line on which all computers can transmit a message for all other computers to hear. Every computer has equal access to the cable and can send a message at any time without warning. To ensure that only one computer transmits at a time, each node follows a protocol called Carrier Sense Multiple Access/Collision Detect (CSMA/CD) when transmitting messages. The name is unwieldy, but the protocol is simple. In fact, it is the same protocol used in everyday telephone conversations, in which only one person can speak at a time or neither is clearly understood. Thus, the phone line carries only one party's voice at a time, and the message is clear. This is the "CSMA" part of CSMA/CD, more commonly referred to as the "listen before talking" protocol.

The "CD" part of the protocol handles the times when two nodes start transmissions simultaneously. To understand this part of the protocol, think of what happens during a telephone conversation when both parties begin talking at the same time. Typically, each person stops talking and begins again a few moments later, hoping that this time one party begins sooner than the other. With CSMA/CD, if two (or more) nodes begin transmitting at the same time, the messages "collide" on the network. The nodes monitor for such a collision, and when one is detected, all nodes stop transmitting and begin again after a pause of random length. Usually, one node begins its retransmission before the other, which allows it to gain control of the network.

As with token-ring networks, multiple physical cable options, including coaxial, twisted-pair, and fiber-optic cables, are available with Ethernet. Coaxial cable, the most popular, has a thick and a thin variation. Thick cables support a distance of up to 2,800 meters and a maximum of 1,024 workstations; thin cables support a maximum distance of 925 meters and up to 1,024 workstations. Currently, Ethernet supports a transfer rate of 10 million bits per second and Fast Ethernet supports up to 100 million bits per second. In 1993, 62% of S/390establishments had Ethernet LANs installed. There is no question that Ethernet, Fast Ethernet, or Gigabit Ethernet will be a large player in the future networking technologies.

Fiber Distributed Data Interface (FDDI) is an ANSI standard (X3T9.5) for a 100-million-bit-per-second LAN using fiber-optic cabling (copper twisted-pair is also supported). This standard is based on a ring topology and uses an early release token-passing access method (similar to the token-ring capability described earlier). The FDDI technology is based on a set of counter-rotating rings that provide a high degree of reliability. In normal operation, the primary ring carries data and the second ring is used for automatic recovery in case of a single point of failure in the primary ring. The FDDI standard specifies that stations can be up to 2 km apart and that a total network can cover up to 100 km. Estimates indicate that 25% of S/390 establishments had FDDI LANs installed by year-end 1994.

Asynchronous Transfer Mode (ATM) has emerged to be a worldwide network protocol that offers very high bandwidth (up to billions of bits per second). This technology was expected to provide a foundation for network computing, where large blocks of multimedia data are required to be moved with required deliver characteristics. Now, ATM has become a core networking technology when reliability and predictability are key concerns. ATM provides a flexible and fast cell-switching service. Data traffic, which can be voice, data, and video from multiple channels, is "multiplexed" (multiple forms and packets of data are transmitted simultaneously) to provide better bandwidth utilization.

Packets within ATM are called cells, and each cell contains 48 bytes of data. Each cell is preceded by a 5-byte header, making the total packet 53 bytes in size. Existing LAN technologies can be emulated using ATM LAN Emulation (LANE), enabling current LAN-based applications to use ATM technology without change but without some of the benefits of ATM. Native ATM exploitation, also provided via OSA 2, positions S/390 to fully participate in all ATM network environments.

The S/390 and zSeries Open Systems Adapter (discussed earlier in this chapter) helps provide cost-effective communications to your business; OSA 1, OSA 2, and now OSA-E are designed to deliver integrated industry-standard connectivity in a nearly seamless manner. This enables the adapter to provide connectivity to LANs, LAN backbones, high-speed workstations, intelligent hubs, bridges, and routers in a mixed (heterogeneous) environment. The adapters deliver traditional SNA, APPN, HPR, and TCP/IP access to S/390 and z900 servers.

OSA 1, announced in November 1994, provides integrated FDDI, token-ring, and Ethernet support. OSA 2, introduced in 1995, provides support for SNA Passthru, TCP/IP Passthru, LPAR support, FDDI, token-ring, and Ethernet (10 Mbit/s and 100 Mbit/s) industry-standard LAN connectivity. OSA-E is the new platform from which S/390 G6 and z900 supports native and LAN-emulation ATM implementations. OSA-E will be discussed in more detail in Chapter 5.

Additional Integrated Function

Although S/390's core hardware and software technologies have steadily improved over the years, perhaps the most significant business benefits are found in its systemwide integration of these technologies. The following sections describe several of the ways in which your business can benefit from this integration. The topics are presented in more detail in subsequent chapters.

UNIX Services

For businesses running traditional S/390-based applications, UNIX Services, formerly known as OpenEdition MVS, is IBM's response to this need. Introduced in MVS/ESA SP Version 4, Release 3, this function added a set of services that comply with IEEE Portable Operating System Interface for Computer Environments (POSIX) standards. These services consist of an Application Programming Interface (API) for the C language, an extended user interface, a hierarchical file system, a command shell and utilities, and a debugger. Users familiar with UNIX commands can use their skills immediately with UNIX Services.

UNIX Services is a set of open, vendor-independent standards incorporated into MVS/ESA Version 5 and now z/OS and OS/390. These standards provide features that bring application portability and system interoperability to the S/390 world of operating systems. The demand for open systems grew out of business's desire for choice and flexibility. Changes within the business environment required that applications be developed or acquired and delivered quickly when needed. Existing infrastructures should not slow down this capability.

A later level of the support, in MVS/ESA Version 5, Release 2.2, enables users to port UNIX applications to S/390, expand the scope of POSIX applications to include new UNIX functions, develop and use DCE client/server applications on S/390, support UNIX applications that need to share data in a heterogeneous environment, and use existing OS/390 databases in a heterogeneous network environment.

Object Technology

The dynamics of the business environment and the speed with which technology evolves drive the need for flexibility in applications. As businesses reengineer, restructure, and resize to become more competitive, object technology (to be discussed more fully in Chapter 4) changes the economics of application development. It holds the promise of taking a complex business problem and providing a solution using software components that are extendible and reusable. Object technology applications will closely model the business problems they are designed to solve, will be easier to develop, and will be more flexible to maintain. Java and the wealth of technologies surrounding it, such as JavaBeans, are providing significant value in this area.

By definition, object technology is well suited for distributed systems because the business logic (that is, methods or procedures) and the data are contained within a single software element in an application.

These elements (often referred to as components) are the objects that are used in designing and implementing software. Objects represent real-world items, such as a bank account, a customer order, or an employee record. Objects can be located anywhere within a distributed network and will be isolated from most specific platform characteristics. The focus of application development falls on understanding the market-place, the customer interactions, and business processes, rather than on technical elements of program development. The real value, however, is in the programming model, with local/remote transparency and life cycle management, including tools, combined with industry standards such as CORBA/IIOP.

With markets moving toward shorter product life cycles, businesses will find object technology attractive both for reducing the time required to develop applications and for designing flexible applications that create competitive advantage. With object-oriented applications, businesses will be able to respond more aggressively to shifts within the industry.

Data Management Alternatives

Like the information technology industry as a whole, data management also is experiencing rapid change. Network computing provides a wide variety of clients with access to large computer systems. Parallel technology in both hardware and software is attracting strong interest. These trends allow businesses to exploit their data in ways that were not possible or affordable just five years ago. Data mining and data warehouses (discussed in Chapter 4) are only two examples of increased business dependence on data management.

The complexity of managing data increases the demand for cost-effective scalable solutions that provide good performance and high availability. Also, businesses want to be able to decentralize data usage, but not necessarily data storage, using multiple vendor products while retaining control and management of that data. These needs are driving a more varied set of data type definitions such as text, sound, image, and video. Relational databases now have richer support for structured data as object-oriented databases complement support of user-defined data structures. Databases will use parallel processing techniques in addition to supporting parallel functions in operating systems and hardware. Around-the-clock availability demands more backup and recovery features applying to data at a more granular level. Data replication, two-phase commit, distributed queries, and heterogeneous data access are each extending the business use of data. Chapters 4 and 6 describe IBM's investments in tools that are accelerating the evolution of data management.

Enterprise Multimedia Servers

Text, graphics, images, audio, and video are the media for business communications today. Vital computing systems will provide added value to businesses by supporting these critical technologies. S/390 is again keeping pace.

Enterprise multimedia capability requires the storage, processing, and transmission of multimedia (all the forms listed earlier) information throughout and beyond the business. Integrating this capability with existing applications will make multimedia a powerful and major extension of existing client/server technologies. Business applications for which multimedia provides value include

- **Folder Management.** In many businesses, much of the clerical and administrative work is related to handling correspondence, notes, documents, photographs, and faxes. These are often contained in a folder placed in a filing cabinet. They are bulky, are costly to store and retrieve, and sometimes get misplaced. Electronic image-based folders bring substantial business benefit, already being achieved by some insurance companies.

- **Direct Retailing.** Glossy catalogues are widely used as one of today's solutions to direct selling. Making them available in digital form as an interactive multimedia application with enhanced images, video clips, and sound reduces the direct selling cost and extends the retailer's reach to new customers. Prototypical applications are under development today.

- **Motor Insurance Claims Handling.** Scanning copies of accident reports and repair estimates into a multimedia server enables online handling of the approval process. Video films of actual damage improve the assessment and result in quick agreement on the amount. Insurance companies reduce costs because assessors travel less, and customers benefit by faster response.

- **Media Inventory.** A business that produces and sells music and video CDs can hold hundreds of thousands of music tracks. Today these are stored on magnetic tape that is aging, placing the sound track at risk. Changing the analog tape to digital form enables the data to be compressed and stored on a combination of magnetic disk, optical disk, and automated library tape. Because it is digital, it can be copied flawlessly many times. The possibilities for users to search this data, choose appropriate sound tracks and video clips, and create their own CDs opens new business opportunities.

The S/390 and z900 are the cornerstone for the movement to the World Wide Web. With over 80% of the world's data located on an S/390 or z900 platforms, access to the data is critical. The zSeries now offers users a logical path to grow into larger, more sophisticated and more reliable server systems either in conjunction with their S/390 or consolidated on one or more new z900s.

Performance Overview

One important aspect of a computer system is the rate at which it completes its assigned work, known as the performance of the computer. The higher the performance, the more work the computer does in a given time period. Many things, including the central processor(s), central storage, expanded storage, I/O channel or bus configurations, DASDs, communications line speeds, and programming efficiencies affect the performance of a computer system. This complexity makes it difficult, and often misleading, to predict the overall performance of a computer system by looking at selected specifications of the individual components.

Because these servers have peripheral devices in common, it is possible to focus on the performance differences between the various servers without too much oversimplification. Even with a focus on processor unit performance, however, there are many elements that together determine the level of performance a server delivers. Central processor cycle time, number of execution units within a central processor, rate of instruction execution (often measured in Millions of Instructions Per Second, or MIPS), the function of the instruction set, central storage size and speed, and expanded storage size and speed are all major factors in server performance. Although each of these is important, none of them individually defines processor unit performance.

Benchmark testing compares the overall performance of different servers. This involves loading each benchmark computer with the same number of users, running the same programs, and measuring how the system behaves under the load. Through this benchmark testing, all of the elements come into play, and the overall performance of selected servers is compared meaningfully. It is important to choose a benchmark that is representative of the type of workload supported by the computer.

Existing types of industry benchmarks are classified into two categories:

1. Industry-standard benchmarks are usually run in batch mode, exercise the arithmetic capabilities of the computer, and report results in MIPS (Millions of Instructions Per Second). Dhrystone MIPS uses 100 C-language source statements, which are chosen by statistical analysis and execute using no memory access or I/O. SPECmark-I and SPECmark-F are industry-standard benchmarks for scientific computing. They measure integer and floating-point performance, and are run in batch mode.

2. Independent commercial benchmarks, such as the Transaction Processing Performance Council's TPC-A, TPC-B, TPC-C, TPC-D, and RAMP-C, usually report results in number of transactions per unit of time. TPC-A is a simple "on-line" benchmark, TPC-B measures performance in batch mode, TPC-C measures performance of complex transaction-processing workloads, and TPC-D measures a decision support environment.

IBM has conducted benchmark testing to compare the relative performance of the various S/390 and z900 models with one another. This testing was done by loading the computers with various mixes of specially designed programs, called workloads, that exercise the processors as they would operate in various hypothetical business environments. To perform benchmark testing, the test group must make assumptions about the kind of work being done and the behavior of the users at each workstation. For this reason, no testing can say exactly how a processor performs under an individual application. Because all assumptions are the same for all models included in the benchmark testing, however, the test provides an excellent measure of the relative performance of the various models. The following sections describe the types of performance measurement IBM uses for S/390 and z900.

Large System Performance Reference (LSPR)

The IBM Large System Performance Reference (LSPR) ratios are IBM's assessment of relative processor capacity in an unconstrained environment for specific benchmark workloads and system control programs. The results are based on both measurements and analysis. Each workload is run such that it can be compared with other measurements of the same workload. Nothing is done to favor any specific processor. When a suitable testing environment is not available, analysis is used to address these methodology concerns.

Since consistency in workloads is required, and since it is impractical to actually test with tens of thousands of "real" workstations, a terminal simulator is used for interactive workload measurements. For each simulated remote VTAM terminal for OS/390, the simulator must assign scripts, generate end-user inputs (with think time and think time distribution applied), and wait for the response before sending the next input. IBM's simulator performs these functions without any significant impact on the host measurement. The CPU cost of generating transactions is included in the overall processing of the transaction when computing an Internal Throughput Rate (ITR).

The LSPR measurement tools make transactions appear to the system exactly as if they had come in from a local or a remote terminal. Internal instruction paths and interrupts to process the transaction are identical to those that occur in production environments.

The performance of the S/390 and z900 servers is measured in terms of throughput, or the amount of work the server does in a given period of time. To isolate the processor unit performance from that of other subsystems necessary to make a complete server system, the Internal Throughput Rate (ITR) is measured. The ITR is the amount of work done during the portions of the testing period in which the processor unit is actually performing work (rather than waiting for external devices to respond). It is a measure of the number of completed transactions divided by the amount of time the central processor(s) is busy. To compare the performance of the various servers the workloads are run under OS/390 Version 2, Release 10 and the raw ITR for each processor is converted to a ratio. To calculate the ITR ratio, the zSeries 900 and S/390 G5/G6 models are divided by the ITR of the zSeries 900 Model 1C1. This ITR ratio is used to compare the performance of the various models.

The performance level of the zSeries 900 Model 1C1 is arbitrarily given the value of 1 in each operating system environment and under all workloads. The larger the ITR ratio, when greater than 1.0, the higher the performance of that server is over the Model 1C1 model server. If the ITR ratio for that server is less than 1.0, that server has a lower performance than the Model 1C1. A general-purpose Model 116 mixed ITR is 10.78 versus 1.0 for the Capacity Model 1C1. In a CBW2 workload the ITR is 15.19. At the other extreme a G5 RA6 mixed ITR is 0.34 versus a z900 Model 1C1 and the equivalent G5 Turbo model mixed ITR is 0.60. The S/390 G6 Turbo Model ZZ7, the 12-way, mixed ITR is 6.87. In addition to OS/390 Version 2, Release 10, ITRs were developed for VM CMS, VSE CICS, and CICS as a VM guest. Appendix B is a pictoral relative performance comparison of the S/390 G5/G6 and the z900.

Workloads selected during the MVS/ESA benchmark testing reflect the different types of workloads found in today's computing environment. They include Engineering/Scientific Batch (FPC1), Commercial Batch (CBW2 and CB84), Time Sharing Option (TSO) On-line, Customer Information Control System (CICS) On-line, Database 2 (DB2) On-line, and Information Management System (IMS) On-line. These characterize workloads of the System/370 and S/390 families with standard features; therefore, the engineering/scientific workload was not implemented to take advantage of the Integrated Vector Facility, which typically improves performance for this type of work.

For more information concerning the workload environments, the metrics of measurement, using performance data, and validating a new processor's capacity expectations, see the IBM Large Systems Performance Reference (LSPR), SC28-1187, or visit the IBM LSPR Web site at *http://www-1.com/servers/eserver/zseries/lspr/*.

Using the Transaction Processing Performance Council (TPC)

The Transaction Processing Performance Council, of which IBM has been a member since November 1988, consists of computer vendors seeking to produce industry-standard benchmarks for the on-line transaction-processing environment. Manufacturers run the benchmarks at their own expense and conform to a set of rules defined by the TPC. Results require TPC-approved auditing and are published in a full disclosure report written by the vendor.

TPC metrics include a transaction rate expressed in transactions per second (tps) or transactions per minute (tpm) and a cost per transaction per unit of time. This cost is calculated by dividing the five-year cost of the tested system by the transaction rate. The five-year cost includes elements such as terminals, terminal controllers, network controllers, channels, processor, tapes, disks, software, and maintenance. Each TPC benchmark also includes several nonperformance tests to ensure that the tested systems have a reasonable level of robustness. Four benchmarks, described later, have been defined and made available, and three additional TPC benchmarks (measuring client/server, server only, and enterprise workload applications) are in process.

The TPC-A benchmark standardized measurements of the DebitCredit banking application and provided specifications on how to implement, measure, and report results using that workload. The TPC-B benchmark is the "batch" version of the TPC-A benchmark; that is, it does not include the front-end transaction manager, reducing the path length per transaction. The TPC-C benchmark represents some typical transactions of a commercial business engaged in selling and distributing a product. The workload consists of five unique transactions, with each being selected at defined frequencies. The frequency of only one of the five transactions is reported as transactions per minute (tpmC). The TPC-D benchmark represents a decision support environment consisting of 17 queries and 2 batch update jobs. The TPC-D benchmark became available in April 1995.

Summary

In an era when the life span of technology is measured in months, the IBM large eServers stand alone in business servers with an evolutionary history spanning four decades. As technologies have modified each component of the server system, from the processor to the storage hierarchy, to communications, to peripherals, and to operating system and application software, these servers have adapted to those changes, and they continue to deliver new advanced functions critical to business growth. The IBM large eServers have been a force for change, delivering added value to its users. The remaining chapters of this book detail the increased value businesses can realize today with S/390 and zSeries.

3

Peripherals—Fueling a Revolution

If servers are the engines driving business processes and business growth, data is the fuel that powers those engines. Whether your business performs scientific or commercial computing, each of your applications and processes has one element in common—data. Data available where it is needed, when it is needed, in appropriate quantity, and in a suitable form is key to driving business processes.

This chapter focuses on technology and several older generation and new generation products that move data into and out of servers and provide storage for data when it is not actively being used by the server. Input/output (I/O) channels (or simply, channels), which provide the means of connecting devices to servers, were introduced in the previous chapter. This chapter explores the three primary channel types, parallel, Enterprise System CONnection (ESCON), and FIber CONnection (FICON). For networking attachment to the S/390 and the z900, this chapter and Chapter 5 will discuss the Open Systems Adapter, which provides a means for industry-standard communications attachment to the S/390 and especially with the z900 infrastructure.

Devices called peripherals are used to gather, display, and store data in a variety of formats and for a variety of business purposes. (See "Storage Hierarchy" in Chapter 2 for additional information.) Peripheral devices are attached to S/390 or zSeries servers (usually via a cable to an installed feature) and perform functions under the computer's control. Disks, tape drives, printers, and plotters fall into this category.

Historically, computing has used data as a finished product to be packaged and used virtually in the same form in which it was captured. A variety of display formats were provided to simplify the presentation of data, but little was done to the data itself. In the past 10 years, with the rapid evolution of personal and office computing, the focus has moved from using data as a finished product to using data as raw material. Although still valued in its own right, data is increasingly viewed as valuable for the information that can be derived from its analysis. The finished product is now the information, or knowledge, that is derived from the data, and that advance, stimulated and supported by the technology of peripherals, is fueling a revolution in the use of data to achieve business advantage.

This change in the perception of data has dramatically changed how data is processed, stored, and displayed. Data analysis, for example, requires a different processing scheme than does the processing of transactions that use small amounts of data. This in turn drives the need to feed processors large amounts of data and to present the summary of that data in user-friendly displays or printouts. Because data is now viewed for its contributions to business information, retaining large amounts of historical data while ensuring its accuracy and integrity is increasingly important to business operations. The advent of the Internet has driven the need for new access to the data stored on the S/390. Numerous methods have been developed to provide access to the data while maintaining its security and integrity.

Chapter 2 addressed the revolutionary changes in server capability. This chapter explores equally revolutionary changes in peripherals. Chapter 4 presents the software structures built on top of this foundation. Together, these chapters describe the interactions among the hardware and software portions of a server system and present the magnitude of the revolution that has occurred in central-site server systems. Adding the communication layer, which is to be discussed in Chapter 5, expands the scope of the revolution to your whole business.

This chapter does not provide comprehensive coverage of all peripherals that can be used with S/390 and zSeries servers. It does, however, introduce several currently used or new device types that represent those most commonly used in an up-to-date business environment. We begin by exploring the architecture and technology that connect those devices to processors. Because the channel technology and peripheral device applications are similar for both the S/390 and z900 and were described in Chapter 2, the discussions in this chapter apply equally to both server generations unless differences are specifically noted.

Input/Output (I/O) Channel Architecture

The input/output (I/O) channels in z900, or S/390, servers provide a pipeline through which information is exchanged between the server processor unit and external devices. The most common type of device attached to a channel is a control unit (or controller). The control unit is a device that houses circuitry designed to manipulate one or more specific types of I/O device. Figure 3.1 illustrates how I/O devices and control units are attached to channels.

In the figure, an S/390 processor unit is equipped with several channels. The first channel (channel 1) is attached to an old 3174 Establishment Controller (this category of control unit, called communications controllers, is discussed in Chapter 5), which is attached to a group of terminals and a printer. Another channel (channel 2) is attached to a

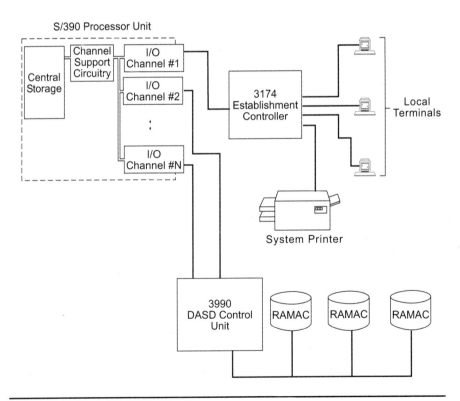

Figure 3.1. I/O devices attach to S/390 processors via channels.

3990 DASD Control Unit, which is attached to RAMAC DASDs. In another application of channels (not shown in the figure), a channel in one server can be attached to a channel in another server through a Multisystem Channel Communication Unit (MCCU), enabling high-speed information exchange between two or more server processor units.

Each channel is a small computer in its own right, consisting of a specially programmed microprocessor and associated circuitry. This microprocessor sends and receives packets of information in prescribed formats called Channel Command Words (CCWs) and Channel Status Words (CSWs). Through CCWs and CSWs, the channels manipulate the attached control units, and thus their I/O devices, under the control of the operating system and application programs executing within the server processor unit.

Using Figure 3.1, we can trace the steps necessary for a Central Processor (CP) to read information from a DASD. When the need for additional information is detected in the CP and the information is not found in central (or expanded storage), the operating system, on behalf of the application program, generates a list of CCWs (in effect, a small program that the channel's microprocessor executes) designed to retrieve the needed information. This list is placed in a special area in central storage associated with the appropriate channel, channel 2 in this case. The operating system then notifies channel 2 via an interrupt-driven scheme that it has work to do and returns to its other CP activities.

Channel 2's microprocessor retrieves the list of CCWs from its area of central storage and sends it to the attached 3990 DASD Control Unit. The DASD Control Unit instructs the DASD units to retrieve the necessary information, and it responds with status information (CSWs) as required by the channel protocol. The DASD units read the required information from disk and provide it to the DASD Control Unit, which in turn provides it to channel 2. Channel 2 effects the transfer of the information into a designated area of central storage, using the channel support circuitry. Channel 2 then notifies the operating system via an interrupt that the required information is available in central storage for access by the CP, and the CP resumes where it left off.

Even in this simplified view of channel information flow, you see that a lot of activity must occur in order for information to move up the storage hierarchy from DASD to central storage (discussed in Chapter 2). The more cycles a server system spends doing input/output (I/O) activity, the fewer cycles are left, in a given amount of time, to do work for the users--thus lowering the effective workload throughput of the system. For this reason, it is best to keep as much information as possible (especially information that is likely to be needed soon) as high in the storage hierarchy as possible. Even though I/O channels operate at very high speeds compared to other types of data communications, a performance penalty is paid every time the needed information is not already in the processor unit (either in central or expanded storage). The following sections look more closely at three different types of channels used in the subject servers: the older traditional parallel channels, Enterprise System Connection (ESCON) channels, and the newer Fiber Connect (FICON) channels.

Parallel Channels

The parallel channels used with these servers are essentially the same as those used by the earlier System/370 family of computers. Figure 3.2 illustrates devices attached to S/390 computers through parallel channels. Two copper wire cables connect a parallel channel to a control unit. One cable, called the bus cable, carries the data as it flows between the channel and the control unit(s). The other cable, called the tag cable, carries control signals that implement the communications protocol used between the channel and the control unit(s). Multiple control units are attached to a single parallel channel in a daisy-chained fashion over a maximum distance of 400 feet (122 meters). With an optional 3044 Fiber Optic Extender Link for parallel channels, the distance between the channel and the control unit can be extended an additional 1.8 miles (3 km). Up to 256 devices can connect and simultaneously operate on one parallel channel.

As the term "parallel" implies, information is transferred 8 bits at a time over multiple wires (in parallel) in the bus cable. Data is exchanged between a parallel channel and a control unit in either byte multiplex mode or block multiplex mode. In byte multiplex mode, individual bytes (8 bits) are transferred one at a time or in small groups containing up to 64 bytes. This mode is a relatively slow method of exchanging information (40 KB/s to 1 MB/s) and is used only with slower I/O devices. In block multiplex mode, multiple bytes of information are transferred in large groups with transmission speeds ranging from 1.5 to 4.5 MB/s. A channel's mode of operation is set by the system operator through the I/O Configuration Program (IOCP) and must match that of the attached control unit(s). Parallel channels are used while the S/390 computer is operating in either System/370 mode or ESA/390 mode.

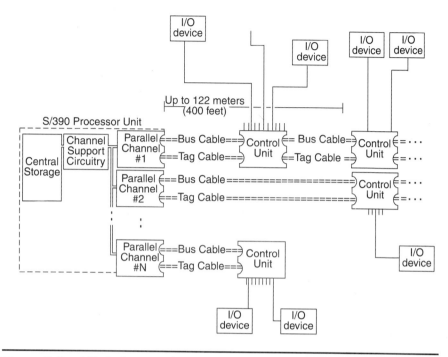

Figure 3.2. I/O devices attach to S/390 processors via traditional parallel channels.

ESCON Channels

Rather than using the bus and tag cables of parallel channels, ESCON channels use fiber-optic cables, which carry light pulses rather than electrical signals. Figure 3.3 illustrates the first difference between the cables. The single fiber-optic cable used with ESCON channels is much smaller than the bus and tag cables used with parallel channels. Also, because the fiber-optic cables use light, they are not susceptible to ElectroMagnetic Interference (EMI), to Radio-Frequency Interference (RFI), or to ground shifts. This immunity offers faster transmission speed and greater maximum distance. The sheer bulk of bus and tag cables always represented a major effort in planning and fitting-up a data center. That and other environmentals for older technology servers were the cause for the use of raised floors in data centers. Fiber-optic cabling, discussed in Chapter 2, is significantly less bulky and represents the cabling medium of preference.

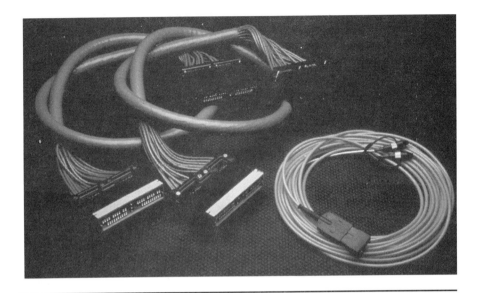

Figure 3.3. Left, traditional bus and tag cables used with parallel channels. Right, fiber-optic cable used with ESCON channels.

With fiber-optic cables, ESCON channels exchange information with control units at a rate of either 10 or 17 MB/s. The data rate varies based on the server type supported. Within the coupling-capable groups of processors, the ES/9121 511-based processors support 10 MB/s and the ES/9021 711-based and the S/390 and z900 servers support a data rate of 17 MB/s.

Distances supported by ESCON channels are a function of the type of fiber supported. Multimode fiber of 50/125 microns in diameter supports a distance of up to 2 km before the signal must be repeated or redriven. Multimode fiber 62.5/125 microns in diameter supports distances of up to 3 km. Single-mode fiber supports distances of up to 20 km. With the ESCON eXtended Distance Feature (XDF), S/390 and z900 servers can exchange information with control units at a distance of up to 20 km. Some features of XDF were withdrawn from marketing by IBM in 1995, but XDF continues to be offered on the ESCON Director s and ESCON Channel Extenders.

ESCON channels are part of the ESA/390 architecture, introduced with the S/390 family. There are four implementations of ESCON channels: native ESCON channels, ESCON Channel-To-Channel (CTC),

ESCON with parallel control units, and ESCON with byte support. They differ in the means of connecting to another channel (CTC, for example) and in the type of control unit they support. Figure 3.4 illustrates how devices are attached.

The fiber cable attaches one ESCON channel directly to one ESCON-compatible control unit, as shown at the bottom of Figure 3.4. Alternatively, an ESCON channel attaches to an ESCON Director (this and other ESCON devices are discussed later in this chapter), which, in turn, attaches to multiple ESCON-compatible control units, also shown in Figure 3.4. The ESCON Director provides a switching function that allows any attached ESCON channel to access any attached control unit. Through one ESCON Director, up to 256 devices and 32 control units are supported per ESCON channel.

This has several ramifications. First, because any channel can get to any device, any channel can act as a backup path for any failing chan-

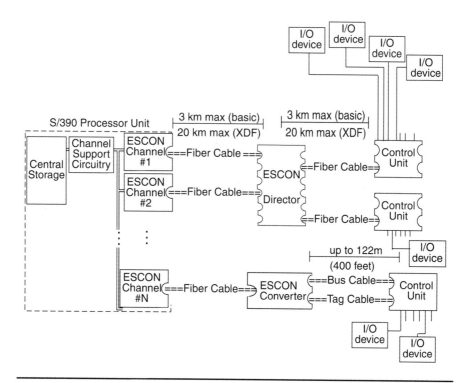

Figure 3.4. I/O devices attach to S/390 processors via ESCON channels.

nel, improving availability and reliability. Although redundant paths also are commonplace with parallel channels, the ESCON Director provides a more flexible configuration. Further, with ESCON channels the workload is more evenly divided over a group of channels, because an idle channel can handle an I/O activity request for another channel. In fact, this switching function allows one channel to send a request to a control unit and another channel to handle the information transfer after the control unit has retrieved the data from its attached I/O device. This is helpful when the channel handling the original request becomes busy before the control unit can respond. The net effect is that the needed information often arrives in central storage more quickly, improving the overall system performance.

Because the distance between ESCON Director s can be up to 14.3 miles (23 km) (ESCON XDF) and two chained ESCON Director s (or three channel extenders) can be used in the connection, the maximum distance from a processor unit to an I/O control unit is 37.3 miles (60 km). However, various I/O control units have their own distance limitations independent of the ESCON XDF capability. For example, a 3990 Model 6 Tape Control Unit can only be located up to 20 km away. The 3490 Tape Control Unit and Tape Library can be up to 23 km from the server, and other controllers can be up to 43 km away.

ESCON channels are used only in an S/390 computer operating in ESA/390 mode or Logical PARtition (LPAR) mode, or on any z900. When operating in ESA/390 LPAR mode, ESCON channels provide a unique capability. ESCON channels are shared across logical partitions, reducing the number of channels required to add new partitions or applications. Sharing channels allows LPARs to connect to I/O devices using significantly fewer cables. This facility is supported on all coupling-capable processors, allowing support of shared coupling links for parallel sysplex. Figure 3.5 shows an example of the sharing that EMIF provides.

With ESCON channels, information is transferred 1 bit at a time over the fiber cable. That is, ESCON channels are serial channels. The slower byte mode of parallel channels is supported with ESCON channels via a 9034 ESCON Converter with byte-device attachment support (for devices such as the 3745 Communications Controller). As with parallel channels, an ESCON channel on one S/390 server can attach to an ESCON channel on another S/390 or z900 server to effect high-speed information transfer between the two systems as long as the distance between the servers is within the supported limits.

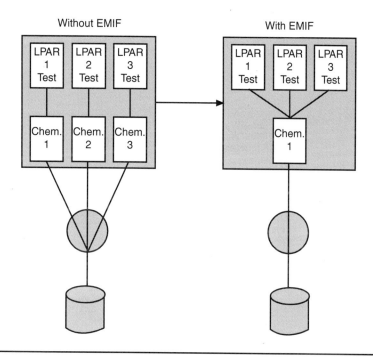

Figure 3.5. EMIF reduces channel connection requirements.

ESCON channels and ESCON Director s directly attach only to ESCON-compatible control units. However, Figure 3.6 shows a configuration that allows non-ESCON control units to attach to ESCON channels through a 9034 ESCON Converter. This device attaches directly to an ESCON channel via fiber-optic cable and to a non-ESCON control unit via traditional bus and tag cables. Alternatively, both parallel and ESCON channels can coexist in a single server.

ESCON Directors
ESCON Directors provide dynamic (that is, "on-the-fly") switching and lengthen links for ESCON (basic and XDF) connections. Each ESCON Director has from 8 to 248 fiber-optic ports that attach to either an I/O control unit or an ESCON channel. As shown in Figures 3.4 and 3.6, ESCON Director s are located between several ESCON I/O channels in a server and several I/O control units, and they route the information flow based on ESCON link configuration information loaded by the

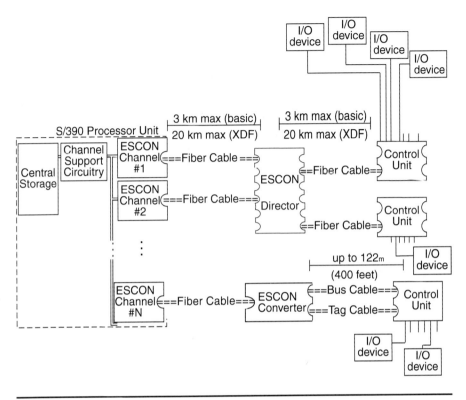

Figure 3.6.   ESCON channels attach to non-ESCON control units via an ESCON converter.

server operator. The ESCON Directors act as high-speed traffic cops, accepting information from one port, interpreting the destination address, and routing the information to the appropriate port. ESCON Director s also perform this switching function in channel-to-channel configurations, in which information is transferred directly between two servers through an ESCON Director link.

Three ESCON Director models are used with S/390 or z900 servers: the 9033 ESCON Director Model 4 (which replaces the Model 1) and the 9032 ESCON Director s Models 3 and 5. The 9033 is a tabletop unit that provides 8, 12, or 16 ports, any of which attach to either ESCON I/O channels or I/O control units. Any 9033 with less than 16 ports expands at any time (in increments of 4 ports) to a total of 16 ports. The 9032 models (see Figure 3.7) are floor-standing units that

Figure 3.7. ESCON Director Model 3.

support from 28 to 248 ports, any of which can be attached to either ESCON I/O channels or I/O control units. The 9032 models can be expanded at any time (in increments of 4 or 8 ports, depending on the model) to the maximum number of up to 124 or 248 ports depending on the model.

On any ESCON Director, individual ports can be configured to be dedicated connections—between an ESCON I/O channel and an I/O control unit, for example, or isolated to permit only specific connections. Up to two ESCON Directors can be connected together (using a dedicated port on each ESCON Director) in a single link. ESCON Directors can be used in conjunction with the 9034 ESCON Converter (discussed later) to attach non-ESCON-capable I/O control units to ESCON I/O channels.

ESCON Directors provide flexibility in establishing links between a set of ESCON I/O channels and I/O control units. Without an ESCON Director, one ESCON channel attaches to only one I/O control unit (a point-to-point ESCON implementation). With an ESCON Director, one ESCON channel can send and receive information with many different I/O control units as the ESCON Director performs the switching necessary to route the information to any I/O control unit attached to that ESCON Director. When attached to multiple ESCON I/O channels, an ESCON Director moves information more efficiently between the server and attached I/O control units by using any of the available I/O channels to communicate with the I/O control unit, eliminating the need to wait for a specific channel to complete any in-process activity before communicating.

A PC (not provided with the ESCON Director) configures and manages an ESCON Director. Configuration functions can be restricted and password protected to prevent unauthorized tampering with an ESCON Director. ESCON I/O channels or I/O control units can be added or removed from an ESCON Director without disrupting the normal operation of other devices attached to that ESCON Director. The ESCON Manager, a licensed software program (discussed in Chapter 7), works with the ESCON Director to simplify the task of managing complex system interconnections.

ESCON Converters

The ESCON Converter Model 1 (9034), shown in Figure 3.8, attaches non-ESCON-capable I/O control units (such as the 3990 DASD Control Unit) to ESCON channels. It converts fiber-optic protocols to parallel protocols. ESCON Converter Model 2 (9035), shown in Figure 3.9, allows ESCON-capable I/O control units to directly attach to parallel I/O channels on older S/370 processors, such as the IBM 3090 and some IBM 4381 systems. It converts parallel protocols to fiber-optic protocols. Both models have a maximum data rate of 4.5 MB/s.

The 9034 is designed for use in environments in which an S/370 or S/390 computer installation is migrating to ESCON over time. It enables most non-ESCON-capable I/O control units to be used on basic ESCON channels in order to benefit from the extended distances afforded by such a connection without having to modify existing application software or databases.

As shown in Figure 3.6, the 9034 attaches to the I/O control unit using the traditional bus and tag cables used with parallel I/O channels.

That is, the 9034 appears to be a parallel I/O channel to the I/O control unit. The 9034 then attaches to a basic ESCON I/O channel configured to operate in ESCON Converter mode. When an ESCON I/O channel operates in ESCON Converter mode, it sends and receives data at 4.5 MB/s (rather than its normal 10 to 17 MB/s rate).

I/O control units using the block multiplex mode of communications and selected byte multiplex mode units (supporting ESCON channels) can be used with this type of connection. The ESCON channel

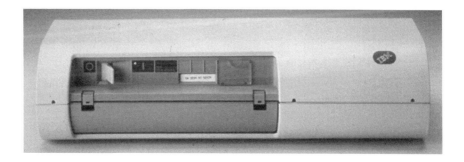

Figure 3.8. 9034 ESCON Converter Model 1.

Figure 3.9. ESCON Converter Model 2.

must be dedicated to the 9034 and its connected I/O control units. Up to eight I/O control units attach to one 9034. Byte multiplexor channel support eliminates the need for parallel channels for these devices and allows for an easy transition to ESCON.

FICON Channels

With the introduction of the S/390 Generation 5 processors in 1998, IBM announced an improvement on the fiber connection standard with FIber CONnection (FICON) channels. FICON technology is compatible with the Fiber Channel PHysical (FC-PH) signaling standard. It extends the maximum distance between the channel and control unit (or director) to 4 km with negligible performance degradation, and it increases the data transfer rate from 20 MB per second to 60 or 80 MB per second, with peak achievable speed of 100 MB per second. In addition, FICON increases the maximum throughput rate from 500 (with ESCON) to 4,000 I/Os per channel per second.

The improved throughput is achieved by several changes. First, of course, is the faster data transfer rate. Second, an ESCON channel operates only in half-duplex mode. That is, data can be going or coming in, but not both at the same time, whereas a FICON channel operates in full-duplex mode, allowing concurrent reads and writes on the same channel. Furthermore, the FICON channel can handle up to eight concurrent I/O operations (from eight control units), while the ESCON channel handles but one. Finally, it is less intrusive to intermix large and small blocks of data on the FICON channel than on the ESCON channel.

There were compelling reasons for IBM to develop the faster FICON channel. The increasing amount of data attached to the server for both operational systems and data warehouses (discussed in Chapter 4), coupled with the dramatic reduction in CMOS cycle time, created a need to keep tape libraries and backup systems at geographically dispersed locations.

At first, FICON channels only connect to 9032 Model 5 ESCON Directors with a FICON Bridge card, which can easily be added to any 9032-5. In future phases, IBM has announced plans to introduce native FICON control units and FICON switches. FICON control units perform the same functions as ESCON control units, but can operate at higher speeds when attached to FICON channels. FICON switches are analogous to ESCON directors, but they enable dynamic connections between multiple FICON channels and multiple FICON control units. Up to 16,384 devices can be attached to one FICON channel, thus reducing the number of channels required.

Even when connected to ESCON directors, the FICON channels greatly simplify configurations. One FICON channel can handle the workload of 8 ESCON channels, thus reducing the number of cables required to connect the server to multiple control units with multiple connections, yet a FICON channel card occupies the same amount of space in the server frame as one ESCON channel card. Up to 24 FICON channels can be installed on a G6 and now up to 96 on a z900. FICON is highly compatible with ESCON, attaching to ESCON Directors and control units, and supporting EMIF as ESCON does.

9729 Optical Wavelength Division Multiplexor (Muxmaster)

The IBM 9729 Optical Wavelength Division Multiplexor provides a mechanism for providing fast, reliable fiber-optic connections between two sites separated by a maximum of 50 km. The 9729 Multiplexor uses optical wavelength division technology to take advantage of the fiber-optic networks that are in place today, replacing multiple, high-speed serial links between sites with a single fiber and then using wave division multiplexing to carry up to 10 separate signals across that single physical connection.

The 9729 Optical Wavelength Division Multiplexor enables multiple bit streams, each possibly using a different communications protocol, bit rate, and frame format, to be multiplexed onto a single optical fiber for transmission between separate locations. The 9729 Multiplexor can multiplex 10 full-duplex bit streams, each at up to 200 Mb/s (million bits per second) over a single optical fiber. The distance between the two locations can be up to 50 km and still support a 200 Mb/s rate per channel.

The 9729 Multiplexor uses 20 optical wavelengths, spaced about 1 nm apart (about 120 GHz) in the 1,550-nm wavelength range. Ten of these channels are used for transmission in one direction and 10 in the opposite direction on the same fiber. Because the actual signal bandwidth that the electronics can handle over one wavelength is such a small fraction of the interchannel spacing, the signals do not interfere with each other and can therefore be multiplexed into a single fiber. The 9729 can be connected to the ESCON channel, as well as to the Sysplex Timer Model 2 to enable interconnectivity of data centers across wider distances. The 9729 comes in two models. The Model 001 is the original product. An entry model, the Model 041, was announced in 1997. The 9729-041 provides for connectivity of up to four connections.

Disk Storage

All S/390 and zSeries servers need some disk storage to complete the computer system. Various combinations of Direct Access Storage Devices (DASDs) provide this storage. The basic anatomy of a DASD was described in Chapter 2. Large servers supporting massive amounts of data have become critical elements in competitive business strategies. Growing volumes of data and increased urgency in accessing data have led to new technologies for ensuring the availability and reliability of data and performance of devices handling data. These technologies include the use of Redundant Arrays of Independent Disks (RAIDs), higher-density devices, and the integration of components to create fault-tolerant and high-availability products. This section presents an overview of these topics.

DASD Performance

It is important to understand a little bit about DASD performance because in most applications it plays an important role in the overall performance of a server system. This is particularly true in commercial environments, in which there is usually heavy transfer of information between a DASD and central storage.

The "performance" of a DASD refers to the rate at which information is located and transferred between the DASD and central storage. The average speed at which a fixed disk positions the read/write head over the proper region of the platter is the average seek time, usually expressed in milliseconds (1/1000 second). After the read/write head is properly positioned, the system must wait as the platter spins until the needed data begins to pass under the read/write head. The average time it takes for the platter to rotate to the proper position for processing the required data is called the average latency, which is also expressed in milliseconds. Finally, once the read/write head is positioned and the data begins to pass by on the spinning platter, the information is transferred from the disk to the controller. The speed at which this is done is called the DASD's data transfer rate. This is usually expressed in millions of bytes per second (MB/s). The shorter the seek time and the latency, and the higher the transfer rate, the better is the performance of the DASD subsystem and, often, that of the overall server system.

In addition to these DASD specifications, other performance considerations apply in configuring the DASD subsystem of a server. These considerations include the number and type of DASD controller(s) being used, the use of intermediate storage areas (cache and nonvolatile storage), and the S/390 or z900 server I/O channel configuration.

RAID Technology

The RAID technology was designed initially as a means of lowering the cost of storage for computing systems (reflected in the term "Redundant Array of *Inexpensive* Disks," which has subsequently been changed to "Redundant Array of *Independent* Disks"). Much of the initial focus was on assessing the advantages of using very low-cost drives at the expense of compensating for their more frequent failures.

IBM's history with disk drives goes back to the development of the first RAMAC device, discussed in Chapter 2. IBM's research on methods for overcoming storage system failures led to the first patent issued, in May 1978, for a disk array (simply put, an organization of multiple disks) subsystem. Thus, it was not surprising that IBM would join, in 1987, with researchers at the University of California at Berkeley looking for ways to lower storage costs while improving reliability and, perhaps, performance.

The original research focused on designs for overcoming the deficiencies of less-reliable, lower-capacity, lower-cost disks by combining large numbers in an array. Large numbers would be needed to match the capacity and performance of a few very large, high-cost storage devices then in use on large computers. Because more disks mean more chance of physical failure, the array design would preserve data availability, offsetting the higher probability of failure in any one of those disks.

The Berkeley project resulted in defining five levels of redundant arrays, three of which (RAID levels 1, 3, and 5) have been implemented by manufacturers. (RAID levels 2 and 4 remain primarily academic architectures). Subsequent to the work done at Berkeley, additional levels of "RAID" technology have been defined. "RAID-0" refers to data striping, in which data is recorded sequentially (in stripes) across several disks rather than continuously on one disk. Although it does not provide protection against failure of a component (that is, it provides no data redundancy), data striping does provide improved I/O performance. "RAID-6" extends parity checking, explained later, to two levels, increasing the complexity of RAID processing while providing increased levels of fault tolerance.

RAID-1, often referred to as data mirroring or dual copy, literally writes the same data to two different storage devices at the same time. This is the simplest and most performance-efficient RAID implementation, but it has the added cost of doubling the storage space required for business data. When used to protect the most valued business data, it is an important dimension of data management.

RAID levels 3, 5, and 6 all require the use of parity information to rebuild missing information when one part of an array of data is lost. For many years, the parity concept has been used to improve the reliability of computer memory. The technique involves the use of sophisticated algorithms to reconstruct missing data from what is known about that data. A simple analogy is found in a basic formula, such as $2 + 6 = x$, in which the numbers represent known data and the x (8) represents parity. As long as any two of the factors in the equation and a statement of their relationship are known, the third element can be found.

The differences in the three RAID levels using parity are seen in the use of the parity information. RAID-3 places data on one set of disks and all parity data on a single separate disk. Although this simplifies the system operation, it can create a bottleneck (contention) at the parity disk when multiple devices are writing to that disk at the same time. RAID-5 spreads parity data across two or more disks, on which it also stores data. This results in multiple write operations to multiple disks, creating a "write penalty" during which the ongoing application can be delayed. It does avoid the contention created by RAID-3, however. RAID-6, not often used in commercial applications, imposes a greater "write penalty" and added complexity because it uses two separate parity schemes to assure data availability, even if two drives should fail.

RAMAC Array Architecture

The first S/390 RAMAC devices were announced and shipped by IBM in 1994. In June 1995, follow-on technology was implemented in RAMAC 2 storage systems. Although RAMAC 2 provides greater-density drives and improves the overall system performance, most product characteristics remain the same. The RAMAC Array architecture is built on four building blocks: the 3.5-inch disk drive, initially introduced as a 2 GB–capacity drive and upgraded with RAMAC 2 to a 4 GB drive; the drawer; the rack; and the 3990 Storage Control. Each of these contributes to the fault-tolerant and high-availability characteristics of the RAMAC and RAMAC 2 Array devices.

In 1996, IBM introduced the RAMAC 3 technology. The RAMAC 3 Array can be combined with one or two Storage Controls (3990) integrated with 2 to 32 RAMAC 3s. A minimum configuration of 45.4 GB includes a single storage control unit and a single storage frame with 2 drawers. Capacity can be added in 22.7 GB increments, resulting in a maximum configuration of 2 storage units and 2 frames with 32 drawers for a total capacity of 726 GB.

The RAMAC 3 storage frame incorporates a new high-speed device adapter, effectively tripling the maximum data rate between the storage control and the drawer to enable overall performance equal to or better than that of RAMAC 2. The RAMAC 3 drawer offers a total of eight logical volumes and enhances performance by incorporating IBM Ultrastar 2XP 3.5-inch 9.1 GB high-performance disk drives. The new drives double the capacity of the previous RAMAC 2 drawer. RAMAC 3 installs on all IBM system software that supports RAMAC 2. The 3990-6 also supports the RAMAC 3 storage frame.

The 3.5-inch Ultrastar 2XP disk drive uses IBM's thin-film MagnetoResistive (MR) head technology, which has a dual-element configuration that allows read and write activities to be optimized independently. MR head technology supports the Ultrastar 2XP's 1 GB per 3.5-inch platter density. Increasing platter densities results in fewer parts and higher reliability and performance. Rotating at 7,200 revolutions per minute (rpm), the Ultrastar 2XP provides an average seek time of 8 milliseconds (ms). The Ultrastar features a maximum synchronous burst transfer rate of 40 MB/s. (See "DASD Performance" earlier in this chapter for explanations of these metrics.) These performance characteristics make it one of the fastest storage devices available.

The RAMAC drawer (shown in Figure 3.10) operates as a high-performance RAID-5 array. Each of the 16 drawers has duplex paths, a battery-supported nonvolatile cache, 32-bit microprocessors, and four 3.5-inch disk drives. In the event of a power failure, the drawer is able to write cache data to disk, ensuring fault-tolerant data availability.

The RAMAC rack (shown in Figure 3.11) supports 16 drawers with redundant power supplies, multiple data paths, redundant cooling fans, and a dual-line cord, further enhancing the availability of data to the application. The rack, for the array DASD models, attaches to the 3990 Storage Control, discussed later. Array subsystem racks contain controller logic and hardware and connect directly to a S/390 channel.

Several design features contribute to high performance and continuous availability in RAMAC storage devices. In addition to the technology characteristics already mentioned, performance is enhanced through sequential data striping, DASD fast write, cache, and concurrent copy. Availability enhancements include dynamic disk reconstruction, fault

Figure 3.10. RAMAC Array Architecture Drawer.

Figure 3.11. RAMAC Array Architecture Rack.

tolerance through component redundancy and NonVolatile Storage (NVS), and dynamic sparing.

Performance Features
Sequential data striping, introduced earlier in the discussion of RAID architecture, improves performance for batched sequential data sets, particularly for sequential write applications, by placing data across multiple volumes in parallel rather than queuing all of the data against a single data volume. In RAMAC's implementation, data is striped across the four drives in each drawer. This function working with RAID-5 data parity contributes to high performance with nearly continuous availability. When successive tracks are striped sequentially, parity information is generated from the content of the newly written data without having to read old data and old parity information. This characteristic contributes to high data rates and reduced elapsed times for sequential write applications. The aggregate data transfer rate becomes the sum of the rates for the total number of volumes assigned to the logical array.

DASD Fast Write enables data intended to be written to relatively slow DASDs to be written instead to NonVolatile Storage (NVS), discussed later, in much less time. This frees the storage subsystem to proceed without having to wait for the relatively long electromechanical delay associated with actually writing the data to a DASD. NVS protects the information from unexpected power outages and writes the information to disk at a time convenient to the subsystem.

As defined earlier, cache is high-speed electronic storage (semiconductor memory) that automatically gathers and holds data likely to be needed soon. Multilevel cache, located in the controller, the rack, and the drawer, enables the subsystem to distribute workload among the different levels, achieving both high performance and availability advantages.

Using a cache as a staging point for reading data from and writing data to a DASD can significantly improve some elements of storage subsystem performance. There are a number of methods, reflecting various trade-offs, for using a cache and a number of places to position a cache. The principle behind using cache storage lies in the fact that when data is read from a DASD (a relatively time-consuming process), additional data likely to be requested in an upcoming read request is near to the last data read. Thus, rather than waiting for the next read, some amount of additional data is read into cache when the requested data is read. If the subsequent read request is satisfied from the additional data already read into cache (a cache hit), significant performance gains are achieved. Clearly, the larger the cache, the more data is read in and the greater is the likelihood of a cache hit. The greater the number of cache hits in relation to the total number of attempts (hit ratio), the better is the overall subsystem performance.

On the other side of the equation are algorithms for minimizing the impact of cache misses (when requested data is not found in cache and a trip to a DASD is required). A significant measure of subsystem efficiency is the frequency with which data must be read from a DASD rather than from a cache. A second measure is the amount of time required to move data from a DASD. Aggregate performance is a factor of both of these measures.

To achieve optimum subsystem throughput, the IBM 3990 Model 6 Storage Control can determine if data would benefit from record caching, track caching, or no caching at all. Because the optimal cache management algorithm (track or record) varies from one application to another, or even with the time of day for the same application, an adaptive design for selecting the best-performing caching mode is important. During batch processing, track caching may provide better performance because many records on the same track are accessed sequentially. During on-line transaction processing, record caching may deliver better performance because requests are for data that is more randomly distributed (data has a poor "locality of reference").

Concurrent copy creates a backup copy of data while allowing other production processing to continue, virtually removing the need for a backup window. Once the concurrent copy initialization process is logically complete, data is available to on-line applications while it is being copied to the backup output media. Performance implications are a function of the extent to which the database is closed to application access during the concurrent copy process. IBM's Data Facility Program (DFP) software is used to "pause" the database without having to "close" it. Closing a database is a time-intensive operation, whereas a "pause" achieves the same objective without the delays associated with "close/open." Thus, DFP ensures virtually no user-perceived impact to data availability. Software subsystems such as DB2, IMS, and CICS use concurrent copy. This function also simplifies the process of DASD-to-DASD copying or of providing database copies for batch processing. Copies can be made to DASDs, tape, or optical devices at ESCON distances.

The RVA 2 Turbo devices introduced an alternative to concurrent copy called SnapShot. SnapShot operates entirely within the RVA 2 and takes a matter of seconds. This is possible because current RAMAC models use the concept of a logical disk volume. A logical disk appears to the operating system as an actual 3390 or 3380 disk volume, but it is implemented in the RVA 2 as a set of pointers to the data. Each read or write operation from the server contains a data address, and the logical disk array manager uses these pointers to translate the (logical) data address into a physical address in the disk array. When SnapShot is invoked on a logical volume, it creates a new logical volume by copying these pointers, which it can do very rapidly. Then when the original "copy" of the data is updated, the updated part is written to another area in the array and the pointers in the original logical volume are updated to reflect the new location. The pointers in the new logical volume are kept as they were, pointing to the older version of the data.

Availability Features

Dynamic disk reconstruction supports replacing a failed disk drive in a drawer without affecting host applications. Also known as "hot plugging," this feature allows a disk drive (also called a Head–Disk Assembly, or HDA) to be replaced while the other disk drives in the drawer remain active. Data is reconstructed on the disk drive when it is replaced. RAID-5 processing ensures access to data while the drive is not functioning.

Component redundancy enables hardware fault tolerance in the RAMAC storage subsystem. Duplicate storage disks, communication paths, power and cooling devices, and power sources add to RAMAC's high-availability characteristics.

NonVolatile Storage (NVS) is a cache that keeps data from being lost when a power outage occurs by switching to a battery backup system. Cached data is retained in this storage area long enough for it to be successfully copied to disk. The 3990 Storage Control provides sufficient battery backup capability to maintain data in a cache for up to 48 hours, more than sufficient to handle day-to-day power outage situations.

Coincident with keeping the NVS powered until data is written to a DASD, the disk drives in RAMAC drawers are powered until the data is destaged. This sustained power supports a "graceful" degradation of DASD function, ensuring appropriate retaining of the data state and preventing the mechanical "head crashes" common with earlier DASDs.

Dynamic sparing uses spare RAMAC drawers to back up drawers that encounter a failure or potential failure. This is an extension of the dual-copy feature, which also ensures the continued availability of the original data. When a drawer is taken out of action, deliberately or not, data from the failing drawer is copied to the spare. The spare drawer reconstructs parity as data is written. Access to data in the original drawer continues during the copying process, preserving full logical data redundancy during that operation.

Direct Access Storage Device (DASD) Characteristics

The RAMAC 2 Array DASD and the RAMAC 2 Array Subsystem implement RAID level 5 technology and also support dual-copy, or mirroring. The 3990 Storage Controller remains the interface to the S/390 for the RAMAC 2 Array DASD as well as for the 3390 DASD. In 1996, the RAMAC 3 Array Subsystem was announced as a further improvement to the RAMAC family of products.

RAMAC 2 Array
The RAMAC Scalable Array 2 (see Figure 3.12) consists of one IBM 9396 Model 200 Control Unit providing the control functions for the

Figure 3.12. RAMAC Array DASD.

subsystem and a single IBM 9396 Storage Frame model from among the 14 available, each providing a different capacity and/or a different performance capability. Models are designated as "2XY," where "X" uniquely identifies the capacity (the number of disk arrays) and "Y" designates the number of Device Controller Pair features that are required on the 9396-200 Control Unit. The 9396 Model 2XY Storage Frame contains the RAID-5 disk arrays, each of which consists of nine drives containing data and one drive containing parity on a rotating basis.

The RAMAC Scalable Array 2 provides data storage capacities that can range from 304 to 1,368 gigabytes (GB) and cache sizes from 1,024 to 4,098 megabytes (MB). Storage capacity can be nondisruptively upgraded on the subsystem. Cache capacity is specified as a feature on the 9396-200 Control Unit and can be upgraded in 1 GB increments. The cache upgrade does interrupt subsystem operation.

The smaller, yet larger-capacity, Ultrastar 2XP Disk Drives used by RAMAC 2 save a significant amount of space. The RAMAC Scalable Array 2 can achieve a maximum capacity with what the original RAMAC Scalable Array required three disk cabinets to achieve. This results in floor space savings and savings in both power consumption and heat generation for all configurations.

When the 9396-200 Control Unit is configured with at least 16 ESCON ports and/or parallel channels, the RAMAC Scalable Array is capable of performing up to 16 concurrent data transfers to the host systems to which it is attached. Parallel channel speeds of up to 3 and 4.5 MB/s and ESCON speeds of up to 10 and 17 MB/s are supported.

When the 9396-200 Control Unit is configured with the maximum of six Device Controller Pairs, the RAMAC Scalable Array is capable of performing 24 concurrent data transfers to the RAID-5 disk arrays in the 9396-2XY Storage Frame. The RAMAC Scalable Array employs RAID-5 technology to provide the back-end storage. In most cases, this means that in the event of the loss of a single disk in an array, data can be recovered through the use of parity data, which is kept for each RAID-5 array in the subsystem. The RAMAC Scalable Array 2 supports up to 512 logical volumes in 3380 and/or 3390 formats. Full volume support for 3380-J and -K and 3390-1, -2, -3, and -9 is provided. The disk arrays are shipped in 3390-3 format.

RAMAC 3 Storage Frame and Drawer
The RAMAC 3 Array Storage System is a direct access magnetic disk storage array unit that has improved high-availability and high-density data storage. The storage frame provides path and other control functions for the storage array, supports attachment to the 9390 or the 3990-6 control, and provides the power control and distribution within the storage frame and the installed drawers. The storage frame supports up to 16 drawers with a minimum requirement of 2 drawers.

The RAMAC 3 Array Storage utilizes the Ultrastar 2XP 3.5-inch disk drive, which supports the packaging of 363 GB of user disk space in a single frame, using half the floor space requirement of RAMAC 2.

RAMAC Virtual Array 2 (RVA 2) Turbo and Turbo X83
The RVA 2 Turbo Storage System expands on the functionality and performance of prior RAMAC array storage systems. Using a new RAID-6

technology that avoids the write performance problems of the past, it supports up to 1,024 logical volumes containing 290 to 1.68 TB of user disk space, in 3380 or 3390 format. It should be noted that the RAMAC technology has replaced the older 3390 and 3380 technology, which is no longer marketed by IBM. Features include 3.5 GB to 6 GB of cache, data compression in the control unit (so data in cache is also in compressed format), up to 16 paths per device, and up to 12 concurrent I/O operations. More recently a newer RVA model was introduced, the RAMAC Virtual Array Turbo Model X83, with a cache size ranging from 3.5 to 6 GB and 1,024 logical volumes containing 290 GB to 1.68 TB of user space.

DFSMSdss and concurrent copy are still supported, but a new SnapShot copying feature, explained earlier, is also available. SnapShot runs in a matter of seconds, while concurrent copy will recognize the RVA 2 Turbo or Model X83 and will invoke SnapShot if the user has requested a concurrent copy within the same disk array. SnapShot is a feature of a new software package called IBM eXtended Facilities Product (IXFP). IXFP also provides dynamic data space release to release unused space in the arrays, capacity and performance monitoring of the disk array subsystem, and a user interface for adding and deleting logical volumes.

A related device is the 9399 Cross Platform Extension (XPE), which allows Windows NT and UNIX servers to connect to a RVA model, which is also attached to a z900 or S/390 server. This not only allows data sharing between the two types of servers, it provides the smaller servers with data storage that can be managed by OS/390 utilities such as SnapShot, concurrent copy, Extended Remote Copy, and Peer-to-Peer Remote Copy.

3990 Storage Control

The 3990 Storage Control Model 6 (see Figure 3.13) manages the flow of information between a server and 3390 (and the older 3380) Direct Access Storage Devices (DASDs) or RAMAC DASD arrays that provide disk storage for S/390 or z900 servers.

In 1996, all prior models of the 3990 Storage Control family were replaced with the Model 6. Based on CMOS technology (discussed in Chapter 2), this model uses 80% fewer chips than the predecessor model, contributing to greater reliability and lower power consumption and cooling requirements.

The Model 6 (illustrated in Figure 3.14) is characterized by one cache and one NonVolatile Storage (NVS). Cache sizes range up to 4

Figure 3.13. 3990 Storage Control.

GB, and NVS sizes range up to 128 MB. Upgrades are field installable. Each of the two storage directors (each contributing two paths to the DASD), the cache, and the NVS is packaged with its own power and service regions, providing four regions in total. This enables service to be performed on one region while other regions continue to support operations.

In the Model 6, all paths serve all attached devices and all caches and NVS are available to each path. The Model 6 operates in DLSE

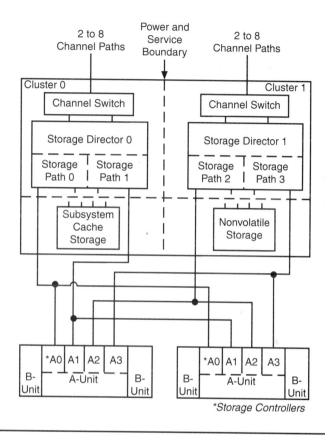

Figure 3.14. 3990 Model 6 attached to 3390s.

mode. It provides for as many as 128 ESCON logical paths. Using ESCON Directors or 9036 ESCON Remote Channel Extenders and the XDF fiber links, the Model 6 can be installed at distances up to 43 km (26.7 miles) from the host. The 3990-6 also supports parallel channel attachments as well as the sysplex processor environment. It connects up to 32 CPUs or LPARs in an S/390 parallel sysplex. All members of the 3390 and RAMAC Array DASD families can attach to the 3990-6.

Functionally, this model is distinguished from the others through its use of advanced cache management techniques that can be activated automatically or by a host application. A dump application, for example, could notify the 3990-6 that it is performing a large-scale sequential operation. The 3990-6 then activates a specific cooperative algorithm based on that input. The 3990-6 itself can activate adaptive cache management techniques, depending on the data access characteristics.

For disaster recovery protection scenarios, the 3990-6 includes a Remote Copy feature that ensures continuous operation when a subsystem, a computer room, or even a whole site is lost. Remote Copy keeps an up-to-date copy of critical data in a remote site in case such a disaster strikes. There are two versions of Remote Copy: Peer-to-Peer Remote Copy (PPRC), for applications that must have an absolutely current backup copy, and eXtended Remote Copy (XRC), for use when the remote data can be a few seconds behind that of the local version.

PPRC provides continuous data shadowing (mirroring) across storage subsystems by sending updates to the recovery 3990 Model 6 in a synchronous cache-to-cache communication via ESCON links. Data at the secondary site will be kept fully in step with data at the primary location. Synchronous writes on two 3990 Model 6 Storage Controls will create a performance impact when the function is in operation. XRC provides function for disaster recovery and workload migration through a combination of 3990 Licensed Internal Code (LIC) and DFSMS/MVS software (discussed in Chapter 6). Data specified at a volume level can be copied asynchronously from a 3990 Model 6 at the primary site to a 3990 at a recovery site.

Depending on the overall system workload, there may be little or no performance impact to the primary site subsystem when using XRC. The primary 3990's DASD writes take place normally, with no delay. Records containing time-sequenced updates are created in the primary 3990's cache, the records are read periodically by the XRC DFSMS/MVS data mover, and the updates are subsequently written to the recovery site's 3990 DASD. Using XRC, you can locate your secondary storage site at a virtually unlimited distance from the primary site through the use of channel extension technology.

Self-diagnostic features of the 3990-6 reduce the amount of time that service personnel spend fixing errors. Periodic Resident Testing (PRT) continuously performs diagnostic checks against DASD components of the subsystem to confirm proper operation. First Failure Support Technology (FFST) performs most of the diagnostic work on all errors so that service technicians can fix problems quickly. The 3990-6 can issue Service Information Messages (SIMs) to alert operations personnel to an error, its cause, the impact on subsystem operation, and the necessary repair action.

Enterprise Storage Server (ESS) (a.k.a. "Shark")

The IBM Enterprise Storage Server, based on IBM's SeaScape architecture, is a high-performance, high-availability, high-capacity storage subsystem considered the natural successor to the IBM 3990. IBM has indicated that future releases of ESS will also offer implementation of their Logic Structured File (LSF) architecture to protect users' investment in RAMAC Virtual Array (RVA). Connectivity to S/390 is by up to 32 ESCON channels. IBM has indicated its intention to deliver native FICON channel support on ESS by mid-2001. With the availability of native FICON attachment, the bandwidth between the ESS Control Unit and the processor will dramatically increase. This will make the ESS an even more ideal high-performance storage subsystem for the S/390 and z900 platform.

The ESS is structured around two 4-way RISC (Reduced Instruction Set Computing) processors with up to 16 GB of cache and 384 MB of nonvolatile storage. ESS provides excellent scalable capacity from 400 GB to over 11 TB. The incremental capacity will require attaching a second frame. Each frame, base and expansion, represents a footprint of about one square meter.

The capacity scalability has been implemented through Snap-In Building Blocks. The user can choose one of 32 standard capacity configurations. The capacity increments are composed of two 9 GB drives, fifteen 18 GB drives and fifteen 36 GB drives.

ESS consolidates the existing Copy Services solutions including

- Peer-to-Peer Remote Copy (PPRC), a separately priced feature using a synchronous protocol that allows real-time mirroring of data from one Logical UNit (LUN) to another LUN. This protocol ensures that the secondary copy is up to date by ensuring that the primary copy is only written once it has received acknowledgment that the secondary copy has been written to. The primary LUN can be in either the same or a different ESS.

- Flash Copy, which makes a single point in time (TO) copy of a LUN taking only a few seconds and is instantly available for use. This is generally a tool for on-line backup, creating a database for data mining or new application testing.

- eXtended Remote Copy (XRC), which provides a copy of OS/390 data to a remote location via telecommunications lines; because it is asynchronous it is not limited by distance.

- Concurrent Copy, a function for OS/390 enabling data center operations staff to take a copy or a data dump while applications are updating that data. It is similar to FlashCopy, creating a TO copy of the source, but Concurrent Copy can act on data sets as well as a full volume.

A performance enhancement feature package (ESS EX Performance Package) of three items is offered especially for S/390:

- Multiple Allegiance (MA) allows ESS to accept an I/O request from each channel path group for a unit address. The request can be concurrent with other I/O requests, which may be queued awaiting initiation. This provides improved ESS throughput and performance by allowing multiple access to a shared volume (Logical Device).

- Parallel Access Volumes (PAV) is a feature allowing access to a CKD volume on an ESS in parallel. Using PAV permits assigning a base address to a CKD logical device using any of the 256 available base device addresses. Then alias addresses for the CKD device can be configured. Alias addresses can be dynamically reassigned.

- I/O Priority Queuing allows the ability to queue in a priority order I/Os from different system images. The OS/390 WorkLoad Manager (WLM) utilizes this priority to favor I/Os from one system over the others when running WLM in Goal mode.

Optical Storage

Information that is infrequently used or that traditionally has been stored on paper or microfiche can be stored cost-effectively using optical storage. Unlike DASDs and tape, which use magnetic recording technology to save information, optical storage uses light from a laser to write and read information on disks that are kept in a robotic library. The IBM 3995 Optical Library C-series Enhanced models provide low-cost, high-capacity, direct access storage for the S/390 and zSeries servers. A single system can provide 270 GB to 2.682 TB of on-line storage. The 3995 C-Series Models with 2.6 GB cartridges are upgradable to the enhanced models with 5.2 GB drives.

Extended multifunction drives provide support for permanent Write-Once, Read-Many (WORM), Magneto-Optical (MO) rewritable, and Continuous Composite Write-Once (CCW) WORM, using 5.25-inch industry-standard 5.2 GB (8×) optical media cartridges. Backward compatibility on any three previous generations enables continued access to data on those previously written cartridges. All three technologies can be used within a single library. The selection of an appropriate type of optical storage depends on application requirements.

WORM storage provides a permanent, unalterable copy of the information being stored. This information is stored on an optical cartridge that is easily inserted into and removed from an optical drive. The optical cartridge consists of a plastic disk coated with a thin layer of reflective alloy material and mounted inside a plastic case.

Information is written on the disk by focusing a laser beam into a tiny spot on the disk. The laser heats up the disk surface at that particular spot and actually melts a hole in the reflective coating. The binary representations of 1s and 0s are formed by turning the laser on and off as the disk rotates. To read information back from the disk, the laser is set at a lower power setting, not sufficient to melt the recording layer. The light from the laser reflects back from the disk, except where the holes are burned through the layer. The reflected light, or the absence of it, carries the data stored on the disk back to the system. This type of storage provides extremely high data recording densities, which makes for relatively inexpensive storage.

A key advantage of WORM storage is that the recording process is permanent. Once the recording surface of a particular portion of the disk is written to, it cannot be changed back to its original state. This makes WORM storage a good choice for applications that demand highly reliable audit trails and that have business or legal needs to keep permanent copies of large amounts of information. Banks, insurance companies, hospitals, and governments benefit from using optical storage to keep images of documents and to save other information that has previously been kept on microfilm, on microfiche, or in rooms full of filing cabinets.

Rewritable optical storage uses a combination of magnetic and optical (magneto-optic) technologies to read, write, and erase data on optical cartridges, similar to the way in which DASDs or tape work. The high storage densities of optical storage make it possible to place up to 5.2 GB of data on a single 5.25-inch (8") optical cartridge. Because disk technology is used, your applications access the information directly.

The optical cartridge used for rewritable optical storage has the same physical characteristics as those for WORM. Magneto-optic technology, however, employs a combination of heat and a magnetic field to record data. The laser is focused to a spot on the disk and heats up the recording surface. When a magnetic field is applied to this heated area, the recording layer is set in the direction of the magnetic field. The data is erased simply by reapplying heat and a magnetic field set in the opposite direction. Again, information is read by bouncing the laser off the disk at a lower power setting. The polarity of the reflected light shifts in one direction or another depending on the direction of the magnetic field at that spot on the disk. This reflected light beam carries the digital information stored on the disk.

The 3995 Optical Library is an automated storage product that consists of storage slots for optical cartridges, a robot for moving the cartridges, and multifunction optical drives. The Data Storage Facility Management Subsystem (DFSMS) and the Object Access Method (OAM) support the 3995 Optical Library. It comes in four base and three optional expansion models:

- The Model C32 provides up to 270 GB (unformatted) of rewritable, permanent WORM and CCW storage capacity. The library includes two 5.2 GB high-capacity extended multifunction optical drives and storage cells for 52 optical cartridges.

- The Model C34 provides up to 540 GB (unformatted) of rewritable, permanent WORM and CCW optical storage capacity. The library includes two 5.2 GB high-capacity extended multifunction optical drives and storage cells for 104 optical cartridges. Two additional internal high-capacity extended multifunction optical drives can be added as an optional feature. This model is field upgradable to a Model C36.

- The Model C36 provides up to 811 GB (unformatted) of rewritable, permanent WORM and CCW optical storage capacity. The library includes four 5.2 GB high-capacity extended multifunction optical drives and storage cells for 156 optical cartridges. Two additional internal high-capacity extended multifunction optical drives can be added as an optional feature.

- The Model C38 provides up to 1.34 TB (unformatted) of rewritable, permanent WORM and CCW optical storage capacity. The library includes four 5.2 GB high-capacity extended multifunction optical drives and storage cells for 258 optical cartridges. Two additional internal high-capacity extended multifunction optical drives can be added as an optional feature.

Additional capacity can be attained through expansion models:

- The Model C12 provides up to 270 GB (unformatted) of rewritable, permanent WORM and CCW optical storage capacity. The library includes two 5.2 GB high-capacity extended multifunction optical drive and storage cells for 52 optical cartridges. The 3995 Model C12 attaches to a Model C32 control unit.

- The Model C16 provides up to 811 GB (unformatted) of rewritable, permanent WORM and CCW optical storage capacity. The library includes four 5.2 GB high-capacity extended multifunction optical drives and storage cells for 156 optical cartridges. Two additional internal high-capacity extended multifunction optical drives can be added as an optional feature. The 3995 Model C16 attaches to a Model C36 control unit.

- The Model C18 provides up to 1.341 TB (unformatted) of rewritable, permanent WORM and CCW optical storage capacity. The library includes four 5.2 GB high-capacity extended multifunction optical drives and storage cells for 258 optical cartridges. Two additional internal high-capacity extended multifunction optical drives can be added as an optional feature. The 3995 Model C18 attaches to a Model C38 control unit.

Tape Storage

Server systems are woven deeply into today's business processes and usually become the core of day-to-day operations. The information stored on the server system is a valuable corporate asset that must be protected. Magnetic tape storage provides a cost-effective and efficient means of backing up the information on the disk storage. The following sections discuss the most current tape storage peripherals used with S/390 and z900 servers.

3590 High-Performance Tape Subsystem

The 3590 High-Performance Tape Subsystem (see Figure 3.15), featuring the Magstar tape drive, is a tape processing system that replaces the IBM 3480, 3490, and 3490E tape subsystems. The Magstar 3590 Tape Subsystem is available in two series, the B and E models. The B Models provide a tape drive data rate of 9 MB/s, a capacity of 10 GB (30 GB with 3:1 compaction) per cartridge, and data integrity of 100 times that of the 3480 products. The more recent E Models' data rate is 14 MB/s, and the drive has a capacity of 20 GB (60 GB with 3:1 compaction) per cartridge. The IBM Magstar drives can be configured in racks or frames,

Figure 3.15.   3590 High-Performance Tape Subsystem.

inside or outside an IBM Automated Tape library system. The components of the B or E series of 3590 High-Performance Tape Subsystem include two tape drive models, a control unit, a frame model, and the tape cartridge. New technology, known as Seascape technology, is used throughout the architecture of this subsystem. The 3590 Tape Drive comes in four models. The B models are the 3590-B1A (Magstar) and the 3590-B11. The E models are the E1A (Magstar) and the 3590-E11. It should be noted that the Magstar B1A can be field updated to the E models. The B11 or E11 are rack mountable and include a 10-cartridge Automatic Cartridge Facility (ACF), which can be quickly loaded using a new magazine. The B1A or E1A models are designed for installation in the 3494 Tape Library Dataserver and therefore have no ACF.

The Automatic Cartridge Loader (ACL) is quite different from the 3480 ACL and the IBM 3490 Integrated Cartridge Loader (ICL). Mounted on the ACF housing are a liquid crystal display panel and controls for operator use. In addition to the 10 tape positions (cells), the ACF provides an eleventh slot (the priority cell), into which specific mounts can be inserted without affecting the cartridges in the magazine. A 10-slot cartridge magazine is used to transport tapes and to load the ACF. Transport mechanisms within the ACF move the cartridges between the drive, the magazine, and the priority cell, and allow for random recall of any cartridge.

Within the 3590, the movable head assembly and logic each use new technology. In addition to its very compact size (8.8 inches wide × 29.8 inches deep × 10.5 inches high) and its high-speed characteristics (2 m/s tape speed, 5 m/s search and rewind speed, with full cartridge rewind time of 60 s), the Magstar tape drive offers other functions.

It attaches directly to a 16-bit, fast and wide SCSI (Small Computer System Interface) differential interface and, using a control unit, to ESCON or FICON channels. The B models have a native data rate of 9 MB/s, the E model 14 MB/s. This and an improved data compression algorithm enable it to use more fully the 20 MB/s SCSI or 17 MB/s ESCON channel, or up to a maximum of 100 MB/s full duplex with FICON channel. Each 3590 Tape Drive has its own integrated Ultra-SCSI control unit (with two channel interfaces for multihost attachment), removing potential contention for drives and potential bottlenecks in the control unit that existed in earlier models.

The 3590 A14 Frame with up to two integrated 3590 Model A60s provides a frame attachment of up to four Magstar 3590 Model B11/E11 Tape Drives, with their 10-cartridge automatic cartridge facility for operator usage. The 3590 A60 can also be integrated in a 3494 Tape Library Model D14 to automate up to four 3590 Model B1A or E1A Tape Drives.

The 3590 Model C12 or C14 Silo Compatible Frame is for the attachment of four Magstar 3590 Tape Drives in a StorageTek Automated Cartridge System (ACS) to ESCON or FICON channels. The Magstar 3590 drives are connected to ESCON or FICON channels through one or two Magstar 3590 Controllers installed in the Model C14 or external to the Model C12 Silo Compatible Frame. The 3590 supports attachment to standard ESCON (17 MB/s instantaneous data rate) channels or FICON (100 MB/s) channels. The controller can be at a maximum channel distance of 43 km (27 miles) from the host when using fiber-optic cable between ESCON Directors and is designed for remote servicing.

For maximum performance and throughput, the four drives can be connected to two controllers, each with two ESCON/SCSI or FICON/SCSI adapters, allowing each drive to be dedicated to an adapter. The C14 is designed to allow installation of one or two controllers inside the C14 without requiring a separate rack. This subsystem will enable new levels of reliability and cartridge capacity compared to existing 18- or 36-track technology. Tapes are written in 3590 media format, and most software will use the full capacity of the tape. Magstar 3590 tape drives in the Model C14 Silo-Compatible Frame attached via a 3590 Model Controller may be used to migrate from 18- or 36-track technology in a StorageTek ACS to Magstar using fewer cartridges.

The Magstar 3590 Model A60 Controller improves 3590 Tape Subsystem performance by incorporating IBM Seascape architecture. This architecture removes bottlenecks typically found in tape subsystems. The Model A60 can be configured with up to eight ESCON interfaces or up to two FICON interfaces. The 3590 A60 Tape Controller is the first storage device to provide a direct FICON interface. The FICON interfaces can coexist with ESCON interfaces on the same box.

The Model A60 Controller has remote support capabilities enabling quick diagnostics, problem determination and verification, and a means to upgrade 3590 microcode from remote sites via modem. IBM supplies the modem to enable remote support.

The Magstar 3590 Model A60 is a reusable storage asset that can be placed in multiple 3590 storage solutions. With the up to 20 GB capacity of the newer 3590 High-Performance Tape Cartridge, the capacity of the IBM 3494 ranges from 4.8 TB (14.4 TB with 3:1 compaction) up to 248 TB (748 TB with 3:1 compaction). A 3494 can be configured with up to sixteen 3590 Model A60 Controllers and 62 Magstar 3590 Tape Drives.

The 3590 High-Performance Tape Cartridge and media are different and not compatible with other IBM tape subsystems. The 3590 tape drive can neither read from nor write to previous IBM tape cartridge formats, in other words, 18- or 36-track formats. Physically, the tape cartridge has the same external size and shape as the IBM 3480 cartridge. However, the capacity of the high-performance tape cartridge is 10 GB for uncompacted data or as much as 30 GB if the data is suitable for compaction. The tape itself is half an inch wide and 300 meters long.

The cartridge casing is also the same physical size and shape as the 3480 cartridges and is physically compatible, in terms of robotic handling and storage, with those cartridges. Slight but significant modifications improve the physical handling and ensure proper identification of the tapes for use in appropriate configurations. Two colored plastic inserts with two possible indentations provide the means for identifying up to 16 different cartridge types. The 3590 hardware is able to recognize the presence or absence of these indicators and mount or reject the tapes as appropriate.

Two newer technologies significant to tape processing are the metal particle medium and interleaved longitudinal recording. The metal particle medium used in the 3590 tape cartridge produces a significantly higher data recording density than that of the 3480 and 3490 cartridges. The newer cartridges have a much greater ability to maintain a magnetic field (coercivity), allowing more information to be recorded on the medium. The linear density of the cartridges is about three times that of the 3480 and 3490 devices. Track density is improved by a factor of four.

The new 16-track serpentine interleaved longitudinal recording technology significantly improves tape performance and transfer rates without changing the tape speed (2 m/s). Using a buffer to compress data before it is written to the tape contributes some of the speed improvement. Typical tape damage results from folding the tape (vertical damage) or scratching along the tape (horizontal damage), both of which can occur during tape movement. By interleaving information (spreading the bits of a unit of information along the tape in a staggered fashion), IBM increases the probability of recovering from either vertical or horizontal damage. Only a few bits within many bytes would be damaged, simplifying recovery and improving the probability of reading a damaged tape.

A thin-film MagnetoResistive (MR) head technology, together with the new tape medium, supports higher-density recording, both in number of bits and in number of tracks per inch. Data is written in 256 KB units using a 16-track format. The first set of 16 tracks is written until the physical end of the tape is reached. Using the electronic head switch, 16 different interleaved tracks are written while the tape moves back to the beginning. The head is then indexed (physically moved a fraction of a millimeter) to the next set of 16 tracks and the process is repeated. Eight sets of interleaved tracks are written, for a total of 128 tracks. Improved Error Correction Code (ECC) and servo tracks prewritten on the tape ensure data integrity. The Magstar tape drive is designed for up to a 100-fold increase in data integrity compared to the 3490E.

3494 Automated Tape Library (ATL) Dataserver

The Magstar 3494 library components include the library manager, console, cartridge accessor, optional convenience I/O stations, optional tape units, barcode reader, optional ESCON controller, and up to 240 cartridge storage cells. The Model L10 has up to two 3490E Tape Drives; the Model L12 has up to two Magstar 3590 Tape Drives; and the Model L14 has up to two Magstar 3590 Tape Drives and an ESCON controller.

The Magstar 3494 drive units provide the capability for adding tape units and up to 400 cartridge storage cells. The Model D10 has up to two 3490E Tape Drives; the Model D12 has up to six SCSI-attached Magstar 3590 Tape Drives; and the Model D14 has up to four Magstar 3590 Tape Drives and an ESCON controller.

The Magstar 3494 Storage Unit provides the capability for adding cartridge storage. The Model S10 supports up to 400 cartridge cells. The Magstar 3494 Virtual Tape Server is designed to stack multiple host-created volumes (logical volumes) onto a Magstar 3590 cartridge, thus maximizing the amount of data stored on a physical volume. The Models B16 and B18 contain the Magstar Virtual Tape Server controller, up to 400 cartridge storage cells, and up to 288 GB of fault-tolerant RAID disk cache storage. All data sent to the tape server is written first to disk cache, which is much faster than tape, and is transferred from cache to tape cartridges later. Likewise, data sent from the tape server is always written to cache first and the physical tape drive is freed for other work.

In practice, most tape reads occur soon after the tape volume was written, so frequently the requested (logical) volume will still be in cache when it is read. Another advantage of the cache is to permit concurrent access to several logical tape volumes. The Model B16 requires an adjacent Model D12 that has cartridge storage and contains from three to six Magstar 3590 drives that are used by the Virtual Tape Server. The B16 and adjacent D12 can be in any position of a Magstar 3494 system configuration unit that can coexist with drive frame units that contain 3490E or Magstar 3590 Tape Drives. The model B18 also requires a Model D12, but the D12 can be up to 14 meters away. The Magstar Virtual Tape Server connects to S/390 and z900 servers through one or two ESCON attachments.

The Magstar 3494 Library Manager controls accessing of cartridges, placing cartridges in racks, movement of cartridges, automatic drive cleaning, tape handling priorities, and error recovery and error logging. The library manager database can optionally be duplexed on two disks. Two library managers are installed with the high-availability model.

The Magstar 3494 Model HA1 High-Availability Unit consists of two service bay frames with one added at each end of a configuration to provide an accessor service area and a parking area. A second library manager, in the same service bay as the second accessor, is added to the subsystem to improve library availability in the event of a library manager failure. The dual library manager design also adds a second accessor so that the library can automatically continue operations in the event of an accessor failure. One accessor will be active at a time; the second is available as a hot standby. Either accessor can push the other into its service bay. Concurrent maintenance on an accessor is supported. The library can continue to function as a failed accessor is being serviced. This also minimizes library down time when library manager code is being installed. A new library manager PC will be included to enhance performance. A second hard drive is required in both library managers for duplication of library database information.

Magstar 3494 Tape Library configurations of 1 to 8, 10, 12, or 16 frames are allowed. When a Model HA1 High-Availability Unit is attached, configurations of 3, 4, 6, 8, 10, 12, and 16 frames are allowed in addition to the two Model HA1 service bays. The Model B16 Virtual Tape Server can now be installed anywhere within the 16 frames. The Model D10, D12, and D14 Drive Unit frames and the Model S10 Storage Unit frames can also be installed in any location in the Magstar 3494 Tape Library. A maximum of 62 Magstar 3590 Tape Drives are now supported using Magstar 3590 Model A60 Controllers (in 15 Model D14s and 1 Model L14). Remote console support using DCAF for both library managers is also available.

3490 Magnetic Tape Subsystems

The 3490 Magnetic Tape Subsystem utilizes a compact half-inch tape cartridge. Information is read from or written to the cartridge at up to 3 MB/s. Enhanced-capability models with an enhanced buffer can support an instantaneous data transfer rate of up to 9 MB/s when using compaction and when attached to an ESCON channel. All IBM 3490 frame models consist of a control unit (Model AXX) and a drive unit (Model BXX). Multiple B units can be controlled from a single A unit. Models A01, A02, and B04 support the base 3490 tape subsystem. Models A10, A20, and B40 support the 3490E tape subsystem.

The 3490E Models A10 and A20 (see Figure 3.16) are multiple microprocessor–driven control units with an 8 MB dynamic data buffer per logical control unit, a performance-enhanced Improved Data Recording

Figure 3.16. 3490 Enhanced Capability Magnetic Tape Subsystem.

Capability (IDRC), and a flexible number of ESCON and parallel channel adapters. The Model A10 Control Unit provides for connection of up to eight tape transports and can be upgraded to a 3490 Model A20 Control Unit. The Model A20 Control Unit contains two logical control units, each with an 8 MB dynamic buffer. It attaches up to 16 tape transports. The 3490E Model B40 is a tape drive unit that contains four compact self-threading tape transports. The integrated cartridge loader is standard on all Model B40 tape units, which also have an articulating operator display on top of each unit.

All 3490E models discussed here are enhanced-capability models, which support an enhanced buffer and 36-track recording technology. The new recording technology doubles the cartridge capacity over previous 3480 or 3490 base models. In combination with the Improved Data Recording Capability (IDRC), the enhanced-capability models increase cartridge system tape capacity by up to 10 times (up to 20 times, if compared to uncompacted cartridges written in 18-track format). A compaction ratio of 3 to 1 allows up to 2.4 GB of data to be stored on a single enhanced capacity cartridge.

The 3490E Model F1A mounts in the IBM 3494 Magnetic Tape Library and can be installed in any IBM 3494 L10 or IBM 3494 D10 frame. The 3490E Model CXA and F1A drives cannot be intermixed in the same L10 or D10 frame. The 3490E Model F1A features a tape path that minimizes tape wear and increases long-term data integrity. Effective data rates up to 6.8 MB/s, sustained data rates of 3 MB/s, and burst data rates of 20 MB/s can be attained on the SCSI-2 fast and wide, 16-bit interface.

Display Stations

The original devices that people used to interact with S/390 computers were known as display stations or simply displays. These devices have become known as "dumb heads" in computing circles. Although millions of these devices are in use worldwide, they are being replaced by graphically oriented data displays, presenting data in a manner much like what we see on the World Wide Web. Simple text is replaced with combinations of graphics. Keyboard input is augmented with that from pointing devices. Even in cases where applications are incapable of providing anything other than line-oriented, "green screen" display of data, methods are now available to trap the information, reformat it, and display it in a more user-friendly manner.

Even the traditional S/390 attachment, known as the 3270 display, is now often emulated by desktop application software. Research indicates that there are well over 10 million 3270 displays or emulators currently in use worldwide. Methods have been developed to enable a 3270 capability over traditional SNA networks, Novell Netware networks, and even TCP/IP networks.

The traditional S/390 server display was a TV-like device that converted the server's electrical signals into light images that convey information to the user. These displays were typically incapable of graphics. Instead they presented data using, for example, up to 24 lines of data, generally with 80 characters of data per line. Displays had a keyboard that allowed the user to send information back to the server, but there was no mouse attachment. If a display station was located near the server, for example in the same building, it was locally attached to a workstation controller (such as a 3174 Establishment Controller or an Integrated Workstation Subsystem Controller). The controller was in turn attached to the server. If the display station was not near the server, for example in another state, workstations were first attached to a workstation controller that was subsequently remotely attached to the server over communications lines. Either way, the function provided to the display station user is the same. Some type of display station is required to allow the user to interact with a server. In 1997, IBM provided an innovative approach to S/390 access. Through eNetwork Host on Demand, a user at any Java-enabled Web browser can access the S/390 using 3270 technology and a 100% Java-developed solution over intranets and internets, including mobile and remote access.

With the evolution of intelligent workstations, interaction with the server is no longer restricted to the older traditional displays. Many varied forms of graphical interconnection are now possible. Because those devices are covered in tremendous detail in many other sources, we will not discuss them further.

Printers

Printers are electromechanical devices that print a computer's electronically encoded information onto paper. So many printers can work with

S/390 and zSeries servers that exhaustive coverage of all of them is beyond the scope of this book. Our discussion here is limited to some representative printers that fit the needs of many environments.

With the evolution of printing technology, printers have become both more compact and more sophisticated. Many today include memory that provides a wide variety of functional capabilities. Printers also have progressed in the sophistication of the printing technology. We will look at representative printers in several categories:

- Character Printers

- Line Printers

- Page Printers

As with display stations, printers located near the server, for example in the same building, are locally attached to the server via a cable. If the printer is not near but remote from the server, it is remotely attached over communications lines. Either way, the functions provided by the printer are the same.

Character Printers

The dot-matrix printing technique creates an image by causing a series of small pins contained in the print head to strike a ribbon, which in turn strikes the paper. Through selection of the proper pins, a fine dot pattern is generated. As with the dot pattern illuminated on a TV set or computer display, the human eye naturally blends these printed dots to form the desired image. Most dot-matrix printers operate in alphanumeric mode or All-Points-Addressable (APA) mode. In alphanumeric mode, the printer generates any alphanumeric character (letters and numbers) and some special symbols from a predefined library, called the character set. In APA mode, virtually any combination of dots can be generated to produce complex images.

The 4230 Printer is an example of a character printer. It is a tabletop printer that produces data processing quality (Fast Draft mode) documents at a speed of 375 to 600 characters per second (cps), depending on the model. In Data Processing (DP), Data Processing text (DP text), and Near-Letter-Quality (NLQ) modes, the clarity of the documents produced is improved at the cost of reduced printing speed. At only 53 dBA, the 4230's noise level makes it suited for a high-speed office printer, and its small footprint allows it to be placed wherever a printer is needed.

Three 4230 versions (Models 2XX, 4XX, and 5XX) are supported on S/390 zSeries servers and controllers. Model 201 has a maximum speed of 375 cps (Fast Draft mode) and provides a print buffer 32 KB in size. This print buffer acts as a temporary storage area, improving the efficiency of information flow between the printer and the computer system. The 4230 Model 202 produces Fast Draft mode documents at a rate of up to 480 cps and comes with a 128 KB print buffer. The print buffer expands by adding the 512 KB Extended Memory Feature. Model 202 also supports the Intelligent Printer Data Stream (IPDS), allowing it to print more advanced images such as bar codes and graphics. Model 201 can be upgraded to a Model 202 at any time. Models 4X3 and 5X3 increase the maximum rate to 600 cps.

A dual-purpose paper module provides a tractor feed that moves continuous forms through the printer. These forms include blank paper, preprinted forms, and multipart forms (up to six parts). Because of variations in multipart forms, however, specific forms should be tested before a decision is made to purchase the printer. This is especially true for five- and six-part forms. The dual-purpose paper module also supports the Document on Demand function, which allows the user to tear off a form just printed without having to wait for the next form to be printed or having to eject a blank form and thus create waste. With Document on Demand, the user can temporarily eject some blank forms, tear off the one needed, and then roll the remaining forms back into printing position with a few keystrokes. Another option automatically feeds individual sheets of paper (cut sheets) from a stack into the printer.

Line Printers

The band-matrix printing technique is a hybrid technology in that it is similar to the dot-matrix printing technique, creating an image by causing a series of small dots to strike a ribbon, which in turn strikes the paper, but images are printed more quickly because multiple characters are being printed simultaneously. With the print band printing technique, the dot-matrix approach is no longer used. A metal band engraved with the character set spins at high speeds within the printer. As the needed character on the spinning print band aligns with the correct spot on the paper, an impression is made. Printing the entire character at once, rather than building it through a series of dots, provides for high-quality printing. No APA graphics are supported, however, because only the characters on the print band being used can be printed on the paper.

- The 4234 Printer uses the band-matrix printing technique. It is called a line printer because it prints an entire line of text at one time rather than one character at a time. The 4234 is designed to stand on the floor and to print draft-quality documents at a speed of up to 410 (Model 1), 475 (Model 8), or 800 (Model 11) lines per minute (lpm). When operating in either near-letter-quality or data-processing-quality modes, the clarity of the document produced is improved at the cost of reduced printing speed.

- The 6400 Models 005 and 05P utilize the IBM 6400 print mechanism to print at up to 500 lines per minute (lpm). The "P" in the model designation refers to the pedestal configuration. As compared to the enclosed cabinet design of the 6400 Model 005, the 05P configuration is an "open" design. This design maximizes forms access and minimizes floor space requirements. The 6400 05P offers both the standard rear exit of forms and the option of an exit through the top for quick access.

- The 6400 Models 009 and 09P utilize the IBM 6400 print mechanism to print at up to 900 lines per minute (lpm). The 6400 09P offers both the standard rear exit of forms, plus the option of an exit through the top for quick access.

- The 6400 Model 014 is a high-performance impact printer that utilizes the IBM 6400 print mechanism to print at up to 1400 lines per minute (lpm). The Model 014 uses a cabinet design that significantly enhances the printer acoustics, making this printer suitable for an office environment.

Page Printers

The other printers just discussed print documents one character or one line at a time. The page printer, as the name describes, produces a whole page at a time. It prints on individual sheets of paper or cut sheets, not on continuous forms as do the other printers discussed so far. It can handle a workload of 2 to 23 million impressions (pages) per month. These printers use the laser/ElectroPhotographic (EP) process in which the laser produces a charged image on a drum inside the printer. Ink (toner) is attracted to the charged portions of the drum and is then transferred to the paper, as in a copy machine. This produces high-quality, high-speed printing, but because laser/EP is a nonimpact technique, it cannot print on multipart forms, which depend on the impact to produce carbon copies.

- The IBM InfoPrint 2000 Multifunctional Production System is designed for a balance of speed, capacity, and resolution in a black-and-white cut-sheet printing application. It prints up to 110 impressions per minute (ipm) at 600 dots per inch (dpi). The InfoPrint 2000 is available in three models. The Model RP1 is a high-speed, multifunctional digital duplicator with upgradable features including network connectivity. The Model NP1 is a high-speed PostScript, PCL, and PDF network printer with upgradable features including production-copying capabilities. Lastly, the Model DP1 is a high-speed, cut sheet production publisher and can be configured with either an AFCCU or Xerox data stream enablement with network connectivity and support for PostScript, PCL, and PDF.

- The IBM InfoPrint 3000 Advanced Function Printing (Figure 3.17) is a high-speed, continuous forms, advanced double-dotting electrophotographic printing system. Models ED1/ED2 print at throughput speeds of up to 344 impressions per minute (ipm) for a 2-up 8.5 × 11-inch page. The Model ES1 provides half the throughput performance of the ED models. The system permits 240 or 300 dpi data streams and can print them at 480 or 600 dpi resolution in both simplex and duplex modes.

- The IBM InfoPrint 4000 Advanced Function Simplex Printing System is a high-speed, high-volume continuous forms printer switchable between 240 and 300 dpi resolution. The first of two models is the IS1, which prints at speeds of up to 354 ipm for 2-up 8.5 × 11-inch paper. The Model IS2 comparable speed is 501 ipm.

- The IBM InfoPrint 4000 Advanced Function Duplex Printing System (Figure 3.18) is a high-quality, high-speed, continuous-forms dual-simplex or duplex printer for high-volume applications. It offers multiple and switchable resolutions of 240 dpi, 300 dpi, or 240/300 dpi at up to 708 ipm or 1,002 ipm for a 2-up 8.5 × 11-inch page depending on the model. The simplex models are ID1 and ID3, and the duplex models are ID2 (up to 708 ipm) and ID4 (up to 1,002 ipm). The InfoPrint 4000 ID models utilize the new Advanced Function Common Control Unit (AFCCU). Two additional models, ID5 and ID6, were introduced for even better print quality. These new models provide a choice of 480/680 dpi switchable resolution. Even at the high throughput of 1,002 ipm, the ID5/ID6 provide the capability to choose the optimum output resolution to print 240, 300, or 600 dpi input datastreams. The business's investment has been protected as upgrades from currently installed wide models of

Figure 3.17. InfoPrint 3000 Advanced Function Printer.

Figure 3.18.   InfoPrint 4000 Advanced Function Duplex Printing System.

3900 or 4000 Simplex or Duplex printers to the Infoprint 4000 Duplex Printing Systems is available.

- The IBM InfoPrint High Resolution Duplex Printing System IR models are high-speed, high-volume, cost-effective, duplex continuous-forms printers also based on the enhanced Advanced Function Common Control Unit (AFCCU). They digitally print high-resolution, Adobe PostScript 600 dpi documents and Advanced Function Presentation (AFP) 480–600 dpi documents at speeds of up to 708 ipm on the Models IR3 and IR4 for a 2-up 8.5 × 11-inch page. The Models IR1 and IR2 comparable print speed is 464 ipm. The control unit processor speed allows the use of Fiber Distributed Data Interface (FDDI), a fiber-optic LAN attachment enabling quick processing of jobs from the print queue to the printer.

Serial Storage Architecture

With all of the inherent power and performance of the channels previously discussed, more performance is required to move larger volumes of data more quickly among more demanding peripherals and processors. Serial Storage Architecture (SSA) is an evolving architecture that will meet those needs. SSA is a high-performance, low-cost serial interface for connecting storage devices, storage subsystems, servers, and workstations. It has many networking and other features that enable innovative approaches to connectivity for many applications. Although it is of greatest interest as a replacement for smaller-capacity peripherals, it is applicable to large systems as well.

The first SSA interface (called the 9333 I/O Channel) was developed by IBM as a proprietary interface for high-performance storage applications. Today thousands of these units are installed. In 1991, IBM made the technology available to the computer industry as one of the serial storage options for the Small Computer Systems Interface (SCSI-3). Since 1994, SSA standardization and documentation has been under the control of the ANSI committee responsible for SCSI-3, and since January 1995, the SSA Industry Association has been actively promoting the technical and economic benefits of SSA to the computer industry.

Without getting too deeply into the SSA technology, the following sections identify the benefits of this architecture and some of its features. More information is available from IBM and from the SSA Industry Association. An excellent overview is available from IBM on the Internet at *http://www.storage.ibm.com/storage/hardsoft/ssaovu.htm.*

Business Benefits of SSA

Imagine a world in which a single I/O interface effectively addresses the needs of the entire spectrum of servers, from personal computers to supercomputers. SSA is such an interface, providing unparalleled connection to a wide array of peripheral products. It has been specifically designed to connect disk drives, tape drives, CD-ROMs, optical drives, printers, scanners, and other peripherals to workstations, servers, and storage subsystems. It differs from traditional parallel interfaces in several basic ways.

First, it is predominantly a loop-based interface, in contrast to SCSI, which is a linear or string interface. No external drivers or receivers are required; these functions are embedded within a CMOS protocol chip. Only 4 signal wires are required, compared to 68 for the closest SCSI equivalent. SSA interfaces require no address switches and no discrete terminators. SSA supports three interconnection (network) topologies (configurations): string, loop, and switch. As described later, SSA supports up to 129 nodes in a string, 127 nodes in a loop, and a virtually unlimited number of nodes if switches are used. This contrasts with parallel SCSI, which supports only 8 or 16 devices.

String topologies are the simplest topologies, using interfaces to connect up to 129 devices (nodes) in a continuous string. The nodes at either end of the string can be single-port nodes, dual-port nodes with one port not operational, or switches. The intermediate nodes, if any, are always dual-port nodes. Each link between nodes operates independently and manages its own data flow control and error recovery. An error in one link does not affect other links. A break at any point in the string, however, makes all nodes beyond the break unusable.

The loop topology (illustrated in Figure 3.19) removes that single point of failure by providing alternate paths to each node in the network (up to 127 dual-port nodes). A single break in the loop continues to allow communication among all nodes via what has become a string interface. The loop also provides the advantage of allowing a node to be inserted into or removed from the loop dynamically without preventing communication between the other nodes. Even though the network must be reconfigured, the loop remains functional.

The switch topology is the most complicated and requires additional hardware for its implementation. Switches support up to 96 ports, but because they allow a number of strings to be connected, they achieve an almost unlimited number of nodes (that is, a virtually unlimited network configuration). The switch supports alternate paths to achieve fault tolerance.

A second difference is the significant increase in bandwidth that SSA enables. The fundamental building block of SSA is a single port capable of carrying on two simultaneous 20 MB/s conversations, one inbound and one outbound. This is referred to as the link speed, the total traffic on either line, and equates to a port speed of 40 MB/s total bandwidth in full-duplex mode.

Because an SSA connection uses two ports (both of which can be duplexed), it is capable of carrying on four simultaneous conversations (sending and receiving through each port) for a total available bandwidth of 80 MB/s. Achieving this theoretical capacity requires spatial

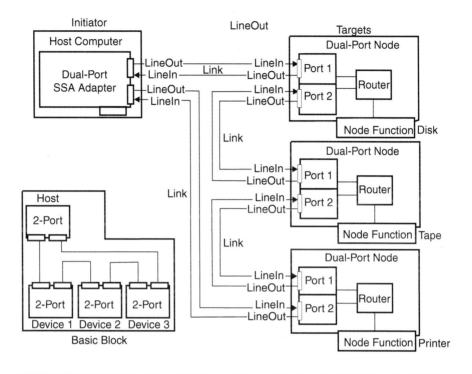

Figure 3.19. Loop topology characteristics of the SSA architecture.

reuse (described later) and full-duplex transfers. These in turn require advanced hardware and programming behind the SSA interface. Because the SSA architecture is open ended, higher speeds (up to 40 and 100 MB/s) can be supported.

The fact that there are no bus phases (such as arbitration, selection, and reselection, in which packets of information vie for access to channels) reduces the overhead associated with SSA to around 6%. That is, 94% of the data on the interface is your business data (SSA is about 94% efficient). The third difference comes through spatial reuse, which enables separate SSA links (peripheral devices) to perform operations simultaneously. Additional detail is provided later.

SSA's dual-port, full-duplex architecture allows peripherals to be connected in configurations with no single point of failure. Because multiple paths are inherent in the design, increased fault tolerance is far easier to implement. SSA provides "hot plugging" of devices and automatic reconfiguration, allowing devices to be added or removed while others continue to operate. For configuration flexibility, SSA nodes can be up to 20 meters apart, using low-cost, copper, shielded twisted-pair cables (instead of the more typical 68-wire cable). If fiber-optic cables are used, the maximum distance between nodes increases to 680 meters. SSA also uses existing CMOS technology, ensuring that its cost will be no higher than existing SCSI costs.

Features of SSA

Network configuration (interconnecting two or more nodes) is built into the SSA standard, enabling automatic configuration and dynamic changing. This section reviews the basic structures of a SSA network, some of which have been introduced earlier. Two features, routing and spatial reuse, are explored in more detail.

Network Characteristics
The most basic network consists of a single-port (gateway) host adapter connected to a single-port peripheral. The serial connection consists of six wires, four of which are used to transmit frames of information. A frame is a unit, with an exact format, that is used to transfer all information across the serial link. There are three types of frames, varying by the type of information they transfer. An application frame transfers data (up to 128 bytes) and any message structure information (up to 32 bytes) used for commands, data, status, and vendor-specific information. A privileged frame transfers configuration and error recovery data. A control frame is used only for node or link resets. The application and privileged frames consist of a sequence of at least seven data characters delimited at each end by special characters. The control frame follows the same format but with no data field.

A link, as described earlier, is a dedicated connection between two single-port nodes. When it is idle (that is, when no frames are being transferred), synchronizing characters are sent between the single-port nodes, keeping the links synchronized and allowing the network to instantly detect a link failure.

A node is a system, controller, or device with one or more serial links. Each node has a specific responsibility, task, or use (that is, function) that defines its reason for existing. The three types of nodes are single port, dual port, and switch port. A port consists of the hardware and firmware to support one end of a link. Most of a port's function is already available in current technology chips.

Nodes operate in one of two modes, initiator and target. In Initiator mode, the node within a device determines what task needs to be executed and which node will perform the desired task. It creates frames of information to be sent across the link and confirms that the node performed the task assigned to it.

One initiator in the network must be designated as the master node. This node performs the configuration process of the network. Although only one initiator is selected as the master, any initiator in the SSA network must be capable of performing this function. This requirement protects the network if the current master breaks or some other initiator exercises its option (master priority) to become the master.

The master is responsible for informing other nodes of their location in the network by issuing special configuration messages. Other initiator nodes in the network also perform a configuration process to discover the links and nodes that are operational within the network. This results in a configuration table that lists all the nodes with pointers to represent the physical links. Initiators then select a primary path address to each node and calculate the corresponding return path. Dual-port nodes provide alternative paths from the initiator, giving the interface redundancy and spatial reuse benefits.

In Target mode, the node informs the initiator that it is ready to receive a frame of information and acknowledges receipt of those frames. A target node may have up to 128 Logical Units (LUs) attached to it. An LU is a physical or virtual peripheral device that is the basic addressable unit on a target. Logical units can be a portion of the peripheral device (a partition, for example). The LUs provide the function for which the node is responsible.

Frame Routing

The router (see in Figure 3.19) is responsible for forwarding frames to the devices supported by the node function or to the outbound line of another port in the node. The address field of the inbound frame determines which action it takes. When the node originates a frame, it instructs the router to transmit the frame on a specified port. All message and data frames relating to a particular command use the same port. The routing capability demonstrates a main feature of the SSA interface—all routing is done in hardware. Neither firmware nor software is involved in the forwarding of frames, providing high speed through a node.

Spatial Reuse

As defined earlier, spatial reuse enables separate SSA links (peripheral devices) to perform operations simultaneously. This simultaneous multitasking capability within a single network enables multiple network initiators to transmit different processes to different targets simultaneously.

Because each link between nodes (and between the node and the host server) functions independently, several transfers occur concurrently at the full bandwidth described earlier, provided that each transfer uses a different link. This allows much higher aggregate throughput than a token ring or a bus. A practical illustration of this results when one disk drive on a string or loop is backed up to tape while another drive on the same string copies data from a CD-ROM and yet another drive sends data to a printer.

Summary

The revolution in enterprise server business computing is furthered by the evolution in storage architectures and subsystems. Fully developed ESCON and FICON channel architectures that move data at 17 MB/s (or as high as 100 MB/s in the case of FICON) complement the server's growing appetite for data. Disk, tape, and optical storage devices, although shrinking in physical size, hold orders of magnitude more data. Graphical displays provide easy-to-use, user-friendly interfaces. They provide the look and feel appropriate to your business application needs. Printers provide flexibility, quietness, and ease of use that allows large-volume printing in your business production environments. The days of users waiting for overnight delivery of printer output or for access to a remote printer are long past, being replaced instead by instant access to the server data. Today's peripheral devices fuel your business computing revolution and provide your e-business server performance and capability by providing highly secure rapid access to enormous volumes of data where and when your business needs dictate.

4

S/390—zSeries Software

A major phenomenon of the computing world in the past several years is the rapid emergence of the Internet. IBM, with its subsidiaries Lotus and Tivoli, is the world's largest hardware, consulting, and software company, helping customers to build leading-edge systems for business around the world, across all key industries, and across a wide range of computing platforms. From this experience a framework was created for a solutions development methodology for building and deploying e-business applications. The e-business in simple terms is the marriage of the Internet with the IT systems infrastructure that S/390 and the zSeries servers so adequately provides.

Our focus in previous chapters was on the hardware: a server system's foundation or skeletal structure. We closely examined the evolution of processor units and peripherals used by S/390 and the zSeries servers. Now our focus shifts to the shapes and substance on top of the foundation, the elements that put the hardware to work. In the first part of this chapter, we introduce you to the role of application programs, both prewritten and custom developed, in a large server environment. In the latter part, we provide specific information on the three major eServer zSeries operating systems and their role in providing support for the various applications required to meet your business needs. First, however, we will look at IBM's efforts to ensure continuing value in software investments by maintaining software compatibility.

Software Compatibility

Computers implementing the popular S/390 (and the earlier System/370) computer architecture, such as the S/390 Parallel Enterprise Servers and the earlier generations, have been in use for many years, especially in medium to large businesses. As a result, businesses have invested tremendous amounts of time, money, and skill in designing and implementing custom application programs to meet their specific needs. In addition, many Independent Software Vendors (ISVs) have written S/390 application programs, providing a library of solutions to fill business needs. To preserve the enormous investments in these application programs, the new emerging z/Architecture retains compatibility with the S/390 architecture and its application programs, ensuring that most application programs written for System/370 and S/390 servers will run without modification on a zSeries server. There is further discussion of the IBM forward and backward compatibility protocol later in this chapter.

Application Program Compatibility

Compatibility refers to the ability of application programs to communicate, or interact, with the rest of the computer system. Application programs typically represent the primary share of a business's software development, purchase, data collection, and user training investment. Abandoning an application program because of incompatibilities (that is, the application program is unable to communicate with the operating system) may mean throwing away substantial amounts of data, training, and experience accumulated with that application program. Application compatibility is also important because it gives users the option of meeting business needs by choosing from the many application programs developed for the prior generation of systems architecture. Incompatibility at the application program level would render these programs virtually useless. Two attributes that enable application compatibility are the software architecture and the Application Programming Interface (API).

In the S/390, the software architecture is the ESA/390 architecture. This architecture defines the set of programming instructions (called the instruction set), the basic building blocks provided by the computer system architecture, used to build application programs. The API is the set of services provided by other software layers through which an application program communicates with the other software layers to get work done. Figure 4.1 shows that the application program interacts directly with the operating system layer; thus, the operating system provides the API for application programs in S/390 servers.

To maintain compatibility at the application program level, preserving both the software architecture and the API presented by the computer system is crucial. Because S/390 computers implement the ESA/390 software architecture, they retain compatibility with the earlier System/370 architecture (which in turn is compatible with the earlier System/360 architecture). The zSeries servers have the same capability for accommodating previous generations because they are trimodal (they will run in 24-bit and 31-bit as well as 64-bit mode). Thus, the first requirement for application program compatibility, preserved software architecture, is met. In addition to the preservation of application program investment, the back-level compatibility allows for a simple migration to the new server hardware followed by an orderly safe migration to the new operating system architecture, as is the case with S/390 and the zSeries servers.

What about preserving the API presented by the operating system? Maintaining compatibility at the operating system software level is as important as application program compatibility, but it is usually handled transparently (without impact to the application). That is, new levels of the operating system continue to support the functions provided in the earlier level while delivering new functions enabled by the new architecture. The zSeries operating system delivers functions that could not be considered by programmers using the S/390. The zSeries introduces new versions of the same operating systems, z/OS and z/VM, used with S/390. They provide a compatible API with ESA architectured operating systems. Therefore, the second requirement of application program compatibility is preserved. There is further discussion of the IBM operating system compatibility protocol for the zSeries later in this chapter.

Software Frameworks

In today's business world, computers are used in many types of environments for a variety of tasks. To meet these different needs, several IBM

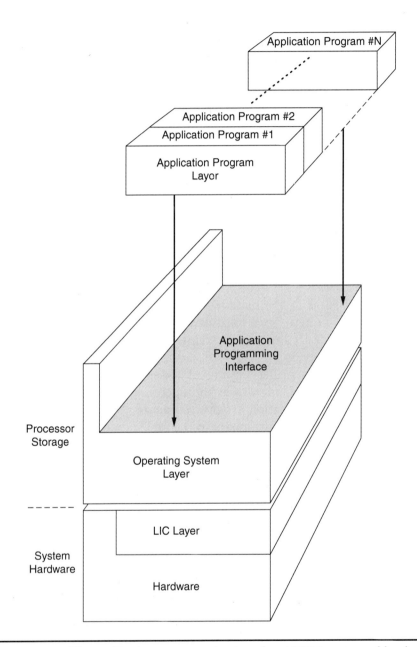

Figure 4.1.   The application programming interface (API) is presented by the operating system and is used by application programs to perform various tasks more easily.

computer system families and multiple operating systems have evolved. For example, the S/390 family can use the OS/390 (formerly known as MVS/ESA), √M/ESA, or VSE/ESA operating system; the IBM AS/400 computer family uses the OS/400 operating system; and the PC family uses OS/2 or Microsoft's Windows operating systems. As long as a user stays within one server family and operating system, it is relatively easy to change or migrate from one model to a more powerful or newer model and to bring along (port) any application programs purchased or developed for the initial system. When migrating from one server family to another, however, the user is often forced to modify, or even completely rewrite, existing application programs. IBM has helped alleviate this problem for S/390 and the zSeries by adding the ability to use UNIX, Linux, and NT applications on the both generations of servers.

Movement between operating systems within the same family may require some change to the application, but it generally does not require a significant rewrite of the application. In the S/390 and more so in the zSeries, much of this difference is handled automatically by the operating system.

The Network Computing Framework

The Network Computing Framework (NCF; see Figure 4.2) provides the foundation for successfully tackling the challenges development teams face—not from a theoretical point of view, but from a very practical point of view about how these applications are best built and deployed.

The NCF provides a system whereby applications can be up and running in months rather than the years it might have taken in the past. The solutions are developed such that they can be expanded as the needs expand. So, for example, what begins as a relatively straightforward on-line catalog for customers soon becomes an integrated system that lets customers place orders, integrating the system into existing inventory, accounting, and workflow systems to manage customer orders.

Announced by IBM in 1997, the NCF provides a framework for building e-business solutions. It enables development teams to rapidly build and deploy e-business applications. The framework is implemented using JavaBeans and a comprehensive set of network-based services for ease of development and extensibility, and by a powerful set of development tools. The NCF contains six key elements:

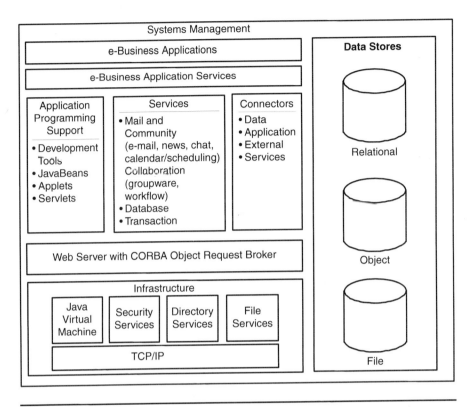

Figure 4.2.   The Network Computing Framework.

1. An infrastructure and a set of services whose capabilities can be accessed via open, standard protocols and a standard component interface, JavaBeans.

2. Clients based on a Web browser Java applet model that support universal access, a thin client paradigm, and exploitation of "just-in-time" delivery of components to provide a rich user interaction with the server.

3. A programming model and tools that create and exploit JavaBean components to build e-business applications. As a result, any tool can produce a component to access any service.

4. Internet-ready support for protocols such as HTTP and IIOP that link JavaBean components.

5. A set of "connector" services that provide access to existing data, applications, and external services.

6. A set of built-in collaboration, commerce, and content services that provide a foundation for an industry of partner-built solutions and customizable applications for e-business.

Application Programs on the S/390

Chapter 2 introduced the three basic software layers in the subject servers and how they cooperate to perform useful work for the user. This section concentrates on the top layer of the model, application programs (see Figure 4.3). It is the application program that actually "applies" the computational power of the server to a particular business task. The many approaches to computing and the variety of application program types all have the same objectives: to get the maximum amount of work done in the least amount of time at the lowest price with continuous availability to the business. These objectives lead to different combinations of computing elements to solve different types of application needs.

Some workloads require sequential processing. That is, each step of work depends on the successful completion of a step preceding it. Batch processing workloads, such as those performed by banks reconciling accounts at the end of a business day, typify this type of application. Other workloads can be segmented into parts that can execute simultaneously (in parallel) on different processors. Queries, whether simple or complex, fall into this category. Because these typically access tables from several databases, or portions of a single database, the query can be segmented into pieces that each access a different database. The result is much faster response time. Transactions, on the other hand, are independent work units. Typically of short duration, both in terms of the entered request for information (input) and the resulting response (output), transactions require a "manager" that feeds the requests to processor resources as they become available. Transaction processing systems usually must handle large volumes of simultaneous requests generated from multiple sources and requiring output sent to multiple locations. For these applications, throughput (the ability to quickly process requests) is critical.

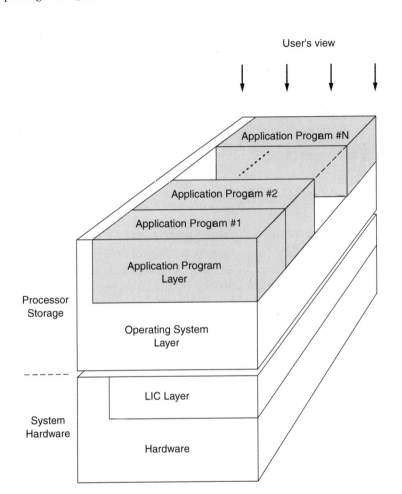

Figure 4.3. The application program layer of the S/390 software model.

Many businesses use application programs designed, written, and sold by other companies. This is becoming more and more the case as special-purpose packages of programs become available to solve specific industry problems, such as business reengineering. These are called prewritten application programs. In many cases, companies choose to design and write their own custom application programs or to use a combination of prewritten and custom application programs.

This section looks at both application program alternatives. Some prewritten application programs for the servers are discussed, but this chapter does not provide a complete guide to all prewritten application software. Comprehensive coverage of the many products available today would fill many books, each of which would be obsolete by the time it was published. Instead, this chapter helps you to make more informed purchasing decisions by giving examples of prewritten application programs and by briefly describing the custom application program alternative.

Prewritten Programs

Today's prewritten application programs range from simple programs that concentrate on a very specific task to powerful and complex groups of programs designed to work together. They perform a myriad of functions as diverse as the environments in which computers are found today. Many prewritten application programs are usable in most business environments (for example, word processing and electronic mail). These are known as cross-industry application programs, because they are not specific to any particular industry segment. Other prewritten applications address the specialized needs of a particular industry (for example, manufacturing or utilities). These are called industry-specific application programs. As an example, there have been several thousand new or improved applications for the S/390 since 1995.

Cross-Industry Application Programs

Prewritten cross-industry application programs are designed to fill the needs of many different types of businesses. There are a large number of programs available; examples are Lotus Domino, Query Management Facility (QMF), Application System (AS), and ImagePlus. There is one important IBM offering related to e-business software infrastructure development, where IBM has invested over several billion dollars in the last two to three years. This is a good indication of the seriousness with which IBM views the requirements and opportunity of businesses' need to reengineer their e-business infrastructure. IBM has strengthened, rebranded, and integrated its e-business infrastructure solution stack under the WebSphere brand name. The next section will describe how IBM got its start with S/390 and how it has grown to be the industry leading application framework for e-business.

IBM WebSphere Software Platform

As background to the evolution of the IBM WebSphere Software Platform for e-business, we need to look back to the middle and late 1990s and what transpired over the years to follow.

Lotus Domino for S/390 provided the industry's leading groupware solution. In 1996 and 1997, IBM converted several of its internal systems to Lotus Domino, installed on the IBM S/390 Parallel Enterprise Server. The Lotus Domino platform enables users to rapidly build, deploy, and manage applications that help colleagues, partners, and customers coordinate business activities on the Internet or an intranet. For example, development engineers in different locations can use Domino to collaborate and pool resources to design a new product.

The S/390 server's security, scalability, reliability, and throughput strengths made it an ideal server platform for Web applications and e-business activities. Lotus Domino on the S/390 complements other e-business enhancements and solutions for S/390, including digital certificate support, cryptography capabilities, Net.Commerce, and firewall technologies. The addition of Lotus groupware to the S/390 e-business portfolio made the S/390 server an even stronger foundation for companies to communicate, collaborate, and conduct commerce via the Internet.

Domino applications that were developed for other platforms began to be ported to the S/390 by Lotus Business Partners. These solutions included sales and services automation applications, application development tools, and project management applications. The IBM S/390 StarterPak for Lotus Domino was a service offering for Domino for S/390 Workloads that combined services, hardware, and preloaded software, including OS/390. It supported e-mail users and Lotus Notes database applications in a pilot or small production environment. It was designed to allow users to test applications and then deploy them on a larger S/390 server without affecting customers' production environments. Users could also use StarterPak to test OS/390 solutions from other vendors.

WebSphere Application Server for OS/390 and z/OS

Domino Go Webserver for OS/390, offered with the introduction of OS/390 Version 2, Release 5, provided an integrated Web server for the S/390, replacing its predecessor, Internet Connection Secure Server for OS/390. The name was subsequently changed in the release of OS/390 Version 2, Release 6 to WebSphere Application Server for OS/390. The proven strengths of S/390—continuous computing, secure transactions, large business databases, scalable servers, and easy access to needed data—made the S/390 an ideal location for a Web server. In September 1998, WebSphere Application Server for OS/390 was integrated into OS/390 Version 2, Release 6 and enabled the delivery of information, products, and services to the millions of users with Web browsers. With the increasing importance of electronic commerce, the security feature provided a means of conducting secure business transactions on the Internet with Web browsers enabled with Secure Sockets Layer (SSL).

In June of 2000 IBM made the major announcement that WebSphere would be the basis for their application framework for e-business architecture. IBM's WebSphere is based on open standards–based technology, allowing it to be implemented on all platforms. It has been built around Enterprise JavaBeans (EJB), and WebSphere has moved IBM into an in-dustry-leading position as an open-platform provider. All of IBM's server development organizations have been directed to embrace Enterprise JavaBeans to design their WebSphere implementation. The WebSphere package is composed of highly integrated bundles of software products that are designed to help users build and manage their e-businesses by providing them with much easier and faster tools to develop, deploy, and deliver e-business solutions and to manage them through their life cycle at lower cost. Initially the intent of the offering was to provide a package of core Application Server products, but now it has been significantly expanded to include the whole core stack of IBM e-business software for all platforms—S/390-zSeries, RS/6000, AS/400, and PCs. The WebSphere offering is made up of four elements:

- WebSphere Application Server Standard Edition

- WebSphere Application Server Advanced Edition

- WebSphere Application Server Enterprise Edition

- MQ Series

Within these base products the software product content is broken into the Foundation bundle, the Foundation Extensions bundle, and the Application Accelerators bundle.

IBM is committed to encouraging partners to add value and comple-ment the WebSphere offering through a wide range of applications, solutions, and e-business services. The WebSphere Software Platform is based on open industry standards such as Java, XML(eXtensible Mark-Up Language), LDAP (Lightweight Directory Access Protocol), and WAP (Wireless Application Protocol), which makes it safe and easy for partner adaptation. The list of partners will continue to grow, but some current examples are Ariba, Siebel, i2, Extricity, Razorfish, Macromedia, Rational, Red Hat, Novell, and Ernst & Young. IBM has more than 20,000 business partners, including nearly 10,000 ISVs. The WebSphere Software Platform is generally considered to be the most universal platform, supporting the most hardware and operating system environments in the industry.

OS/390 proxy servers, which make requests on behalf of clients, can simplify network design, provide additional privacy, and improve responsiveness by caching frequently accessed information. HyperText Markup Language (HTML) documents and binary resources (images, sound clips, and video clips) to be stored on an OS/390 repository may originate anywhere. Typically, image, sound, and video data are originated by multimedia workstations. HTML text can be created by using any suitable authoring tool available on workstations, or by using editors and text processors available on OS/390. Multiple servers can be operated simultaneously on the S/390, with the Interactive Network Dispatcher used to load balance between the servers. Some additional features and functions that provide this capability are

- Use of the OS/390 System Authorization Facility (SAF).

- Inputs to OS/390 System Management Facility logs.

- Easy-to-use configuration tools.

- Proxy authentication.

- Local file caching.

- Default code page support.

- S/390 Cryptographic Hardware support.

- Workload Manager (WLM) enablement.

- Web Usage Mining.

- Common Gateway Interface (CGI) support for C, REXX, Perl, and Java.

- PICS, SNMP subagent, and SOCKS support.

- Fast CGI, ICAPI, Servlet support.

- Client authentication.

- OS/390 Data Set Support.

Query Management Facility

For large amounts of information to be dealt with efficiently, the information needs to be organized in a uniform manner. For example, the information in a telephone book is organized into an alphabetical list of names, addresses, and telephone numbers. If you have ever lifted a Manhattan telephone book, you know that phone books contain a fair amount of information.

For efficient handling, the information stored within a computer system also needs to be organized. One common way of organizing is to enter the information into a database with files, records, and fields as subsets. This is exactly how the information in a phone book is structured. Figure 4.4 shows an example of a telephone book listing

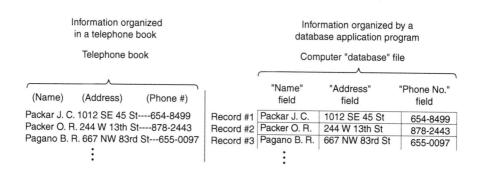

Figure 4.4. Information in a database is organized much like the information in a telephone book.

and the corresponding computer database structure. The white pages and yellow pages of the phone book are analogous to files or sets of information, also called database files. The information about one person in the phone book is analogous to a record. The records contain the information for a given entry, and each record contains the same type of information about its respective entry. In this case, a record contains the name, address, and phone number of the person. Each of these three items is analogous to a field within a record. For example, the address part of a phone book entry would be called the "address field."

Databases contain information about inventory in a store, a book in a library, personnel records, medical records, or virtually any other type of information. Organizations such as banks, airlines, and insurance companies commonly use extremely large databases shared by many users. Office workers and executives use databases to maintain personal telephone books, appointment calendars, and so on.

Manually looking up information in a phone book quickly becomes fatiguing. The same is true for manipulating any large body of information. Once the information is entered into an electronic database, however, it can be retrieved quickly and easily by a program designed to access the database. The IBM Query Management Facility (QMF) is an application program designed to give S/390 users and programmers access to the information stored in a database (Figure 4.5) through a query, a set of rules against which every record in a database is compared. Information that complies with the set of rules is copied from the database file into a report that is organized according to the user's guidelines. In other words, a query is a request to create a report containing the information from a database that meets certain criteria. For example, a personnel manager performs a query to get a list of names of all employees who have been with the company for 25 years or more, or a banker performs a query to get a list of all accounts with a balance of more than $100,000.

Query Management Facility (QMF) is a query and reporting tool for IBM's DB2 relational database management system family. It has been extended to provide new capabilities for the workstation environment and enhancements for the S/390. QMF Version 3, Release 3 enables you to work with data all over the enterprise—from OS/390, VSE, and VM to workstation servers running OS/2, Windows NT, AIX, and other UNIX operating systems, to massively parallel processors. QMF and the QMF HPO/Shuttle feature include the capability

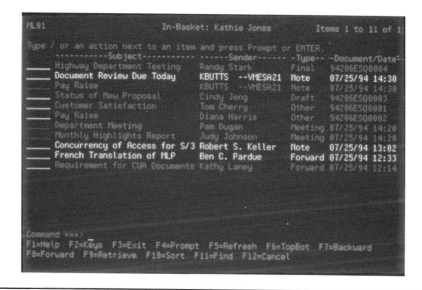

Figure 4.5. Screen presented by the Query Management Facility program product.

for accessing large amounts of data, sharing central repositories of queries and enterprise reports, and/or implementing tightly controlled distributed or client/server solutions. Web enablement, usability, and application-enabling enhancements, and improvements to the QMF HPO/Shuttle feature for Windows, including TCP/IP support, prompted query GUI interface, and static Structured Query Language (SQL) are now included in the product.

Customers using Lotus Approach 97 and Lotus SmartSuite 97 can exploit QMF. The QMF Approach Client allows you to display the results of QMF Queries and Procedures in Approach views, as well as to import QMF Queries and Forms to create an Approach report or cross-tab view. Approach can be used for the following procedures:

- **QMF Query.** When you select a QMF Query, the query is run on the QMF server. The results appear in the Approach form and worksheet. The data is read-only.

- **QMF Procedure.** When you select a QMF Procedure, the procedure is run on the QMF Server. The last data result produced by the procedure appears in the Approach form and worksheet. The data is read-only.

Approach can import these files:

- **QMF Form.** When you select a QMF form to import, the form is downloaded from the QMF server. Its attributes are used to create a new Approach report or cross-tab view.

- **QMF Query.** If you have the DB2 data source defined, you can import a QMF Query using the SQL Assistant. The SQL statement of the QMF Query is downloaded from the QMF server. The DB2 data source is used to connect to DB2 and submit the SQL statements to DB2 directly.

Application System

Application System (AS) is IBM's decision support system for the S/390 environment. It provides client/server solutions through the AS intelligent server. AS provides the tools to enable decisions to be based on facts rather than guesswork. AS traditionally runs in a S/390 environment under OS/390 (TSO/E, CICS/ESA) and VM/ESA. Over the last few years, AS has evolved as an intelligent server with PC clients under OS/2 and Windows.

The AS PC clients offer a choice of a graphical user interface (GUI) or a programming interface (C or C++). The AS PC clients can be used standalone or integrated with the user's product of choice (Lotus SmartSuite, for example) by using open interfaces, including ODBC, DDE, and CSV. AS also enables a World Wide Web (WWW) Internet sample solution, which can deliver the full power of the AS intelligent server to a Web browser. Alternatively, for the Internet service provider, AS can automatically generate Web pages using HTML.

AS provides comprehensive data analysis and manipulation as well as a wide range of data access. AS enables multidimensional analysis against a wide range of data sources. For data mining solutions, AS enables preprocessing as well as the presentation of the results of data mining. AS provides tools and facilities to help manipulate, analyze, and present enterprise data. AS has a rapid application development environment that provides developers the opportunity to combine any of the tools and facilities to deliver solutions for presentation at traditional terminals or as fully integrated client/server solutions.

ImagePlus

Although server systems have become the preferred way of collecting, managing, and distributing information in business, a lot of paper continues to circulate in offices, because much of the information needed to support daily business operations does not lend itself to being encoded in traditional computer systems. Examples of such information are signed documents, photographs, and documents that contain both text and drawings. Because of this hard-to-manage information, many highly computerized businesses still have to resort to manual methods of doing business for some tasks. They must still deal with rows of filing cabinets, overflowing in-baskets, envelopes, stamps, mail delays, wastebaskets, couriers, and folders. Often, handling this hard-to-manage information creates bottlenecks in an office's productivity and can significantly delay the entire business cycle. Recent advances in computer performance and optical storage technology have resulted in products, such as IBM's ImagePlus family, to handle this hard-to-manage information.

ImagePlus is a family of hardware and software products designed to capture, store, and manipulate images. An image is basically an electronic photograph of a document that is stored inside a computer. Virtually any type of document can be easily captured inside a server system as an image. ImagePlus facilitates the office changeover from a paper system to an electronic image system. That is, ImagePlus does for hard-to-manage documents what word processing did for standard letters and reports.

Tracing some hard-to-manage documents through a hypothetical insurance company using ImagePlus will help to clarify the concepts. For the purposes of our example, we will process a claim made by Mr. Payne (a client) for the repair of damage caused by a recent hurricane. Figure 4.6 shows the ImagePlus system used by our insurance company to process claims.

First, the insurance company's mailroom receives three estimates from various contractors for the repair of Mr. Payne's home. Because these are signed estimates with handwritten notes and include photographs of the damage, they fall into the category of hard-to-manage documents. They are first sent to the operator of the scan workstation so that an image of each estimate document can be created in the computer. The scan workstation consists of a workstation running OS/2 or Windows with the ImagePlus workstation program, a display, and a scanner (a printer may be added so that the workstation

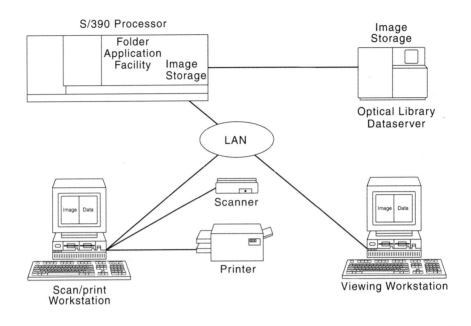

Figure 4.6. Example of ImagePlus in an OS/390 environment.

can double as a print workstation, as shown in the figure). The scanner is similar to a copy machine, but rather than producing a duplicate image on another sheet of paper, the scanner electronically produces a duplicate digital image in the workstation's memory. Once the image is in the workstation, the image quality is enhanced by the ImagePlus workstation portion, edited as necessary, and compressed to conserve valuable disk space. The images are then sent to the S/390 server and stored in S/390 Disk Storage.

After these steps, an application program specially written to use the facilities of the ImagePlus system takes over. This application indexes and stores the images. This indexing associates the images with Mr. Payne's account number and other pertinent information to facilitate their quick retrieval. That is, all information related to Mr. Payne's claim is linked together inside the server system. The system also sends a copy of the images to the Optical Library Dataserver.

In this example, the application allows the claims supervisor to prioritize Mr. Payne's claim with the other active claims and assign it to a claims processor working at a view workstation. Like the scan workstation, the view workstation is based on a workstation running ImagePlus workstation support. There is no need for a scanner or a printer at the view workstation. The claims processor at the view workstation can now easily view all of the information associated with Mr. Payne's case. During the processing of Mr. Payne's claim, the claims processor can suspend the case while waiting for additional information, suspend the case for a specified number of days, or complete the processing and close the case.

Because the information about Mr. Payne's case is all in order, the claims processor completes the necessary processing and closes the case. For now, the images pertaining to Mr. Payne's case are removed from S/390 disk storage to free space for other active claims, but the Optical Library Dataserver keeps a permanent record on optical disk for audit purposes. Later, if some of Mr. Payne's case images are needed, they can be recalled from the Optical Library Dataserver. They can be displayed on a view workstation as before, or they can be sent to a print workstation if hard copies are required, such as for external correspondence.

This is one simple example of an ImagePlus environment. An important feature of the whole ImagePlus system's architecture is that it is designed to accommodate other application programs. That is, it provides an application program interface that allows a programmer to develop custom application programs that use image capture, manipulation, storage, indexing, and printing functions provided by the ImagePlus family of products. This allows a business to build image-processing capabilities into its mainstream business application programs. For example, a real estate office can capture photographs of the exteriors and interiors of the houses that are for sale and store them in an ImagePlus system. With these computer images, a real estate agent can essentially "walk" prospective buyers through the house before they ever leave the real estate office, saving everyone a lot of time. Image processing will play a role of increasing importance in businesses of the future.

Industry-Specific Application Programs

In most cases, a business has needs that are more specialized to its particular industry. Therefore, a prewritten industry-specific application program may be desirable. This type of application program is specifically designed to address the needs of a well-defined business type such as a construction company or a hospital. Many software companies put great effort into developing industry-specific programs for the servers in our discussion, providing many options for addressing specific business and professional environments.

In most cases, a business has needs that are more specialized to its particular industry. Therefore, a prewritten industry-specific application program may be desirable. This type of application program is specially designed to address the needs of a well-defined business type such as a construction company or a hospital. Many software companies put great effort into developing industry-specific programs for the servers in our discussion, providing many options for addressing specific business and professional environments.

SAP R/3

SAP R/3's suite of client/server data processing products is based on the concept of combining all the business activities and technical processes of a company into a single, integrated software solution. SAP enables real-time integration, linking a company's business processes and applications, and supporting immediate responses to change throughout the organization. Its applications cover a wide variety of areas, including financials, asset management, controlling, project planning, sales and distribution, manufacturing, production planning, quality assurance, and human resources. SAP R/3 a uniform view of its results across international geographies. The business technology of SAP R/3, which is a three-tier client/server architecture, allows for Internet integration. The integrated workflow, application logic, and business object technologies of the R/3 System form the basis of this infrastructure. The Web browser can serve as an alternative user interface for R/3 business applications.

SAP R/3 is supported on S/390 in a three-tier client/server implementation. The S/390 or z900 provides the database server function with the client/server technology benefits such as distributed processing and extensive scalability. In a three-tier R/3 configuration, RS/6000 or Windows systems provide the application server function, and Windows desktop computers are used for presentation.

Presentation requests from the clients are sent to the application servers that process SAP R/3 system transactions. The application server runs these transactions and either reads data from local memory or initiates database requests. In an R/3 system, each application server can provide different functions or each can be defined as a logical grouping of users, such as a department or geography. A large number of different application servers can work in parallel with one another, accessing data stored in the database server. To spread the computing load as evenly as possible among the individual computers while optimizing overall performance, specialized application servers can also be defined for certain areas, such as sales and distribution, financial accounting, and human resources management. The application programs and user data, including data and process models, are stored on the database server. SAP R/3 uses DB2, which can manage large amounts of data on behalf of many users, as the database server. To run the database server on S/390 or z/900 requires SAP R/3 Release 3.0 or later on the application server and the database server.

IBM – Siebel Global Strategic Alliance

IBM is alligning itself with a number of industry leading developers, mentioned in Chapter 1. In October 1999, Siebel Systems and IBM announced a significant enhancement to their relationship, the IBM - Siebel Global Strategic Alliance. The mutual objective is to integrate Siebel System's multi-channel Customer Relationship Management (CRM) software applications with IBM's e-business capabilities including worldwide joint marketing, collaborative selling, software integration, and joint development. The integration of Siebel's Web-based applications with IBM expertise and products provides a powerful platform designed to reduce users cost and risk while accelerating deployment and improving the users return on investment.

The Siebel Customer Relationship Management solutions fully support the IBM application framework for e-business encompassing IBM middleware and component-based technologies including WebSphere Application Server. The Siebel e-business applications are completely compatible with IBM's DB2 Universal Database and the Siebel applications are therefore optimized for the four IBM eServer families described in Chapter 1. The IBM DB2 Universal Database is recognized as offering industry leading scalability, reliability, and availability.

IBM Global Services, described in Chapter 6, is a Siebel Strategic Alliance Partner, supporting users for Siebel's Web-based Front Office Applications including sales, marketing, service, telesales, telemarketing, field service, and Internet-based e-commerce.

IBM Global Financing, also described in Chapter 6, offers total solution financing for Siebel products allowing Siebel product users to acquire and implement e-business IT solutions across their enterprise.

Custom Application Programs

Prewritten application programs fit many needs. They are often well-written, flexible, and convenient tools. In some cases, however, users may find that the fit of their application program needs to be more customized. This is especially true in environments in which the server is employed to perform unusual and specific tasks, there is a need to conform to existing company procedures, or competitive advantage can be gained. In these cases, it may be better to develop custom application programs written to the user's exact specifications.

Custom application programs are usually designed and written by a staff of programmers employed by the company or by consultants contracted just for that purpose. In either case, the basic development steps are usually the same. First, a software specification is developed that describes what each program does. After the specification is completed, a preliminary version of the program is written that demonstrates the function that will eventually be in the final program. This preliminary version is evaluated by the user, and the specification is altered to reflect any needed changes. As a last step, the final program and user manuals are written and put in place at the user's location.

Typically, user training will be provided by the developer and any problems will be ironed out. Once the user accepts the program, the software has to be supported—users will need a place to go when they have questions not addressed by the manuals. Support also includes making necessary changes to the application program, as the changing business environment will often require. This kind of ongoing support is critical to the success of any computer automation project.

In many cases, custom application program development is initially more expensive and time-consuming than the prewritten application program approach. In many environments, however, the additional expense and time are quickly recovered by the increased productivity that can result from custom applications that precisely fit the needs of the environment. An additional benefit of custom application programs is their ability to change as a company changes. Getting major modifications to prewritten application programs may be difficult or even impossible. However, as described earlier, the downside of user application programs is the maintenance that is required. This can not only be costly but necessitates excellent documentation and ongoing in-house skills. The cycle of custom application program development can be very trying, especially with large or multiple projects. The complexities of today's application programs make it challenging to maintain existing custom application programs, let alone develop more. For this reason, many application development staffs find themselves very busy maintaining existing applications or working on projects that were requested two years ago, activities that hinder their ability to deliver new application programs needed by the users today.

Much attention is being given to the problem. With the S/390 and zSeries capability to support additional environments such as Lotus Domino, UNIX, Linux, NT, and Java, and with the creation of frameworks such as the Network Computing Framework, there are now many new possibilities for application development. For example, applications developed on or for other platforms can now be more easily ported to or simply run on the subject servers, changing the traditional view of application development on the S/390 and now the z900.

Custom Application Program Development

There are many different tools and approaches intended to improve the process of custom application development, with varying levels of success. In fact, the diversity of tools available today to address the challenge of custom application program development can itself lead to incompatibilities and a fragmented development process. The IBM strategy focuses on tools that address the global application development issues of implementing network computing applications, development of applications using object-oriented technology, and expansion of application development to multiple IBM and non-IBM development and execution platforms. One important dimension of this approach is the flexibility to develop an application in a computing environment that is different from the environment in which it will run. Application developers have a number of choices when it comes to developing large server-based or network computing applications that run in an S/390 or zSeries environment. The following sections look at these options in more detail.

Front-Ending Existing Applications

This process increases productivity by making existing applications easier to use without changing the actual applications. Adding new, user-friendly, graphical front ends to existing applications is an efficient way to improve user productivity without the increased expense or time consumption required to develop new applications. Here are examples of some of the tools that have been available:

- *VisualAge*, identified by several computer journals as an outstanding application development product, is an object-oriented visual-programming tool that provides a library of application components (or objects). Developers can use the existing objects or create new ones to build workstation programs that invoke existing server applications or access data stored on other systems across the network. VisualAge for Java is the development tool to use when building Java-compatible applications, applets, servlets, and JavaBean components. VisualAge for Java can also be used as a development environment for building Lotus Domino applications.

- *OnDemand for OS/390* is a set of programs that enable the automatic capture, index, archive, retrieval, presentation, and output of large volumes of computer generated documents, such as line data, Advanced Function Presentation (AFP) data, and images. Once documents are indexed and stored, the OnDemand 3270, client/server, or Internet interface allows users to easily search, retrieve, view, print, and fax documents. OnDemand provides Computer Output to Laser Disk (COLD) functions and is a component of the IBM Enterprise Document Management Suite (EDMSuite).

- The *Interactive System Productivity Facility (ISPF) for OS/390* provides a tool for modernizing host applications with Common User Access (CUA) constructs and client/server support. It is IBM's host-based Application Development (AD) environment that enables users to drive the development of host-only as well as client/server applications from the same host-based environment. The ISPF manages from the host traditional CICS, IMS, DB/2, and other applications. With it, applications are changed into distributed presentation applications by distributing the presentation function to individual workstations using OS/2, Windows, RS/6000, or Hewlett-Packard's HP-UX. Version 4, Release 1 provides a new graphical user interface (GUI) for ISPF applications without requiring any programming effort. ISPF Version 4, Release 2, Modification 1 (4.2.1) expands GUI platform coverage to include the 32-bit Windows NT and Windows 95 platforms as well as the Solaris 2.3 platform.

Version 4, Release 2 adds functions and flexibility for creating high-productivity user interfaces for applications. It provides the ability to automatically enhance and move to the workstation the user interface of host applications. Using this product to write GUI interfaces provides all the advantages of host applications, including security, central distribution, 3270 support, and maintenance, while keeping the advantages of having the GUI at the workstation.

ISPF for OS/390 Release 5 provides Web access enhancements, including an ISPF Application Server and ISPF Workstation Agent Applet, that allow new and existing ISPF applications to be accessed from the World Wide Web. This allows ISPF applications to be run from a network computer or workstation browser utilizing Java 1.1.1. VisualAge ISPF, a visual development solution utilizing the composition editor of IBM VisualAge technology, is used to create new ISPF panels and modify existing ISPF panels for use on 3270 and GUI screens. This allows customers the flexibility of creating or modifying ISPF panels without needing to know the syntax of the ISPF panel language or ISPF Dialog Tag Language (DTL). An OS/390 license will allow unlimited downloads of VisualAge ISPF.

- *CICS Gateway for Java* is designed to link the world of S/390 enterprise computing data with the Internet. Java is the key that gives access to the Internet. The CICS Gateway for Java enables Network Computers and PCs to transact business over the Internet. The CICS Gateway for Java is provided for the OS/390, OS/2, Windows NT, AIX, and Solaris platforms.

- *MQSeries Client for Java* is an MQSeries client written in the Java programming language for communicating via TCP/IP. It enables Web browsers and Java applets to issue calls and queries to MQSeries, giving access to mainframe and legacy applications over the internet without the need for any other MQSeries code on the client machine. With MQSeries Client for Java the user of an Internet terminal can become a true participant in transactions, rather than a just a giver and receiver of information.

- *Net.Data* provides database connectivity for Internet and intranet applications enabling the connection of relational data on a variety of platforms, from workstation to mainframe. Web applications can access DB2, Oracle, Sybase, and ODBC data sources as well as flat file data. Net.Data provides for high-performance applications and robust application development functionality, including development with Java, REXX, Perl, and C/C++.

Procedural Application Development Tools

Many application developers create applications using a procedural methodology. Frequently, these applications access IMS DB- and DB2-family databases. Many of them provide on-line transaction processing support against these databases. IBM provides a wide range of compiler choices, which provide interfaces to the databases to minimize the application code necessary.

The compiler provides the base for developing and enhancing programs. Solutions also require mainframe and workstation tools that can improve S/390 application development productivity as well as help to reengineer existing applications, automate program testing, and promote code reuse. These tools include debuggers, language-sensitive editors, and test facilities that are tightly coupled to the compiler. With the addition of UNIX Services (discussed later in this chapter), application developers have access to UNIX functions. Users have access to the following tools on S/390:

- *Language Environment for MVS and VM, Release 5* (formerly *LE/370*) combines essential run-time services such as message handling, condition handling, and storage management routines into one product. It provides common services and language-specific routines in a single run-time environment for applications generated with the IBM COBOL for MVS and VM, IBM C/C++ for MVS/ESA, FORTRAN, and IBM PL/1 for MVS and

VM high-level language compilers. This product also provides support for the PL/1 multitasking facility and additional object and load module support for OS PL/1. IBM Language Environment for MVS and VM Release 5 provides a common set of services in a single run-time environment. Additional support for object-oriented, distributed client/server, and open standards application development technologies simultaneously enhances the run-time environment. Language Environment is now an integrated part of OS/390.

- *IBM COBOL for OS/390 and VM* enhances the COBOL object-oriented programming support on OS/390 that was introduced in IBM COBOL for MVS and VM. IBM COBOL for OS/390 and VM is based on IBM COBOL for MVS and VM, including features such as COBOL 85 Standard language support, intrinsic functions, year 2000 support, interlanguage communications, and the mainframe interactive debugging tool. IBM COBOL for OS/390 and VM Version 2 provides COBOL support for Dynamic Link Library (DLL) generation for OS/390 applications. Application programmers can use DLLs to split their applications into smaller units and direct these units to be loaded only when required. Object-oriented applications can separate client code and class libraries into separate load modules. Also, the System Object Model (SOM) kernel and class libraries are accessed as DLLs. Support is also provided for SOMobjects for OS/390 Release 3.

- *IBM COBOL for VSE* brings new functions to the VSE environment, including intrinsic functions, access to all elements in a table at once, consistent interlanguage communications, common services and functions, improved dynamic calls, and support for the year 2000.

- *Workstation Interactive Test Tool (WITT and X/WITT)* automates program testing by creating test scripts that can be reused to ensure high-quality program maintenance. WITT runs on OS/2 and Windows, and X/WITT runs on X Windows. Each product records, plays back, and compares execution of a client/server application.

Advanced Application Generator Tools

This process provides an integrated application development environment that generates applications from a higher-level specification or a rules-based language. Using advanced application generators speeds application development, reducing application backlog and responding more quickly to business changes. Because the process is iterative, users can provide feedback at each development stage. *VisualGen* is an OS/2-based application development solution for applications that run in a variety of workstation and host environments. It provides the capability to define, test, and generate, in the same development environment, graphical user interface client applications, server applications, and single-system applications. It is designed to meet the needs of businesses that are implementing second generation client/server applications for On-Line Transaction Processing (OLTP) environments.

Object-Oriented Application Development

Today's complex business environment demands flexibility and adaptability in the tools with which the business is managed. Applications that both capture and analyze business information also require far more flexibility than those of even a few years ago. Object-Oriented (OO) Programming (OOP) enables a business to rapidly build, deploy, maintain, and modify application programs. A key element differentiating this technology from earlier programming technologies is the capturing of real-world business entities (such as products, orders, bills, and names) and mapping them to the processes and relationships with which they are involved. Once a business process is modeled, needed changes are incorporated with minimum disruption. Prototypes are improved incrementally until they meet production requirements. Object-oriented program development offers advantages in the areas of code reuse, high program quality, reduced development time, and rapid deployment of objects across a network of interconnected systems.

Java for OS/390 provides Sun Microsystems' Java Development Kit (JDK) on the S/390 platform. For increased performance, a Just-In-Time (JIT) compiler built specifically for OS/390 is included. The OS/390 JIT compiler is comparable to JIT compilers on other server platforms. Java for OS/390 provides a Java execution environment on all versions and releases of OS/390 with function equivalent to that available on any other server platform. Java for OS/390 fulfills the Java Compliance Suite compliance requirement. Now Enterprise JavaBeans (EJB) has become the Java platform that all eServer Series (z, i, x, and t) design within. Access to DB2 relational data through Java DataBase Connect (JDBC), access to CICS and IMS subsystems, and access to record-oriented data through these subsystems and MQ are also available.

Given that Component Broker Series (CBS) is the OS/390 object server architecture, Java will be treated as an object-oriented application development language that fits into the CBS architecture. Therefore, Java objects can participate in and be managed by CBS. Java can also be used to build Internet/intranet applications that use standard interfaces like Common Gateway Interface (CGI) and Internet Connection Application Programming Interface (ICAPI).

The portability aspects of Java make it attractive. Developers can write software to run on OS/390 without having to invest in S/390 hardware and software. They can develop applications on their existing platform and run them without having to make changes to those applications on S/390 servers. The portability of Java allows you to write, debug, and maintain one version of the application that runs anywhere in your network.

Component Broker is an implementation of CORBA (Common Object Request Broker Architecture) standards–based object technology that is available during 1998. The Component Broker programming model makes application development much easier. The programming model and tools developed to support it hide complicated details from the programmer that relate to locking, caching, transactions, data location, navigation, and storage. Component Broker exploits OS/390's support of parallel sysplex.

Support Services for S/390 and z900 Application Development
The IBM Solution Developer Program is a service that provides the information and services needed to develop applications for network computing, or e-business. Partnering with IBM through the IBM Solution Developer Program enables a strategic focus on network computing, and all of the products make up a network infrastructure. The IBM Solution Developer Program provides the business, technical, and marketing services needed to write applications for the network computing environment. These services enable ISVs to write and market applications as quickly and profitably as possible.

The VisualAge Object Connection program is designed to encourage commercial software developers to explore the business of building VisualAge-enabled and Java reusable software componentry. In addition to component development, the Object Connection program supports independent software vendors building VisualAge-complementary tools and end-user applications.

SmoothStart for Domino for S/390 is an installation service offered by IBM Global Services. Customers can take advantage of IBM specialists to install and configure Domino to their IT specifications and ensure a successful transition to Domino for S/390. The SmoothStart service provides installation planning, OS/390 system customization, on-site installation and testing of the Domino code, and skills instruction.

Application Enablers—Extending the API

Application programs interact directly with the operating system to perform different tasks such as reading and writing disk storage or sending information over a communications network. The interaction between the operating system and application programs takes place through the Application Programming Interface (API) presented by the operating system (Figure 4.7). Program products (Figure 4.8), called application enablers, extend the API presented by the operating system. Application enablers add function to the API, thus offering more services to application programs. As the figure shows, application enablers reside between the operating system and the application program layers of our software model, and they actively communicate with both layers.

Adding additional services to the API makes the job of application program development easier. Because software development companies can more easily develop prewritten application programs, S/390 users have more prewritten application programs from which to choose. In the same way, the productivity of developing custom application programs is improved because the application enablers provide many functions that would otherwise have to be written from scratch during the custom application development project. The following sections look at categories of application enablers used with S/390 computers: transaction-processing application enablers, database application enablers, including an overview of IBM's database strategy, and special-purpose application enablers.

Transaction-Processing Application Enablers

Traditionally, S/390 users interacted with the computer system by typing a request on a workstation's keyboard and then viewing the computer system's response on the workstation's display screen. Although

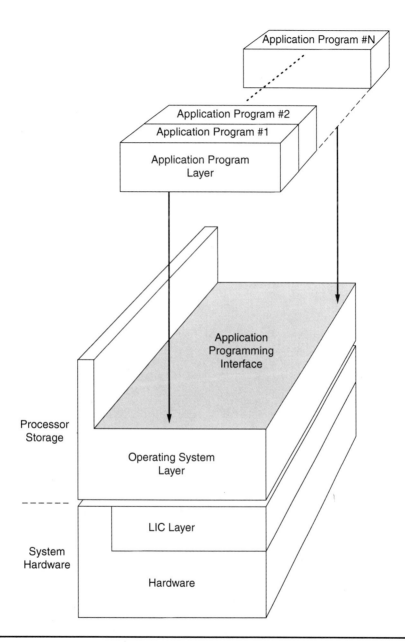

Figure 4.7. The application programming interface (API) is presented by the operating system and is used by application programs to perform various tasks more easily.

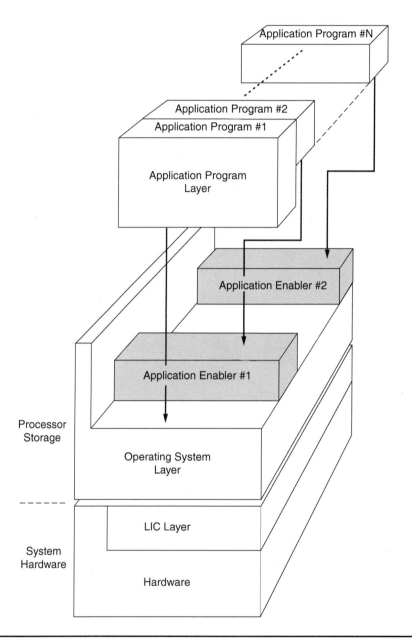

Figure 4.8. Application enablers build on the API of the operating system, offering additional services to application programs.

the technique may in some cases have been replaced with a graphical interface, the underlying concept remains the same. For example, a front desk clerk at the Uptown Hotel may enter a request for information about Mr. Vann's reservation and then see the information presented on the display screen. This type of interaction is called a transaction. Although transactions seem simple on the surface, the clerk at the Uptown Hotel sets off a flurry of activity within the system when he or she requests information about Mr. Vann's reservation: the request must be interpreted; the proper database file must be accessed; Mr. Vann's record in the database must be found; and the requested information must be sent back, formatted, and directed to the display station.

Now consider that there probably are multiple hotel clerks at the Uptown Hotel, all checking in and checking out different customers. Moreover, there are nationwide telephone operators, located in another city, all simultaneously making, canceling, and changing reservations for the entire chain of Uptown Hotels throughout the world. Thus, the transaction load can quickly increase the demands on the computer system, which could mean slow response times for the hotel clerks, which means long lines at the checkout desk and angry customers. You can also see how damaging it would be when the server system is down.

Our example is a hotel-oriented transaction, but most businesses use transactions. Thus, there is a need to provide S/390 users with a transaction-processing capability that delivers access to information, good performance levels (i.e., fast response times), and reliability (little computer down time). In providing this transaction-processing environment, there are common needs for any type of transaction, such as communicating with a pool of display stations, handling multiple and simultaneous transactions, and accessing files.

The Customer Information Control System (CICS) is a family of application enablers that provide these services for application programs, freeing the application program developer from having to worry about transaction mechanics. That is, the services provided by the CICS allow the programmer to spend time writing application programs that meet the business's needs rather than wading through the mechanics of a transaction. As an application enabler, the CICS resides between the operating system and the transaction-based application programs. The programmer then writes an application program to the API provided by the CICS and lets the CICS do the necessary interaction with the operating system. One copy of the CICS running in the computer system can handle the transactions of many different users and many different transaction-based application programs. Alternatively, multiple copies of the CICS can be active in a single S/390 computer and can freely communicate with one another (that is, share data). Further, multiple copies of the CICS can be installed in different computer systems (S/390s or others) and can communicate freely. The data acted upon by the CICS can be held in a database, in a standard data file, or within the CICS itself.

There are different versions of the CICS for the various S/390 operating system environments. CICS Transaction Server for OS/390 is for the OS/390 operating system; CICS/VSE is for the VSE/ESA operating system; and CICS/VM is for the VM/ESA operating system. An important feature of the CICS is the common application program interface (API), which allows applications to be ported easily from one platform to another. Application functions can be distributed across different elements in a network, allowing the best use of hardware investments. In a PC, for example, application programs written to the CICS API can access data stored on the PC's own disk storage or on that of a connected computer system (for example, a CICS S/390 system) in a cooperative processing configuration. The CICS supports the S/390 parallel sysplex, including IMS DB data sharing, VSAM (Virtual Storage Access Method) record level sharing, and dynamic workload balancing. The CICS also provides support for multiple network protocols, including SNA and TCP/IP, transparent use of LANs and WANs, and concurrent sharing of data with complete integrity. CICS Transaction Server for OS/390 is the base for large-scale or complex transaction processing. CICS Transaction Server for OS/390, orderable as a single package, contains CICS-enabling functions.

The CICS supports a single image in sysplex configurations without a coupling facility (non–parallel sysplex) and standalone OS/390 system (single-system sysplex). It supports a new interface that allows 3270-based CICS transactions to run unchanged without a 3270 terminal. It includes an interface to the World Wide Web (WWW) with support for 3270-based transactions. Parallel sysplex support is extended with the new system management facility for defining and installing CICS resources across multiple CICS occurrences that are managed by the CICSPlex SM function on S/390 systems. To enable higher availability, the CICS supports new DB2 resource definitions with Resource Definition On-line (RDO) as alternative to the traditional Resource Control Table (RCT) definitions. The package also includes support for client partner LU6.2 applications across TCP/IP networks. CICS was the first S/390 product to implement the MultiNode Persistent Sessions support that enables application fault tolerance across hardware, operating system, or application failures.

CICSPlex System Manager/ESA (CICSPlex SM) provides a system manager for CICS/ESA system programmers, system administrators, and master terminal operators. It provides a real-time, single-system image of the multiple CICS/ESA systems that make up the transaction processing environment in many businesses. From a single point of control, CICSPlex SM monitors and operates the CICS address-spaces and resources throughout the business enterprise. It also provides management by exception capability, automatically warning of deviations from intended performance, and workload management, which provides workload balancing across CICS systems.

The Business Application Services (BAS) facility provides a single point of definition and installation for CICS resources across multiple CICS occurrences on S/390 systems managed by CICSPlex System Manager. The aim of BAS is to provide a logical, single-system image solution to CICS resource definition.

Database Application Enablers

As we saw earlier in this chapter, a database is a body of information stored within a server system in such a way that the information can be efficiently manipulated. There are different types of databases, but all provide a structure in which information can be stored in a coherent and consistent manner. Databases are used widely for storing different types of information, such as airline reservations, personnel records, bills of material, sales figures, characteristics of fishes, insurance claims, or melting points of various chemicals. To aid in the development of S/390 databases and the application programs that manipulate them, various database application enablers have been developed. They fall into groups of relational, hierarchical, and parallel database enablers

Relational Database Enablers: DB2 and SQL

IBM's relational database technology incorporates highly efficient optimizing technology, object extensions to combine relational technology with emerging object and multimedia technologies, and traditional relational database management functions. The DB2 family of relational database products offers industrial-strength database management for decision support, transaction processing, and an extensive range of business applications. The DB2 family spans AS/400 systems, RISC System/6000 hardware, S/390, non-IBM machines from Hewlett-Packard and Sun Microsystems, and operating systems such as OS/2, Windows and Windows NT, AIX, HP-UX, UNIX, SCO OpenServer, and Solaris Operating Environment. It supports growth from a small number of users to environments requiring support of thousands of users.

DB2 is an application enabler that provides a mechanism to build and manage a relational database on a system running under OS/390. A relational database uses a flexible, tabular format for storing information that lends itself to ad hoc question-and-answer dialogs between the user and the computer system. DB2 by itself facilitates the development of custom application programs that access the information via Structured Query Language (SQL). SQL is an English-like language used to search, modify, create, and delete information in a database. SQL statements can be embedded in custom application programs or issued directly by users with the help of prewritten application programs such as the Query Management Facility (QMF) and Application System (AS), discussed earlier in this chapter.

Enhancements in DB2 allow programs to access data at multiple sites for the same transaction. DB2 ensures data integrity while the application makes updates at multiple sites. This process, called distributed two-phase commit, also enables IMS and CICS applications to perform updates to data stored at remote locations. This enhancement is made within the Distributed Relational Database Architecture (DRDA). DRDA provides a set of protocols that define how client and server systems can interoperate with each other to provide access to remote data. It is an open architecture that enables client systems to access and manipulate data on any DRDA-enabled server, whether provided by the same vendor or by different vendors. Functions included are single-site access definitions, multisite updates with enforced data integrity, and the use of stored procedures and DCE (Data Base2) security.

DRDA clients can be used directly by applications or together with systems software for added transparency and function. DRDA provides enabling technology for data access for users, applications, data replication, and systems management. IBM provides DRDA clients and servers throughout the DB2 family. Other enhancements allow parallel I/O operations to reduce query response time when accessing large partitioned data tables. Also, data compression provides improvements in DASD (Direct Access Storage Device) storage, controller, channels, and central storage at some cost in processor time. Use of the hardware compression feature (see Chapter 2) minimizes the impact on processor time. Stored SQL procedures also provide significant performance improvement.

DB2 for OS/390 Version 5 expands DB2 capabilities by delivering function built on advanced database technology. DB2 capitalizes on improvements in communication bandwidth and growth in lower-cost microprocessors and disk storage. Open connectivity gives easy access to historical and operational data. The latest enhancements better enable DB2 as an effective platform for a large data warehouse. DB2 Version 5 delivers more client/server function, more support for open industry standards, including JDBC, and greater performance and availability. This release expands the parallel database technology by enhancing function for DB2 data sharing with parallel sysplex technology. This support enables DB2 data sharing applications to run on more than one DB2 subsystem and read/write from a common shared database. This feature uses coupled systems technology made available through the enhanced sysplex environment.

Hierarchical Database Enablers
IBM's hierarchical database manager technology provides support for business-critical on-line operational applications when support for high availability, high performance, and high capacity with low cost per transaction are key factors. IMS DB, which can be accessed from IMS/ESA Transaction Manager and the CICS, provides this support through full-function databases. These allow complex data relationships and predefined structures to be handled with efficient I/O operations. It also supports Fast Path databases that offer more efficient access to data and higher performance.

Information Management System/Enterprise System Architecture (IMS/ESA) is a different type of database application enabler that is used on S/390 computers running OS/390 or the MVS operating system. Whereas DB2 enablers are used for relational databases, IMS/ESA provides a mechanism to build and manage a hierarchical database in which pieces of information are stored in an inverted tree structure with predefined relationships to each other. These predefined relationships improve the performance of database transactions at the cost of reduced flexibility compared to the tabular structure of a relational database.

IMS/ESA facilitates the development of custom application programs that access the information via Data Language/1 (DL/1). DL/1 is used to search, modify, create, and delete information in a database. DL/1 statements are embedded in custom application programs. In Version 5 of IMS/ESA, DL/1 calls allow automated operator programs to issue commands, improving productivity. Made available in the second quarter of 1995, Version 5 includes enhancements to the two existing components of IMS, Database Manager, and Transaction Manager, and adds a third component, Remote Site Recovery (RSR). This version also takes advantage of OS/390 UNIX Services support and object-oriented technology support. IMS/ESA Version 5 also operates in a VM virtual machine under the control of MVS/SP Version 4, Release 2. In this environment, it is intended for program development and testing. Restrictions apply to this capability.

IMS/ESA Database Manager (IMS/ESA DB) provides performance, integrity, capacity, and availability for the IMS database used by the IMS Transaction Manager and CICS/ESA users. Through use of the IMS Resource Lock Manager (IRLM) and the parallel sysplex (hardware and software), IMS DB provides N-way data sharing. Fast Path performance improvements allow slightly fewer than 10,000 Fast Path Area data sets and slightly fewer than 8,183 full-function database data sets to be concurrently open. Support is provided for the OS/390 Workload Manager, enabling more efficient control of the workload mix. A major concern for many businesses as they approach the twenty-first century is whether their applications will be impacted by dates beyond 1999. IMS/ESA Versions 5 and 6 enable testing for year 2000 problems and for correcting applications that are impacted. Both are fully year 2000 compliant. IMS Version 6 Database Manager provides improved object programming and Internet access to data for Network Computing, and improved availability and capacity, such as the ability to avoid a restart during the daylight savings time change.

The optional IMS/ESA Transaction Manager (IMS/ESA TM) provides transaction-processing facilities similar to those of the CICS discussed earlier in this chapter. Alternatively, IMS/ESA databases can be used with the CICS as the transaction manager. The IMS TOC (TCP/IP OTMA Connection) provides connectivity to IMS TM from any TCP/IP client application. The IMS Client for Java provides code for preparing a Java program to access IMS applications and data running on an S/390. IMS Version 6 Transaction Manager offers improved integrity, security, and Internet access for network computing, and improved capacity and availability. IMS TM provides many functions, including

- Enabling support for Advanced Program-to-Program Communications (APPC) with applications on a programmable workstation and other products that support APPC/MVS.

- Managing and securing the IMS TM terminal network.

- Routing messages from terminal to terminal, from application to application, and between application programs and terminals.

- Queuing input and output messages.

- Providing message integrity.

- Scheduling application programs.

The IMS Shared Message Queue (SMQ) solution in Version 6 allows IMS customers to take advantage of the S/390 Parallel Sysplex Coupling Facility to store and share the IMS message queues among multiple IMS TM systems. Incoming messages from an IMS TM on one Central Processor Complex (CPC) in the sysplex can be placed on a shared queue in the Coupling Facility by the IMS Common Queue Server (CQS) for processing by an IMS TM on another CPC in the sysplex. This can provide increased capacity and availability for IMS systems. This SMQ solution takes advantage of the MVS function Cross System Extended Services (XES) to access the Coupling Facility and the Automatic Restart Manager (ARM) to improve availability by automatically restarting the components in place or on another CPC. With shared queues, a message can be processed by any IMS sharing the queues. This can result in automatic workload distribution because the messages can be processed by whichever IMS subsystem has the capacity to handle the message. The OS/390 Workload Manager (WLM) can be used to classify the incoming messages and can be relied upon to help control the assignment of MVS resources, as it does today for IMS. The IMS SMQ solution allows IMS customers to take advantage of the sysplex environment, enabling increased capacity and incremental horizontal growth.

The IMS Connectors provide connectivity from the Web to transactions and data in IMS. These solutions allow customers to match their communications infrastructures, used with IMS, to their Web server configuration. The IMS WWW Templates contain templates for providing Web access to IMS TM that accept APPC connections. The IMS Web uses a TCP/IP communication infrastructure and middle-tier Web servers to make IMS transactions available on the Web. The IMS TCP/IP OTMA Connection provides enhanced communication linkages between remote workstations and IMS. The IMS Client for Java provides code for preparing a Java program to access IMS applications and data running in an S/390.

Developing Usable Business Information

The ultimate business goal of transaction and database enabling is the creation and capture of data and its transformation into usable business information. Recent technologies, both software and hardware, have made this practical and increasingly important in gaining and maintaining competitive advantage. IBM's database strategy incorporates these new technologies.

As a business evolves and grows over time, many different databases are typically developed and maintained on the business's computer systems. Unfortunately, each database is often limited in structure, format, and flexibility. For example, a personnel program may build a database of employee information that can be accessed only by a particular application program due to the data format used. A database might be stored on a user's own computer and not be easily accessible to the other users who may eventually need it. Inconsistencies of this kind made Decision Support Systems (DSS) difficult and unreliable for a long time. Eventually, the noted database consultant William H. Inmon developed the theory of the atomic database and methods for the practical design of a data warehouse. An atomic database is a single repository of the lowest level of detail that will ever be needed. A data warehouse includes the atomic database and methods for populating it and retrieving information from it in a useful manner.

Based on these concepts, IBM addressed the need to improve access to information by developing the Information Warehouse Solution (depicted in Figure 4.9). This solution provides capabilities for building a data warehouse as a means of enhancing business decision making. Traditional business applications (operational applications) access small amounts of data while processing transactions for order entry, point-of-sale, payroll, and other business functions. These applications create and use data that change frequently and that are related to a particular application. A data warehouse includes a store of data that is optimized for applications (called informational applications) that support analytical processing and decision making. Applications such as query and reporting, point-in-time data analysis, trend analysis, and data mining use this data as a means of discovering new information useful to a business.

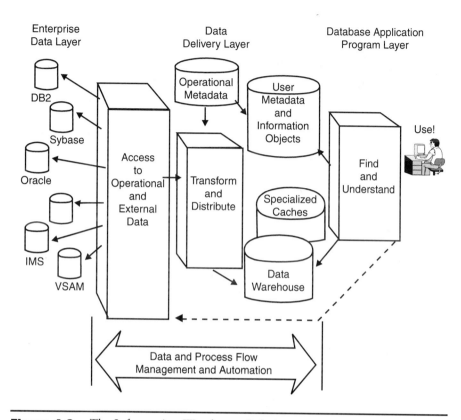

Figure 4.9. The Information Warehouse Solution.

Because operational applications and informational applications and their data are fundamentally different, most businesses will evolve two different environments, each optimized to support one type of application. The original data source for both types of applications, however, is the same. It may be internal to the business or be extracted from external sources. In either case, before the data is useful to the informational applications, it requires transformation to a different format and cleaning to remove data useful only in operational environments. The data types used in both applications include the following:

- Real-time data is typically used only by operational applications. This contains detailed data reflecting only the most current level of activity. It may exist in multiple locations throughout the business without synchronization.

- Reconciled data contains detail records from the real-time level, but it has been cleaned, adjusted, or enhanced so that the data can be used in informational applications. All inconsistencies have been reconciled.

- Derived data generally appears as summaries of reconciled data. These summaries can be in the form of averages or aggregates from multiple sources of real-time or reconciled data. Derived data is more useful for informational applications because it improves processing efficiency.

- Changed data has evolved over time. This data is time-stamped to record when the change was made. A changed-data store contains a record of the changes (adds, deletes, updates), enabling any level of point-in-time analysis.

- Metadata is descriptive information about other data elements or data types. It is important as users attempt to access data and develop their own information applications. They need to understand what data exists for them to access, exactly what that data represents, how current it is, and so on. Metadata provides these answers, usually through data dictionaries, database catalogs, programs, and copy libraries.

IBM's Data Warehousing provides a solution for building and managing data warehouses and data marts that scale from personal size to the largest enterprise. The solution consists of

- *Visual Warehouse*, a fast-start package for building and maintaining a data warehouse in a LAN environment.

- *DataGuide*, a catalog solution to help business users locate, understand, and access enterprise data.

- *TeamConnection DataAtlas*, a data modeling, database design, and data dictionary for DB2 for OS/390, DB2 Common Server, and IMS databases.

- *Data Propagator*, a data replication system that includes support for business plans that include movement to client/server environments, data warehousing, and business reengineering.

Decision Support systems include the following:

- *Intelligent Decision Server (IDS)*, a client/server decision support tool with powerful reporting, analysis, and application construction facilities. IDS helps network computing users find and analyze massive amounts of data in an enterprise. With IDS, data analysis applications can be accessed from Web browsers, Lotus Notes, and clients running on Windows, Windows NT, OS/2, AIX, and Solaris.

- *Application System (AS)*, a full decision support host-based solution for accessing a wide variety of database sources. AS is a key component in the IBM solution to address the needs of Decision Support, Enterprise, Business, and Management Information Systems divisions.

- *Lotus Approach and Domino Web Server*, which provide access to both DB2 and Approach databases with a single interface.

- *WebSphere Application Server*, in which DB2 Universal Database (not on OS/390), Net.Data, and WebSphere operate together to make DB2 data available to any Web browser. Data such as numbers and text, images, and sounds can be retrieved.

- *Query Management Facility (QMF)*, a query and report-writing tool set for accessing the DB2 family of databases and managing the query environment.

- *Visualizer*, an easy-to-use query tool that requires no SQL knowledge. Users can browse their results and perform analysis using reports and charts.

- *Ultimedia Manager*, which finds images stored within the database by color, shape, texture, and related business data. Images can be in many formats including OS/2 2.0 bitmap, Windows 3.x bitmap, PCX, Intel and Motorola TIFF, TARGA TGA, Audio Visual Connection (AVC), TIFF (FAX), GIF, and Kodak Photo-CD.

Data Mining

A new dimension of decision support systems is added through the use of data mining to discover in large databases associations and sequential patterns that reveal unforeseen patterns of behavior. Finding these hidden patterns can represent a competitive opportunity for your business. Using unique data-driven algorithms, this technology makes no assumptions about anticipated results, as opposed to other technologies that create hypotheses and seek data to verify them. IBM has defined four classes of data mining techniques based on patent-pending technology:

- The Association Detection Algorithm reveals all associations (affinities) that one set of items in a transaction imply about other items in that transaction. For example, a food chain may discover that a significant portion of its customers who buy salmon and dill also buy white wine. This insight might allow the chain to better forecast sales of each item, to create a theme for merchandising the items, or to offer a unique promotion featuring those items.

- Sequential patterns involve analyzing purchases or events occurring in a sequence to detect frequently occurring patterns. A retailer, for example, might find that customers who purchase sheets and pillowcases followed by a comforter tend to purchase drapes 70% of the time. This insight might lead to redefining the store layout or targeting a promotion for drapes at customers who have purchased sheets and pillowcases in the last two months.

- Classifiers are functions used to examine a set of records to produce descriptions of the characteristics of each record and to sort them by classes, which are predetermined and associated with each record. The embodiment of the class descriptions is called a model. Classification models include linear regression models, decision tree models, rules-based models, and neural network models. Classifiers are suited to credit card analysis, in which each customer record contains a number of descriptors. For customers whose credit history is known, each record can be classified (tagged) with good, medium, or poor, reflecting the degree of credit risk. A classifier can then examine the tagged records and produce an explicit description of each of the three classes (for example, good credit risks are between the ages of 45 and 55, have incomes in excess of $35,000, and live in XYZ neighborhood).

- Clustering uses a set of records with no classes (tags) associated. The classes are generated by the clustering tool. This process is useful in market segmentation analysis, in discovering affinity groups, or in defect analysis.

Data mining comprises three distinct phases or steps: data preparation, mining operations, and presentation. Information discovery is a process that iterates through these three phases. The first phase, data preparation, consists of data integration followed by data selection and preanalysis. Data integration refers to merging data that typically resides in multiple files or databases in an operational environment. Activities required here are similar to those required in building a data warehouse. Data selection and preanalysis create subsets of the data, which improves the quality of the data mining operation and avoids limitations that may exist in data mining tools. Data in the warehouse may be accessed through a standard SQL interface or through alternate interfaces such as a Web browser.

IBM's data mining technology uses DB2 databases as well as flat files containing data extracted from relational databases or generated from operational systems. A Graphical User Interface (GUI) enables users to browse through the results or to compare them with previous results. Defining and extracting a data set once enables users to mine different parts of the data set or the same set several times without redefining it. Solutions include *Intelligent Miner*, a productivity tool for discovering hidden information in vast amounts of data, and *MediaMiner*, which provides an open framework for building applications based on multimedia information sources.

Special-Purpose Application Enablers

The transaction-processing and database application enablers discussed so far are general in their usage. Other application enablers extend the operating system's API to meet very specific needs. Included among these are the following:

- *Enterprise Document Management Suite (EDMSuite)* is a group of Web-enabled products that includes imaging, Computer Output to Laser Disk (COLD), and document and workflow management. The IBM EDMSuite products enable management of and access to digital documents stored in systems across an organization through the use of network computing. Access is provided through familiar Web browsers, Lotus Notes clients, and sophisticated production clients. EDMSuite includes the functions of the FlowMark and ImagePlus applications. EDMSuite provides for the storage, retrieval, and distribution of virtually all types of documents. From a Web browser, images, faxes, computer-generated statements, word processing documents, spreadsheets, and more can be retrieved from multiple different repositories.

- *ImagePlus*, IBM's image management software, enables organizations to replace paper-based information with electronic images. ImagePlus products allow images and other electronic documents to be captured, indexed, and stored, using a specified workflow or process. Word processing, spreadsheets, and graphics, as well as audio and video, can all be grouped to form a comprehensive folder. With ImagePlus, paper documents, photos, or drawings are scanned or captured as electronic images, organized into folders, linked to business applications, routed through the work process, and presented to users. Application enablers are available to make it easier for programmers to integrate image technology into application programs. Images can be thought of as electronic snapshots of papers, photos, receipts, or other documents. These electronic snapshots are stored along with more traditional data (customer names, dates, or prices, for example) using large-capacity optical storage devices. Having data and images immediately available in a computer system facilitates the logistics of logging, filing, locating, and moving large quantities of documents.

- *FlowMark,* IBM's work process manager, enables organizations to define, implement, and track the processes used within their business. FlowMark links people, information, and applications to streamline business processes.

Operating System Alternatives

S/390 and zSeries 900 servers may be used with a variety of operating systems, each creating a different application execution environment with its own set of advantages and disadvantages. These environments vary primarily in the interfaces (Application Program Interfaces, or APIs) between the application and the operating systems. They also differ in how central storage is used and the virtual storage structure is created, as well as other characteristics. The best environment for your business choice depends on considerations such as compatibility with application programs, the workload characteristics, the number and type of users, and, more important, positioning to move to the most secure, most available, highest-performance, and most scalable platform, the zSeries, as business capabilities permit.

IBM's large-system operating systems cover a wide variety of environments. Over the years, the operating systems have evolved through several generations (System/360, System/370, S/390, and now zSeries 900) and have included multiple architectures. Generally, as architectures and operating systems have evolved, they have maintained compatibility with earlier versions and with applications written to work with those versions. To gain the full advantage of the systems using the latest architecture, that is, the z/Architecture, new versions of the operating system are required. Through the S/390 compatibility modes, operating systems designed for use with the S/390 family of servers can be used directly on the newer z900 servers. This section provides an historical overview and an update of the most commonly used operating system alternatives.

- Multiple Virtual Storage/Enterprise System Architecture (MVS/ESA)

- Operating S/390 (OS/390)

- z/OS

- Virtual Machine/Enterprise System Architecture (VM/ESA)

- z/VM

- Virtual Storage Extended/Enterprise System Architecture (VSE/ESA)

In addition to these most common operating systems, the section closes with a brief review of some other operating system alternatives, of which the Linux operating system has emerged as one of the most widely used.

Evolution of OS/390

MVS/ESA

Terms such as "industrial strength" and "business critical" are just now becoming applicable to some UNIX-based operating systems, but they are terms that have been applied to the Multiple Virtual Storage/Enterprise System Architecture (MVS/ESA) operating system for several decades. "Bulletproof" is another term that has been applied to MVS/ESA, and only MVS/ESA can be labeled as such. In fact, MVS/ESA has become the de facto standard by which other industrial-strength operating systems measure their usefulness as business solutions. The following sections of this chapter will help you understand why this is so.

MVS/ESA has been the strategic operating system for IBM's S/390 computers, ranging from midsize to the largest possible configurations, for decades. MVS/ESA technology is at the core of the system for the S/390, called OS/390 and now referred to as z/OS. It provides the most comprehensive, most reliable, and most powerful environment available for an S/390 computer. A quick look at the history of MVS/ESA helps to understand the environment it creates within an S/390 or z900 server.

Operating System/Multiprogramming with Variable Tasks (OS/MVT)
MVS/ESA is the descendant of the Operating System/360 (OS/360) family introduced for IBM System/360 computers in 1964. Multiple versions of OS/360 offered different levels of function. The most interesting version of OS/360 for our MVS/ESA discussion was called Operating System/Multiprogramming with Variable Tasks (OS/MVT). OS/MVT supported multiprogramming and ran up to 15 application programs at the same time. All application programs and OS/MVT itself shared whatever central storage was installed in the computer system. To facilitate this sharing, OS/MVT divided the central storage into multiple partitions (up to 15). Each program ran in one of these partitions. With

OS/MVT, the central storage size allocated to each partition (that is, each application program or task) could grow or shrink automatically according to the needs of that particular partition at any moment. This is where the name "Multiprogramming with Variable Tasks" in OS/MVT comes from—in contrast to a less powerful cousin of OS/MVT, called OS/Multiprogramming with a Fixed number of Tasks (OS/MFT), which could not dynamically resize the central storage allocated to a job.

Operating System/Virtual Storage 2 (OS/VS2)

With the advent of virtual storage in 1972, a new version of OS/MVT called Operating System/Virtual Storage 2 (OS/VS2), also known as Single Virtual Storage (SVS), was introduced. The most important enhancement introduced with SVS was support for virtual storage. (Chapter 2 described virtual storage as a process for translating storage addresses that makes a computer system seem to have more central storage than it actually does.) Even though SVS could manage up to 16 MB of central storage, most systems had less than 16 MB installed.

SVS took whatever central storage was installed and "stretched it" to appear to be 16 MB in size using the virtual storage technique. The 16 MB of virtual storage was then divided into independent partitions like those of the OS/MVT environment. The illusion of more storage created by virtual storage meant that more and larger application programs could run simultaneously, making for more efficient use of the computer system and thus completing more work in a given period of time.

Multiple Virtual Storage/370 (MVS/370)

The next evolutionary step after SVS came with the introduction of Multiple Virtual Storage/370 (MVS/370), announced in 1973 and first shipped in 1974. Although early versions of MVS/370 supported only up to 16 MB of central storage (24 address bits), the Extended Real Addressing enhancement (26 address bits) was introduced in the late 1970s to allow MVS/370 to support up to 64 MB of central storage (2^{26} bytes = 64 MB). More central storage meant less paging activity between central storage and disk storage, and thus better overall system performance.

As the name "Multiple Virtual Storage" implies, MVS/370 "stretched" the available central storage into multiple virtual address spaces. Then, each application program (either batch or interactive) was given its own virtual address space, which could be up to 16 MB in size. This vastly expanded the amount of available storage, as perceived by application programs, from a single shared 16 MB virtual address space. More virtual storage meant that more and larger batch and interactive jobs could be handled by the MVS/370 operating system. Further, the separate address spaces provided a layer of protective insulation between the application programs or users in different address spaces, helping to prevent the activities in one address space from inadvertently disrupting the activities in the other address spaces. From these earliest days, it was IBM's intent to isolate problems to the smallest possible unit of the system (that is, to fence them off from other user or system units) and to keep the remainder of the system operational. Each address space created by MVS was still limited to 16 MB, however, to preserve compatibility with application programs developed for earlier S/360 and S/370 operating system environments.

The isolation afforded by putting each application program in a separate address space has its advantages, but it also tends to hinder the sharing of common programs and data needed by users working in separate address spaces. To address this need, MVS/370 provided a common area that provided a place to put a copy of programs (for example, TSO or IMS) and data that could then be shared by all authorized address spaces (that is, users and application programs). Further, the common area could be used as a "mailbox" to pass data from one address space to another.

However, the common area approach had some weaknesses. For example, even if only two application programs needed to share or pass data, that data had to be moved into the common area. Thus, the common area would have to grow to accommodate that data, and this would take away additional private virtual storage from all other users.

As the multiple address space concept was exploited more and more, the common area grew steadily to accommodate an increasing number of shared programs and data areas and encroached more and more on the remaining virtual address space designated for private application programs. Further, the common area approach to share information was relatively slow, since it involved operating system services (that is, software) rather than an architectural feature (that is, hardware).

To provide a better way to communicate between address spaces, the Dual-Address-Space Facility, more commonly known as the Cross Memory Facility, was added to the System/370 architecture. Cross memory was implemented by adding to the System/370 architecture a set of new programming instructions that allowed an application program in one virtual address space to access data or pass control to another application program residing in another virtual address space. This allowed for direct sharing or passing data between two application programs residing in different virtual address spaces. Since the cross memory approach did not use operating system services or the common area of virtual storage, it was more efficient and did not require that the common area encroach on private virtual storage. Cross memory circumvented the isolation afforded by having separate virtual address spaces without jeopardizing the built-in protection that keeps application programs from interfering with one another. It accomplished this because the new cross memory programming instructions could be executed only by application programs specifically authorized to do so. In this way, the cross memory enhancement to the System/370 architecture allowed MVS/370 to retain the isolation benefits of having application programs run in separate virtual address spaces and provide for more efficient data sharing/passing between virtual address spaces. Moreover, it achieved this without having to use the crowded common area of virtual storage.

By the end of the 1970s, application program needs had grown so much that the 16 MB limit for a single virtual address space had become a big limitation. IBM was challenged to find a way to increase the virtual address space size without losing compatibility with existing MVS/370 application programs. The 16 MB virtual address spaces were addressed using 24-bit virtual addresses (2^{24} bytes = 16 MB). To expand the size of a virtual address space, virtual address bits had to be added to the current 24-bit virtual address. Extra virtual address bits were available in the System/370 architecture, but application programmers had used these extra bits for their own purposes. If IBM started using the extra virtual address bits to expand virtual storage beyond 16 MB, many of the application programs that used those bits would have to be modified; thus, compatibility with existing MVS/370 application programs would be adversely affected. To resolve this problem, IBM developed the System/370 eXtended Architecture (370-XA) and supported it in a new version of MVS/370, called Multiple Virtual Storage/eXtended Architecture (MVS/XA), announced in 1981 and delivered in 1983.

Multiple Virtual Storage/eXtended Architecture (MVS/XA)
Figure 4.10 shows how MVS/XA managed the central storage of a System/370-XA computer system. Although System/370 Extended Architecture defined central storage of two gigabytes (2 GB), implementation

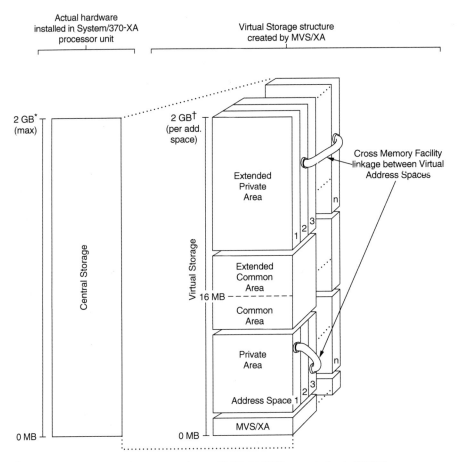

Actual hardware installed in System/370-XA processor unit

Virtual Storage structure created by MVS/XA

2 GB* (max)

Central Storage

0 MB

2 GB† (per add. space)

Virtual Storage

Extended Private Area

Extended Common Area

16 MB -------

Common Area

Private Area

Address Space 1

MVS/XA

0 MB

Cross Memory Facility linkage between Virtual Address Spaces

* Architecture allowed central storage maximum of 2 GB; MVS/XA supported up to 256 MB.
† Maximum virtual address range per address space is $2^{31} = 2$ GB.

Figure 4.10. MVS/XA expanded the maximum size of a virtual address space to 2 GB.

in MVS/XA supported only 256 MB—four times the central storage maximum of 64 MB supported by MVS/370.

More central storage typically means less paging between disk storage and central storage, which usually means better overall system performance. The right side of the figure shows the maximum virtual address space size expanded to 2 GB—a 128-fold increase over MVS/370! This expansion was accomplished by using the extra bits in the System/370 architecture to expand the virtual address from 24 bits to 31 bits (2^{31} bits = 2 GB). But what about compatibility with 24-bit MVS/370 application programs that used those extra bits for their own purposes?

To accommodate those application programs, 370-XA and MVS/XA support two modes of operation: 24-bit mode and 31-bit mode. That is, 24-bit MVS/370 application programs that use the extra address bits for their own purposes can run unchanged in 24-bit mode. Application programs that do not use the extra bits, or application programs designed or modified to run in 31-bit mode, can enjoy the benefits of a vastly expanded virtual address space. In fact, 24-bit application programs and 31-bit application programs can run at the same time under MVS/XA in what is called bimodal operation. MVS/XA and the System/370-XA computer automatically sense which mode is needed as they process each application program. The 24-bit mode allows the data processing staff to migrate operations to MVS/XA and then to migrate their application programs to 31-bit mode at their own pace.

Returning to Figure 4.10, notice that MVS/XA resided at the bottom of virtual storage. Above that is the same private area and common area as in MVS/370. In the new virtual storage area above 16 MB, the common area is extended and there is the extended private area, which creates more virtual storage for each virtual address space. The same cross memory linkage was used to communicate between address spaces.

During the 1980s, the large virtual address spaces provided by MVS/XA allowed more and more work to be loaded into a given computer system. The increasing workload and technological advances led to the next architectural enhancement in the MVS world, namely, Multiple Virtual Storage/Enterprise Systems Architecture (MVS/ESA), announced and delivered in 1988. MVS/ESA was designed to exploit the new capabilities of an enhanced 370-XA architecture called the Enterprise System Architecture/370 (ESA/370), also introduced in 1988.

Multiple Virtual Storage/Enterprise Systems Architecture (MVS/ESA)
Figure 4.11 shows the environment created by MVS/ESA, which supports up to 2 GB of central storage and provides better utilization of expanded storage. Expanded storage was introduced in 1985 on the ES/3090 and used by MVS/XA primarily for paging space and Virtual I/O (VIO). Additional uses of expanded storage included paging, enhanced VIO, and added data spaces, plus services that included the Virtual Lookaside Facility (VLF), Library Look Aside (LLA), the Data

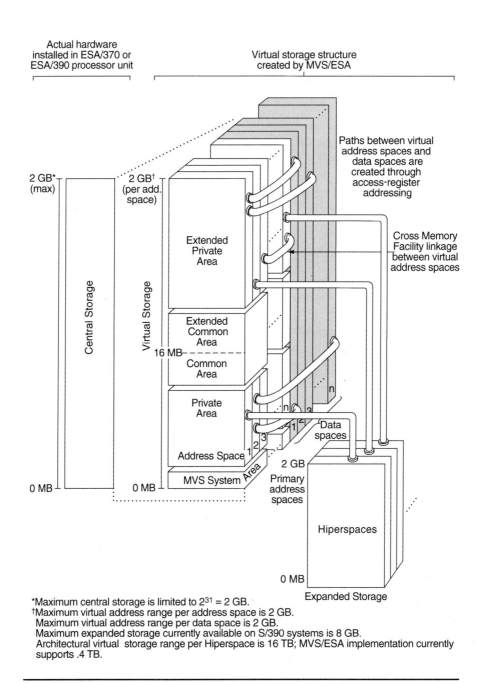

Figure 4.11. MVS/370 handled more central storage than earlier operating systems and supported multiple virtual address spaces.

Lookaside Facility (DLF), and Data Windowing Services (DWS). In a sense, expanded storage augments central storage.

Like central storage, expanded storage is made of circuitry housed in the processor unit. Although expanded storage is slower than central storage (and less expensive), information stored in expanded storage can be provided to central storage much more quickly than can information stored in disk storage. Expanded storage can be thought of as a high-speed storage area for information that would otherwise be stored in disk storage—a kind of disk cache. This helps improve the overall performance of a computer system by keeping as much data as possible as high in the storage hierarchy as possible—a goal of the ESA/370 architecture. Together, central storage and expanded storage are called processor storage (see Chapter 2).

Returning to Figure 4.11, notice that MVS/ESA creates the same 2 GB virtual address spaces as MVS/XA. However, the last virtual address spaces shown in the figure are a new type, called data spaces, introduced with MVS/ESA. A data space is an area of virtual storage, ranging in size from 4 KB to 2 GB, that is byte addressable by an application. In addition to the 2 GB of virtual storage in an application's own address space, application programs store and retrieve information stored in many data spaces. Unlike normal address spaces (now called primary address spaces), which house active application programs and data, data spaces house data only. That is, you cannot load an application program into a data space and start it running, but you can load data into data spaces that can be accessed by application program(s) running in one or more primary address spaces.

To access data in a data space, the application program uses a facility, called access-register addressing, introduced in the ESA/370 architecture. With access-register addressing, the dynamic address translation process described in Chapter 2 is modified so that the access register, rather than the base register, is used in converting from the real to the virtual address. This approach means that an application program can use standard programming instructions to act on data in one or more data spaces without sacrificing compatibility with earlier application programs. As depicted in the figure, access-register addressing provides the connection between application programs and data spaces. Together, data spaces and access-register addressing allow application programs to access/share data in a more flexible and more efficient way. MVS/ESA also provides the same cross memory linkage as earlier MVS versions.

MVS/ESA supports one more type of address space, called a hiperspace (see Figure 4.11). Like a data space, a hiperspace provides additional room for data storage that is accessible to one or more application programs. However, the data in a hiperspace normally resides in expanded storage and must be moved into a primary address space before it can be processed. Information in a hiperspace is moved in 4 KB blocks (one page) under the control of an application program. Through the use of the Move Page hardware enhancement, transfer time between expanded storage and central storage is significantly reduced by eliminating much of the software management required in determining which page frame is free to accept the 4 KB block being transferred. Hiperspaces provide an application program with more flexibility in the quest to keep data as high in the storage hierarchy as possible.

Multiple Virtual Storage/Enterprise Systems Architecture, System Product Version 4 (MVS/ESA SP Version 4)
In September 1990, IBM introduced the Enterprise System Architecture/390 (ESA/390), the ES/9000 S/390 family of computers, and Multiple Virtual Storage/Enterprise Systems Architecture System Product Version 4 (MVS/ESA SP Version 4). The enhancements in this new version were geared to support new facilities including ESCON I/O channels (for example, dynamic I/O reconfiguration) and the Sysplex Timer (used to synchronize the time-of-day clocks on multiple processors working together).

Many installations require more than one processor within a data center because, for example, a single processor does not have sufficient capacity or the installation may want backup capability. With this release it was possible to hook those systems together and view them as a single logical entity or sysplex, a term derived from the two words "*sys*tem com*plex*" (see Chapter 2 for additional information). A sysplex requires a combination of S/390 hardware and software components to connect multiple system images together. The systems were initially linked via Channel-To-Channel (CTC) connections, either with fiber-optic ESCON CTCs or with an IBM 3088 Multisystem Channel Communication Unit (MCCU). The Sysplex Timer synchronizes the time-of-day clocks on each system and provides a common time reference for system monitoring and problem determination. Up to ten systems can be connected in this fashion to form the sysplex.

The MVS/ESA console services allow the installation to operate MVS systems in the sysplex from one console, either the MVS console or a

NetView console. The Global Resource Serialization (GRS) function of MVS is required and has been enhanced to support sysplex in a dynamic fashion. Processors can be added or removed from a Global Resource Serialization ring, and Resource Name Lists can be updated dynamically.

Within MVS/ESA Version 4, a new software function, called Cross System Coupling Facility (XCF), was added. XCF provides the application programming interface and services to allow communication among application groups on the separate processors and provides a monitoring ("heartbeat") and signaling capability. Shared DASDs are also required to provide a heartbeat coordination among the processors. The XCF application programming interface is for authorized programs.

Job Entry Subsystem 2 (JES2), in a MultiAccess Spool (MAS) environment, uses XCF to automatically reset the JES2 software lock and to restart jobs for the failed MAS system. OPC/ESA, the IBM job scheduling product (discussed in Chapter 6), uses XCF in a similar fashion. It reschedules jobs on a different processor if either hardware or software on the processor where the application was originally running fails. Further, CICS/ESA eXtended Recovery Facility (XRF) uses XCF to automate the process of transferring workload to an alternate system.

Some internal MVS/ESA components also use XCF to improve availability. Partitioned Data Set Extended (PDSE) can be shared for input or output by all the systems within the sysplex. Multisystem Dump Analysis and Elimination (DAE) allows sysplex-wide suppression of SVC (Switched Virtual Circuits) dumps (printouts reflecting the contents of some or all parts of storage) and SYSMDUMPs (printouts of a part of system controlled storage). Systems in the sysplex share a DAE data set in which all dump symptoms are kept. The Virtual Lookaside Facility (VLF) NOTE command has been automated to allow the VLF data-in-memory cache in each system within the sysplex to be updated with one command. Prior to automation, the VLFNOTE command had to be issued separately (via TSO/E) on each system. Component Trace uses XCF to provide merged trace information, and SLIP uses XCF to set system traps on all sysplex processors.

The later releases of MVS/ESA Version 4 also include enhanced communications capabilities, called Advanced Program-to-Program Communications/MVS (APPC/MVS). APPC supports cooperative processing and distributed processing for MVS/ESA by enabling application programs running on different computers to cooperate without user intervention. APPC/MVS enhances the interoperability between MVS applications and other applications and systems (IBM or non-IBM) that support SNA LU 6.2 protocols. These facilities complement and coexist with CICS, IMS, TSO, and batch processing. APPC was designed by IBM's networking architects to enhance the productivity of programmers who were writing transaction-driven programs. It allowed them to concentrate on the business functions of the program and be less concerned with the internal workings of the computer. We discuss Advanced Peer-to-Peer Networking (APPN), the most commonly used network architecture to support APPC, in Chapter 5.

APPC/MVS applications can be written to the SAA (System Application Architecture) Common Programming Interface for Communication (CPI-C), which improves portability of MVS applications to and from other SAA systems. The original APPC/MVS conversations were half-duplex between client and server. APPC/MVS Server Facilities allow resident servers to manage resources, data, and services more efficiently. The Server Facilities also allow client and server to establish parallel conversations, simulating full-duplex conversations. (See Chapter 5 for additional details.)

These releases also include new functions (block paging, working set management, and the Asynchronous Pageout Facility) that can improve the engineering/scientific, numerically intensive computing environments. Data for numerically intensive applications often span more than one page of virtual storage. When that data is referenced, several page faults can occur, causing each page of data to be brought into storage separately. The objective of block paging is to identify related pages as a block and bring into storage the whole block when the first page in the block is referenced, rather than bringing them in individually. This reduces I/O activity and some associated application wait time. Working set management offers performance improvement for large applications. When the combined working sets of all address spaces do not fit into central storage, MVS/ESA takes the size and reference behavior of the address spaces into consideration when making central storage allocation, swapping decisions, and multiprogramming level adjustments. The Asynchronous Pageout Facility provides a more efficient method of transferring pages from central storage to expanded storage. After initiating each page transfer, the processor can immediately set up the movement of the next page to be transferred. The processor wait time associated with page transfer completion is eliminated, and the page setup activity is overlapped, improving the page migration process.

These enhancements improve the system efficiency for scalar operations. When coupled with new Vector Facility enhancements (see Chapter 2), the 2 GB of central storage, the 8 GB of expanded storage, VS Fortran (Version 2, Release 5) support of data spaces, the VS Fortran automatic parallelization option to use multiple processors, and transparent Vector Facility use by VS Fortran and APL2, the S/390 computer with MVS/ESA Version 4 is placed into full supercomputer status.

In Version 4, MVS/ESA also added support for subsystem storage protection, the POSIX-compliant Application Programming Interface (API), and a Common Storage Tracker. Subsystem storage protection extends the concept of storage key protection for the protection of subsystem code and control blocks. Its first use is to isolate CICS/ESA applications, preventing them from overwriting CICS code and data. Overwriting of CICS code is relatively common. Subsystem storage protection reduces CICS storage violation outages by up to 50%.

Release 3 of Version 4 moves MVS/ESA into the open systems environment with the addition of the POSIX-compliant API. Occasionally a running MVS/ESA system may experience a shortage of common virtual storage. MVS/ESA provides a new service, the Common Storage Tracker, that tracks storage as it is allocated, providing early detection of common storage problems and allowing corrective action to be deferred.

MVS/ESA Version 5
In 1994, IBM announced Version 5 of MVS/ESA. Release 1 of this version completed the function required for a fully operational parallel sysplex and was required on the Parallel Enterprise Server (9672) attached to the Coupling Facility (discussed in Chapter 2).

Key enhancements in Version 5, Release 1 included support for parallel sysplex services supporting up to 32 MVS/ESA systems, each of which can be a multiprocessor. MVS provides service for subsystems and authorized applications using the Coupling Facility. The coupling technology (discussed in detail in Chapter 2) made high-performance sysplex data sharing possible in MVS/ESA Version 5. The WorkLoad Manager (WLM), introduced with this release, enabled operations management to define processing goals that reflect specific business needs instead of defining detailed system-related parameters to control workload. MVS uses the WLM to adapt the workload to meet those goals. Its use has been widely extended since its introduction.

Most businesses today use a service-level agreement as the vehicle for negotiating support with the user community. Once the service-level agreement is set, the support staff must translate the business objectives into a series of technical terms telling the system how to achieve the objectives. The WLM minimized human intervention by allowing broadly defined objectives to be put directly into the system.

One of the three main objectives of the WLM was to simplify the interfaces to the Systems Resource Manager (SRM) by specifying broader policy-oriented performance goals. The WLM assumes responsibility for deciding how much work should run at which point and with what resources.

The Workload Manager determines system activity, system load, and levels of performance, and gives recommendations to the network manager (Communications Server, VTAM, and TCP/IP), the transaction manager (IMS and CICS, among others), and batch managers (JES and OPCA/ESA, for example) to balance the workload. Consequently, all MVS images participating in a parallel sysplex can communicate with each other, using the coupling facility (discussed in Chapter 2), about the current load and about their ability to accept new work.

The second objective is to gather performance data, which is reported to performance monitoring products such as the Resource Management Facility (RMF), which was modified to report data according to the business goals.

The final objective is to provide information to subsystems to assist them in balancing their own workloads. By providing information to CICSPlex/SM, WLM enables CICS transactions to be balanced across the parallel sysplex. Although WLM does not distribute this workload itself, it enables the subsystems to perform this function. CICS/ESA Version 4 fully exploits the WLM and requires CICSPlex/SM to provide the workload balancing function. IMS, in support of WLM, provides a monitoring environment that the WLM can monitor to determine if executing IMS transactions or batch jobs are meeting response time goals. WLM adjusts the system resources to achieve appropriate goals.

With the introduction in 1995 of MVS/ESA Version 5 Release 2.2, IBM further expanded the capability of this operating system by including support for the XPG4 Base Specification and the X/Open Single UNIX Specification, thereby enhancing the portability of applications. UNIX, POSIX, and DCE Client/Server applications all benefit from this added support. Also, support was added to allow ASCII terminals to attach to MVS/ESA. The application programming interfaces were expanded to include significant UNIX function, allowing businesses to have a broader range of applications that run on S/390. With MVS Open Edition, or UNIX Services as it is now called, businesses have additional options when evaluating "make or buy" decisions about applications.

The discussion thus far has focused on two major elements of MVS/ESA: MVS/ESA System Product (SP) Base Control Program (BCP), which provides the functions for controlling the resources of the S/390 computers, channels, central storage, expanded storage, and virtual storage; and Job Entry Subsystem 2 (JES2), which manages and schedules the flow of work (that is, jobs) to the MVS/ESA SP Base Control Program and manages the output of each of the jobs. The following discussion deals with additional, optional components of MVS/ESA.

BatchPipes/MVS (5655-065) is packaged as a solution consisting of a new licensed product, BatchPipes/MVS, and an integrated service offering (Measured Usage License Charge, discussed in Chapter 6). The product reduces the elapsed time requirements of batch job streams running under the Basic Sequential Access Method (BSAM) or the Queued Sequential Access Method (QSAM) with in-storage connections between jobs. It uses a data-in-memory service to allow replacement of intermediate sequential data sets in those batch job streams. This can reduce elapsed time for sets of jobs that now execute serially but that can execute in parallel on the same S/390 system using this product.

The integrated services offering is designed to assist users to quickly realize the benefits of BatchPipes/MVS. Assistance, for example, is provided in identifying jobs that meet the requirements for exploiting this product, in performing job-flow analysis, and in developing implementation recommendations. Savings can be achieved through running serial batch jobs in parallel (see Figure 4.12), eliminating I/O by passing intermediate results through memory instead of through DASDs or tape data sets, or reducing tapes and tape mounts, DASD usage, and reruns due to media failure by eliminating intermediate data sets. These benefits are achievable with simple Job Control Language (JCL) changes and job scheduling changes without rewriting applications.

BatchPipes/MVS is one of several MVS/ESA functions useful in improving elapsed time for batch jobs. Virtual I/O (VIO) to expanded storage and BatchPipes both eliminate wait times that occur when I/O transfers to and from storage devices. BatchPipes allows concurrent running of the writer and reader jobs, improving elapsed time over VIO, but VIO supports both random and sequential access to data whereas BatchPipes supports only sequential access.

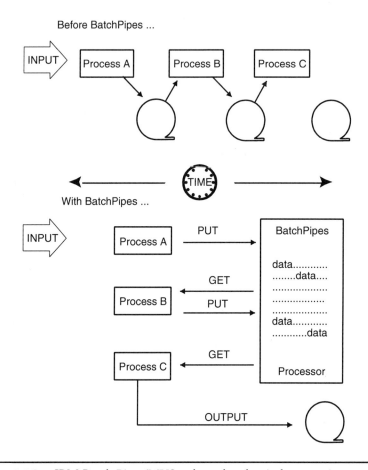

Figure 4.12. IBM Batch Pipes/MVS reduces batch window requirements.

Hiperbatch (derived from *high performance batch*) targets a different type of batch application than BatchPipes. It targets applications in which many readers simultaneously access data from an existing data set. It is a data-in-memory solution in which multiple batch jobs share data in a hiperspace, reducing or eliminating physical I/O delays. All of the shared data resides in processor storage and on DASDs, and the data persists (remains) after being read. BatchPipes applications, in contrast, have one writer passing data to one reader and hold very little data in processor storage at one time. The output from the writer is temporary. With hiperbatch, readers run simultaneously with each other but not with a writer. With BatchPipes, writer and reader jobs run simultaneously.

Batch Local Shared Resources (BLSR) also targets applications that differ from those targeted by BatchPipes. BLSR targets applications using direct or keyed VSAM in a nonsequential access pattern. BatchPipes supports only QSAM and BSAM in a completely sequential access pattern. For data integrity reasons, BLSR writers and readers run serially whereas BatchPipes writers and readers must run concurrently.

Sequential Data Striping and BatchPipes both improve the processing of jobs that spend much time sequentially reading or writing large DASD files. Sequential Data Striping substantially improves I/O access times to DASDs. For temporary data, BatchPipes can eliminate I/O and enable concurrent processing.

Time Sharing Option/Extensions (TSO/E) allows display station users to interact directly with the system to perform systems management tasks and start application programs.

The eNetwork Communications Server for OS/390 manages the communications traffic associated with terminals, manages printers, and permits communications between systems within the network. It supports both System Network Architecture (SNA) and TCP/IP communications networks. It is discussed in more detail in Chapter 5. eNetwork Communications Server for OS/390 is an integrated part of OS/390 Version 2, Release 5.

LAN Resource Extension and Services (LANRES) establishes a server environment that provides NetWare workstation users transparent access to S/390 resources (see Figure 4.13). With MVS/ESA Version 5, Release 2, LANRES is integrated into MVS/ESA and is a no-charge feature. LANRES is also supported by the VM operating system, and IBM has announced support for the VSE/ESA operating system environment.

LANRES provides the following functions:

- *Disk serving* allows NetWare workstation users to store files on the host system, gaining increased disk storage capacity, reliability, a central control of storage devices, availability of automated backup procedures, and physical security. Multiple NetWare servers connected to a single MVS host can share disks stored on MVS in read-only mode.

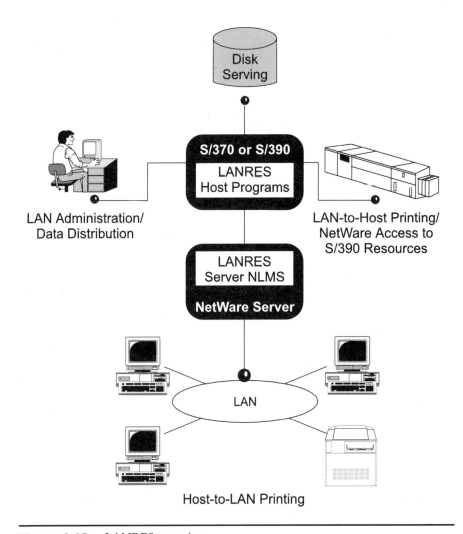

Figure 4.13. LANRES overview.

- *Print serving* supports transparent access to the host system for printing, gaining the advantage of "any-to-any" printing, an easy-to-use end-user interface, and flexibility to add print enhancements as required by work environments. Netware end users can route print jobs through Netware to the host for printing. Host system users can route print jobs to NetWare for printing on NetWare-attached printers.

- *LAN administration* allows authorized system administrators to add, delete, and rename users on the LAN from a central site, reducing resource expense and adding the security of a central data processing center. Administrators can also set passwords and password restrictions, limit space use, control file and directory access, and perform other functions.

- *Data distribution* allows system administrators to manipulate data on LANs connected to host systems by distributing and retrieving data from a server, listing, creating, and deleting files and directories on the server, distributing data from the central location, and creating applications for moving data between the host system and the LAN.

  LANRES connectivity ties the NetWare servers closely to the host while preserving the autonomy and operating independence of the LAN. LANRES supports direct parallel or ESCON channel attachment, SNA LU6.2 (over channel or network), and TCP/IP connectivity. It also supports the Open Systems Adapter (OSA), described in Chapter 5.

The requirement that LANRES and ADSM each have a dedicated high-performance connection from a given server to the host has been removed. Both LANRES and ADSM can share the same channel path. This improves cost effectiveness in arrangements when, for example, LANRES users benefit from use of the direct channel during regular working hours and ADSM uses the same bandwidth during off shift hours for NetWare data backup.

With MVS/ESA Version 5, Release 2, LAN File Services/ESA is integrated into MVS/ESA as a no-charge feature with the name *LAN Server for MVS. LAN Server for MVS* enables LAN-based workstation users to gain rapid access to S/390 disk space in MVS/ESA, OS/390, and VM/ESA operating system environments (see Figure 4.14). It replaces the need for users to share information by downloading with the ability to share current, centrally stored levels of data. Text, graphics, images, video, and sound can all be stored on one system and accessed by many workstation users. Also, LAN administrators have one interface to all the LANs connected to the S/390.

This product supports DOS, OS/2, AIX, and UNIX file formats and operations. It supports TCP/IP, SNA, and channel-attached network

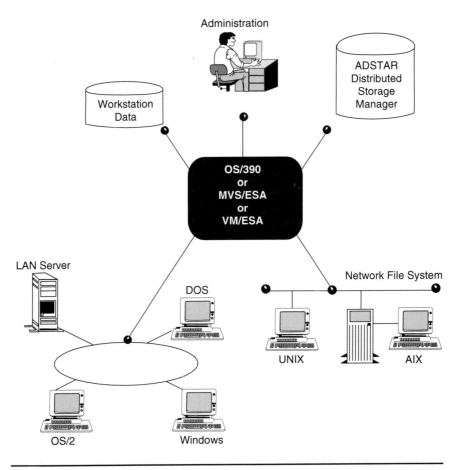

Figure 4.14. LAN File Services schematic.

protocols. It supports OS/2, DOS, Microsoft Windows, AIX on RISC System/6000, and SunOS clients. In an OS/2 environment, services are provided through an OS/2 LAN Server Version 3.0/Advanced System.

With direct ESCON attachment from the 3172-3 or 2216 Model 400 platform, fiber-optic links extend the distance between channels and control units up to 23 km (14.3 miles). "Chained" ESCON Directors increase this range to 43 km (26.7 miles) and expand the channel-to-channel range up to 60 km (37.3 miles). Servers can now be placed much closer to the LANs they support. Fiber Distributed Data Interfaces (FDDIs) support up to 32 LAN attachments through OSA.

Use of the LAN Server for MVS is not visible to end users accustomed to receiving services from workstation-based servers. The performance compares favorably to the performance of a local workstation-based server. This function is composed of an S/390 component and one client component, the OS/2 LAN Server client running on the OS/2 LAN Server 3.0 or 4.0—Advanced. The S/390 component provides storage for workstation format files. This repository supports hierarchical directories, long names, byte-level locking, and extended attributes, which can be used by DOS and OS/2 users connected to the OS/2 LAN Server.

Workstation data is sharable among multiple OS/2 LAN Servers. A channel attachment between the OS/2 LAN Server and the S/390 provides high-speed data transfer for the OS/2 LAN Server user. The IBM 2216 MultiAccess Controller was the recommended networking platform for providing token-ring, Ethernet, and Fiber Distributed Data Interface (FDDI) LAN connectivity to the S/390 using an ESCON or parallel channel.

With the NFS file serving capabilities of LAN Server for MVS, TCP/IP NFS users also can store data in the S/390 workstation repository. OS/2 LAN Server users and NFS users can share data stored on S/390. The full suite of NFS Version 2 Remote Procedure Calls (RPCs) is supported. In a TCP/IP environment, *LAN Server for MVS* provides standard NFS Version 2 services through TCP/IP Version 2 or later.

The AdStar Distributed Storage Manager (ADSM), described in Chapter 6, provides support for the LAN Server for MVS through a special ADSM client. Using this client, files managed by the LAN Server for MVS can be backed up directly into ADSM-managed repositories, reducing elapsed time for file backup tasks. LAN administrators have only one interface to all the LANs connected to the S/390. Through this interface, they control and monitor access to the files stored under LAN File Services/ESA, import and export host files between the workstation file system and the host formatted file system, and back up and restore files and directories through an interface to ADSM.

UNIX Services

Open systems is an area of increasing importance. Today many corporations find themselves with a mix of operating system platforms, software products, transmission protocols, hardware technologies, and multiple vendors scattered throughout the corporation. They may have departmental LANs, wide area networks, remote sites individually connected to the host mainframe, standalone PCs, and other specialized machines. Often these machines and their software are not able to communicate or exchange data, and applications developed for one system often do not run on another. In this environment, IBM's S/390 architecture was viewed as closed or proprietary, primarily because systems built on it could not interoperate with UNIX-based systems. AIX was originally developed as IBM's offering to participate in the UNIX world, but there was a big demand that MVS and VM also participate. Over the past several years, both products have added support to allow interoperability and portability among traditional IBM software platforms. These efforts, however, did not allow integration with many of the other vendors' applications and systems platforms in use in businesses.

This chaotic situation led to the formation of many standards organizations. Hardware manufacturers, software developers, and users tried to develop standards to define interoperability among the different systems and to provide for portability of applications, data, and skills from one system to another. To provide fully open systems, IBM adopted the definitions for interoperability and portability used by the IEEE. Interoperability is the ability of hardware and software from different vendors to work together. IBM's Networking Blueprint and Open Blueprint, as well as the X/Open Distributed Computing Structure, define structures that enable multiple vendor products to work together successfully. A variety of programming models, such as Remote Procedure Call (RPC) and the Message and Queuing Model, provide rules for successful communication. Other protocols define rules for sharing data.

Portability is the ability to move applications, data, and users and support personnel freely across these different systems. This implies that the skills a user needs on one system also "port" to the new system. Common interfaces and facilities, usually defined as standards, make portability possible. The IEEE-defined POSIX standards form one of the building blocks of open systems portability. The X/Open Portability Guides (XPG) build on this standard. Users familiar with UNIX commands can use their skills immediately with OS/390 UNIX Services, originally known as OpenEdition MVS. Access to this interactive environment, the POSIX shell with associated utilities, initially was through the TSO environment.

The extended user interface for the C language and the API support MVS/ESA system calls from POSIX-compliant programs to request standardized MVS/ESA system services through a new interface. The system calls also provide C language functions for controlling processes.

The POSIX standard provides for a variety of functions for process creation, control, and communication. Effectively, these functions are a subset of the UNIX kernel functions now included in OS/390. They can access the Hierarchical File System (HFS), device- and class-specific functions, input/output primitives, C language–specific services, and data interchange/archive format. Although not part of the standard, MVS/ESA added assembler language interfaces to many of the POSIX functions for more application development flexibility.

The Hierarchical File System (HFS) is familiar to UNIX programmers and is common across all POSIX-conforming systems. All files are byte oriented, whereas standard MVS/ESA files are record oriented. The HFS allows for long file names in mixed case—up to 1,023 bytes for a fully qualified name. It uses hierarchical directories, treats all data as byte streams, provides utilities for handling the files, provides permission control, supports concurrent write to the same file from multiple address spaces, and provides still more features as defined in the POSIX standard. Within MVS/ESA, the HFS is implemented through DFSMS/MVS, which means that the file system can be automatically backed up and periodically archived. TSO/E commands and ISPF panels were added to allow a user to copy an HFS data set to an MVS sequential or partitioned data set and to copy other directories. The integration of the POSIX-defined HFS with existing OS/390 file management services provided automated file management capabilities. Security for the HFS is integrated with the RACF (Resource Access Control Facility) security services (see Chapter 6).

In MVS/ESA Version 5, Release 1, IBM extended the support for systems and application interoperability with the support for DCE and integrated sockets (defined later). Additionally, the C run-time environment was packaged as a part of MVS/ESA. Introducing DCE Base Services to MVS/ESA Version 5, Release 1 enhanced access to applications and to data on multiple platforms. This, in turn, enhanced the implementation of client/server applications. DCE addressed business needs to share data and applications, secure information stored in and passed through networks, simplify administration of resources and security, port applications, and reduce programming effort for client/server applications. New functions enabling these capabilities include the following:

- The Network File System (NFS) allows a workstation to access files that may remain elsewhere in a network but seem as if they were resident on the workstation. With this NFS support, a client application can see the OpenEdition Hierarchical File System (HFS) as an extension of the workstation's file system.

- Integrated Sockets support is a socket API that includes the functionality of BSD 4.3 UNIX sockets integrated into the POSIX 1003.1 environment. Sockets are communications channels that enable unrelated processes (applications) to exchange data, whether the processes are on a single system or on multiple systems. This enables full support for X-windows clients within the UNIX Services environment.

- Distributed Computing Environment (DCE) services include Remote Procedure Call (RPC), security, directory, and time management. To achieve interoperability, all systems and their resources must be widely available. Computer services must be provided to applications regardless of location.

  The Open Software Foundation's Distributed Computing Environment (OSF/DCE) is a comprehensive, integrated set of services that support the development, use, and maintenance of distributed applications. RPC automatically invokes directory, security, and communications services for the application programmer. All communication code error handling and data conversions are handled transparently, reducing the amount of time required to code a distributed application. RPC extends the typical procedure calls by supporting direct calls to procedures on remote systems.

  In addition, *Time Service* periodically synchronizes clocks on different nodes in a distributed network, providing applications with a single time reference to schedule activity and to determine event sequencing and duration. *Directory Service* identifies objects (such as users, systems, and resources associated with systems) within the network by name and allows user access to them without the users needing to know where the resources are in the network. A logically centralized, physically distributed directory stores this information. *Security Service* provides the network with authentication, authorization, and user account management services, ensuring integrity and privacy within the network.

  With the facilities and interfaces added to MVS/ESA, end users familiar with other POSIX-compliant systems can use OS/390. They will have the underlying resources, power, availability, and recovery features of MVS/ESA without the need to understand MVS/ESA's regular interfaces. Users can also switch to the regular MVS/ESA interfaces for capability not available through the POSIX-defined interfaces, but portability of applications is lost. Users may also trade portability for capability by using the MVS/ESA extensions to the C language functions.

Although not technically included in the product set, Network Queuing System/MVS (NQS/MVS) complements the environment. NQS/MVS provides MVS/ESA batch capabilities to AIX- and UNIX-based systems. NQS/MVS is an implementation of the AIX or UNIX remote batch submission protocol. It runs on MVS/ESA (JES2 or JES2 multiaccess spool systems) as a server and provides AIX- or UNIX-based workstations the capability to submit batch applications to MVS/ESA using TCP/IP, with the ability to monitor and control those applications using a selected set of NQS commands. It provides AIX- and UNIX-based systems a method of utilizing S/390 computer resources and power. NQS/MVS is the basis for the distributed batch queuing environments portion of the IEEE POSIX standard 1003.15 Batch System Administration, another part of the series under development by the IEEE for open systems.

With OS/390 UNIX Services, portability of applications is further enhanced by integrating all functions required for the XPG4 Base Specification plus 90% of the functions defined by the XPG4.2 Single UNIX Specification. Additional support for interoperability is provided.

The X/Open Corporation, Ltd., working with a set of platform and application vendors, defined a set of UNIX specifications, referred to as Spec 1170, using XPG4 as a base. Subsequently, X/Open published a new specification, XPG4.2, referred to as the Single UNIX Specification. MVS/ESA Version 5, Release 2.2 supports more than 1,100 UNIX functions. Support is also provided for sharing the Hierarchical File System within a parallel sysplex and providing additional exploitation of dynamic workload balancing capability.

The support introduced with Version 5, Release 2.2 includes application programming interfaces supporting the C language; a shell interface that has the "look and feel" of a UNIX system and supports porting UNIX skills; an enhanced Hierarchical File System as a function of DFSMS/MVS Version 1, Release 2; extended integrated socket support to enable both IBM-supplied sockets applications and customer applications to run across multiple transport providers in an open environment; ASCII byte-oriented terminals supported through attachment to a RISC

System/6000 running the new Communications Server, which is downloaded from MVS/ESA Version 5, Release 2.2; and UNIX full-screen support for applications using curses. S/390 UNIX applications can even send and receive a 3270 data stream to and from 3270 displays.

IBM's Open Blueprint maps open system functions to key supporting products and product features. Although some applications will be written using only XPG functions to allow portability across XPG-compliant platforms, others will use additional MVS functions to optimize the application. An application that mixes accesses both to MVS data sets and to the XPG-compliant Hierarchical File System is an example.

SOMobjects for MVS

IBM's System Object Model (SOM) consists of a compiler, an object manager, and base class libraries that are used to build, package, and manipulate binary-compatible application class libraries. Binary compatibility, not available in many object-oriented environments, allows class libraries to be modified or replaced without requiring recompilation of applications. A class can be added to the library without having to recompile all of the classes in that environment. SOMobjects for MVS, now integrated into OS/390, allows applications written in different programming languages to use a common class library. Thus, programs written in one language can use objects written in another. SOMobjects for MVS applications run in CICS, IMS, APPC, batch, and TSO environments. Application development benefits provided through SOMobjects for MVS include the following:

- Faster development and revision of critical business applications.

- Natural mappings between real-world objects and application program objects and support for reusing concepts and components, both of which contribute to improving developer productivity.

- Speeded delivery of applications to users by using existing class libraries and application frameworks to shorten development time.

- Improved program quality through the use of existing, pretested components.

- The ability to port application source code because of the common development base shared with OS/2 and AIX.

This last point becomes increasingly critical as client/server computing becomes more pervasive. Applications must be able to communicate and share data across platforms. With Distributed SOM (DSOM), applications can access and share objects that reside in different systems, and location with implementation of the object is transparent to the user.

OS/390

When OS/390 was previewed in the autumn of 1995, it represented a new concept in large-system, large-enterprise operating system software. OS/390 offered integration, functionality, and investment protection by packaging many of the separate, but generally required, products needed for S/390 operation in what was previously known as a MVS/ESA environment into a single package. OS/390 also included the functions previously available under the OpenEdition MVS operating systems.

OS/390 is a network-ready, integrated operational environment for S/390. The base operating system functions of key products in the MVS environment are installed and tested as one product prior to customer delivery. Installation of OS/390 provides the base operating system, an open communications server, and distributed data and file services. Other integrated functions include the latest technological enhancements of the existing systems, including parallel sysplex support, object-oriented programming, the OSF Distributed Computing Environment (DCE), multimedia, and open application interfaces. A set of optional functions can be installed as an integrated and tested part of OS/390. As a result, the server operating system platform is developed, tested, and delivered as a single product.

OS/390 operates on all models of the S/390 Parallel Enterprise Servers or S/390 Parallel Transaction Servers, all models of the IBM ES/9000 Processor Unit 9021, the 9121, or the PC Server S/390 or RS/6000 with S/390 Server-on-Board, and S/390 Multiprise 2000 and Multiprise 3000 systems, and on the zSeries 900 in 24-bit and 31-bit mode.

OS/390 contains a set of base system services. These include

- Systems Management Services

- Application Enablement Services

- UNIX Services (X/Open UNIX functions)

- Distributed Computing Services

- Communications Server

- LAN Services

- Network Computing Services

- Softcopy Services

OS/390 also contains a set of optional features. Some optional features are not priced; others are additionally priced. Priced as well as unpriced features are included in OS/390 integration testing. OS/390 Release 1 transformed MVS into a server operating system delivering a set of server functions including open and industry standards, integrated client/server functions, network computing support, integrated S/390 and UNIX application environment support, and object technology support. It reduced complexity by integrating existing functions of more than 30 products in the MVS environment, providing simplified installation, and provided comprehensive testing of the integrated product before shipment.

OS/390 Release 2 added new elements such as the 3270 PC File Transfer Program in the base product. It included several optionally priced features such as GDDM-PGF (Graphical Data Display Manager - Presentation Graphic Feature), DFSORT (Data Facility Sort), and the System Display Search Facility (SDSF). It provides new RMF Postprocessor Cache Activity report and SMP/E enhancements. For application growth, it extended the support for the UNIX environment. VisualLift was also included, providing an improved application front end and an enhanced graphical editor. For network computing, function was added for OSA/SF supporting high-bandwidth ATM connectivity (155 Mbits/s), GDDM support for GIF formatting for files transmitted on the Internet, and Network File System (NFS) Client on MVS.

OS/390 Release 3, announced in September 1996, included ServerPac enhancements for reduced complexity, BCP and SMP/E enhancements for improved productivity, VisualLift RTE enhancements, SOM/DSOM support, and extended language support for the C language environment, including enhancements to the IBM Open Class (TM) Library and improved execution for C++ applications, and Logger and Workload Manager (WLM) enhancements for continuous computing/transaction growth. The UNIX Services environment was extended to support

OpenEdition DCE Distributed File Service record data access, allowing UNIX applications running on workstations or other S/390 systems to access and share sequential, VSAM, PDS, and PDSE data sets exported by a Distributed File Service (DFS) server running on an S/390 system. In addition, OS/390 Release 3 enhanced the usability of the Security Server with support that enables the RACF to be administered by the Tivoli User Administration product. Significant focus was given to improving TCP/IP and SNA functionality and performance in this release. For the first time, Internet Connection Secure Server (ICSS) was made available as an optional feature, providing a Web server for the S/390 environment. OS/390 Release 3 was the first release to support the S/390 application high-availability function known as Multinode Persistent Sessions, allowing applications such as those based on CICS to provide recovery for system or application failures within a parallel sysplex with minimal end-user impact.

The OS/390 BonusPak II was made available with OS/390 Release 3. It offered proven techniques for establishing a secure Internet or intranet presence using the OS/390 Web Server. It was shipped to all OS/390 Release 3 customers in softcopy format at no additional charge. BonusPak II supported both the IBM Internet Connection Secure Server (ICSS) Version 2, Release 1 and Version 2, Release 2 for OS/390.

OS/390 Version 2 is the latest version of the S/390's strategic open server operating system. OS/390 Release 4, announced in March 1997, was the first release of Version 2. OS/390 Version 2 provides a Secure Network Server for application development. Domino Go Webserver (now named WebSphere Application Server) for OS/390 is provided by the IBM Network Computing Framework as a scalable high-performance Web server that includes state-of-the-art security, site indexing capabilities, and advanced server statistics. It incorporates the technology from the Internet Connection Secure Server (ICSS) with Web Usage Mining. Domino Go Webserver for OS/390 provided client authentication, incorporates the function of NetQuestion, a robust text search engine, and can detect the presence of IBM crypto hardware on the S/390 system and, if it is present, exploit it for the encryption and decryption function using the Integrated Cryptographic Service Facility (ICSF) software, thereby improving overall performance, throughput, and security. ICSF support includes Trusted Key Entry (TKE), Commercial Data Masking Facility (CDMF), and Public Key API (PKA support).

From a communications server perspective, OS/390's new TCP/IP protocol stack provides improved performance for UNIX and MVS application environments. TCP/IP's dynamic stack configuration capability improves usability. Also included is a totally new Domain Name Server (DNS) enabled for parallel sysplex technology, allowing load balancing for TCP/IP-based applications running within the parallel sysplex.

For systems management, the integration of Tivoli's TME 10 Framework into OS/390 enables TME applications to provide network computing management from OS/390. Tivoli TME 10 is IBM's strategic distributed computing management solution and replaces SystemView. TME 10 is based on an open, architected, object-oriented framework and provides end-to-end, cross system solutions for managing distributed computing environments.

For distributed computing, the addition of the ENCINA Toolkit Executive, DCE Application Support, and enhancements to DCE Base Services further extends OS/390 distributed computing. ENCINA Toolkit Executive and DCE Application Support provide transactional RPC to enable the building of reliable, distributed, transactional applications using two-phase commit for IMS transaction applications. S/390 Version 2 also includes Lightweight Directory Access Protocol (LDAP) client support, thereby allowing programs running on OS/390 to enter and extract information into and from an LDAP Version 2 Directory Service on another platform.

For system services, support includes enhancements to WorkLoad Manager (WLM) for JES2 batch management, enabling algorithmic decision making using real-time, state, and topology information. For S/390 I/O Configuration Management in Version 2, the OS/390 Hardware Configuration Manager (HCM) is available as an optionally priced feature. The combination of Hardware Configuration Definition (HCD) and HCM provides S/390 Hardware Configuration support, enabling the definition of both the logical and physical configuration within the enterprise.

For support of the UNIX environment, UNIX Application Services (Shell, Utilities, and Debugger) provide the standard command interface familiar to interactive UNIX users. OS/390 R4 includes all of the commands and utilities specified in the X/Open Company's Single UNIX Specification, also known as UNIX 95 or XPG4.2. This feature will allow UNIX programmers and other users to interact with OS/390 as a UNIX system without necessarily having to learn the OS/390 command language or other interactive interfaces. The OS/390 UNIX Services Debugger provides a set of commands that allow a C language program to be debugged interactively. The command set is familiar to many UNIX users. UNIX System Services add the world of open UNIX-based computing to the OS/390 operating system. With Language Environment, they support industry standards for C programming, shell and utilities, client/server applications, and the majority of the standards for thread management and the X/Open Single UNIX Specification. Application developers and interactive users using these interfaces can exploit the capabilities of OS/390 without having to understand OS/390 itself. The combination of open computing and OS/390 allows the transparent exchange of data, easy portability of applications, cross-network management of data and applications, and the exploitation of traditional MVS system strengths in an open environment.

OS/390 Release 5 continued the improvements. For Network Computing, OS/390 Version 2, Release 5 support of the Network Computing initiative includes an updated Domino Go Webserver and substantially improved TCP/IP networking function (improved in performance, scalability, and usability). A new Telnet server provides "TN3270E" support, to support the largest networks. Full Dynamic IP support automates registration of clients to DNS without manual administration. Native support for ATM over TCP/IP using the OSA 2 adapter is provided.

As an Application Server, improved Component Broker for OS/390 Application Enabling Technology, Domino Go Webserver (now WebSphere Application Server) support, and IBM Network Station support are provided. Substantial improvements are included for the ISPF to better enable the function in a Web environment. DCE Base services are improved with Kerberos Version 5 and DCE Distributed File Service enhancements.

New releases of OS/390 Version 2, Releases 5 through 9, continued every six months through March 2000, including support of new hardware and operating system function. The major new S/390 hardware function support in OS/390 was FICON channel support, introduced with S/390 G5/G6 and retrofitted via a PTF back to OS/390 Release 3 or higher. This was required because the Resource Management Facility (RMF) reports on the Peripheral Component Interconnect (PCI) bus utilization as well as port bandwidth for performance management and capacity planning. The remaining key enhancements for these OS/390 releases started in September 1998 with the release of Version 2, Release 6 with changes to eNetwork Communications Server support, enhancements to the Parallel Sysplex Technology function, and enhancements to RMF, WLM, and HCD. Part of Version 2, Release 7 in March 1999 was the addition of the Tivoli Management Agent, once again enhancements to eNetwork CS and the Parallel Sysplex Technology. In September 1999, with of Release 8, there were enhancements to UNIX System Services Security through a new RACF user type and control of a super user. Also included were the SecureWay Communications Server with new security functions such as IKE, Triple DES, and TN3270 SSL as well as WLM management of JES3 initiators and ISPF application development enhancements. Finally, in March 2000, Release 9 included the addition of the PCI Cryptographic function and further enhancements to the WebSphere Application Server.

z/OS Version 1, Release 1 and OS/390 Version 2, Release 10

In October 2000, coincident with the zSeries announcement, the new 64-bit follow-on version of OS/390 was released, named z/OS. z/OS Version 1, Release 1 is the initial release supporting the new 64-bit z/Architecture on the z900 servers. The most advanced zSeries functions are exploited by z/OS to best respond to the demanding quality of service needs in an enterprise e-business environment. z/OS provides a highly secure, scalable, high-performance and always available base on which to build and deploy Internet and Java-enabled applications. The zSeries servers and the z/OS operating system provide the needed protection of users' investment in S/390 applications by providing the capability of easily integrating existing applications within the businesses e-business infrastructure. z/OS supports new technologies including Enterprise JavaBeans, XML, HTML, and Unicode, while supporting the technological advances in parallel sysplex processing and TCP/IP networking. The base z/OS operating system includes the z/OS Communications Server, enabling world-class TCP/IP and SNA networking support, including enterprise class dependability, performance, scalability, secure connectivity, and multiple protocol support. OS/390 Version 2, Release 10 will run on S/390 or z900 servers but is bimodal in that it will run in 24-bit or 31-bit mode. z/OS Version 1, Release 1 is essentially the same product as OS/390 Version 2, Release 10.

There are four major new features in z/OS supporting the users' challenge to design their next generation IT infrastructure.

- z/OS Version 1, Release 1 provides 64-bit real storage support for the z900 servers. With 64-bit addressing capability, z/Architecture removes the paging constraints due to the 2 GB addressing threshold, which is a consequence of the 31-bit S/390 architecture. z/Architecture may allow users to consolidate current systems into fewer LPARs or to a single native image. z/OS functions that have been enhanced to exploit 64-bit real storage addressing above 2 GB are traditional access methods such as BSAM, QSAM, and VSAM for extended format data sets, Hierarchical File System (HFS), and eXtended Remote Copy (XRC). In addition, IBM products enhanced to exploit 64-bit real storage above 2 GB are DB2 Version 6 (with PTF) and IMS Version 7. IBM and ISV software products that run 31-bit mode under OS/390 Version 2, Release 6 through Release 10 will run unchanged on zServers servers under OS/390 Version 2, Release 6 through Version 2, Release 10. IBM is working with many software vendors to enhance 64-bit exploitation in their products.

• The Intelligent Resource Director (IRD) is a new z/Architecture feature extending the WorkLoad Manager (WLM) to work with PR/SM on z900 servers. This feature permits z/OS to now dynamically manage resources across an LPAR, which is the subset of the systems that are running as LPARs on the same central electronic complex. WLM can alter processor capacity, channel paths, and I/O requests across LPARs based on the business's goals and without operator intervention.

IRD assigns the appropriate resources to the application. The ability for the system to automatically and dynamically allocate resources to respond to the changing application needs is an evolutionary step and a major contributor to reducing the total cost of the system by combining the strengths of the z900 LPARs, parallel sysplex, and z/OS WLM. IRD is made up of three functions that work together to respond to the ever increasing demands of e-business.

– LPAR CPU Management allows WLM operating in goal mode to manage the processor weighting and logical processors across LPARs. It dynamically moves processor resources toward LPARs with the greatest need. Additionally, WLM will manage the available processors by dynamically adjusting the number of logical CPs in each

LPAR. z/OS has more control over the allocation of CP resources to better meet the businesses goals.

- Dynamic Channel Path Management is a change to the allocation methodology of I/O paths as was implemented in previous architectures. In the past I/O paths were defined as a fixed path relationship between processors and devices. In the zSeries and z/OS the paths may be dynamically assigned to control units to adjust to the changing I/O load. The system programmer defines control unit channel paths but indicates the number of additional channels from a pool of managed channels DCM may add should the workload arise to require more channels. As the work shifts to other control units, channels can be reassigned. This capability reduces the requirement for more than 256 channels.

- Channel Subsystem Priority Queuing is an extension into the I/O channel subsystem, using IRD, of the I/O Priority Queuing function already in place in OS/390. This accommodates moving I/O devices in support of higher-priority workloads running in an LPAR cluster. LPAR priorities are managed by WLM in Goal mode. This allows the user to share I/O connectivity, with no concern that low-priority I/O-intensive workloads will preempt higher-priority workloads. This function complements the Enterprise Storage Subsystem capability to manage I/O priority across central electronic complexes. It is possible that high-priority workloads will benefit with improved performance if there has been I/O contention with lower-priority workloads. Initially this function is implemented for Parallel OEMI and ESCON channels. With IRD, the combination of z/OS and the z900 working in synergy extends workload management to ensure that the most important work on a server meets its goals, to increase the efficiency of existing hardware, and to reduce the amount of intervention in a constantly changing environment.

• In z/OS, msys for Setup is the first step of a major ease-of-manageability initiative. It offers a new approach for installing and configuring the products running on z/OS, resulting in productivity improvements allowing usage of consistent interfaces with wizard-like configuration dialogs. The new dialogs reduce the skill requirements for product setup and will free up scarce and valuable personnel for other tasks.

After configuration parameters have been set, msys for Setup can automatically update the system configuration directly. The user is able to view the details of the changes before they are made, and msys for Setup will then provide an LDAP-based z/OS management directory that becomes the central repository for all configuration data.

Setting up a parallel sysplex resource sharing environment becomes much quicker and easier by defining and implementing the required policies, parmlib specifications, and security.

• Workload License Charges represent the newest IBM software pricing strategy designed to support e-business. Users pay only for the software capacity that they need, allowing users to grow a single workload at a time with ease and granularity by charging according to submachine capacity rather than machine capacity. This enables users to add excess capacity without incurring software charges and to define and pay for software on their average (four-hour rolling) requirement instead of the peak requirement.

Users can modify the licensing terms in their IBM License Manager (ILM) as often as desired to control their software bill on a monthly basis. This can all be done from the Windows-based License Manager Administration Tool. The IBM ILM and Workload License Charges will be discussed in more detail in Chapter 6.

TCP/IP Networking Enhancements
z/OS can provide nearly continuous availability for TCP/IP applications with two new features, Sysplex Distributor and VIPA (Virtual Internet Protocol Addressing) Nondisruptive Takeover. The integration of these functions in hardware and software brings very high resiliency and availability to the z900 and S/390 Networking environment.

The Virtual IP Address (VIPA) Nondisruptive Takeover represents an IP address that is not tied to a specific hardware adapter address so that if an adapter fails, the IP protocol can find an alternate path to the same software. VIPA was introduced in OS/390 Version 2, Release 8, and it supported movement to a backup IP stack on a different server in a parallel sysplex if there was a failure in the primary IP stack. VIPA Nondisruptive Takeover enhances the initial Release 8 functions by providing VIPA takeback support, moving workload back from the alternate to the primary IP stack.

Sysplex Distributor, introduced in OS/390 Version 2, Release 10, is a software-only means of distributing IP workload across a parallel sysplex cluster. Clients appear to be connected to a single IP address, yet the connections are routed to servers on different z900 or S/390 servers. This simplifies the task of moving applications within a parallel sysplex environment.

Some Exploiters of z/Architecture

The current but continuously expanding list of exploiters of z/Architecture for z/OS and OS/390 Release 10 include DB2 Universal Database Server for OS/390, IMS, Hierarchical File System (HFS), Virtual Storage Access Method (VSAM), Remote Dual Copy (XRC), and DASD and tape access methods. IBM is working with many software vendors to enhance 64-bit exploitation. IBM and ISV software products that run 31-bit mode under OS/390 Version 2, Release 6 through Version 2, Release 10 will run unchanged on the z900 under OS/390 Version 2, Release 6 through Release 10.

Migration Considerations

The ease of migration to the z900 64-bit environment is dependent on the current server installed. The most likely starting point is a G5/G6 server running OS/390 Version 2, Release 6 to Release 9 or VM/ESA. Although VM is discussed later, the migration considerations will be covered following the OS migration examples. It is not recommended to migrate the server and the operating at the same time, so the following represent likely one-step-at-a-time migration examples for these two operating system platforms.

OS/390 and z/OS Example

Using the examples shown in Figure 4.15, the business will want to move from the currently installed position (A) to the full migration po-

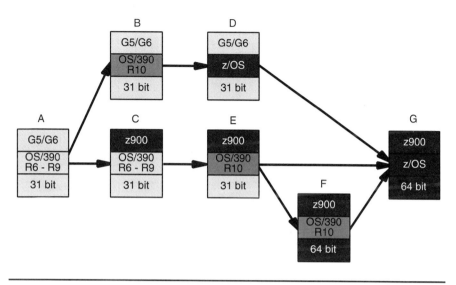

Figure 4.15. OS, one-step-at-a-time migration.

sition, a z900 running z/OS (G). In this example there are two recommended paths to accomplish the migration with minimum application impact. The first alternative is to migrate the OS operating system, OS/390, to Release 10 and then to z/OS (A–B–D) before upgrading the server to a z900 (D–G). The alternative approach would be to move first to the new z900 server (A–C) and then migrate to OS/390 Version 2 R10 (C–E). The business then would have the option to migrate to 64-bit mode under OS/390 Release 10 before migrating to z/OS (E–F–G) or migrate directly to 64-bit mode z/OS in one step (E–G). Because the 64-bit mode conversion under z/OS is rather automated by z/OS, it is a relatively safe step to take.

VM/ESA and z/VM example
Figure 4.16 indicates the migration path examples a business would follow if it was currently running on the VM/ESA platform. If the business's current VM/ESA can run on the z900, the recommended migration path would be to first upgrade to the z900 server (step a) and then migrate to z/VM in 32-bit mode (step b) before moving to 64-bit mode (c). However, if the currently running VM/ESA is unable to run on a z900, it is recommended to first migrate to z/VM (step d) before

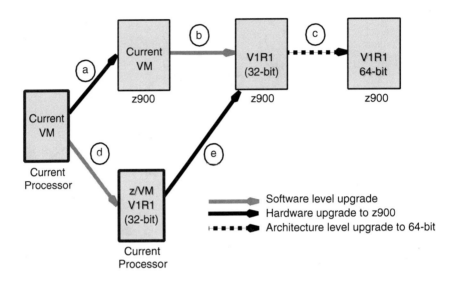

Figure 4.16.   VM, one-step-at-a-time migration path examples.

moving to the z900 (e). In this example the final migration step is to implement 64-bit mode (c).

LPAR Coexistence
Changing the architectures in an LPAR (Figure 4.17) does not affect other LPARs because going to 64-bit or returning to 32-bit mode is nondisruptive to other LPARs. LPAR coexistence means that 64-bit LPARs coexist with 32-bit LPARs on the same z900 server.

OS Release Coexistence
Coexistence is the ability for two or more systems to share resources at the same time. Normally, four consecutive OS/390 releases may coexist in a multisystem configuration and would last for a period of two years based on the current six-month release cycle. It should be noted that for OS/390 Version 2, Release 10 there is a special provision that five consecutive releases may coexist (Figure 4.18), which are Releases 6 through 10. The z/OS coexistence policy is also four consecutive releases but measured forward and backward. In this case it should be remembered that OS/390 Version 2, Release 10 and z/OS Version 1, Release 1 are considered as one coexistence level.

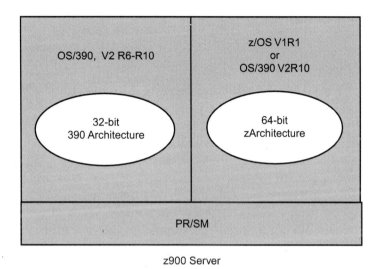

Figure 4.17. 32-bit and 64-bit LP coexistence.

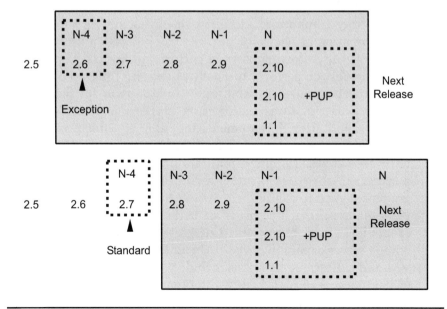

Figure 4.18. OS/390—z/OS coexistence.

Evolution of VM

VM/ESA

The Virtual Machine/Enterprise System Architecture (VM/ESA) operating system builds on the virtual storage concept to subdivide a single computer system into multiple, virtual computer systems, each with its own processor storage, disk storage, tape storage, and other I/O devices. That is, VM/ESA uses software techniques to make a single S/390 server appear to be multiple server systems. Each of these servers, simulated in software and called a virtual machine, acts as an independent and complete computer system. In some cases, a virtual machine acts like an S/390-compatible "personal computer" with a single-user operating system serving the needs of a single user (or application program). A group of single-user virtual machines can be linked together to create a virtual "local area network" of S/390 servers within a single system (depicted in Figure 4.19), all simulated in software. Alternatively, a single virtual machine can run a multiuser operating system (for example, MVS/ESA) and serve the needs of many users.

VM/ESA's unique approach to resource management (that is, subdividing a single system into multiple virtual systems, each with its own resources) makes it especially useful for interactive computing, client/server computing, and guest operating system support. Interactive computing provides for flexible dialog between users and application programs, allowing users to perform ad hoc queries to databases, write memos, or perform mechanical design. Today, VM's large-scale interactive computing capabilities include support for thousands of office users, data analysis and decision support, advanced database processing, application development, and ad hoc problem solving.

Client/server computing is facilitated by allowing a virtual machine to be dedicated to running a program that provides services (thus called a server) to the users of other virtual machines (called clients). Programs designed to run in their own virtual machine and to provide services to virtual machine users are called service virtual machines. VM capabilities enable businesses to integrate mainframe strengths with VM-unique server capabilities and LAN and workstation technologies. The VM and mainframe strengths include very fast access to large volumes of data, access to high-bandwidth communications and high-capacity devices, and efficient and secure administration of large numbers of users and applications.

S/390 system running VM/ESA

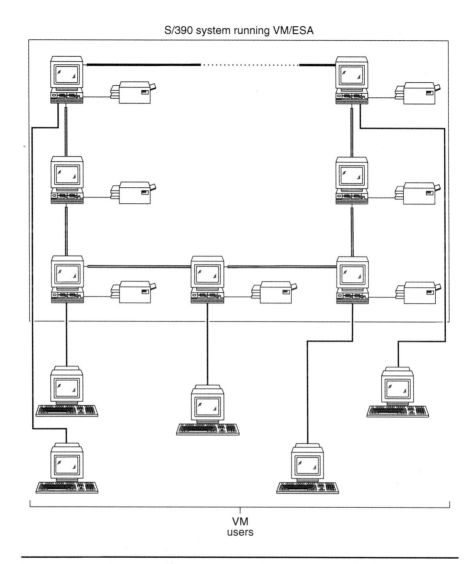

VM
users

Figure 4.19. Conceptually, VM creates a local area network of single-user computers within an S/390 system.

Finally, each virtual machine runs one of several different operating systems in addition to (or on top of) VM itself. This frees each user to run the operating system (for example, CMS, VSE, or MVS) that is required or best suited to the application program. Other operating systems running under VM in a virtual machine are called guest operating systems. The efficiencies generated through VM acting as a hypervisor or "host" system, in which resources are shared among multiple different systems on a single processor, make it practical to use VM to create, test, and run applications from any S/390 operating environment. This simplifies migration and experimentation with new platforms and functions. Today, the VM operating system spans the entire range of S/390 processors. As many as 9 million people are estimated to use VM every day.

Origins of VM/ESA

VM/ESA has roots dating back to 1964, when a group of researchers at IBM's Cambridge Scientific Center conceived the virtual machine model. With this computing model, the hardware resources of a computer system were managed by one computer program, called the Control Program (CP), while the users' activities were managed by an operating system. One such operating system, called the Conversational Monitor System (CMS), comes with VM/ESA. Figure 4.20 shows a cutaway view of our software model depicting the relationship between the CP, operating systems, application programs, and virtual machines. (Note that several applications can run on the single VSE guest.)

The CP creates a virtual machine image in software for each user of the computer system. The virtual machine image appears to be actual computer hardware to the programs running in that virtual machine, including operating systems (such as CMS, VSE/ESA, or OS/390) and application programs. Since the CP has the ability to create a software image identical to that presented by computer hardware, it is called a hypervisor. By giving a virtual machine to each user, the CP provides effective protection to prevent one user from accidentally (or intentionally) interfering with another.

The Conversational Monitor System (CMS) is a single-user operating system that runs on top of the CP and interacts with the user and any application program running in that virtual machine. As shown in Figure 4.20, other operating systems (such as VSE/ESA or OS/390) also run on top of the CP as guests—a capability that the other S/390 operating systems cannot match. The guest operating system capability, along with the interuser protection provided by the virtual machine concept, makes VM a natural environment in which to test or migrate to new versions of operating systems and new application programs without risking the current production environment.

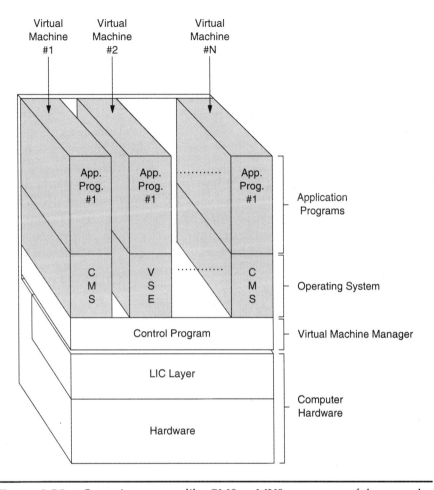

Figure 4.20. Operating systems like CMS or MVS run on top of the control program component of VM.

The evolution of VM as an operating system is shown in a time line in Figure 4.21. The first embodiment of the virtual machine concept was a hypervisor called Control Program–40 (CP-40), developed as an experiment to study the time-sharing techniques and hardware requirements for the IBM System/360 family of computers. Time sharing, as discussed earlier, allows a single computer system to work on multiple active application programs, giving a slice of processing time to each. CP-40 first ran on a specially modified System/360 computer, which also served as the development platform for what was then called the Cambridge Monitor System (CMS), which was being developed independently. In 1966, CMS and CP-40 were combined to form a time-sharing system that would form the basis for the VM/370 operating system. As shown in Figure 4.21, the VM/370 operating system evolved during the early 1980s into several unique products, which were developed based on the needs of the different environments in which VM was used.

VM/SP served the S/370 hardware, including dual and dyadic processors, that was then available, with a maximum of 16 MB of main storage. The VM/SP High-Performance Option (HPO), introduced in 1981, provided performance and capacity enhancements to the VM/SP System/370 environment by recoding some areas and moving some functions into processor microcode. This version supported 64 MB of memory and 32 channels. Whereas VM/SP supported tens of users, HPO supported hundreds of users. It also provided support for MVS/370 as a guest operating system at near native performance.

Meanwhile, in 1981 the System/370 eXtended Architecture (XA), supporting 31-bit addressing, was announced. This architecture supported more storage, more processors, more channels, and the dynamic I/O subsystem, enabling significantly faster response times for users. A

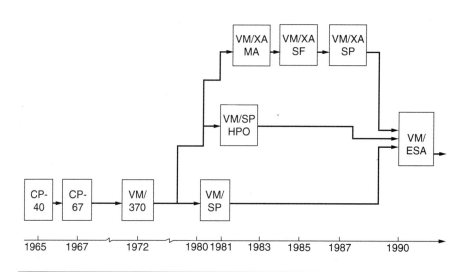

Figure 4.21. VM's lineage.

series of solutions enabled VM to make the transition to this new programming environment. The VM/XA Migration Aid was first shipped in 1983 to provide test and migration capabilities for MVS/XA guests. The VM/XA System Facility added more capability in 1985, but it was not until the VM/XA System Product shipped in 1987 that full VM capability was provided on IBM's large processors. In contrast to VM/SP with HPO, VM/XA SP supported thousands of users and many guests.

VM/ESA Version 1
Now IBM had three different VM operating systems addressing three different customer sets. Each new operating system function had to be coded for each system. Because constraints were encountered in VM/SP and VM/SP HPO that could not be relieved in the S/370 architecture, IBM decided to create a single VM operating system using the new ESA/390 architecture and chose VM/XA SP as the base. Migration studies were undertaken, and inhibitors were removed or solutions incorporated into that base to ensure the highest possible compatibility for the end users of the new system, called VM/ESA. (VM/SP, VM/SP HPO, and VM/XA SP were withdrawn from marketing and service support in 1994.)

In 1990 VM/ESA was announced along with the S/390 family, converging the VM family of products into a single offering. This simplified the packaging and systems management for VM users while allowing IBM to better focus VM development resources. A smooth migration path was established to this new operating system, a system that contained more functions, better manageability, and better reliability. The one piece missing from the first release, Fixed Block Architecture (FBA) support, was added in VM/ESA Release 2.

The major components of VM/ESA and their functions include the following:

- The Control Program (CP) manages the hardware elements of the computer system and creates virtual machines for users and application programs.

- The Conversational Monitor System (CMS) is a single-user operating system for virtual machines running under the CP.

- The Group Control System (GCS) manages virtual machines running VM subsystems associated with SNA communications networks.

- APPC/VM Virtual Telecommunications Access Method Support (AVS) runs in a virtual machine and provides communications between VM application programs using the Advanced Program-to-Program (APPC) protocol over an SNA communications network using the Advanced Communications Function/Virtual Telecommunications Access Method (ACF/VTAM).

- Transparent Services Access Facility (TSAF) runs in a virtual machine and provides communications between VM application programs using the Advanced Program-to-Program (APPC) protocol over a bisync or channel-to-channel communications network without requiring the ACF/VTAM subsystem.

- Procedures Language VM/REXX interprets and executes programs written in the English-like REstructured eXtended eXecutor (REXX) programming language. REXX is used to write custom application programs or to build a list of commands used to perform various system tasks.

- CMS Pipelines, integrated into VM/ESA Version 1, Release 1.1, provide a method of writing simple, reusable programs and connecting them so that the output of one program (or pipeline stage) is the input to the next program (or pipeline stage). The individual pipelines are independent of one another, are device independent, and each does its own job with no concern for where the data comes from or where it is going. The output of one program can be connected to the input of any other. This function provides a 15% to 300% improvement in productivity when writing REXX applications.

- With Version 2 Release 1, CMS Pipelines provides six new stages and provides assembler macros that perform basic pipeline functions and are the building blocks for writing assembler stage commands. CMS pipeline users can now write stages in assembler languages, and vendor products can provide a pipeline interface to their product. With VM/ESA Version 2, Release 3.0 (discussed later), the Pipelines PRPQ is integrated into the base of VM/ESA. New support includes toleration for Pipelines program execution in a multitasking environment, TCP connectivity, and documentation of more Pipelines stages.

- Virtual Machine Serviceability Enhancements Staged/Extended (VMSES/E) is an automated tool for updating the installation and applying service. It automatically builds the parts of the system that are the most time-consuming to build by hand. It is the single installation and service tool across all VM/ESA releases, and it also supports the 370 Accommodation Feature. It eases verification of system levels, and it allows the system programmer to "try out" the installation to see if it is correct before actually changing the system. Once installation is complete, VMSES/E automatically updates the system software inventory, noting what release and service level of the operating system is installed.

- The Dump Viewing Facility allows a system programmer to examine system information helpful in diagnosing system problems.

The rest of this section looks at the way VM/ESA manages S/390 computers. Figure 4.22 shows one example of how VM/ESA Version 1, Release 1 manages the central storage of an ES/9000 processor. As with the other operating systems, VM/ESA uses the virtual storage concept, with multiple 2 GB virtual address spaces, to expand the available central storage so that programs perceive a much larger storage structure. The way in which VM/ESA uses virtual storage, however, differs. The Control Program (CP) component of VM/ESA is loaded into the first section of virtual storage. When a user signs on to the system, the CP creates a virtual machine for that user and loads an operating system. In our example, several virtual machines are running the CMS operating system and one virtual machine is running the VSE/ESA operating system. Next, one or more application programs are loaded into each virtual machine. Since the VSE/ESA virtual machine provides the same environment when running on top of VM/ESA as it does when running by itself, the VSE/ESA virtual machine can run any VSE application program.

As we have seen in our exploration of MVS/ESA, the ESA/390 architecture introduced expanded virtual storage structures. Prior to the ESA/390 architecture, virtual address spaces could not exceed 2 GB, and sharing information between address spaces was cumbersome. ESA/390 addressed these two limitations with data spaces, which are available to application programs through an access-register addressing scheme. In addition to the 2 GB in an application's own address space, authorized application programs can access the information stored in many data

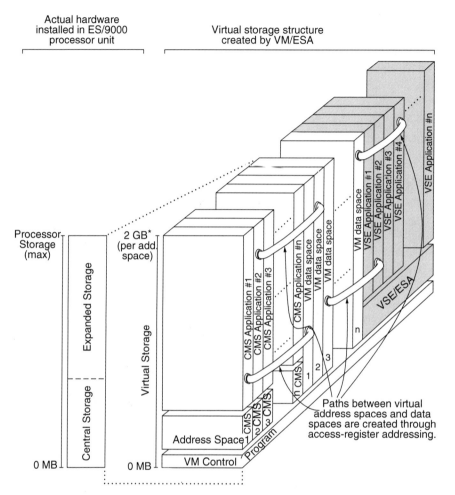

Figure 4.22. Example of how VM/ESA manages the central storage of an ES/9000 processor.

* Maximum virtual address range per address space is 2 GB. In addition, an application running in one address space can access up to 2 TB of data stored in multiple data spaces (2 GB each) and residing outside the application program's address space.

spaces, each of which can be up to 2 GB in size. Further, through access-register addressing, multiple application programs can share the data space without relying on the operating system to intervene.

To exploit these improvements, VM/ESA and the ESA/390 architecture were modified to support data spaces and access-register addressing. To maintain compatibility with current CMS application programs and to provide improved communications between virtual machines, IBM also modified CP to exploit these features. More specifically, the virtual machines created by CP in VM/ESA can use a new virtual machine architecture, called the Enterprise Systems Architecture/eXtended Configuration (ESA/XC). This new architecture builds on the enhancements introduced with the ESA/390 architecture to provide virtual machines that support data spaces and access-register addressing without compromising compatibility with CMS application programs. Figure 4.22 shows that each virtual machine (that is, each address space) is still limited to a maximum of 2 GB. Each virtual machine runs its own copy of the CMS operating system and some CMS application program. Immediately behind the CMS virtual machines are the data spaces that hold data available (through access-register addressing) to any authorized virtual machine(s). Because each data space is up to 2 GB in size, the data storage available to a CMS application program is vastly expanded. The access-register addressing, depicted as a pipe, provides a path through which authorized CMS application programs share data and communicate with one another.

Another way in which VM/ESA encourages sharing information is through the Shared File System (SFS), introduced with the VM/SP product in 1988. Before the SFS, disk storage was split into minidisks, allocated to specific users and managed by the CMS operating system running in that user's virtual machine. The minidisk file system had several problems. First, a minidisk is permanently allocated to a user's virtual machine and is reserved regardless of how much disk space the user needs at any given time. This wasted disk storage that was allocated to a user's virtual machine but not fully utilized by that user. Another limitation with minidisks is that they do not lend themselves to being shared by more than one user. The SFS moves the file management function to a separate virtual machine, which acts as a server managing the disk storage used by all CMS virtual machines. Each CMS virtual machine no longer manages its own disk space. The SFS maintains a high degree of compatibility with the old minidisk file system while making it much easier to share CMS files kept in disk storage among a group of authorized users. The SFS also supports expanded storage, improving the overall I/O performance by keeping data higher in the storage hierarchy (see Chapter 2).

VM/ESA supports ESCON I/O channels and the ESCON Multiple Image Facility (EMIF). When VM/ESA runs in a logical partition, it utilizes EMIF to share ESCON physical channel paths with operating systems running in other logical partitions. VM/ESA also supports Subsystem Storage Protection to help maintain data integrity for subsystems, such as CICS/ESA on an MVS/ESA or VSE/ESA guest, and it supports the Asynchronous Pageout Facility, the in-storage paging capability for demand paging environments such as numerically intensive computing. In addition, VM/ESA added a POWEROFF option to the SHUTDOWN command so that system shutdown could be initiated from a remote location for the newer generation of servers.

In 1994 IBM announced VM/ESA Version 1, Release 2.2, with improvements in basic functions, systems management, guest system support, and hardware support. The improved functions include an automated common access tool (VMLINK) for increasing user productivity, a performance boost and added flexibility for caching CMS and guest minidisks, and a new LOGON BY function to improve security. Hardware support covered the full range of ES/9000 processors including the 9221 211-based models and the 9021 9X2 10-way processor. A "Distributed VM" capability enabled VM's support of parallel computing. Guest system support was enhanced with support of the Asynchronous Data Mover and Subspace Group, two ES/9000 architecture facilities. Enhanced data-in-memory techniques improved guest response time and elapsed batch time by up to 50% for any VM guest and up to 60% when using minidisk caching. System management enhancements included a new SPXTAPE command that speeds up, by up to 10 times, the spool backup process. Also, the system can "cap" processor resources consumed by a user and distribute excess processor resources proportionally. Installation and service processes are further automated, reducing VM/ESA system maintenance costs.

VM/ESA Version 2
Announced in June 1995, Version 2, Release 1 provided significant functional enhancements to the VM operating environment, including provisions for OpenEdition for VM/ESA (described later). Systems management, portability and interoperability of applications among different platforms, dynamic configurability, distributed client/server computing, and additional features simplifying user access to VM and non-VM resources are all part of the new version.

This version of VM/ESA provided support for the new S/390 Parallel Enterprise Server models, discussed in detail in Chapter 3. Support for the new Open Systems Adapter (OSA) feature enabled VM/ESA to provide fully integrated native open systems connectivity to Ethernet, token-ring, and Fiber Distributed Data Interface (FDDI) LANs. Through OSA, Systems Network Architecture/Advanced Peer-to-Peer Networking (SNA/APPN) and Transmission Control Protocol/Internet Protocol (TCP/IP) host processor and server applications gain direct access to LAN-connected SNA/APPN and TCP/IP clients. This direct connectivity to open systems LAN interfaces makes the use of S/390 host resources more efficient. The OSA feature offers integrated industry-standard LAN connectivity in a heterogeneous, multivendor environment. VSE/ESA environments can access the S/390 OSA when operating as a guest of VM/ESA Version 2, Release 1.

Automatic compression and expansion of VSAM data allows VSAM customers to save space on DASDs. The automatic support in Version 2, Release 1 is transparent to users, who can define certain types of VSAM clusters as compressed. VSE/VSAM for VM automatically compresses and expands user data when it is accessed. CMS and GCS users can read and write to the compressed files. This support automatically exploits the S/390 hardware compression feature, if present, to further improve performance.

Dynamic partitioning allows devices such as tape units to be serially shared among multiple hosts via commands issued by the sharing host. Version 2, Release 1 permits these devices to be assigned to the VM host when they are brought on-line. This improves flexibility for dynamic partitioning over the earlier process, which required waiting for a device to be attached to a guest system before assigning it to a host system.

The Control Program (CP) in VM/ESA Version 2, Release 1 became more configurable. The I/O configuration for VM/ESA and an S/390 processor could be altered without requiring shutdown and power-on reset of the system. Channel paths, control units, and I/O devices could be added, modified, or deleted within the running system. Hardware configuration changes could be made for an entire S/390 processor, even when VM/ESA was running in a logical partition.

For end users, VM/ESA Version 2, Release 1 provides a new VM Graphical User Interface (GUI) facility, enabling host-resident applications to combine the efficiency of 3270 terminal emulation with the power of a modern GUI. Through the use of a new programming API, VM applications can specify most elements of a Common User Access (CUA)–compliant interface when creating an end-user interface. This API interacts with code on the workstation, known as the VM Workstation Agent, to display the interface to the end user. The Workstation

Agent in turn translates the API requests from VM into the appropriate native workstation requests. The VM GUI API is an object-oriented API that can be called from procedural or object-oriented languages. Initially, Version 2, Release 1 supports OS/2 over TCP/IP or SNA LU 6.2, Microsoft Windows over TCP/IP, and AIX over TCP/IP.

LAN Resource Extension and Services (LANRES) and the LAN File Service/ESA provide NetWare and LAN Server environments with transparent access to VM/ESA storage resources. LANRES provides disk and print serving and central administration for NetWare LANs. LANRES and LAN File Services are integrated into VM/ESA Version 2, Release 1 as no-charge features. They are available as charged, standalone products (5684-142 for LANRES and 5648-039 for LAN File Server) for users of VM/ESA Version 1, Release 2.2 or earlier. All further enhancements will be implemented on the Version 2, Release 1 features.

Other programs that extend the function of VM/ESA and their roles include the following:

- The Advanced Communications Function/Virtual Telecommunications Access Method (ACF/VTAM), discussed in Chapter 6, manages the communications traffic associated with terminals, printers, and System Network Architecture (SNA) communications networks, including support for Advanced Peer-to-Peer Networking (APPN).

- Transmission Control Protocol/Internet Protocol (TCP/IP) for VM allows VM users to communicate and interoperate with other systems in a multivendor network using the TCP/IP protocol set. Applications include sending mail, transferring files, logging on to a remote host, and using other network and client server functions.

- The Remote Spooling Communications Subsystem (RSCS) Version 3, Release 2 supports 31-bit addressing and can therefore use storage above the 16 MB line. Removing this storage constraint allows users to expand a network to many additional links without adding the complexity of additional servers. This version also enhances access to the Internet. TCP/IP line drivers allow the RSCS to use a TCP/IP network. In addition to the exchange of e-mail, available in Version 3, Release 1.1, print files from the RSCS network can be routed to line printer daemons for distribution anywhere in the Internet Protocol (IP) network. A line printer driver provides support for PostScript print files, and a new ASCII printer driver provides access to ASCII print devices connected via TCP/IP. For file transfer networking flexibility, the RSCS transmits Network Job Entry (NJE) data packets using TCP/IP as a transfer medium. Currently supported SNA connections continue to be supported.

- Directory Maintenance (DirMaint) Version 1, Release 5 provides service and installation in VMSES/E format to improve serviceability and maintainability. Menu enhancements, DASD management enhancements, Shared File System support, XA exploitation, and constraint relief provide added value to the system administrator.

- VSE/VSAM for VM was originally the access method for the VSE operating system. It is now widely accepted by VM users and is a prerequisite for some VM products. It is designed to operate with direct access devices and to support both direct and sequential processing. Version 6, Release 1 is extracted from VSE/ESA Central Functions Version 6, Release 1, a base program of VSE/ESA Version 2, Release 1. It supports hardware-assisted data compression and expansion for VSAM data sets on native VM and VM guests. You can select which data sets should be stored and held in memory as compressed data sets and which data sets should remain expanded. This provides significant reductions in required disk space, reduces channel traffic, and stores more data records within a 4 GB file. Version 6, Release 1 also further exploits 31-bit addressing by moving control blocks above the 16 MB line. Software emulation to compress or expand data is offered in VM/ESA if no hardware assistance is available.

VM/ESA in an Open Systems Environment (OpenEdition for VM/ESA)
The OpenEdition for VM/ESA is a part of VM/ESA Version 2, Release 1. With this function, VM expands its interoperability with the Open Software Foundation's (OSF's) Distributed Computing Environment (DCE). This permits VM/ESA systems to participate in DCE cells with other DCE-compliant systems, including OS/390, AIX/6000, and non-IBM UNIX systems. OpenEdition for VM/ESA also increases the port-

ability of applications to and from VM/ESA through support of key IEEE Portable Operating System Interface (POSIX) standards, providing common system and user interfaces for application development.

VM/ESA Version 2 supports the IEEE POSIX 1003.1 standard that defines the base operating system interfaces and an environment for application programs written in the C language. POSIX 1003.1 describes C language functions that an application programmer encodes to obtain services from the base operating system. VM/ESA Version 2 includes the C/370 Library component and the Common Execution Library (CEL) interface from the Language Environment for MVS and VM (discussed earlier in this chapter).

VM/ESA provides a full implementation of POSIX 1003.1 with the exception of implementing the spawn() function in place of the fork() function (different methods to enable the propagation of multithreaded processes). The spawn() function provides a fast, low-overhead mechanism for creating a new POSIX process to run a new program. Process control and environments, files and directory functions, and access to the databases are supported by POSIX 1003.1 functions.

Among those functions is the "byte file system," a repository with a set of administration commands and utilities that is common across POSIX-conforming systems. Support for this file system is provided with the CMS Shared File System (SFS), which supports byte files and the existing CMS record file data with common administration tasks and system-managed storage. The SFS byte file system also allows references from the byte file system to SFS record files and to CMS minidisk files. This permits POSIX applications to access traditional CMS files without performing data conversion. Existing data can be ported to a wide range of platforms.

In OpenEdition for VM/ESA, programs are CMS files. These can reside on minidisks, in the SFS, or in the OpenEdition Byte File System (BFS). When a module is on an accessed minidisk or SFS directory, it can be executed like any other CMS module. When it resides in the BFS, it can be executed through the "shell" (discussed later) or through the CMS. POSIX-compliant applications can be ported to OpenEdition for VM/ESA with little reworking as long as they strictly conform to the POSIX standards; that is, they issue no system calls other than those identified in those standards. CMS allows an application to issue both POSIX and non-POSIX calls, with CMS defining the rules for the interaction of the two classes. OpenEdition for VM/ESA also supports secure file access. Authorization for file access is validated by checking the POSIX security values of the requester against those permitted to access the file. An external security interface is provided for those wishing to have an external security manager, such as RACF for VM, to provide the POSIX group and user database information, and to authorize access to it.

OpenEdition for VM/ESA provides support for Sockets, a protocol for client/server communication. Sockets are application programming interfaces to TCP/IP to allow interoperability. In OpenEdition for VM/ESA the Sockets are a set of C language functions that correspond closely to the Sockets used by UNIX applications. The Sockets API provides support for both UNIX-domain Sockets, which allow communication among processes on a single system, and Internet-domain Sockets, which allow application programs to communicate with others in the network. The OpenEdition for VM/ESA Shell and Utilities feature provides tools to support application development tasks and porting of POSIX applications. This priced feature defines a standard interface and environment for application programs that require the services of a shell command language interpreter and a set of common utility programs.

The POSIX 1003.2 shell is a command interpreter that accepts commands defined in that standard. For some command requests, the shell calls other programs, called utilities. The shell and utilities programs are familiar to UNIX system programmers. Application programmers on VM/ESA can develop application solutions previously applicable to other POSIX-compliant systems. This function will give VM users the feel of using a UNIX system for POSIX-based applications.

In early 1996, the IBM OpenEdition Distributed Computing Environment (DCE) for VM/ESA was released. Support covered POSIX, the DCE feature, and the CMS GUI and GUI API. OSF's DCE is a layer of software between the operating system, the network, and the distributed application. For application developers, it masks the complexity of the network and different system architectures when writing and deploying open distributed or client/server applications. With this feature, programmers can develop applications on any platform supporting the DCE architecture and those applications, using the VM DCE services, can interoperate with other DCE-compliant systems. Data can be shared through the directory service with anyone else authorized in the system. With the addition of these DCE features, VM/ESA integrates with IBM's Open Blueprint Distributed Services.

This function will enable VM/ESA to participate in a DCE Cell and to support DCE Remote Procedure Call (RPC)–based client and server applications. RPC provides a facility for calling a procedure on a remote system as if it were on a local system, providing programmers with several powerful tools to build client/server applications. RPC handles all communications code, error handling, and data conversions transparently, substantially reducing the time required to code a distributed application as well as the amount of code required for that application. It generates code that transforms procedure calls into network messages and vice versa. RPC services mask the differences between data representations on different machines, allowing programs to work across heterogeneous systems.

The DCE Cell Directory Service (CDS) client provides access to the DCE CDS Server on another system in the DCE Cell. Users can identify resources such as RPC-based servers, files, or print queues by name and gain access to them without needing to know their location in the network. The DCE Cell and the transmission of data are protected by the DCE Security Service client, which provides the API to access the DCE security server on another system in the DCE Cell. DCE applications can run on VM with access to functions provided by the DCE Security Service, including user registration, authorization, and authentication. This combination provides a cross-vendor, cross-platform security capability. With the DCE Threads API, DCE applications can exploit multitasking in the DCE environment. The DCE Threads service allows a user to create and control multiple threads of execution within a single process.

VM/ESA Version 2, Release 3.0
Shipping in 1998, VM/ESA Version 2, Release 3 provided a S/390 platform consisting of network computing, guest operating system support, client/server computing, and interactive processing. An integrated TCP/IP suite, Network File System (NFS) access to VM files, Java Virtual Machine capability, and Message Queuing Interface (MQI) support are provided for VM/ESA in networked environments. VM/ESA Version 2, Release 3.0 provides both the boot server and management elements for the network computer desktop platform replacement.

In addition to expanded network computing support, VM/ESA Version 2, Release 3.0 provides OS/390 parallel sysplex testing support, enabling users to test entire OS/390 sysplex clusters as a set of guest virtual machines on selected processors. It also provides integrated Language Environment (LE) and additional UNIX interfaces to simplify application enablement and porting support for IBM's S/390 server hardware, the S/390 Multiprise 2000 and S/390 Enterprise Servers—Generation 3 or Generation 4.

UNIX application support includes the addition of more application programming interfaces and accommodation of certain uses of the UNIX fork() function. Approximately 150 additional UNIX APIs are supported by VM/ESA Version 2, Release 3.0. These interfaces are a subset of the XPG4.2 (X/Open Portability Guide) specification and were selected based on the input of users and solution providers interested in porting applications from UNIX systems to VM/ESA. In combination with VM/ESA's preexisting POSIX API support, application developers and solution providers can use the UNIX environment on VM for their development and porting efforts.

z/VM Version 3, Release 1

z/VM Version 3, Release 1 was also a key element of the October 2000 eServer zSeries announcement and is the follow-on product for VM/ESA users, providing them with new enhancements in support of their applications, database systems, and e-business solutions.

When running z/VM on a z900 it is possible to run 64-bit-capable OS/390 Version 2, Release 10, z/OS, and Linux for zSeries as guest systems of z/VM. In addition, 31-bit guest operating system support is provided for OS/390, VSE/ESA, TPF, and Linux for S/390.

z/VM exploits the new 64-bit z/Architecture, and through support of guest coupling users can develop and test their 64-bit applications before putting them into production. z/VM reduces the storage constraints by eliminating the 2 GB central storage limitation, giving the users the significant headroom needed to accommodate their increasing e-business demands and growing back-office applications within a single machine image. z/VM will also provide real storage constraint relief by running in 64-bit mode on a z900. This constraint relief is provided for 31-bit guest operating systems such as TPF, which is common in a page-constrained 31-bit-capable VM/ESA mode. Users running a large number of Linux for S/390 guest systems will likely benefit from the large real memory constraint relief afforded under z/VM.

In addition to the z900, z/VM will also support a wide variety of existing S/390 servers, offering existing VM/ESA users the ability to maintain their current VM environments on the latest technology and position themselves to grow into the zSeries.

Current OS/390 users migrating to z/OS may find there is a flexibility advantage to using z/VM for their test and migration work. z/VM supports the guest execution of 64-bit operating systems including OS/390 Version 2, Release 10 and z/OS running on the z900.

In enhanced TCP/IP, an improved FTP server, a new SSL server, and IP multicast support has been added in z/VM. z/VM offers enhanced support for Queued Direct I/O (QDIO) hardware facility, allowing a program to directly exchange data with an I/O device without performing traditional I/O instructions. VM/ESA users desiring SSL-secure TCP/IP network traffic, such as Telnet sessions, will be able to do so with z/VM.

Real-Time Monitor (RTM) VM/ESA and VM Performance Reporting Facility (VM PRF) have been enhanced for new and changed monitor records in z/VM.

z/VM supports Flash Copy and Parallel Access Volumes (PAV) for Enterprise Storage Server (ESS) for high-speed data copy. Additional guest support is provided for the 3494 Virtual Tape Server and FICON attached 3590 A60 tape controllers. z/VM delivers exceptional connectivity support for FICON channels, high-speed communications adapters, and advanced storage solutions.

Evolution of VSE

VSE/ESA

The Virtual Storage Extended/Enterprise System Architecture (VSE/ESA) operating system is used primarily in small to midsized S/390 computers. The easiest way to understand the environment that VSE/ESA creates within S/390 computers is to review its history.

Disk Operating System (DOS)

VSE/ESA is the descendant of the Disk Operating System/360 (DOS), introduced in 1965 for use with the smaller models of the System/360 mainframe computer family. Figure 4.23 shows how DOS organized the central storage of a System/360 computer into four regions called partitions. DOS itself was loaded from disk storage into the first partition. The next partition, labeled "Batch #1" in the figure, was used to execute a single batch application program.

Earlier, we saw that batch jobs in the System/360 days were typically submitted to the computer by placing a stack of computer punch cards into a card reader, which would transfer the information (that is,

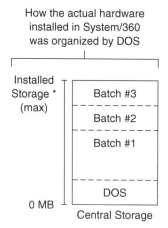

How the actual hardware
installed in System/360
was organized by DOS

Installed
Storage *
(max)

| Batch #3 |
| Batch #2 |
| Batch #1 |
| DOS |

0 MB

Central Storage

*Maximum central storage varied based on the expansion capabilities
of the particular System/360 processor unit model of interest.

Figure 4.23.   DOS divided the central storage of System/360 computers into four partitions.

the batch job instructions) into the computer. System/360 batch application programs usually presented their results in the form of a printed report. Initially, DOS supported only one batch partition. Later, however, the other two batch partitions shown in the figure were added to allow the System/360 computer to execute up to three batch programs simultaneously (marking the beginning of multiapplication support, which allowed the System/360 to handle a group of batch jobs more efficiently).

Disk Operating System/Virtual Storage (DOS/VS)

The next evolutionary step after DOS was the Disk Operating System/Virtual Storage (DOS/VS) operating system, introduced in 1972 for the System/370 family of computers. It was also around this time that interactive processing, in which users have a direct dialog with a computer program through a workstation, was catching on. As more and larger batch programs were developed and the workload of interactive users increased, so did the need for more central storage—a very expensive commodity at the time.

A major enhancement made in DOS/VS to help relieve the central storage squeeze was support for virtual storage (described in Chapter 2), an implementation in the operating system that makes a computer system seem to have more central storage than it actually does. In the DOS environment, computer programmers and users had to concern themselves with the physical amount of central storage available on the computer system that they were using. Once all of the installed central storage was in use, the computer system simply could not start any additional activities (batch or interactive). The virtual storage technique introduced with DOS/VS provided a means for the operating system to manage the storage hierarchy so that central storage seemed "larger than life," relieving users of this concern.

Figure 4.24 shows how DOS/VS managed a System/370 processor's central storage. DOS/VS could manage up to 8 MB of central storage

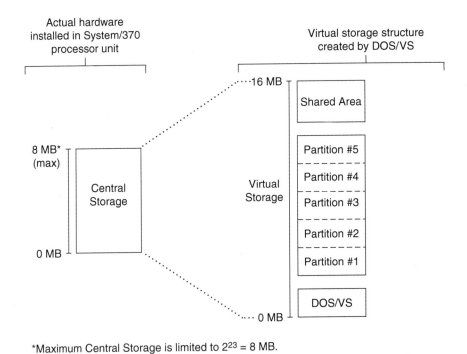

*Maximum Central Storage is limited to 2^{23} = 8 MB.

Figure 4.24. DOS/VS used virtual storage techniques to "stretch" central storage.

physically installed in the System/370 processor (even though no System/370 models were yet available to provide that much). DOS/VS took whatever central storage was installed and, using the virtual storage technique, "stretched it" to appear to be 16 MB in size. The 16 MB of virtual storage was then divided into independent partitions like those of the DOS environment.

However, DOS/VS could support up to five simultaneously active partitions, each of which could be used to run either a batch or an interactive application program for the users. (One partition could be used to execute an interactive application program that would simultaneously serve the needs of multiple users.) Again, we see in the figure that DOS/VS itself is loaded into the first part of virtual storage.

Another difference between DOS and DOS/VS is the introduction of the shared area seen in our figure at the top of virtual storage. In DOS, application programs and data in one partition could not be used by (accessed by) the programs of any other partition. This meant that each partition to perform common functions like printing and communicating over networks had to load its own copy of the programs and data needed by all partitions. Having identical copies of the same programs and data in each partition wasted virtual storage, which was quickly becoming a critical resource. DOS/VS's shared area provided a place to put one copy of the programs and data that could be shared by all partitions, saving space in each partition. In 1979, an improved version of DOS/VS called Disk Operating System/Virtual Storage Extended (DOS/VSE) was introduced. DOS/VSE could support up to 16 MB of central storage and up to 12 partitions.

Virtual Storage Extended/System Package (VSE/SP)
The next evolutionary step after DOS/VSE came in 1983 with the introduction of Virtual Storage Extended/System Package (VSE/SP). Even though the letters "DOS" were dropped from the name, VSE/SP was an enhanced version of DOS/VSE. Version 2 of VSE/SP was introduced in 1985. With Version 2, VSE/SP began to differentiate itself from the other operating systems with key advances in systems integration. Prior to 1985, each of the operating systems had used Installation Productivity Option (IPO) and, later, System Installation Productivity Option (SIPO) as a means of simplifying installation of the basic operating system. Although the installation options provided the necessary software on a single tape (that is, the software was "physically integrated"), they provided little assistance in administering day-to-day operations.

With VSE/SP Version 2, the physically integrated software components were also "logically integrated." Once the predefined installation routines completed the basic installation (which typically took no more than two hours), a specially designed, user-oriented dialog stepped the operator through the remaining installation tasks. Subsequently, the dialog concept was extended to assist administrators in dealing with tasks such as adding users to the system, managing the spooler queues, administering VSAM data files, tailoring subsystems, adding new hardware, and monitoring system performance.

A second enhancement that simplified VSE/SP operations came through the Fast Service Upgrade (FSU) feature. FSU also uses a dialog to assist operators in replacing system code on a production system without disturbing the business application code. Prior to being made available to customers, each FSU was serviced and system tested by laboratory experts. Putting the FSU on the system required repopulating existing libraries and data structures rather than re-creating them, as a reinstallation would require. With enhancements, FSU became the mode of operation for moving from one release of VSE to another. With the advent of 31-bit addressing in VSE/ESA Version 1, Release 3 (described later), the FSU concept was further expanded to support upgrades to new versions as well as release-to-release upgrades. Figure 4.24 shows how VSE/SP (Version 3.2) handled System/370 central storage. Like DOS/VSE, VSE/SP supports up to 16 MB of central storage. However, VSE/SP stretched whatever central storage was installed into 128 MB of virtual storage (the original VSE/SP supported 40 MB of virtual storage).

Since the virtual address was kept at 24 bits in length to preserve compatibility with DOS/VSE application programs, why wasn't VSE/SP limited to 16 MB (2^{24} bytes = 16 MB) of virtual storage, as DOS/VSE was? The answer lies in the Virtual Addressability Extensions (VAE) feature introduced with VSE/SP. This allows VSE/SP to define multiple 16 MB virtual address spaces, each identical to the single 16 MB virtual address space provided by DOS/VSE. Early versions of VSE/SP supported up to three virtual address spaces, whereas the latest version supported up to nine spaces, as shown in Figure 4.24. Having multiple address spaces provided a much-needed expansion of virtual storage without losing compatibility with existing application programs. More virtual storage meant the VSE/SP system could handle more and larger batch and interactive jobs. Further, the separate address spaces provided a layer of protective insulation between the application programs or users in different address spaces, helping to prevent the activities in one address space from inadvertently disrupting the activities in the others. Despite this advance, VSE/SP was still limited to a total of 12 partitions (one application program per partition) across all virtual address spaces.

Although the inter–address space isolation afforded by VAE's multiple address spaces had advantages, it also made it more difficult for the programs or users in one address space to share data with programs or users in another address space. It was possible for two application programs in different address spaces to share data residing in the "shared area" at the top of virtual storage. The trouble was, the shared area was already growing to hold the many other things needed by all address spaces. The larger the shared area grew, the smaller the private area had to become. For this reason, the Cross-Partition Communication Control (XPCC) was built into VSE/SP. With XPCC, the application programs in separate address spaces wishing to share data had first to ask VSE/SP to use XPCC to build a connection between them. This connection would effectively build a path (via the operating system) between the two application programs, allowing them to share data without taking up room in the shared area of Virtual Storage. An example of such a path, between address space 3 and address space 8, is shown in Figure 4.25.

Virtual Storage Extended/Enterprise System Architecture (VSE/ESA) Version 1
Virtual Storage Extended/Enterprise System Architecture (VSE/ESA) Version 1 was introduced with the S/390 family of computers in September 1990. Figure 4.26 shows how VSE/ESA Version 1 handles an S/390 processor's central storage. This is in keeping with the general ESA/390 strategy of improving overall system performance by keeping programs and data as high in the storage hierarchy as possible. However, in VSE/ESA Version 1, Releases 1 and 2 central storage is limited to a size of 384 MB. VSE/ESA stretches whatever amount of central storage there is into a virtual storage size of up to 32 GB spread over multiple address spaces of 16 MB each.

VSE/ESA still supports the same 12 partitions as VSE/SP in order to preserve compatibility with earlier application programs. However, VSE/ESA gets past the 12-partition barrier through its support of a new kind of partition, called a dynamic partition. Dynamic partitions are automatically created when an application program is started in that partition and automatically deleted when the application program is terminated. To differentiate them, the original 12 partitions are called

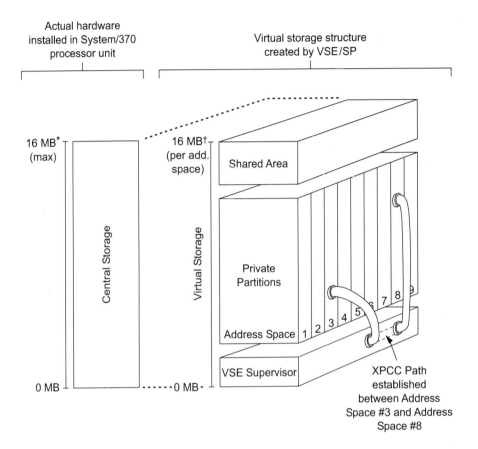

Actual hardware
installed in System/370
processor unit

Virtual storage structure
created by VSE/SP

16 MB* (max)

16 MB† (per add. space)

Shared Area

Central Storage

Virtual Storage

Private Partitions

Address Space 1 2 3 4 5 6 7 8 9

VSE Supervisor

XPCC Path
established
between Address
Space #3 and Address
Space #8

0 MB — 0 MB

* Maximum central storage is limited to 2^{24} = 16 MB.
† Maximum virtual address range per address space is 2^{24} = 16 MB.
 Total virtual storage (all address spaces) supported is 128 MB.

Figure 4.25. VSE/SP created multiple virtual address spaces.

static partitions, since they are defined during installation and cannot be changed "on the fly." The design of the VSE/ESA operating system is such that it can theoretically support up to 200 independent application programs in 200 dynamic partitions. This theoretical maximum is likely to be reduced when constrained by processor speed, system configuration, and application program characteristics. Each dynamic partition resides in its own address space.

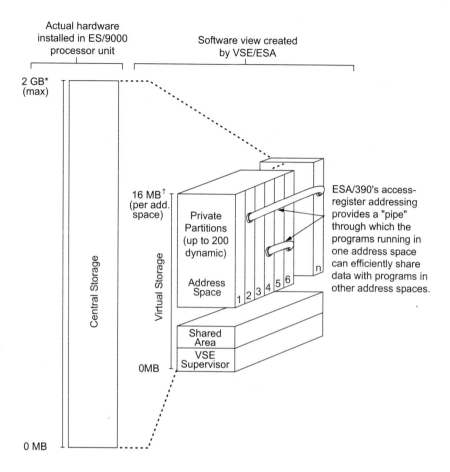

Figure 4.26. VSE/ESA handles more central storage and more virtual storage than earlier versions and introduces dynamic partitions.

The support for more central storage, more virtual storage, and dynamic partitions allows VSE/ESA to execute more and larger application programs than any of its predecessors. Having more simultaneously active users and application programs typically means a greater need to share data between application programs. One way to meet this need, as we have seen, is through the shared area of virtual storage. However, as the already sizable shared area of virtual storage grows, it takes away virtual storage space needed by the application programs in private partitions. With 200 active application programs, the shared area quickly squeezes out the very application programs it is there to serve. Although the Cross Partition Communication Control (XPCC) function allows two application programs in different address spaces to share information without consuming any of the shared virtual storage area, it must effect this sharing through operating system functions (that is, through software).

As the need for data sharing across address spaces increases, so does the need for a more efficient (that is, hardware-based) solution that does not limit the performance of the computer system. For this reason, a new means of sharing data between application programs in different address spaces was designed into the ESA/370 and ESA/390 architectures, namely, access-register addressing. With access-register addressing, the dynamic address translation process is modified so that the access register, rather than the base register, is used to convert from the real to virtual address. That is, an application program, through access-register addressing, efficiently uses data that resides in another address space. This allows an application program to share data efficiently with other application programs in as many as 15 other address spaces (even more by reloading the access register).

Access-register addressing was implemented in all S/390 computers and in the VSE/ESA operating system. Although VSE/ESA runs on System/370-based processor units, it cannot use access-register addressing on them because they do not have the necessary hardware support. VSE/ESA therefore resorts to a slower, software-based method for data sharing among different address spaces in System/370-based processor units. Example paths provided by access-register addressing are shown in Figure 4.27.

VSE/ESA Version 1 supports the Dynamic Channel Subsystem, which provides for dynamic channel path selection and dynamic path reconnection for more efficient I/O. Up to 256 channels are supported, 16 times the previous limit. Up to 8 paths are supported to a single device. VSE/ESA Version 1, Release 3 (V1R3) introduced 31-bit virtual addressing and ESA/390 data spaces, greatly increasing the amount of virtual storage available in the VSE/ESA environment. The basic structure of static and dynamic partitions remains the same (12 static parti-

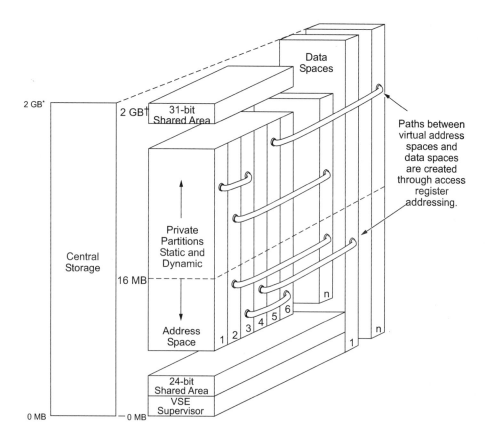

2 GB*

2 GB†

31-bit
Shared Area

Data
Spaces

Central
Storage

Private
Partitions
Static and
Dynamic

16 MB

Address
Space

1 2 3 4 5 6

n

1

n

Paths between
virtual address
spaces and
data spaces
are created
through access
register
addressing.

24-bit
Shared Area

VSE
Supervisor

0 MB

0 MB

*Maximum central storage is architecturally limited to 2 GB.
VSE/ESA design limit is 2 GB; but central storage supported
is the lesser of processor central storage or 2 GB.
†Maximum virtual address range for an address space or a data space.

Figure 4.27. VSE/ESA Version 1, Release 3 supports 31-bit addressing and ESA/390 data spaces.

tions in 12 address spaces, plus up to 200 dynamic partitions each in its own address space), but the size of address space has increased from 16 MB of virtual storage to 2 GB, a 128-fold increase. This increased amount of virtual storage provides an opportunity to relieve virtual storage constraints that had developed in the 16 MB address space. Functions providing constraint relief by reducing shared storage requirements below

16 MB virtual include ACF/VTAM, which has been moved from shared storage to a private address space, and VSE/POWER, which can be moved from shared storage if additional private address space room is required by an application.

The new virtual storage structure is shown in Figure 4.27. Virtual storage is divided into areas below and above 16 MB virtual. The VSE Supervisor, a shared area, and private space remain below 16 MB, just as in the past releases. This provides compatibility for applications that run in 24-bit addressing mode. Note that the shared area is now called the 24-bit shared area. The area from 16 MB up to 2 GB contains a 31-bit private space and a 31-bit shared area. Many applications do not need a 2 GB address space. An IPL (Initial Program Load) parameter allows the private area size to be defined.

A new type of virtual space, called a data space, can be defined up to 2 GB in size. It is different from an address space because no code execution is possible from this virtual space; it was designed to hold data only. Applications written with the new high-level assembler language can access the data within the data space at the byte level. The information held in these spaces is accessed through a new access register, defined by the ESA/390 architecture.

VSE/ESA Version 1, Release 3 increased the amount of central storage supported from 384 MB to 2 GB. VSE/ESA spreads the 12 static and up to 200 dynamic partitions plus data spaces into whatever amount of central storage is attached to the processor. VSE/ESA enhanced performance with a virtual disk, which allows data that otherwise would be stored on DASDs to reside in ESA/390 data spaces in central storage. Virtual disk usage is for temporary data, such as compile and sort jobs or temporary intermediate results of a calculation. It is also useful for fast access to read-only data, which must be copied to the virtual disk before usage. A virtual disk appears to an application like an ordinary Fixed Block Architecture (FBA) DASD; therefore, it can be used without application change. This release of VSE/ESA also added support for the ESCON Director and increased the number of channel-attached devices from 254 to 1,024.

Applications developed for CICS run under both VSE/ESA and OS/390. VSE/ESA may run as a remote system, managed by OS/390 through TME 10 NetView for OS/390 and the Target System Control Facility (TSCF). VSE/ESA continues to build on its unique relationship with OS/390. Specific enhancements include support for hardware data compression, standard on all S/390 processors since the ES/9000.

VSE/ESA Version 1, Release 4 (5750-ACD) shares the same base program of CICS/VSE Version 2, Release 3 as VSE/ESA Version 2, Release 1 (5690-VSE). Many new optional products introduced with VSE/ESA Version 2.1 are also available for VSE/ESA Version 1.4. Significant ones include LE COBOL and PL/I, VisualGen, VisualLift, QMF, ADSM/VSE, and DFSORT/VSE. VSE/ESA Version 1.4 offers the same CICS migration facilities as Version 2, Release 1. VSE/ESA Version 1, Release 4 was offered as a interim release for VSE/ESA users not wanting, for whatever reason, to migrate to Version 2.

Virtual Storage Extended/Enterprise System Architecture (VSE/ESA) Version 2

With this version, VSE/ESA acquires many of the functions supported by MVS and VM. In addition to the support for the S/390 Parallel Enterprise Servers, VSE provides multiprocessor support through the VSE/ESA Turbo Dispatcher. This function exploits multiple processors within one CEC by distributing work on the available processors on a partition basis. Today's concept of storage protection by partition is maintained. There are no additional storage management considerations to support this function.

The Turbo Dispatcher adds new logic to the VSE supervisor, enabling it to assign work to more than one processor within a shared central complex (CEC). The next eligible work unit of a job is assigned to the next processor unit waiting for work. When no processor is waiting and work is available, a lower-priority job will be interrupted and the pending work assigned to that processor. This support differs from the MVS/ESA N-way support. In MVS, several tasks from the same job can execute on different processors at the same time. With the VSE/ESA Turbo Dispatcher, the job and all the tasks associated with it are assigned to a single processor. The Turbo Dispatcher handles this work transparently to the application and user. No application changes are required.

Although not as complex or as sophisticated as the MVS function, Turbo Dispatcher does enhance the growth potential for systems using VSE. Previously, VSE users were constrained by the availability of uniprocessors. To exploit low-end dyadic processors required running multiple copies of VSE as guests under the VM operating system or running multiple copies of VSE in separate Logical PARtitions (LPARs). These solutions imposed significant management and performance constraints. Now, with Turbo Dispatcher, VSE/ESA users can exploit the largest dyadic processor models and the Parallel Enterprise Server models.

Although Turbo Dispatcher can theoretically support between 150 and 200 processors, the design of the CICS imposes limitations that reduce practical use of Turbo Dispatcher to no more than four parallel processors. Although any number of parallel work units can proceed simultaneously, only one nonparallel work unit can proceed at any point in time within a processor complex. Nonparallel functions include system functions like SVCs, POWER, or anything running in a protect Key 0. This makes nonparallel work a potential bottleneck when attempting to run more than four processors in a single complex. Some applications may be able to effectively use more than four processors; others will use fewer.

Hardware compression of VSAM data sets (KSDS, VRDS, and ESDS) reduces the cost of DASD storage (providing DASD savings in the range of 40% to 50%), reduces channel traffic, reduces CPU time required compared to a software compression technique, and provides relief to VSAM data sets that have reached their 4 GB addressability limit. VSE/ESA users can use the latest levels of IBM peripheral storage.

The advances in simplifying and improving the Interactive User Interface that VSE began with VSE/SP and the Fast Service Upgrade have continued into Version 2. In this version, the workstation completes the migration from the 3270 "green on black" passive screen to a full-function graphical user interface. The VSE Workdesk provides a graphical interactive user interface for VSE/ESA on the workstation using GUI controls. Spin dials, action bars, pull-down menus, pushbuttons, and check boxes are supported. It runs on an OS/2 or Windows PC, providing the same look and feel as workstation applications.

Many of the products already discussed with MVS/ESA and VM/ESA are also supported by VSE/ESA and enhance its participation in the client/server environment. LANRES, AdStar Distributed Storage Manager (ADSM), VisualLift for the 3270 workstation interface, Language Environment/370 (LE/370), SQL/DS, VTAM, APPN, and CICS are among these. Together with other products, they represent a significant increase in VSE/ESA's participation in IBM's Open Blueprint.

VSE/ESA Version 2, Release 3 provides an integrated system package with network computing and client/server, on-line transaction, and full-function batch capabilities. VSE/ESA Version 2, Release 3 adds standard TCP/IP connectivity and interoperability. TCP/IP for VSE/ESA Web server capability enables VSE/ESA systems to service many new application opportunities. VSE/ESA Version 2, Release 4 represents a significant milestone in building affinity between VSE/ESA and OS/390. With

VSE/ESA Version 2, Release 4, a new CICS Transaction Server for VSE/ESA is introduced. It is based on CICS for MVS/ESA.

Other VSE/ESA Components
Transaction Server for VSE/ESA provides improved integrity, new function and usability, increased capacity, and a firm foundation for ongoing enhancements. In addition, subsystem storage protection, a standard feature of S/390 servers, is exploited to improve availability. VSE/ESA Version 2, Release 4 delivers the CICS Transaction Server for VSE/ESA as well as CICS/VSE Version 2, Release 3. Both systems may be run in a "CICS Coexistence Environment" to help with the transition from older CICS systems to the new CICS Transaction Server for VSE/ESA. CICS Transaction Server for VSE/ESA has been extensively reengineered to improve its functionality and reliability.

Some other components are

- VSE/Advanced Functions (VSE/AF), which has the base VSE/ESA operating system programs.

- VSE/System Product, which provides an interactive user interface and basic functions to help install and automate the startup of the computer system.

- VSE/POWER, which controls the VSE/ESA partitions (static and dynamic) and manages the flow of information from input devices to output devices. For example, it accepts the output of an application program and then gradually feeds it to a printer at the rate the printer can handle (called spooling a file to a printer). Files can also be spooled back and forth over communications networks between computer systems.

- VSE/Virtual Storage Access Method (VSE/VSAM), which helps organize the information kept in disk storage and provides application programs with a consistent way to access information contained in disk storage.

- Advanced Communications Function/Virtual Telecommunications Access Method (ACF/VTAM), which manages the communications traffic associated with terminals, printers, and System Network Architecture (SNA) communication networks of computers and Advanced Peer-to-Peer Networking (APPN) support in both client server and traditional network environments. S/390 data compression is also exploited.

- VSE/Interactive Compute and Control Facility (VSE/ICCF), which is a tool that helps the computer's operator run the system and helps programmers write and then execute custom programs.

- REstructured eXtended eXecutor (REXX/VSE) programming language (5686-058), which was introduced along with VSE/ESA Version 1, Release 3 and allows programs to be written in a clear and structured manner. It includes powerful character string manipulation, automatic data typing, and high-precision arithmetic. REXX/VSE supports both interpreted and compiled EXECs. The product includes both a full REXX interpreter and the REXX compiler run-time library. The compiler library allows REXX programs compiled on TSO/E or CMS to be executed.

Other Operating Systems

In addition to the three major operating systems just described, other operating systems can be used with S/390 and zSeries servers. This section reviews four of these.

Advanced Interactive eXecutive/Enterprise Systems Architecture (AIX/ESA)

This was IBM's first operating system for the open systems environment, in which computer systems of many different types need to communicate freely with one another. Building on the base of a UNIX operating system, IBM offers a family of AIX operating systems, including AIX versions for PCs and RISC System/6000, System/370, and S/390 computers. AIX/ESA was withdrawn in 1996 and replaced by the OpenEdition MVS component of MVS/ESA Version 5, Release 2.2, which is now superseded by the UNIX Services function of OS/390.

Linux Operating System

Linux is a relatively new UNIX-like operating system that was developed by a young student, Linus Torvalds, while he attended the University of Helsinki in Finland. Linus wanted to improve on the Minix UNIX system and proceeded to develop and release his system, Version 0.02, in 1991. He continued to improve his system design until 1994, when Version 1.0 of the Linux Kernal was released. The current full-featured version is 2.4 and was released January 2001. Linux is continuously being developed and tested by an open source community under the GNU General Public License, and its source code is freely available to users. Linux can be used for networking, for software development, and as an end-user platform. The number of Linux users is growing rapidly and in 2000 was estimated by the IDC to be 9 million.

In December 1999, IBM shocked the industry when it released source code that supported the Linux operating system on the S/390. Where a business utilizes the S/390 server platform it can be expected to run all or nearly all of the businesses enterprise data on the S/390. The advantage of also running Linux on an S/390 gives the business user the ability for Linux applications to access all of that enterprise data. The S/390's large capacity, greater security, and reliability make it the perfect platform to help simplify the IT infrastructure, reducing costs by cutting the number of servers employed. This blend of server and operating system offers the ideal platform for a highly integrated e-business solution.

As with the open flexibility of the S/390, the z900 servers offer additional levels of flexibility to manage numerous operating systems on a single server including z/OS, OS/390, z/VM, VM/ESA, VSE/ESA, TPF, Linux for zSeries, and Linux for S/390. Linux for S/390 will run 31-bit applications, and Linux for zSeries will support the new 64-bit architecture on z900 servers. The z900 can run the same Linux for S/390 as the previous S/390 servers can, but porting S/390 Linux to the z900 will not take full advantage of the z900. The new SuSE Linux AG distribution includes the Linux version capable of full 64-bit memory addressing. Multiple Linux systems can be easily managed on the zSeries 900 with z/VM, and the Linux images can share the resources and internal high-speed communications inherent in the z900. Additional Linux workload processing capacity can be purchased exclusively for Linux with no effect on the z900 model designation, therefore without increasing charges for zSeries or S/390 non-Linux-related software on the rest of the server. The zSeries flexibility and management characteristics make it possible to add new Linux images in minutes rather than days, and with the zSeries server scalability the overall number of servers required by the business can be minimized.

There is an interesting example of the effect of IBM's pricing model, the details of which can be seen on their z900 Web site. The example is a z900 sample configuration running 2,500 Linux instances. The cost of the system, excluding peripherals, is around $1.2 million and amortized over the 2,500 Linux instances results in a cost per virtual Linux machine of about $500. This is very competitive with low-end desktop computers and less costly than many entry-level rack mounts.

Transaction Processing Facility (TPF)

The TPF operating system (once known as the AirLine Control System, or ALCS) is designed for businesses and organizations that have high on-line transaction volumes and large networks. Its high capacity and availability characteristics make it IBM's strategic, real-time, High-Volume Transaction Processing (HVTP) platform. Customer reports indicate production workloads of over 5,200 messages per second. The majority of customers operate at 99.9 to 100% availability for sustained periods of time (one customer has run nearly two years without any planned or unplanned outages).

Originally the result of an early 1960s project between IBM and several airlines, TPF has attracted customers throughout the world, spread across several industries, including airlines, lodgings, banks, and financial institutions. Their common characteristic is an environment in which transaction growth is expected to be very fast or there are peak periods of intense transaction activity. TPF provides those businesses with significant competitive advantage by enabling high capacity with very low cost per transaction.

Designed for the S/390 environment, TPF supports loosely coupled parallel processors. It is suited to take advantage of the 9672 parallel servers. TPF's architecture supports very large communication networks and is designed to recover from most computer outages in only a few seconds, without incurring a loss of the network.

A new function in TPF Version 4.1 was virtual storage support, providing transaction protection through program isolation, which improves overall system capacity. New methods of loading application programs to the TPF system improved system availability and operability in the same release. Optional file addressing techniques increased the size of databases supported under TPF to 4 billion records. Communication enhancements provide increased connectivity and application portability through LU 6.2 parallel sessions. New system diagnostics ease problem determination and correction through exploitation of hardware trace facilities and improved software traces. The MVS/ESA subsystem (TPF/MVS) enables the TPF API to be used by MVS/ESA customers. TCP/IP connectivity is available using the IBM 3172 and the TPF SOCKETS/CLAW interface.

Distributed Processing Programming eXecutive/370 (DPPX/370)

DPPX/370 was originally developed to provide a way for users of IBM's 8100 computer family (based on the DPPX operating system) to more easily migrate to the System/370 family of computers. DPPX/370 maintained a high degree of compatibility with the application programs originally written for an 8100 DPPX system. DPPX/370 was useful in environments where users wished to install small S/390 processors at multiple remote offices and manage those processors from a larger S/390 computer (running MVS/ESA) at a central site.

Summary

In this chapter, we have presented the fundamental difference between the S/390 and zSeries as a server environment for business-critical applications and other open systems. Prior to the industry and business focus on open systems, S/390 was delivering full-function support for business applications. S/390 systems scaled from processors smaller than today's servers to very powerful multiprocessors many hundred times larger. They possessed all of the functions critical to successful business operation. What the early S/390 server generations had in compute function, however, they lacked in user (and business) friendliness. (We will discuss pricing in Chapter 6.) Then came open systems, network computing, and now the Internet. These systems began solving fundamental business problems of scaling to larger systems, supporting more complex business applications and enabling more users to share system resources securely and manageably. S/390 and the new zSeries servers have focused on improving usability characteristics and building interfaces to alternative platforms, making them a complete part of an overall solution.

Today you can evaluate the outcome. First, S/390 with OS/390 and specifically UNIX Services, and finally the introduction of the Linux operating system platform, provided nearly full-function support for applications that needed to run in an open environment yet access the whole of the enterprise data base. Now the zSeries and z/Architecture with their increased scalability, reliability, and manageability, and further with their enhanced Linux capabilities, have taken the next evolutionary step in the open world. These servers do so with a single integrated system that provides its historical, industrial-strength, business-support environment, which supports both your application development needs and your production workloads. Many businesses entrust some applications to other open systems, but the most critical ones continue to be found on S/390 and now the zSeries servers.

5

Communications—
Accessing the Data

For decades technology focused alternately between speeding up processors to enable them to handle greater workflow and speeding up devices storing data to keep them from becoming a bottleneck. Communications, to the extent that it existed beyond the bounds of the host system, was seldom a concern. Host-centric or data-centric defined both the architecture and the attitude.

Today, "network computing" has entered our vocabulary. The Internet will forever change how the masses of data and the transaction processing that are accessible on the S/390 or z900 will be used. To compete effectively, businesses have gathered data rapidly from all parts and provided it to users, wherever they were. Basic communication via the Internet has rapidly expanded across the United States and throughout the world. Nearly every advertisement by even the smallest of companies today mentions the Web address for that corporation. The need and desire to gain access while continuing to build on existing application bases are driving considerable change into server communications. The change has been captured in a simple term, "electronic business" (e-business), which combines the simplicity and reach of the Web with core business operations: e-business = Web + IT.

End-user access via the Internet is not all that is important. Corporations remain committed to the traditional server communications method based on the Systems Network Architecture (SNA). Trillions of dollars' worth of application program code have been developed around applications using this communications method. The key success of e-business is to bridge the secure, predictable access provided by SNA with the underlying technology of the Internet, which is based on TCP/IP.

The rapid spread of high-powered personal computers and workstations increased the demand for useful local data and the ability to process it in the most remote areas. New techniques evolved for distributing massive amounts of data to these new systems. With the new techniques came a wide variety of communication protocols (rules and procedures). Faced with the potential for communications chaos, businesses and users rapidly converged on sets of standards to guide this emerging aspect of computing past technical, procedural, and communications barriers. As with the processing elements themselves, networking and communications have emerged into a new, open world.

In this chapter we will explore many of the technologies, protocols, and standards that guide the field of communications today, starting with the limited-scope local area network. We then introduce the concept of networked computing, which requires a comprehensive infrastructure to incorporate the traditional communication architectures and network types with the Internet. Finally, we introduce several key elements of an effective communications network.

Local Area Networks

Although servers can communicate with each other over great distances, some business environments require communication links among server systems that are all located in one place. This is particularly true for smaller businesses or businesses in which server needs are satisfied within a single location, such as a campus environment. Such a need commonly arises when a community of local users needs access to application programs or information located on a central server system located in the same building or on the same campus. A financial analyst, for example, may need the flexibility and ease of use offered by running spreadsheet and business graphics application programs on a workstation. The analyst may also need access to the financial database and electronic mail hosted on the company's server. One way to provide this access is to establish a communications link between the workstation and the host server.

Since all participating servers in this example are in the same location, this type of communications link is called a Local Area Network (LAN). Although LANs at other locations can be linked together with traditional communications lines, the server systems on any one LAN must be in the same building or on the same campus. This distance limitation is the price you pay for getting the high speeds associated with LANs.

The IBM Token-Ring Network provides one way for a local group of servers to communicate very efficiently (4 or 16 Mbits/s). Because of physical limitations, this type of communications link is not used directly between distant or remote servers. Two common methods for interconnecting remote LANs together over the wide area network are bridges and routers, which provide the appearance that remote separate LANs are accessible by all users connected to any of the LANs.

Figure 5.1 shows the basic architecture of a token-ring network. Each computer that participates in the network is called a network station, and it shares information, programs, and server system with other nodes in the network. The nodes of the network are logically arranged in a "ring" pattern, giving the network its name.

Although various types of wiring can be used to implement a token-ring network, a twisted-pair (two-wire) cable is most commonly used. The cable connects a server system's token-ring adapter card directly to a Controller Access Unit (CAU). The CAU is the device, typically located in a wiring closet, that actually makes the electrical connections from the cables to each node in the network. One CAU, for example, supports the attachment of up to 92 nodes and supports a choice of remote management software packages. A modular jack is used to attach each network node to the CAU, which lets nodes be added to or removed from the network. In the event that one segment of the token-ring network fails, the CAU automatically reroutes traffic over a backup path to keep the network going. With today's more complex networks, technologies such as hubs, switches, and routers are used to interconnect LANs, providing the ability to quickly exchange messages between the LANs while enabling control over which messages are exchanged. Networking hubs now typically replace CAUs as the token-ring technology, and the sophistication that it requires has advanced.

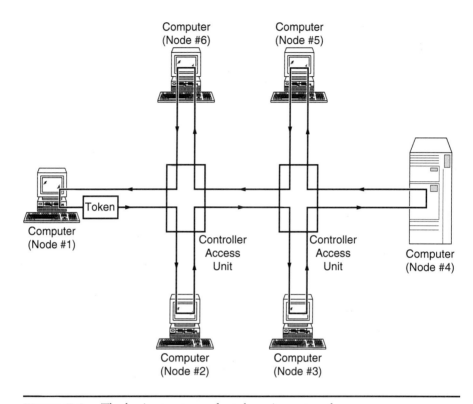

Figure 5.1. The basic structure of a token-ring network.

AS/400 servers, RISC System/6000 servers, multiple S/390 or zSeries servers, and other types/makes of servers can all participate in a single token-ring network. S/390 and zSeries servers can also communicate with many different types of servers over other types of local area networks, such as Ethernet or ATM LANs. With this overview of the token-ring network, we now examine two examples of personal computers cooperating with a central S/390 server over a token-ring network. In the first example (Figure 5.2), the S/390 provides file and print server support to the network. In the second example (Figure 5.3), the S/390 and the PCs work more closely together in a cooperative processing environment.

Figure 5.2 shows a small local area network consisting of workstations (PCs, Apple Macintosh computers, UNIX computers) and an S/390 server. The connection between the S/390 and the LAN is provided by

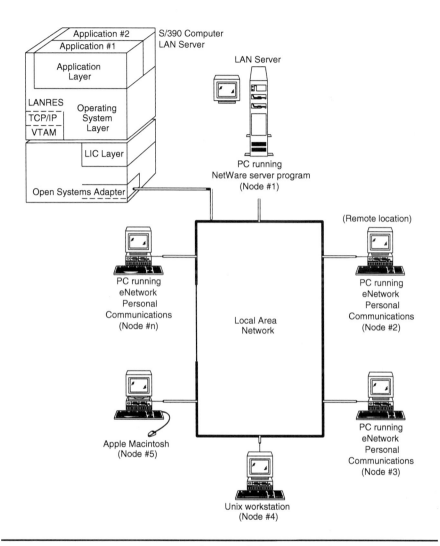

Figure 5.2. An S/390 system can share its disk storage and printers with other computer systems on a local area network.

the Open Systems Adapter (OSA). The OSA could be used for connection to a token-ring, Ethernet, Fast Ethernet, FDDI, or Asynchronous Transfer Mode (ATM) network. The programming necessary to communicate with the other nodes in the network is provided by the communications component of the S/390 operating system, eNetwork

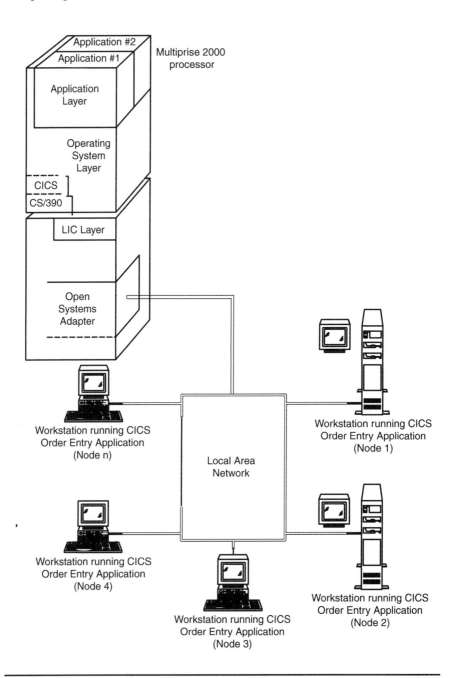

Figure 5.3. Example communications configuration that allows for cooperative processing between the S/390 application programs and workstation application programs.

Communications Server for OS/390, which was previously known as the Virtual Telecommunications Access Method (VTAM), and TCP/IP for MVS/ESA. The Novell NetWare Server program in the attached PC allows the PC to be a LAN server. As a LAN server, this PC shares its fixed disk storage, printers, and communications links with the other servers, LAN clients, in the LAN. These LAN clients can be PCs running DOS, Windows, or OS/2, or they can be other types of computers, such as Apple Macintoshes or UNIX workstations.

The eNetwork Personal Communications (PCOMM) program operating on the workstations allows them to emulate a 3270 display station. This means that a workstation user can sign on to the S/390 server as a normal 3270-type display station and can interact with S/390 application programs. While the PC is emulating a 3270-type display, it still keeps its ability to run other workstation programs. It also can transfer files between the PC and the S/390.

The integrated LAN Resource Extension and Services (LANRES) function of the OS/390 operating system works closely with the Novell NetWare LAN Server(s) in the network. Together, LANRES and Novell NetWare Servers provide centralized LAN administration functions. Through the LANRES program, the S/390 can become a LAN server, sharing its resources with the other servers in the LAN. These resources include S/390 disk storage, which becomes an extension of the disk storage of the servers in the LAN. PC users can store and retrieve information in S/390 disk storage the same way they store information on the PC's fixed disk (making the S/390 a file server). This vastly expands the amount of fixed disk storage available to the workstation user, it facilitates data sharing with other authorized users in the LAN, and it allows the data processing staff to see that critical information is consistently backed up and secure. If printers are shared, the S/390 becomes a print server, enabling printers attached to the S/390 to print the output of application programs running on the workstations in the LAN.

The LANRES programs also allow the LAN administrator to create/delete user IDs, priorities, and access privileges for all the users on the LAN from one S/390 display station. Further, the LAN administrator can distribute updated programs and data from the S/390 computer to any of the LAN servers in the network. In fact, many LAN administration and information distribution tasks can be automated by embedding the necessary commands in S/390 programs (for example, a REXX exec in VM/ESA) that can be scheduled to run unattended.

We have just seen how an S/390 can share disk storage and printers with other computers participating in a LAN and help with LAN administration. Now we explore an example of an S/390 and a group of PC computers working even more closely together, using a LAN designed to handle a business's telephone order entry needs. Figure 5.3 is an example of another cooperative processing arrangement with the S/390. In our example, the S/390 or z900 server is directly attached to the local area network via the Open Systems Adapter, but it could be attached just as well via an I/O channel and a 3174 Establishment Controller or the IBM 2216 Multiaccess Connector. eNetwork Communications Server for OS/390 or z/OS again provides the programming necessary for the server to participate in the token-ring network. Also loaded on our server is the Customer Information Control System (CICS) transaction-processing application enabler and some custom CICS application programs, used by a pool of order entry clerks. Each clerk uses one of the PCs attached to the LAN. The PCs are all running CICS and custom PC application programs designed to work with CICS. eNetwork Personal Communications provides the communications programming necessary for the PC to communicate (as LAN clients) with the server over the token-ring network. CICS provides the foundation for building transaction-based application programs, such as order entry.

The order entry clerks use their PCs to enter orders that they receive over the telephone. Under normal circumstances, the orders entered through the PC-resident application programs are immediately forwarded to the server order entry application program. Since both the PC order entry program and the z900 order entry program are CICS based, they communicate naturally. The order entry clerks could use displays to communicate directly with the z900 order entry application program, but there are advantages to using the PCs as a front end to the system. First, the PC's custom order entry application programs provide a graphical user interface. This simplifies and shortens a new clerk's learning curve, and it makes the program easier and more pleasing to use for all order entry clerks. Another advantage of the PC front end is that, if communication with the server goes down for any reason, the order entry clerks can continue to enter orders into the PC-based order entry application program without interruption. Rather than being forwarded immediately to the z900 order entry application program, the new orders are stored on the PC's local fixed disk storage. Later, when the server is back on-line, the PC order entry application program automatically sends the new orders up to the order entry application program on the z900 without user intervention.

When PC application programs interact directly with S/390 application programs, as in the preceding example, they are in a cooperative processing environment. Cooperative processing allows the users to benefit from the independent processing capabilities, graphical strengths, and quick response time of PC systems without giving up the storage capacity, data security, and applications of an z900 server. In addition to PC systems, S/390 and z900 servers participate in cooperative processing with other z900 or S/390s, with RISC System/6000 systems, with AS/400 systems, with Windows-based computers, and with other types and makes of computers.

Distributed Computer Communications

In many cases, using multiple computer systems best satisfies the needs of a business. Instead of providing remote users with standalone workstations or terminals connected to a central computer, a business may provide them with their own small computer system(s). For example, a large retail chain may want a computer system at each retail location as well as a computer system at headquarters. These systems are joined through a communications network that allows them to move information (for example, daily cash register receipts) easily from place to place as necessary. This communication structure is called a distributed computer network.

Distributing computer systems to the sites where they are needed provides several advantages. First, since all users are locally attached to their respective computer system, they often enjoy improved system performance (reduced response time) compared with remotely attached workstations, which are slowed down by communications line limitations. Further, the distributed computer system consolidates communications, a particular benefit at very large remote locations that may need a large number of communications lines to support all the remote workstations. With a distributed computing approach, remote users can be locally attached to their distributed system, which can then communicate with other computers through a single communications line.

The disadvantage of a distributed computer system is that it is often more difficult to manage than a single-computer system. Because S/390 servers were designed for a distributed computer communications environment, however, there are network management tools that ease this task. S/390 computers can participate in distributed computer networks with other S/390s, AS/400 systems, personal computers or workstations, network computers, RISC System/6000 systems, computers made by other manufacturers, or virtually any combination of these.

Distributed Networks

Multiple S/390, z900, or combinations of both servers can be attached together through communications links to create a distributed network (illustrated in Figure 5.4). In this example, multiple z900 or S/390 systems are each distributed to a remote location and a larger z900 is located at the business's headquarters. The S/390, installed at a San Francisco location and shown in the lower left corner of the figure, is one of the remote installations. To accommodate the needs of the local users, it is equipped with a workstation controller that allows for direct attachment of displays and printers to the processor. A communications adapter and modem allow the S/390 to communicate over a leased telephone line with the z900 at the company's headquarters in Pittsburgh. This communications link allows the two systems to freely exchange information (that is, transfer files, exchange electronic mail, and so on). It also allows a remote S/390 or z900 user to pass through and log on to the central server system as a remote user. Conversely, a central site user can pass through and log on to the remote S/390 or z900 as a remote user.

At the headquarters end of the connection, a modem and a 3745 Communications Controller are installed. The modem communicates with its counterpart at the remote location over the leased telephone line. The 3745 Communications Controller handles the information traffic between the z900 and all of the remote locations. An old 3174 Establishment Controller could have met the functional requirements at the central site end in this example, but the 3745 can handle the large volume of communications generated by all of the remote locations more efficiently.

Much like the z900 and S/390, the connectivity to these servers is evolving. In previous years, connectivity was almost surely provided by the 3745 Communications Controller but today connectivity can be provided by several new options, including the 3746 Models 900 and 950 and the Open Systems Adapter (OSA). It is very likely that other

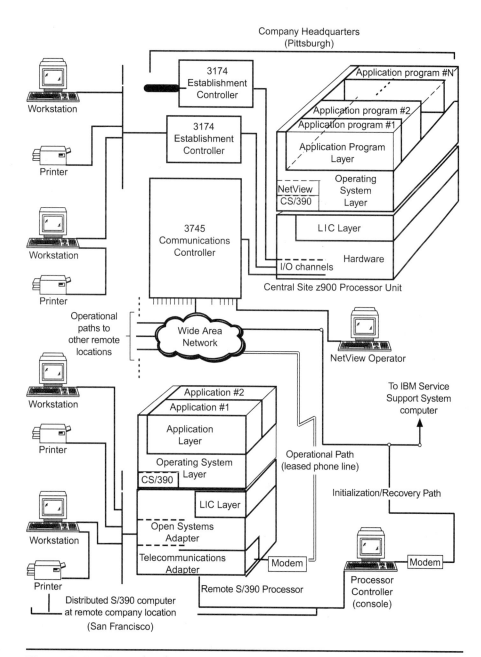

Figure 5.4. Example of communications configuration used to attach distributed S/390 servers to a central S/390 server.

controller types are still installed and in use, but several of them, such as the 3172, 3174, and 2216, are no longer available. The 3745 Models 170, 170A, 31A, and 61A as well as the 3746 Models 900 and 950 are still available, but their usefulness is phasing out in favor of OSA-2 and now OSA-Express, which is the preferred connectivity option for S/390 and z900.

Having remote S/390 or z900 servers participate in a distributed communications network is one thing, but managing that communications network is something else. Network management tasks include problem detection, problem resolution, restarting the system after a problem is resolved, making network configuration changes, and much more. The network management functions needed vary depending on the type of communications network involved. IBM's approach to managing distributed networks containing multiple S/390 and z900 servers centers around NetView, now known as TME 10 NetView, which can be seen in the figure loaded on the S/390 at headquarters. NetView takes advantage of the Remote Operator Facility built into the processors to remotely perform tasks that would otherwise require on-site data processing personnel.

A second communications link, the Initialization/Recovery Path (bottom right corner of Figure 5.4), between the headquarters in Pittsburgh and the remote location in San Francisco supports two-way communications between the remote processor controller and NetView on the central z900. The Initialization/Recovery Path typically uses a lower-cost switched telephone line rather than a leased telephone line. That is, the Initialization/Recovery Path is established only when needed by having a modem (discussed later in this chapter) dial the phone number of the other modem. When the necessary communication is concluded, the link is simply terminated by having the modems hang up. The switched telephone line also allows one communications link to be used for multiple purposes. In Pittsburgh, for example, one Initialization/Recovery Path line can be used to handle all of the remote locations. In San Francisco, it can be used to call the IBM Service Support System server.

NetView can be used to simplify management of this complex configuration. With an Initialization/Recovery Path set up between San Francisco and Pittsburgh, a network operator in Pittsburgh uses NetView to manage the entire distributed network. The NetView program calls up the S/390 in San Francisco over the Initialization/Recovery Path and powers up the system for normal operation. Since this is part of the daily routine for all remote locations, this procedure has been preprogrammed in NetView to occur automatically, relieving the data processing staff of this task. After the S/390 in San Francisco acknowledges that things are running fine, the Initialization/Recovery communications link is terminated and NetView goes on with its other duties.

Meanwhile, in San Francisco things run fine for awhile but then a problem develops, bringing down the communications path. First, the remote processor console automatically calls NetView in Pittsburgh over the Initialization/Recovery Path and reports the problem to NetView. This is done through an alert message that is automatically sent by the processor controller in San Francisco. NetView is preprogrammed to automatically guide the remote processors through a recovery procedure for many different types of alerts, but this particular alert has not been preprogrammed. The data processing personnel in Pittsburgh analyze the problem and determine that a service call is necessary to replace the failing component. Through NetView commands, the personnel instruct the processor controller in San Francisco to place a service call to the IBM Service Support System server, to terminate the communications link with San Francisco, and to use the Initialization/Recovery Path to place the service call. Later, after the failing component is replaced, the personnel instruct NetView to call San Francisco and restart the remote S/390.

This is one simple example of NetView managing a problem in a distributed network with S/390 or z900 servers. Other NetView capabilities include getting updates to Licensed Internal Code and running diagnostics on various network components. The intent of TME 10 NetView for OS/390 and the Remote Operator Facility is to keep things running smoothly while eliminating the need for on-site data processing skills in a distributed network environment.

S/390 and z900 with Distributed Networks

We have just seen how distributed S/390 and z900 servers can be controlled remotely by one z900, in this example, server located at a company's headquarters. In some cases, however, it is desirable to distribute midrange computers, such as the AS/400 systems or Windows NT systems, while retaining a more powerful z900 server system at headquarters. One reason for this decision would be that the best-fitting application program for the remote locations runs only on the remote platform, say an AS/400, whereas the z900 is needed at headquarters to provide more data storage and processing power than even the largest remote system could provide. In any case, a central z900 can participate in and manage a distributed computer network consisting of other systems.

Figure 5.5 shows how a distributed system might be attached to a central z900 or S/390 system. The communications link acts as an operational path serving day-to-day communications needs, as described in the last section. This link also serves as the Initialization/Recovery Path for the distributed network. The operating system used with AS/400 computers (OS/400) works closely with z900 and S/390 operating systems and the TME 10 NetView network management program. The result is similar to the "remote console" function in S/390 and z900 distributed networks. NetView allows the server data processing staff at headquarters to support the distributed AS/400 systems using the same alert message approach discussed in S/390 distributed networks. Conversely, the AS/400 users sign on and directly interact with the S/390 or z900 server from their AS/400 workstation (5250-type workstation) as if they were using an z900 workstation. Thus, the users of either system have access to any system in the network, if the system's security allows it. OS/400's 3270 Device Emulation support allows an AS/400 workstation to emulate a 3270 Workstation. The AS/400 Communications Utilities are an optional extension to OS/400 that allows an AS/400 user to transfer files and submit batch jobs to the S/390 or z900 through its Remote Job Entry (RJE) Facility.

Our example shows only one simple method of attaching an AS/400 to a S/390 or z900. With the Systems Network Architecture (SNA), TCP/IP support for OS/400, and the implementation of Advanced Peer-to-Peer Networking (APPN) and robust TCP/IP communications capabilities on the S/390 and z900 (discussed later in this chapter), there are now many alternatives for distributed network communications between S/390 or z900 and AS/400 computers.

Open Blueprint Network Services

The information provided thus far barely scratches the surface of all the possible communication alternatives and products that exist, and more are made available every month. Also, the increasing emphasis on open

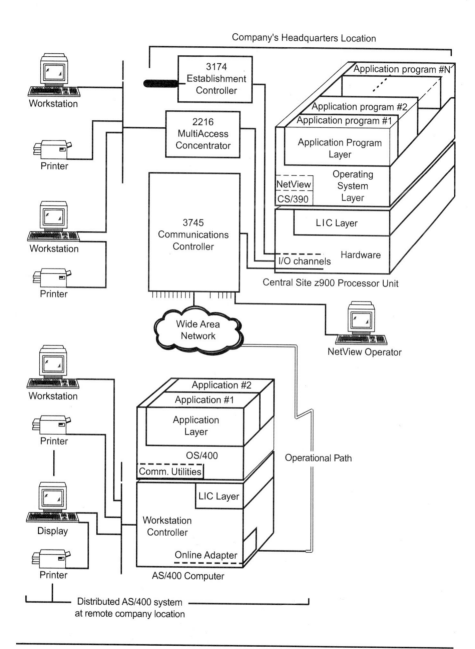

Figure 5.5. Example of communications configuration used to attach distributed AS/400 systems to a central S/390 server.

systems has produced the need for systems and products from multiple vendors to interact with each other. To ensure an orderly evolution of networks and communication links in this dynamic and heterogeneous environment, IBM developed an Open Blueprint (illustrated in Figure 5.6). As with any blueprint, this one defines a structure into which multiple products can fit and provides a schematic for businesses to plan the evolution of their network nodes.

As illustrated, the Open Blueprint is organized into six distinct sets of resource management services. In this chapter, we will address only those resources directly related to communications and networking. These include

- Communication Services, a subcomponent of Distributed Systems Services, which provides mechanisms enabling a single-system (consolidated) view of the network.

- Each of four subcomponents of Network Services, which provide for the transport of data from one system to another.

- An introduction to the Systems Management support associated with networks.

Communication Services
Communication Services includes three multivendor application interfaces and services: Common Programming Interface for Communications (CPI-C), Remote Procedure Call (RPC), and the Message and Queue Interface (MQI). These interfaces present three models that describe how distributed applications or resource managers can talk to each other.

The CPI-C supports communication called conversation between application programs over private logical connections. Conversations are a sophisticated method of communicating that requires simultaneous execution of partner programs. This requires that a network session be established exclusively for the programs to communicate. CPI-C is designed primarily for a structured exchange of information between programs, and CPI-C applications are generally client/server or peer-to-peer implementations. Applications that use the conversational model include distributed transaction processing, distributed relational database access, and bulk data transfer operations involving multiple transmis-

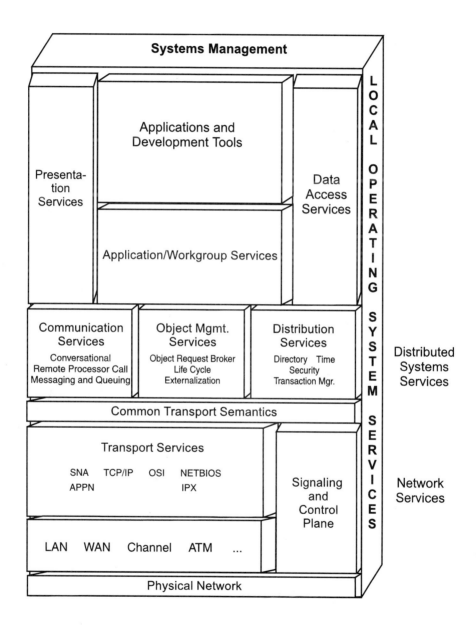

Figure 5.6. Open Blueprint networking components.

sions. ISO chose the conversational model as the basis for the OSI Transaction Processing protocol specification, which is based on the SNA APPC (Advanced Program-to-Program Communication) architecture.

Operating systems use APPC services to assist in implementing conversational (synchronous) applications through CPI-C. In spite of their sophistication, conversational applications are surprisingly easy to implement. APPC/MVS in MVS/ESA and OS/390 offers built-in server functions that can be used in client/server conversations. APPC/MVS services are callable services accessible from a high-level language application without the necessity of writing assembler language routines.

Remote Procedure Call (RPC) uses a call/return mechanism (much like doing Fortran library subroutine calls) to provide communications between client/server applications. The client program (caller) determines the server (called procedure) location in the network, establishes the necessary communication, and passes the required parameters for executing the procedure. The caller waits until the procedure finishes executing (that is, it is a synchronous operation) and the results are passed back. Different vendor implementations of Remote Procedure Call are supported. Today, workstations with applications implementing RPC operate as clients with OS/390 using the Network File System (NFS) server function provided for OS/390. OS/390 also supports Apollo Computers' Network Computing System RPC. The Open Software Foundation (OSF) chose RPC as the fundamental communication model for the Distributed Computing Element (DCE). The OSF/DCE RPC is supported on OS/390 and MVS/ESA SP 4.3 and later releases, enabling support in an open systems environment.

Message Queue Interface (MQI), in contrast to RPC, is an asynchronous program-to-program interface. It supports message-driven, deferred processing communication through queues, not through private connections. Programs that use MQI fill and empty message queues. The calling program places the request in a queue but does not wait for a response; instead, it continues with its processing. When the response arrives, it is placed in another queue to await processing. MQI services route the messages to the appropriate destinations in the network for access by the programs servicing the queue. It provides guaranteed message delivery, recoverability, and, where applicable, sync point participation. MQI applications can be client/server, peer-to-peer, or more complex implementations.

IBM's *MQSeries* (see Figure 5.7) simplifies the process of cross-platform communications by using the MQI, which operates independent

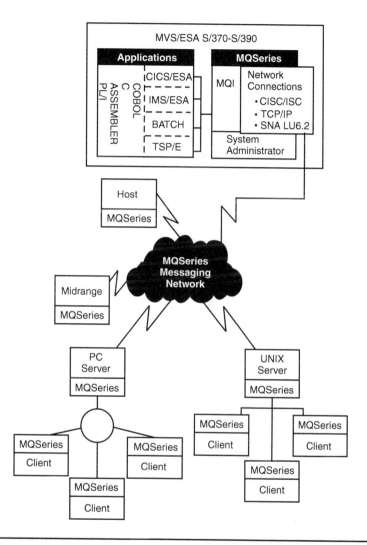

Figure 5.7. IBM's MQSeries simplifies the process of cross-platform communications.

of the underlying network protocol. This program allows developers to design and implement cross-platform links between applications faster than can be done using traditional communications programming techniques. MQSeries handles the communications protocols and recovery after failure, ensuring message delivery. Information can be passed between S/390 and z900-based, server-based, and PC-based applications. MQSeries is ideal for applications that experience long periods of disconnected activity or periods where service is intermittent. These include many existing transaction processing applications using IMS, CICS, and TSO. Bridges for these transaction types enable users on other systems to access mainframe applications without rewriting interfaces to those applications.

MQSeries supports both TCP/PI and SNA APPC communications. Platforms supported include OS/2, AIX, MVS/ESA, OS/390, z/OS, VSE/ESA, OS/400, Digital VMS VAX, Tandem Guardian, HP-UX, SunOS, UNIXWare, SCO UNIX, AT&T GIS UNIX, Sun Solaris, and Tandem Guardian Himalaya. Support is also provided for a Java-based interface to MQSeries. Typically, applications and application services are bound to a specific networking protocol. CPI-C applications are SNA networking; RPC or Sockets applications use TCP/IP; x.400 applications use Open System Interconnection (OSI); other applications use NetBIOS, Internet Packet eXchange (IPX), DECnet, or other protocols.

Network Services
Communications and networking are at the heart of the infrastructure for a distributed system. In earlier generations of computer systems, communication structure strongly influenced the application enabling services and subsystems. In today's distributed, client/server environment, higher-level services and resource managers must support multiple operating system platforms and a wide variety of networking environments. Although the resource managers need services that are useful to their own model, they cannot afford to be tied to specific networking protocols or data link protocols. Thus, today's systems reflect a greater separation of the communication protocols from the network services. This has led to the Network Services structure, found in IBM's Open blueprint, consisting of Common Transport Semantics, Transport Services, Subnetworking, and the Signaling and Control Plane.

Common Transport Semantics
Common Transport Semantics (CTS) insulates the higher-level services (Distributed, Application, and Application Enabling Services) from the underlying transport network. It does this by providing a common view of transport protocols that enables all higher-level services to be transport independent. That is, different transport network drivers can be plugged in under a common implementation of those services. Using

Common Transport Semantics also enables the integration of networks with different protocols through transport gateways, which compensate for differences in the underlying transport networks. This enables the interoperation of client workstations without regard to the LAN medium (token-ring or Ethernet, for example) or LAN transport protocol (IPX, NetBIOS, SNA, or TCP/IP, for example) being used on the workstation.

In the Open Blueprint, Common Transport Semantics is provided through the MultiProtocol Transport Networking (MPTN) architecture and implemented through IBM's family of *AnyNet* products. MPTN architecture is open and general, allowing the elimination of the forced networking protocol bindings between applications and the Transport Services. In other words, the application's APIs and their services can communicate over a protocol other than the one for which they were originally implemented. The applications must be matched pairs, however, both designed to communicate using the same communication protocol. For example, two APPC programs originally designed to communicate over SNA can now communicate over TCP/IP; two Sockets programs originally designed to communicate over TCP/IP can now communicate over SNA; but an APPC program cannot communicate with a Sockets program over either SNA or TCP/IP.

For S/390 environments, ACF/VTAM Version 3, Release 4.2 (and subsequent releases) offers a Multiprotocol Transport Feature called *AnyNet/MVS*, which allows the application to be separated from the network transport and allows a business to reduce the number of protocols that are managed to one or two. This feature was originally an optional priced feature, but it is now included as part of the eNetwork Communications Server offerings across several platforms, including OS/390. Using AnyNet/MVS, CICS/ESA, IMS/ESA TM, DB2, DRDA, or any MVS/ESA APPC, applications communicate with workstations in a TCP/IP network that has the APPC API. The APPC over TCP/IP can be host to workstation, workstation to workstation, or host to host. AnyNet/MVS also supports an interface for Berkeley Software Distribution (BSD) Sockets over SNA.

Estimated by IBM to be installed on more than 95% of its large servers around the world, support for eNetwork Communications Server for OS/390 (and the predecessor VTAM and TCP/IP products) enables communications with the large server. As a central component of IBM's parallel sysplex environment (discussed in Chapter 2), eNetwork Communications Server for OS/390 controls access to applications distributed across multiple processors, which may be located in geographically dispersed areas. It also uses the APPN/HPR technology (discussed later) to enable significantly improved dynamics and availability when accessing the S/390 using SNA technology. For the TCP/IP user, eNetwork Communications Server for OS/390 contains an advanced, high-performing, TCP/IP communications protocol offering developed specifically for the OS/390 environment. With the shipment of OS/390 Version 2, Release 5 in early 1998, eNetwork Communications Server for OS/390 became an integrated component of OS/390.

eNetwork Communications Server for OS/390 and VTAM Version 4, Release 2 or later for MVS/ESA, VM/ESA, and VSE/ESA provide seamless multilevel connectivity for peer-to-peer networking through full support of Advanced Peer-to-Peer Networking (APPN). High-Performance Routing (HPR) support is provided starting with VTAM Version 4, Release 3. This support provides advanced routing, increased network dynamics, enhanced connectivity, and improved performance. Two S/390 nodes can now interconnect without the need for coordinated networking definitions. In fact, within a parallel sysplex, through the facilities of Cross System Coupling Facility (XCF), communication is provided without the need for networking definitions.

Advanced Peer-to-Peer Networking (APPN) and High-Performance Routing provide an evolution from the hierarchical proprietary network architecture of traditional SNA to the more dynamic routing capabilities required by today's networks. APPN/HPR reduces or eliminates much of the network definition required by its predecessor. The HPR function enables controlled yet nondisruptive rerouting of SNA sessions in the event of a network failure. Network resources are defined only at the node at which they are located, and APPN/HPR distributes information about these resources throughout the network as needed. Switching to an APPN network can significantly reduce the cost of an SNA network by enabling the use of newer-generation, more efficient, and lower-cost networking products such as the 3746 Communications Controller (described later). The 3745 Communications Controller can also be used with APPN/HPR assisting in the migration to the newer technology. APPN/HPR technology also better enables the network for coexistence or exploitation of IP router-based networks by SNA applications through the use of IBM's Enterprise Extender technology.

Because APPN and HPR are open standards, available to the industry through the APPN Implementor's Workshop (AIW), any vendor implementing the protocol can participate as a peer with the network.

APPN/HPR products are available for all of the key IBM platforms, as well as from many OEM providers. IBM's Dependent LU Server and Dependent LU Requester provide full support for 3270-based applications over an APPN network.

Full APPN and HPR support as well as traditional subarea support are included with eNetwork Communications Server for OS/390 and are included within the base OS/390 offering. APPN support is also available for z/OS, VM/ESA, z/VM, and VSE/ESA operating systems. Advanced Peer-to-Peer Networking (APPN) and traditional SNA (subarea) networking are viable alternatives for most network environments. HPR support on the S/390 and zSeries also includes the exploitation of native Asynchronous Transfer Mode (ATM) networks directly from the S/390 through the Open Systems Adapter. When using HPR, the SNA Class of Service can be dynamically mapped to the ATM Quality of Service (QOS), enabling all SNA applications to exploit the real power of ATM networks. HPR also enables the use of a single-channel connection either between S/390 images or to channel-attached networking platforms to carry both SNA and TCP/IP network protocols simultaneously, using eNetwork Communication Server for OS/390 MultiPath Channel Plus (MPC+) connectivity, which is a part of the High-Performance Data Transport (HPDT) services within the communications support.

With the AnyNet/MVS function included, SNA applications execute over TCP/IP networks, enabling TCP/IP network users to access SNA applications such as APPC, printers, and emulators. With the inclusion of Enterprise Extender technology across the key IBM communication platforms, Enterprise Extender offers an alternative to AnyNet for SNA applications over an IP network. With AnyNet, TCP/IP Sockets applications could execute over SNA networks, enabling SNA end users on subarea and APPN/HPR networks to access Berkeley Software Distribution C language Sockets applications such as NFS, PING, and X-Windows, or even Lotus Notes. This support enables the addition of applications designed to run over different protocols without changing the applications or modifying hardware.

AnyNet/MVS supports the IBM Open Blueprint and S/390 UNIX Services (formerly called OpenEdition) objective of UNIX application support on S/390 platforms. This feature provides DCE RPC socket application support across APPN/HPR and SNA networks as well as support for integrated Sockets and converged Sockets. Integrated Sockets support enables Sockets applications to choose either AnyNet/MVS or TCP/IP as the network transport. Converged Sockets support enables those applications not only to choose between APPN/SNA or TCP/IP as the transport vehicle but also to dynamically and simultaneously choose to communicate across either APPN/SNA, TCP/IP, or both networks based on whether the host application has a session with an end point on one or the other networks. These enhancements provide UNIX application environments quick and easy access to the resources of the APPN/SNA network.

Transport Services

A variety of network protocols provide information transport over both wide area and local area networks. These include Systems Network Architecture/Advanced Peer-to-Peer Networking (SNA/APPN), described earlier, Transmission Control Protocol/Internet Protocol (TCP/IP), Open System Interconnection (OSI), NetBIOS, and Novell's Internet Packet eXchange (IPX). Each protocol supports interfaces used to access its services. Also included are various end-to-end network monitoring functions that protect data integrity and help to avoid congestion.

Subnetworking

Subnetworking provides a structure that allows networks to evolve to accommodate and exploit new high-speed transmission technologies without jeopardizing existing business application and network investments. It includes products that represent pieces of a larger network, connections to Local Area Networks (LANs), connections to Wide Area Networks (WANs), host channels, and other high-speed transmission services. Many of these products have been discussed earlier in this chapter and in other chapters of this book. Each type offers a unique set of configurability, connectivity, and performance options at varying cost levels. New technology in this area is introduced frequently, and existing technology evolves rapidly, including wireless communication facilities (key to mobile communication), very high-speed Synchronous Optical NETwork (SONET) technologies, and Asynchronous Transfer Mode (ATM) facilities based on high-speed frame relay or cell relay technology.

Asynchronous Transfer Mode (ATM) is a high-speed transmission service with a very high bandwidth (in the gigabit range). In its simplest form, ATM is a new and faster technology that accommodates all existing data communication protocols, including TCP/IP, APPN, and SNA. It will also support existing applications such as e-mail, distributed database, and distributed transaction processing. What makes it dramatically different and unique as an emerging technology is its support of multimedia. Multimedia is the blending together of computer data processing, audio/visual technology, and video display technology in an interactive environment. Evolving applications include enhanced workgroup (collaborative) computing, desktop conferencing, and video-on-demand. Each of these requires network access to shared or common real-time data. Characteristics of multimedia communications include

- Very large amounts of information

- High bandwidth and throughput requirements

- Multicast/broadcast applications

- Continuous streams of information

- Provision of time-sensitive QOS

- Tolerance of lost data

- Real-time (temporal) information

This communication differs from ordinary "fast" data communication in the last three listed characteristics. To ensure a continuous stream of information and to maintain its real-time value, communication service must be guaranteed from input device to output device. This affects every layer of the Open Blueprint. Awareness of the data stream, bandwidth and throughput, loss toleration, latency, and other technical factors must be understood by each component involved in the transmission. ATM is a subnetworking technology that address these requirements by

- Integrating audio, video, and data traffic.

- Separating control elements from data elements.

- Providing high-bandwidth point-to-point and point-to-multipoint connections.

- Providing bandwidth on demand.

- Scaling in speed and distance as needed.

- Managing transmission end to end and guaranteeing quality of service.

ATM nodes provide a fast and flexible packet-switching service using multiplexing for better bandwidth use. The packets within ATM are called "cells," each of which contains 48 data bytes preceded with a 5-byte header, for a total of 53 bytes. By using fixed-size cells, ATM is an excellent protocol for isochronous, or time-sensitive, data transport.

Signaling and Control Plane

Technologies such as video-on-demand, computer-based telephony, and conferencing require direct access to the function provided by the Subnetworking layer. The Signaling and Control Plane has been added to better support the merging worlds of data and telecommunications and to provide the access to the Subnetworking layer. It will provide functions such as call setup/teardown and controls for video or audio conferences.

Signaling, in a communication network, is the collection of procedures used to dynamically make, keep, and end connections that require information exchange between the network users and the switching nodes. The signaling functions define the appropriate sequence and format of messages that are exchanged across the network interface. In an ATM subnetwork environment, for example, a single multimedia application could simultaneously send and receive data using Transport Services such as TCP/IP and set up connections to send and receive video or audio via the Signaling and Control Plane.

The Signaling and Control Plane is based on the International Technical Union—Telecommunications Standardization Sector (ITU-T, formerly the CCITT) Integrated Services Digital Network (ISDN) control plane. It has been generalized, however, to include switch connection support for other network types and to provide the control for the low-level multiplexing of video, audio, and data. Because each different subnetwork has its own unique connection setup interface, the Open Blueprint Signaling and Control Plane is a superset of these various subnetwork connection protocols and subnetwork specific functions.

Systems Management

A key component of the Open Blueprint, Systems Management applies to all Open Blueprint services. Through industry standards, such as SNA management services, TCP/IP Simple Network Management Protocol (SNMP), and OSI Common Management Information Protocol (CMIP), all management disciplines are covered and multiprotocol and multivendor environments are supported. The Open Blueprint defines the framework for providing both centralized and distributed, enterprise-wide systems and network management, planning, coordination, and operations.

As we have seen, the Open Blueprint provides a framework for integrating LAN and WAN networks, for providing management services, and for enabling efficient link utilization, high availability, and predictable response time. The preceding discussion begins to illustrate the complexity of network communications and S/390 or the zSeries 900 are positioned to provide unique advantages to growing businesses especially with the exploitation of the new OSA-Express. Figure 5.8 graphically illustrates the relationship of a large S/390 or zSeries parallel sysplex environment to this networking services structure. The following sections provide more detail on specific elements of the network.

Communications Options

Today's businesses are placing an increasing emphasis on computer communications. This section provides an overview of some communications options used with the S/390 family and/or the zSeries 900. These include integrated communications adapters and standalone boxes that attach to I/O channels. Through these communications options, these series of servers attach to each other and to other types of servers. With the understanding of interfaces and protocols provided in Chapter 2, we are prepared to look at specific communications options available for S/390 and z900 servers. Although this chapter does not provide a comprehensive list of all communications options that are available, it does discuss representative options that fit many common business needs. Because configuration requirements and limitations govern which and how communications options can be used together in a single server system, IBM or an authorized dealer should be consulted when configuring systems. Open Systems Adapter 2 and now the new OSA-Express

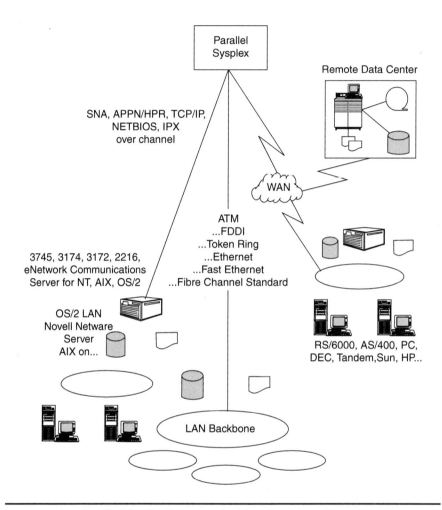

Figure 5.8.   Parallel Sysplex integrated with other computing systems.

feature for the z900 and available for the S/390 G5/G6 servers, described in Chapter 2, are the preferred LAN connectivity technology as HiperSockets are the preferred mode of connectivity between OS images and LPARS in a single z900.

I/O Channel Controllers and Connectivity
Attaching workstations (displays or printers) or interconnecting images within a server or between servers requires the proper communications

channels or links. In the recent past the primary intermediary, server or host to network end users or other devices, was a Communications Controller attached via an ESCON or FICON channel. Having it manage the workstation traffic on the channel freed the central processors in the server to concentrate on running user application programs, completing more work in a given amount of time. The IBM 3745 and 3746 Communication Controllers can continue to provide connectivity to LANs and WANs until a user migrates the data and the transaction workload for e-business to the zSeries 900 to take advantage of the new unique HiperSocket feature or to S/390 G5/G6 and/or z900 to exploit the OSA-E features. OSA-E and HiperSockets were discussed in Chapter 2, but it may be helpful to revisit these feature application highlights here because they relate to solving high-speed e-business requirements. First, we will describe the currently available Communications Controllers, IBM 3745 and 3746. Some companies may still have older controllers—3172, 3174, or a 2216 Multiaccess Connector—actively installed, and they will continue to serve users' needs where high performance is not a requirement.

3745 Communications Controller

As the complexity and size of a computer communications network grew, it often became necessary to handle many different communications protocols, different line types, and much more communications traffic. The 3745 Communications Controller, shown in Figure 5.9, works in concert with an S/390 processor unit and other communications equipment to implement and manage such networks. By handling the processing associated with the network (for example, polling the display stations), the 3745 allowed the S/390 server to focus its effort on running application programs.

A 3745 is a standalone, highly specialized computer system complete with multiple processors, main and disk storage, and its own programming called the Advanced Communications Function/Network Control Program (ACF/NCP). The family of 3745 Communications Controllers consists of four models currently available, Models 170, 170A, 31A, and 61A.

The newer A models add two features to the original 3745 models: a service processor with an extended maintenance and operator subsystem (MOSS-E) and 16 MB of storage, an optional feature available only on certain models. The primary purpose of the newer models is to support the addition of new capability in the 3746 Expansion Units

Figure 5.9. 3745 Communications Controller.

Models 900 and 950. A primary business benefit is realized, however, in the consolidation of front-end processing on fewer 3745s with the introduction of the A models. ESCON channels, extended communication lines, and extended token-ring adapter capacity contribute to the ability to consolidate. Consolidation simplifies the management of the network, reducing associated costs.

The local 3745 attaches to I/O channels of a server on one side and to modems, communications lines, terminals, local area networks, and other communications equipment on the other side. Remote 3745s can connect to the local (S/390 resident) 3745 over communication lines. Multiple 3745s (and their associated 3746 Expansion Units) can be attached in a daisy-chain fashion to create still larger networks. The 3745 Communications Controllers cooperate fully with the TME 10 NetView for OS/390 network management program, which helps monitor and troubleshoot large communications networks.

Figure 5.10 illustrates the use of 3745 Communications Controllers with ACF/NCP to build various communications networks. The 3745 attaches to a local processor through multiple I/O channels and natively attaches to ESCON channels using the 3746-900 expansion unit, improving the overall information flow between it and the S/390 processor unit. The 3745 models have one or two Central Control Units (CCUs), which are its command/control centers. Having two independently operating CCUs, each running its own copy of the ACF/NCP program, improves the performance and flexibility of the 3745. In a twin-CCU configuration, a 3745 can have both CCUs independently active, both active but one acting as a backup, or one active and the other in standby mode. The Model 610 in the figure is still usable but no longer available.

Other frame relay networks and Ethernet LANs connect to large processors through the 3745 Communications Controller, also providing access to host-resident application programs. Though not in the illustration, another S/390 server with a set of local users and a communications processor could attach to this 3745 over a high-speed communications line (for example, a T1 line operating at 1.5 Mbits/s), supporting information exchange between the two S/390 processors. This also allows users to pass through and log onto the partner S/390 server (assuming that they are authorized to do so).

The 3745 can also participate in an APPN/HPR network. While maintaining many of its traditional SNA operational characteristics, the 3745 cooperates with the S/390 to provide a single APPN network node appearance to the remainder of the APPN network. The 3745 in conjunction with the S/390 is known as a Composite Network Node (CNN). Although the 3745 was developed primarily as an SNA networking device, it does provide support for TCP/IP network attachment as well as SNA network attachment.

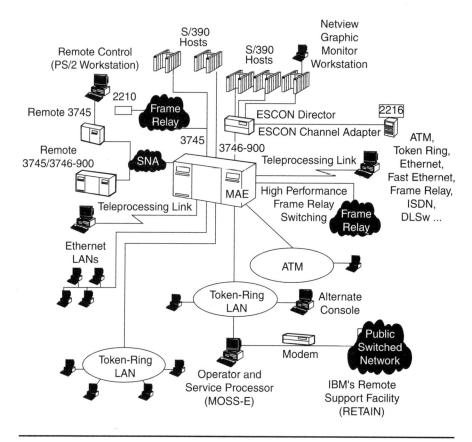

Figure 5.10. 3745 Communications Controllers with ACF/NCP support many types of network attachment.

3746 Model 900 Extension Unit

The 3746-900 increases the 3745's connectivity by offering the possibility of installing one or two adapter enclosures, as communication needs grow, and a choice of three adapter types to meet different communication needs. The basic enclosure houses up to four adapters; the expansion enclosure up to six. The adapter types can be mixed in both enclosures of the 3746.

A Communication Line Adapter (CLA) consists of a Communication Line Processor (CLP) and up to four line interface couplers. Microcode enhancements to the 3746 Model 900 allow each Communication Line Processor (CLP) to activate up to 1,000 physical units, up to 3,000 frame relay permanent virtual circuits, and any mix of up to 120 SDLC and frame relay lines. Communication line adapters of the 3746-900 provide a high-availability option when a pair of communication line processors can be operated in backup mode. In case of failure of a CLP, all its resources (lines and physical units) are automatically switched to the remaining CLP for reactivation via ACF/NCP.

An ESCON channel adapter consists of an ESCON channel processor and an ESCON channel coupler. The ESCON channel adapter attaches the 3745 to a host via fiber optics. Up to 16 host channels can be attached to one ESCON channel adapter using an ESCON Director (discussed in Chapter 3) for dynamic switching. Parallel transmission groups, using two or more ESCON and parallel channels, can be defined in the ACF/NCP software running in the 3745. Channel types can be mixed in a parallel transmission group. Compared with parallel channels, ESCON channels provide greater distance between the host and the 3745 (up to 3 km away but up to 43 km away using an ESCON Director), more configuration flexibility, increased performance, and decreased sensitivity to noise. EMIF function, which allows several Logical PARtitions (LPARs) to share the same ESCON channel, is supported. This permits a single ESCON channel adapter to communicate with several LPARs.

Token-ring adapters consist of a Token-Ring Processor (TRP), with the upgraded versions known as TRP-2 and TRP-3, and one or two token-ring couplers. These can greatly increase the number of token-ring LAN stations that can be attached to the controller. These support very high throughput, close to that of the token-ring medium speed. An advantage of using the 3746-900 for token-ring LAN support is that it frees up adapter positions in the 3745 base frame, which can be used for Ethernet and high-speed line adapters. The 3746-900 adapters can improve the overall performance compared to a standalone 3745. The adapters take over data link control functions from the 3745 ACF/NCP, reducing the workload of the NCP and allowing the 3745 CCU more time for other NCP activities. In a pure token-ring environment, for example, the mixed environment of a 3745 and 3746-900 sustains a maximum data throughput many times that of a standalone 3745. The 3746-900 communication line adapters increase the number of high-speed lines, supporting more users and improving traffic flow between users and applications. The adapter also provides frame relay switching without going through ACF/NCP in the attached 3745, allowing much higher switching throughputs and freeing the 3745 from that traffic load.

The connectivity and the performance of the IBM 3746 Models 900 and 950 adapters were significantly improved in 1996. The improvements allowed up to a 100% connectivity increase for the number of adjacent PUs or APPN/DLUR sessions per adapter, and up to 40% throughput improvement for APPN/Dependent LU traffic. The Communication Line Processor (CLP), Token-Ring Processor Type 2 (TRP2), and ESCON Processor Type 2 (ESCP2) all benefit from the improvement.

The Model 900 supports the APPN network node functions and NCP SNA/subarea or Advanced Peer-to-Peer Networking (APPN) composite network node functions. It uses existing adapters and shares those adapter resources with NCP-controlled traffic. As an APPN/HPR network node, the 3746 automatically registers the topology of the network and updates this topology whenever it changes. It uses this dynamic knowledge of the network to automatically locate any resource and compute possible routes within the network.

The IBM 3746 Model 900 was enhanced to offer the same routing functions as the Model 950 (described next) while retaining its more traditional role as an NCP-controlled communication interface, in pure SNA/subarea networks, or in APPN/HPR composite network nodes. The Model 900 can be field upgraded to support APPN/HPR function and also converted into a standalone 3746 Model 950. It thus offers a flexible and cost-effective evolution path from SNA/subarea to APPN/HPR while providing full support for TCP/IP networks.

3746 N-way Multinetwork Controller Model 950
The 3746 Model 950 offers a new platform for APPN/HPR network nodes and can also provide full, industry-compliant IP router functions. It can also support the additional roles of an SNA traffic router and act as a frame relay node. The 3746 Model 950 is a high-end solution that supports distributed multiprotocol networks, including all the functions of the Model 900, without the need for an attached IBM 3745 Communications Controller and NCP software.

The most important characteristic of an APPN network is its dynamic capability. It has no required hierarchy like that of traditional SNA networks. Nodes can connect and disconnect as needed, and session routes are determined according to the current state of the network. With HPR, failed session routes can be nondisruptively switched. Using the Dependent Logical Unit Requester (DLUR) function, the Model 950 can replace or consolidate one or more IBM 3720s, 3725s, or 3745s.

Routing is distributed in up to ten adapters (with the same three adapter type choices described under the Model 900) while a network node processor performs the directory, topology, and other control point services. The 3746 can also act as a peer APPN network node or IP router node in networks with other IBM networking products providing functions like those of the old IBM 2210 and 2216.

System management for both the Model 900 and the Model 950 uses an intelligent service processor and takes advantage of NetView (described in Chapter 6). The service processor runs the Maintenance and Operator SubSystem Extended (MOSS-E), loads the microcode, stores files containing configuration information, and provides access to the controller configuration and management tool that allows a user to configure and control the network nodes and their resources. The 3746 family of products also supports connecting to X.25, Integrated Service Digital Network (ISDN), and, through the use of the Multiaccess Enclosure, Asynchronous Transfer Mode (ATM) networks.

Open Systems Adapter—Express (OSA-Express)
The OSA-Express feature is available on the S/390 G5/G6 servers but was redesigned for the z900 supporting the new I/O infrastructure of the z900. These features combined with OS/390 and z/OS offer a system solution that maximizes throughput and minimizes host interrupts. The result is a better processor efficiency and much higher-speed connectivity.

As described in Chapter 2, OSA-Express on a z900 supports the Gigabit Ethernet (GbE) feature with a 66 MHz, 64-bit PCI bus that is capable of achieving line speeds of 1 Gbit/s, the first adapter in the industry capable of achieving this line speed, attached to a GbE LAN using the TCP/IP protocol. The OSA-Express (OSA-E) GbE adapter cards use an enhanced hardware platform that is connected to the Central Electronic Complex (CEC) on a z900 through a 333 MB/s STI to two specialized adapter cards. An example of a server system attachment is shown in Figure 5.11. The enhanced z900 infrastructure for Fast Ethernet and 155 ATM use the same common hardware as the FICON channel cards and the PCI-Cryptographic Coprocessor (PCI-CC) cards, providing ATM attachability to a 155 Mbit/s ATM device. OSA-Express ATM features have two physical ports for connection to an ATM Native network or an ATM network with LAN Emulation (LANE) for Ethernet to token-ring clients (Figure 5.12). The OSA-Express Fast EtherNET

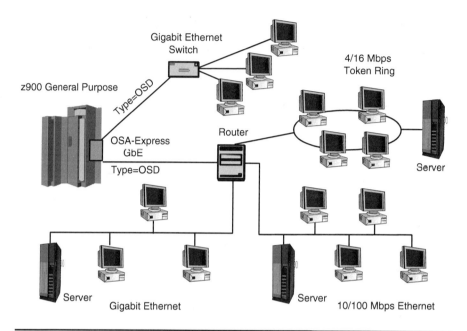

Figure 5.11. OSA-Express GbE attachments.

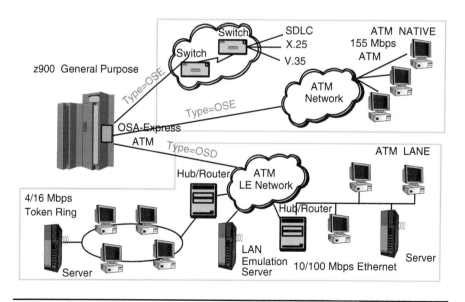

Figure 5.12. OSA-Express ATM attachments.

Adapter (OSA-E FENET) provides direct connection for the z900 through two ports to 100 Mbit/s or 10 Mbit/s Ethernet LANs running in either half- or full-duplex mode (Figure 5.13). OSA-E FENET supports autonegotiation with its attached Ethernet hub, router, or switch.

HiperSockets on the zSeries 900

New and unique with the z900 is the HiperSockets feature, which provides what is called a TCP/IP network in the system. HiperSockets allow for high-speed any-to-any connectivity among Linux and z/OS images, z/OS and z/OS images and Linux, and Linux images all within a single z900, supporting the high-performance data and transaction requirements of the new e-business. These OS images can be directly under an LPAR or under z/VM (second level).

eNetwork Communications Servers

IBM also offers a variety of communications servers for Windows NT, AIX, SCO, and OS/2. These software platforms provide connectivity either directly or indirectly to the S/390 for workstations by providing

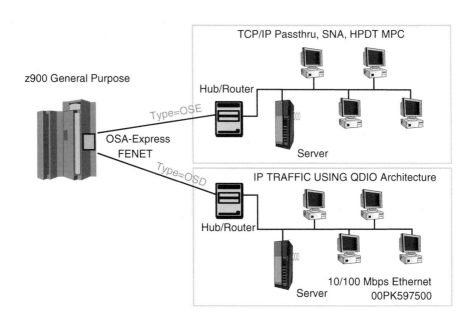

Figure 5.13. OSA-Express FENET attachments.

functions such as terminal pooling, which permits nonsimultaneous sharing of S/390 access by multiple users.

eNetwork Host on Demand

IBM eNetwork Host on Demand gives users secure access to enterprise data using Java through a Web browser. eNetwork Host on Demand enables TN3270, TN5250, VT52, VT100, and VT220 emulation and CICS Gateway for Java access in a single package, and can run in any Java-enabled environment. Because eNetwork Host on Demand is Java based, users in different operating environments—whether they are using network computers, traditional PCs, or advanced workstations get the same look and feel. This consistency reduces retraining costs when users change operating environments and reduces service costs because each user is on the same version of the code. Secure Sockets Layer (SSL) authentication and encryption is used to gain secure access across the Internet.

eNetwork Host on Demand also provides many features that enable users to customize the interface and to transfer data to other desktop applications. File transfer, cut and paste, and print screen are also included. A Java-based programming API for application development is available to customize desktops. National language versions are also available, including versions for double-byte character sets.

Modems

A modem is a device that converts (modulates) computer information into communications signals and transmits them over the telephone lines. At the receiving end, a modem converts (demodulates) the telephone line signals back into computer information. The term "modem" is a combination of the terms "*mo*dulate" and "*dem*odulate."

Why do computers need a modem for telephone line communications? Telephone lines are designed to carry electronically encoded voice messages from one point to another. A device (the telephone) is therefore necessary to convert the speaker's voice into electronic signals suitable for phone line transmission. Although the information in a computer is already electronically encoded, it is not in a form that can be transmitted over the phone lines. For this reason, a device is needed to convert the electronically encoded computer information into electronic signals suitable for telephone line transmission. A modem is like a telephone for a computer. Just as both parties need their own telephone to hold a conversation, both computers must have their own modems to transfer information over the phone lines.

Summary

While the changes to central host computing have positioned S/390 and zSeries servers, peripherals, and software to compete against smaller, easier-to-use open systems, changes to the S/390 communications environment position it as the server for enterprise-wide computing in the open business environment. Client systems today have access to massive amounts of information stored on these large servers. They also have access to the computing power of these servers through cooperative processing, enabled by the latest communication technologies. As those technologies continue to evolve, whether in modems, OSA-Express, OSA-2, HiperSockets, controllers, or networks, they are folded into the S/390 and zSeries, the environment for business in this new age of e-business.

6

Applying z900 and S/390 to Your Business

Although IBM may soon find itself as the sole provider of S/390 and zSeries Server technology, a growing number of vendors supply compatible peripherals, communications equipment, and software for both operations and business applications. Even IBM has three other server technology platforms to choose from, and some businesses will find that a combination of the zServer family and one of the other IBM family servers is the best decision for their environment. Their decision must take into account where they are coming from and where they want to go. Given the alternatives available to a business, acquisition decisions are seldom simple. Evaluations must take into account the complexity of the business's current IT operation, its ability to manage the current and future platform configuration, the services provided by vendors, the usability of hardware and software, and, of course, the cost in terms of price and IT skills. This chapter explores each of these topics.

As you have learned from reading this far, IBM is competing aggressively on every technology front with its S/390 and zSeries Server platform. In this chapter, you will discover that IBM is doing a great deal to ensure that its entire server system offering of the zSeries and S/390 hardware, software, and service is designed and priced to meet your needs for the next decade and beyond. This chapter is by no means a complete guide to introducing or upgrading your S/390 platform, but it provides you with some of the important aspects you will want to consider in developing your business plans.

Choosing Server Configurations

Selecting the proper S/390 and zSeries hardware and software components to fit your needs can be confusing. Traditionally, you must select the processor unit, central storage, expanded storage, disk storage, tape storage, I/O channel/bus configurations, peripherals, operating system(s), operating system extensions, and so on. Assistance in selecting specific zSeries and S/390 configurations is available from IBM or authorized remarketers.

Managing Complexity

Regardless of its present scope, effectively managing your business's server installation is a challenge. That challenge may come from the increasingly heterogeneous mixture of hardware, operating environments, data, and applications, or it may come from explosive growth in network and central site connectivity and information traffic. Further, it may come from increasing demands for continuous systems, network, and data availability, or it may come from new requirements to maintain security and data integrity for expanding sets of users and resources. Almost certainly, you will face some mix of these complex challenges with the added problem of containing, if not reducing, operating costs.

The emerging global e-business economy is intensely competitive. Businesses cannot permit technology and geography to impose limits on growth. Your business, as a part of this global economy, must be free to place data where it fits best, to choose applications based on business objectives, and to implement processes that can effectively manage costs. Users, whether within the company or outside, must have access to data wherever it is kept. That is, they must be able to connect to any existing platform in the company, or beyond, whenever necessary. Your operations staff must have access to tools and procedures that simplify the secure management of these diverse and dispersed resources and networks.

Pressures for access to enterprise data via the Internet are steadily increasing, and businesses have found that they can reduce support costs while improving customer satisfaction through Internet access. An example is seen in the package shipping business. Now all major players provide Internet access to package tracking information, which used to be available, if it was available at all, only through a telephone call to a service agent. The corporate tracking data now becomes available to all (access controls are required). Significant consideration must be given to asset protection while permitting access to the data center.

The remainder of this chapter discusses IBM products and solutions that enable your business to achieve these aims. We have discussed feature and function solutions content, old and new, for processors, peripherals, operating systems, and applications and communications in the preceding chapters. Following are some features and functions that we have not discussed at any length in earlier chapters. A business must choose the function that is applicable to its environment depending on what is currently installed in the business and the business's objectives.

TME 10 NetView

TME 10 Netview, or simply NetView, is a product for managing networks and systems through graphics display and automation 24 hours a day, 7 days a week. It provides these services for both System/370, S/390, and z900 applications. NetView provides a comprehensive set of network management tools and an integrated view of SNA and multiple vendor, heterogeneous networks. It provides the Resource Object Data Manager (RODM) as a single place for information about system resources and attributes with an organized data structure. With NetView, one operator can graphically monitor the network and system resources from a single display. Key features allow operators to quickly analyze and resolve network problems, automate many network and system operations tasks, support dynamic SNA and Logical Unit (LU) topology and status, and provide dynamic NetView operator definition in a Security Access Facility (SAF) environment.

NetView combines the functions of Tivoli's network management products, IBM NetView for MVS/ESA (NetView), IBM NetView MultiSystem Manager (MultiSystem Manager), and IBM Automated Operations Network/MVS (AON/MVS), into a single integrated product with enhanced functionality and performance improvements. By merging the management tools customers need into a single product, NetView provides comprehensive network computing management. NetView offers three packaging options to provide cost competitive and simplified ordering:

- **The Unattended Option.** This provides the automation and management capabilities needed to enable lights-out management from a centrally located staff; no end-user interface is supported.

- **The Procedural Option.** This includes the unattended option functions with expanded management and automation capabilities, including the Automated Operations Network component without the graphical interfaces and without topology management support.

- **The Graphical Enterprise Option.** This is a full-function TME 10 NetView, providing all the management and automation functions including the NetView Graphic Monitor Facility (NGMF), the MultiSystem Manager component, and the Automated Operations Network component.

Among the capabilities that NetView provides are

- Management of a heterogeneous network environment.

- Views of the network at a single glance.

- The ability to manage failed resources directly through exception views.

- Extensive drop-in network automation capabilities.

- Extendable support in both automation and topology discovery.

- Dynamic topology and status information to NetView's Resource Object Data Manager (RODM) in real time for both SNA and non-SNA resources.

- Improved usability, including enhanced NetView help and browse.

- Bidirectional management capability between S/390 or z900 and distributed environments when implemented with TME 10 Global Enterprise Manager

- Object-level security for NetView Graphic Monitor Facility (NGMF) views

The MultiSystem Manager product has been integrated into NetView. It provides the management support for a wide range of networks and can provide dynamic topology discovery and status of non-SNA resources. Its expanded function now supports all of the following types of networks:

- IBM OS/2 LAN Network Manager (LNM) networks

- Novell NetWare networks

- IBM LAN NetView Management Utilities (LMU) networks

- Internet Protocol (IP) networks using IBM NetView for AIX

- NetFinity networks

The MultiSystem Manager component also includes the Open Topology Interface. When used in conjunction with an Open Topology Agent, the Open Topology Manager provides the basis to manage any resource in your network. By using the Open Topology Interface, any agent provider can populate the Resource Object Data Manager (RODM) with resources, enabling graphical display of the status and topology of those resources.

Using the Open Topology Interface, along with the topology features for managing LAN physical media, NetWare servers and requesters, IP resources, LMU resources, NetFinity resources, and ATM resources, NetView provides the ability to manage the resources in the network from a single NetView Graphic Monitor Facility screen. Additional management capability is possible from an MVS (Multiple Virtual Storage) application using MultiSystem Manager Access, a REXX interface to the RODM.

The Automated Operations Network/MVS product has been integrated into TME 10 NetView for OS/390. The Automated Operations

Network (AON) component enables network automation without writing procedures, yet it can be easily extended to meet unique networking requirements. The AON component provides a single, integrated, automated solution for diverse environments, including SNA, TCP/IP, Subarea SNA, X.25, APPN/HPR, and token-ring LANs. It provides the drop-in automation policy and routines necessary to automate network recovery and increase availability of your network. The drop-in automation policy can be easily extended to suit your environment.

Access to the NetView console function is provided by a new Java client function in TME 10 NetView. The NetView console is no longer tied to a 3270 terminal or emulator session. You can now access the command facility, hardware monitor, session monitor, Central Site Control Facility (CSCF), and any NetView console function from any Java-capable workstation such as, OS/2, Windows, or the Network Computer.

System Automation

System Automation for MVS was delivered with Automated Operations Control/MVS Version 1, Release 4 (AOC/MVS); Enterprise Systems Connection (ESCON) Manager (ESCM) Version 1, Release 3; and Target System Control Facility (TSCF) Version 1, Release 2. The three previously separate products were integrated into a single product with additional function to present the operator with a more complete view of enterprise operations. System Automation, Release 2 includes the automation functions for IMS/ESA, CICS/ESA, and OPC/ESA.

As a single product, System Automation consolidates automated system operations, processor operations, and I/O configuration management operations. This is achieved through close integration with NetView and two of its major components, Resource Object Data Manager (RODM) and NetView Graphic Monitor Facility (NGMF). In addition to combining the individual products, significant new functions have been added to System Automation. These functions include additional automation and monitoring capability, new sysplex support functions, integration services, common installation and customization, and integrated publications. System Automation contains important capabilities to help in the management of sysplexes but is also valuable for a nonsysplex environment.

Automated Operations Network/MVS (AON/MVS)

AON/MVS is a NetView-based program, included with TME 10 Netview for OS/390 and z/OS, that provides network automation for the MVS environment. A common set of methodologies (an automation developer's tool kit) is included. AON/MVS provides a number of common routines (such as a generic failure routine, a generic recovery routine, and a generic activity recovery routine) for command input and policy generation, enabling consistency across processors and locations. This enables networked automation in a matter of days, rather than the many months previously devoted to automation-procedure coding.

OS/390 and z/OS Network File System (NFS)

Network File System was formerly known as Data Facility Storage Management Subsystem/MVS (DFSMS/MVS) but was enhanced and renamed with OS/390 Version 2, Release 6. It automates data placement, performance tuning, availability, space usage, and security. It provides for high-performance data transfer, enhances data availability, and simplifies disaster recovery. Its subcomponents include Data Facility Product (DFSMSdfp), the manager of I/O; Data Set Services (DFSMSdss), the manager of data movement; Hierarchical Storage Manager (DFSMShsm), the manager of inactive data; and Removable Media Manager (DFSMSrmm), the manager of removable media. DFSMS/MVS was initially integrated into OS/390 starting with OS/390 Version 2, Release 4. In Release 6 NFS was enhanced to support SUN NFS Versions 2 and 3, support for default filenames for PDS/PDSE was added, and performance for PORTMAP was improved.

Tivoli Storage Manager

The Tivoli Storage Manager, which is the new name for the ADSTAR Distributed Storage Manager (ADSM), provides support for managing data availability and for space management on heterogeneous platforms, both IBM and non-IBM. Tivoli Storage Manager provides a simple, interactive, graphical user interface that simplifies management of distributed systems anywhere in the enterprise. Automatic functions such as backup/restore, archive/retrieval, and space management can be performed without user intervention or participation. Users running on OS/2, NetWare, Windows, DOS, Macintosh, and major UNIX platforms such as SunOS Solaris, DEC Ultrix, SCO UNIX, and HP-UX are supported. Server environments supported include z/OS, z/VM, OS/390, MVS, VM, VSE, RS/6000, AS/400, HP-UX, Sun Solaris, and workstations. ADSM Version 3.1 provided enhancements in the areas of control management, performance, and usability.

- **Control.** As more Tivoli Storage Manager servers are deployed to support system growth, it becomes essential to consolidate the administration and operation of these systems. Tivoli Storage Manager provides centralized control facilities that provide central logging and extensive reporting capabilities using Structured Query Language (SQL) interfaces to access and report on the Tivoli Storage Manager database information. ADSM Version 3.1 adds an optional feature, Server-to-Server Communication, that offers workload balancing across multiple servers and sharing of key storage resources such as large robotic tape libraries and drives.

- **Performance.** With increasingly large databases and file systems, throughput is a critical concern. ADSM Version 3.1 addresses this in several ways. Enhanced buffering technologies improve throughput. A new method of storing files reduces overhead and substantially improves backup and archive performance for small files. A new algorithm for restores has been added that enhances restores and requires less memory resources. In addition, several new fault-tolerant features are provided, including resumption of an interrupted restore.

- **Usability.** ADSM has been completely redesigned and implemented with all new end-user and administrative interfaces based on extensive user-centered design studies. ADSM utilizes World Wide Web (WWW) technology to allow control and operation of ADSM from a Web browser anywhere within the intranet.

Workload management's main objective is to ensure that the work planned for execution is completed to the satisfaction of the user. Achieving this requires answers to questions such as, What are the workload objectives? What scheduling is required for this work? What is the best use of the server resources? What are the potential effects of additional workloads?

InfoPrint Manager

IBM InfoPrint Manager is a software solution for managing a digital printing facility. It combines print management technology with enhanced file management and spooling capabilities to address the requirements of a variety of print markets. Using InfoPrint Manager, diverse file types can be submitted to a single system to be managed, printed, stored, and reprinted, including PostScript, PCL, AFP, PDF, and TIFF. Combining superior enterprise and commercial print functions with built-in Advanced Function Presentation (AFP) and Adobe PostScript support, InfoPrint Manager delivers production-volume, single-copy integrity with PostScript quality. The system's scalability and ease of use also allow it to operate as a digital reprographic printer. The digital reprographics solution allows users to print, store, fax, and e-mail information. The InfoPrint Manager supports datastreams beyond IPDS, and with APF it provides the essential e-business capabilities of electronic document creation and manipulation as well as bidirectional communications.

Performance Management

Tools that enable monitoring and analysis of performance statistics for local or remote systems and balancing the use of fixed system resources by tuning system performance parameters are required. IBM's Resource Measurement Facility (RMF) is one of the most widely used performance-management tools in S/390 installations, providing support both for single systems and for sysplex environments. Through a single logon, RMF displays the entire system as a single image. In real time, your operator can evaluate the performance and usage level of each major system element. It provides quick problem detection to alert users of potential bottlenecks, allowing corrective action before problems become critical.

Enterprise Performance Data Manager/MVS (EPDM/MVS) works with RMF to analyze collected RMF data and to enable more sophisticated projections and presentations. The Service Level Reporter (SLR) also provides a graphical and tabular reporting tool for tracking system, network, CICS, and IMS performance, using data collected by RMF. SLR also tracks network usage and availability using data collected by NetView Performance Monitor (NPM).

NPM provides a base for centralized performance management for a wide variety of products and functions within the communications network. NPM makes it easy to collect, analyze, and display real-time network, session, LAN, and communications performance characteristics using a single graphical workstation. It can also generate alerts to NetView for automation and resolution. Other tools include CICSPlex System Manager (CPSM) and DB2/Performance Manager (DB2/PM).

Problem Management

Tools provided for problem management directly affect system availability, both by enabling quick response to alarms raised before they become problems and by ensuring rapid resolution to problems. A comprehensive set of reports helps operators identify network trouble spots, pinpoint chronic hardware and software failures, monitor vendor responsiveness, and track the status of all open trouble tickets. Automation scripts, which can be triggered by a problem report, help automate many of the tasks associated with a problem request. A change request (such as requesting distribution to a workstation of a software fix) could be initiated from a problem report.

The single point of control provided by OS/390 or z/OS and its system management products is a critical element of effective problem management. By combining this inherent integration with TME 10 NetView's Graphics Monitor Facility (NGMF), you can display and manipulate comprehensive problem records. SLR and EPDM (discussed earlier) work together to provide distributed and centralized problem reporting. This includes tracking AS/400 and RISC System/6000 system performance using data collected by agents on those systems. Other products, such as CICSPlex System Manager, also aid in problem management.

TME 10 Information/Management Version 1, Release 1 provides an integrated platform of tools, services, and interfaces to enforce and automate administrative processes and policies. In addition, TME 10 Information/Management provides a centralized repository capable of storing up to 400 gigabytes of data per database on an MVS/ESA, OS/390 or z/OS platform. It also integrates with many of Tivoli's TME 10 (Tivoli Management Environment) software products. TME 10 Information/ Management Version 1, Release 1 is the first version of Information/ Management that integrates with other Tivoli TME 10 distributed products. TME 10 Global Enterprise Manager (GEM) is instrumented so that it can be managed through TME 10 GEM's Application Policy Manager (APM). Through APM, the status of Information/Management can be viewed. In addition, administrative tasks such as stopping and starting the system can be performed. TME 10 Enterprise Console (TEC) can create, update, and delete information/management problem records based on events received by TEC. TME 10 Software Distribution can remotely install information/management client program interfaces on various target platforms across the enterprise.

Business and Security Management

Although protecting your business has always included securing and ensuring the integrity of your IT resources, the need for this today is greater and more complex. For over two decades, the MVS operating system has had system integrity features built into its design. These features ensure that system facilities that support security cannot be bypassed and users and applications cannot get into portions of the system for which they are not authorized. Integrity is a design point of the MVS system; features such as private address spaces support integrity by isolating programs from each other so that they cannot violate each other's storage. Since 1973, when support for MVS system integrity was formally announced, MVS has provided a highly secure operating environment. This history has continued as MVS has transformed into OS/390.

IBM provides a number of products and functions designed to help keep your resources safe from inadvertent and malicious damage while making user access to applications as convenient as possible and providing network and application security and simplifying network management. The Resource Access Control Facility (RACF) is IBM's strategic access control software for z/OS, OS/390, MVS, and VM operating systems. With z/OS or OS/390, the RACF is an integrated part of the SecureWay Security Server function, formerly called Security Server for OS/390. The SecureWay is an entirely optional feature. The SecureWay includes the RACF and the Open Software Foundation DCE level 1.2 Security Server. With this support, non-DCE applications can use DCE security through the Generic Security Services API, enabling single sign-on to multiple platforms, enterprise-wide security, and a reduction in the administration requirements.

The RACF provides general security services such as user identification, user authentication, and access authorization to resources. Other components or subsystems of the operating system and applications, as well as security administrators, can invoke its services. It allows administrators to update remote RACF databases with a single command, automating the synchronization of separate security databases. The RACF also allows synchronization of all RACF passwords for a given user on the same or remote systems. With RACF Secured Sign-on and a third-party authentication mechanism, users log on once and the system securely logs them onto applications as needed without sending passwords across the network in the clear.

RACF Support for Digital Certificates is also provided with OS/390 and z/OS. Currently, users can access information on an OS/390 or z/OS server via the Internet using the WebSphere Application Server. It uses a digital certificate, which contains information that uniquely identifies the user to enable authentication of the user. With OS/390 Version 2 releases after Release 4, including z/OS Version 1, Release 1, it is possible for the RACF to accept the digital certificate without requiring a RACF user ID and password for each client when Web pages are accessed. Digital certificate security technology can address the problems associated with user and server authentication that are encountered when designing Internet and Web server applications.

NetView Access Services (NVAS) provides eNetwork Communications Server for z/OS and OS/390 (formerly VTAM) SNA Application Session Management and Network Security. Using the IBM Personal Security Card and a cryptographic product, you can protect sensitive data from unauthorized users as it flows across networks. The Transaction Security System or the Integrated Cryptographic Service Feature (ICRF) can provide the needed cryptographic support. The ICRF supports the Data Encryption Standard (DES), the de facto international data encryption standard algorithm. ICRF components themselves are secured with tamper detection features. The ICRF is designed to accommodate high-volume bulk data transfer and transaction processing with complete security.

Operations Planning and Control/ESA (OPC/ESA)

Whether the business operates a single-image MVS/ESA system, a parallel sysplex environment, or a network of complex, multivendor systems, OPC/ESA helps plan, manage, and construct production workloads based on user-supplied descriptions. These plans provide the basis for your service-level agreements and provide a picture of the production workload at any point in time.

From a single point of control, OPC/ESA (see Figure 6.1) analyzes the status of production work and drives the processing of the workload according to the installation's business policies. It submits workload to all systems defined to be under OPC control, collects information about workload execution, and sends status changes to a central point of control. From a central panel, the OPC operator monitors and restarts all work under OPC's control. The operator need not be aware of the system on which a specific piece of workload is executing.

In addition to providing a single point of control, OPC/ESA monitors the production workload in real time, provides security interfaces, permits manual intervention in workload processing, reports current status, and provides information useful in defining service-level agreements. Also, alerts are passed to NetView in response to workload processing situations. These alerts trigger corrective actions. If system failures occur, OPC/ESA can restart processing on another system. In a parallel sysplex environment, a hot standby function automatically transfers control of the production workload to another system in the sysplex. OPC/ESA also offers agents for controlling workload on non-MVS platforms. OPC Tracker Agent features lets you plan, control, and manage the workload on networked non-MVS platforms from the OPC/ESA controlling system.

With Release 3, more precise workload management is achievable. You can now define a specific quantity of resources or alter the quantity, availability, or connection of workstations for different days or for varying time intervals. You can now connect an OPC/ESA special resource to an RODM object (see the earlier discussion of NetView), which lets you schedule operations with the knowledge of actual resource availability. Rule-based run cycles allow powerful and flexible run-time policies that are simple to define. You can define closed intervals handling noncyclic periods outside contiguous business cycles. Job logs can be retrieved on demand or automatically, and viewing of them is provided for all operations.

System Display and Search Facility (SDSF) for OS/390 and z/OS

SDSF provides a tool for simplifying management of a Job Entry Subsystem (JES2). It supports systems programmers, operations personnel, and end users. Whereas system programmers provide the setup and ac-

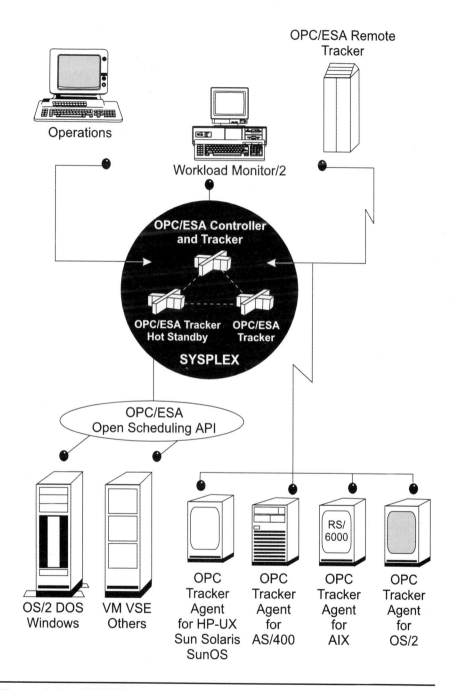

Figure 6.1. OPC/ESA.

cess-control parameters, operations personnel use SDSF to manage the system's resources (printer pools, for example). The fact that system programmers can authorize end users to assume some level of system management makes this product unusual. End-user access can range over a wide set of functions that include managing jobs and output.

Resource Measurement Facility (RMF) for OS/390 and z/OS

Performance management in large systems is key to optimizing the support and satisfaction of users, to reducing the cost of computing, to improving system availability, and, sometimes, to the acceptance of a particular application. RMF, unarguably the most pervasive performance management tool in S/390 installations, provides a wide variety of performance, capacity and long-term planning, and problem-determination tools for single systems and parallel sysplex configurations using the OS/390 and now z/OS operating system.

RMF presents hardcopy data generated through a postprocessor. It also provides two on-line interfaces (Monitor I and Monitor II), with unique layouts and different access characteristics. Although it offers a wide variety in reports and great flexibility, ease of use and productivity requirements are leading IBM to provide more integration among these three interfaces. A first step, to integrate Monitor II and Monitor III into the same on-line interface and to allow the creation of postprocessor reports from the same point of control, is in process. This integration, together with providing the capability to add installation applications to the same ISPF interface, allows users to exploit all RMF reporter functions simultaneously. It also provides a central access point for all performance management functions.

A postprocessor overview report allows an installation to generate output tailored to its own needs. A standard hardcopy output option and a new record layout, which allows results to be processed with additional tools or saved in a performance database, provide flexibility for your reports. These features enable you to reduce the data collected over a long period to only the most significant parameters and to use the results for further analysis.

The growth in popularity of spreadsheets, such as Lotus 1-2-3 and Microsoft Excel, prompted IBM to offer sophisticated tools for data manipulation, evaluation, and display. Some business installations already convert RMF reports to these spreadsheet formats. A new extension to the RMF Postprocessor, the RMF-to-Spreadsheet converter, allows all users to exploit these capabilities. It enables users to convert most RMF Postprocessor reports and many often-used Monitor II and Monitor III reports to Lotus 1-2-3 formats, which can also be read by Microsoft Excel and others.

With the introduction of RMF Version 5, RMF provides a comprehensive function to access all performance data in a sysplex environment and to report on this data from any point in the sysplex. Called the RMF Sysplex Data Server, this function provides access to all SMF and all RMF data in a sysplex. First, the RMF Postprocessor exploits the Sysplex Data Server to allow the user to create RMF reports for the whole sysplex immediately after the data is recorded. At the same time, RMF Monitor III provides on-line multisystem reporting in a sysplex environment.

Global Enterprise Management (GEM)

Tivoli Systems TME 10 Global Enterprise Management (GEM) integrates S/390 and zSeries management and distributed management, providing an end-to-end management solution for network computing enterprises. It unifies management processes by enabling the sharing of management data and the integration of key management functions such as problem management, security administration, event automation, storage, topology management, and operations. TME 10 GEM includes specific integration services for systems management functions. Three examples are problem management, security management, and event automation:

- **Problem Management Service.** This provides the capability of exchanging problem-record information between S/390 or zSeries and distributed environments. A distributed administrator can look at the S/390 Information/Management (Info) database and open a trouble ticket without knowing the S/390 or zSeries language associated with Info.

- **Security Service.** This allows cross-platform administrative tasks from any single point in the network-computing environment.

- **Event/Automation Service with Command Service.** Key events can be automated so that operators and administrators don't need to be involved in the day-to-day operations. The automation can be performed on the S/390, z900 or on a distributed system. TME 10 GEM allows you to pass events and commands back and forth between the two platforms.

The "Open Business" Policy—Protecting Your Assets

A closed business is not a productive business, but of all the reasons for being closed, perhaps the hardest to comprehend in today's computing environment is being closed due to lack of data. An open business can meet revenue or service targets. It lives to see another day. The closed business not only stands to lose that day's revenue but also to lose goodwill, new customers, and perhaps its future growth capability. Being "open" in today's business environment is more than a technology statement; it is a requirement for business continuity and growth.

To achieve those goals, business executives exert great effort to assure both continuous business operations and speedy recovery when a failure occurs. This has been a fundamental charter of processes and operations on both the production and the information systems sides of the business. Failures on either side can be disruptive, at a minimum, or disastrous to business survival in the extreme.

Most businesses that have an identifiable IT organization give that group a charter with the two goals of keeping the business open and of ensuring that people and processes operate efficiently (stay productive). Because these goals might not be prioritized (and perhaps because some goals are easier to achieve), IT organizations often focus on optimizing efficiency and productivity (and lowering costs). This is reflected in one IT manager's observation that "wasted free space on storage devices is the number one enemy of anyone in data processing. It is the number one enemy because it wastes more money than either you or I could imagine." It is not hard to imagine this manager's list of priorities addressing data compression, data compacting, space recovery procedures, and storage management processes.

The production side of the business (that is, the end-users' side), reflects a very different concern from that of saving IT dollars by saving space. Rather, it is saving business time and expense, improving business process flow, and enhancing performance and profitability. To achieve this, users require access to data when and where they need it.

An IT organization sensitive to these business needs will focus attention on functions such as data backup and restore, data integrity and security, data archiving, disaster recovery, and fault-tolerant and continuous operations. Although the IT and production strategies are both relevant to business needs, they will most likely be assigned different priorities. In most cases, a strategy for effective use of storage space will presuppose that a strategy for effectively preserving data already exists.

One area in which both business organizations must come to agreement is that of ensuring that information stored on the computer is seen only by those authorized to see it. Ensuring that policies for access control and for defining levels of confidentiality exist may be an IT responsibility. Ensuring that the policies are followed is everyone's responsibility.

Data Preservation Options

In looking at the total server system, every component (the processor, the network, and the software) provides a possible source of data loss. In this section, we focus only on those solutions specific to storage devices. Other hardware and software data preservation options (such as encryption, component redundancy, and functions for ensuring data integrity) have been discussed in earlier chapters. One crucial observation before we begin: It is important to understand what any solution does for a specific business; what it means for the business's applications, processes, and ultimately the bottom line! This area requires clear communication and close partnership between the process and the IT sides of the business. The relevant topics for quick exploration include

- Backup and restore.

- Archiving.

- Disaster recovery.

Backup and Restore
In a simple yet fundamental form, our daily lives are filled with backup processes. We use a large variety of techniques to back up our memories—memo pads, stick-ups on the refrigerator, and address and telephone notebooks. Mechanical procedures for "backup" include photocopies in our offices, flashlights in our cars, and perhaps, candles

in our homes to back up electrical systems in an emergency. Common characteristics of these and others is that they are required on short notice, are used for brief periods at a time, and create anxiety and frustration if they are absent when needed.

Backing up data for business use shares the same characteristics and adds more. Because data must be available quickly when it is needed and because it must be adaptable to frequent change, restoring data can be as critical as having a backup system. Because not all business data carries the same level of importance, being able to differentiate the data and provide the appropriate level of backup is also important. If preserving the state of data both before and after changes occur is important, techniques more sophisticated than simple backup may be needed. In assessing the level of data backup you need, these questions should be explored:

- What is the nature of the data? "Production" data (in the broadest sense, data that moves the daily business forward) may require more stringent procedures than "temporary work file" data.

- How frequently should data be backed up (every 10 minutes, hour, or day, for example)? Should backup occur each time the data is changed?

- How long should backup data be retained? Is backup storage space recycled every few hours (each shift, for example), at the end of each day, every few days? Is data kept accessible on-line or moved off-line to remote storage?

This last area introduces questions about the long-term value of data. Each business needs a policy that defines the types of data it must keep secured and the specific periods for data retention.

Archiving

The concept of "storage hierarchy" sounds technical and complicated. In fact, our homes are good examples of this concept. We use closets, filing cabinets, desks, and dressers to store frequently used items that we are not overly concerned with losing. Quick and convenient access is the key to this storage location. For seasonal or less often used items (and again with limited or easily replaceable value), we often look to the garage, the basement, or the attic for storage.

For infrequently used valuables with high legal or personal value, however, we find alternative storage solutions. Some build vaults securely into their homes. Many move items off-site to a safe-deposit box; some items, such as wills, are duplicated and left with lawyers or perhaps with family members. Because not even these areas are the most secure and often are not insured against personal loss, irreplaceable items are placed in vaults designed for maximum security where they *are* insured against loss. These can be leased from banks and other companies. Technology enables the same hierarchical approach to data storage.

Archiving refers to procedures for securing over a long period data that is infrequently needed yet valuable. By implication, this data will be stored in a place where lack of access does not interfere with day-to-day operations, that provides levels of security appropriate to the nature of the data, and that supports a medium that is inexpensive to maintain. This drives a key objective of archiving—to free space on faster (more expensive) storage media for data that is needed for current operations. Other forces influencing the need to archive are legal requirements (to preserve corporate, personnel, and contractual data of historical value) and "prudent" needs (preserving corporate history, providing a base for data analysis, and creating a record of critical business transactions, for example). The amount and type of archiving is driven by an acceptable ratio of storage cost to maximum time required to retrieve the data.

The ability to retrieve this data influences where it is kept, the format in which it is kept, the storage medium, and the volume of data to retain. Companies are known to store data in its original form in warehouses, in underground mines, and in locked vaults. Improvements in technology now enable us to store much of this data in electronic form, reducing both the volume and expense of storage while significantly improving the retrieval process.

Disaster Recovery

"Disaster" is a powerful word. It creates images in our minds of shocking, unanticipated emergencies of the highest order. The frequency with which we have witnessed these in recent years does not change the impact each has when it occurs. Disasters can result from careless or accidental actions within the business and sometimes from deliberate efforts to vandalize or even sabotage operations. Most often, however, true disasters occur from uncontrollable events external to the business—some of natural causes (Hurricane Andrew, for example) and others of human origin (the World Trade Center bombing, for example). In each of these instances, the health, and sometimes the survival, of a business depends on the speed with which recovery can be implemented.

There are a number of firms, IBM's Global Services being one of the industry leaders in this arena, that benefit by meeting businesses' needs within the recovery services market, estimated to be in the $1 billion range annually. Some propose a "mobile recovery service" that will travel to the disaster site and set up remote communications, or even better a remote server as part of a parallel sysplex as described in Chapter 2; others will offer office space and equipment at an alternative location reserved specifically for this purpose. Fees for providing this space can range to well over $100,000 per year, just to retain vendor services, and are supplemented with a daily cost that can run into thousands of additional dollars to use the facility during the disaster itself.

Weighed against the growth or survival of the business, this can be a small investment. Industry studies show that banking firms that lose data for as little as 2 days, commercial firms that lose business for 3.5 days, and industrial firms and insurance firms that lose data for 5 to 5.5 days suffer a 25% rate of immediate bankruptcy. Forty percent were bankrupt within 2 years, and almost all were bankrupt after 5 years.

As in personal life, insurance that is affordable by some is not necessarily affordable by all. Many businesses operate daily on the assumption (conscious or not) that a disaster will not strike them. This is often driven by a shortsighted cost–benefit analysis that defines tactical production as more crucial than strategic survival.

The client/server wave placed additional pressures on the problems of retaining backups as key business data moved to remote platforms, often located on a user's desktop. Distributing data adds extreme complexity to the data management problem. Luckily schemes such as the emerging network computer and Web-based data retrieval methods enable the movement of data back to the central computer system, simplifying the data management process.

Ensuring Real-Time Data Recovery

Many of the products discussed earlier in this chapter as well as hardware and software products discussed in earlier chapters contribute both to increasing reliability (failure prevention) and to rapid data and system recovery from failures. Two functions from IBM contribute specifically to disaster recovery scenarios.

Peer-to-Peer Remote Copy (PPRC) is a hardware solution designed for those sites that must have data at the recovery system fully current with the application system and can accept some performance impact on the write operations of applications. With PPRC, no disk data is lost between the last update at the application system and the recovery at the recovery system. A PPRC data copy to the recovery system is synchronous with the primary volume's write operations. PPRC does not consider the application system disk write complete until the recovery system write is complete. Each application system write to the recovery system causes an increase in the response time of the application system. The maximum recommended distance between the application system and the recovery system is 43 km (27 miles).

In real disasters, it is rare that every component of the system fails at once. Data volumes shut down over a period of seconds or even minutes. The challenge during this period is to maintain data integrity by identifying which secondary volumes are in sync with the primaries and which are not. PPRC addresses this problem via two methods. With one option, volumes marked "critical" cannot be updated unless the secondary volume is updated. The second option applies a system Error Recovery Procedure (ERP) that logs error information and copy volume status information before sending completion status back to the processor. If necessary, a copy of this log can be configured at the remote site, providing continuous information as to which volumes are in sync and which are not.

eXtended Remote Copy (XRC) also maintains duplicate copies at locations separated by ESCON distances (up to 43 km) but does so asynchronously (time lapses between updates at the two sites). When teamed with channel extender systems, XRC supports duplicate copies at locations anywhere in the world connected by telecommunications lines. This facility provides to businesses the highest level of application performance at their primary site while supporting a secondary site at a great distance and accepting data at the remote site a few seconds to a few minutes behind the data at the primary site.

Using IBM's Data Facility Storage Management Subsystem (DFSMS/MVS), discussed earlier in this chapter, XRC provides high data integrity, a quality essential for full recovery from a disaster. DFSMS/MVS includes a System Data Mover (SDM) function that scans cache in all of the control units associated with a session. When a server application updates data on the local volumes on the IBM 3990

Controller, a copy of that data is kept in the cache. When scanning the cache, the SDM writes the updated data to the control units at the recovery site. To ensure data integrity, the SDM makes updates at the remote site appear in exactly the same order as data at the primary site, avoiding the possibility of data corruption.

Because XRC is a fully asynchronous solution, in which the second process runs independently of the first, it avoids write operation bottlenecks created when traffic is heavy. Also, during the recovery process following a disaster, XRC identifies any data volumes at the secondary site that are out of sync with their corresponding volumes at the primary site. Another benefit of the XRC function is its ability to support applications while data is migrated from old to new storage products in the background, without causing a major disruption to system operations. Only a brief interrupt is required to redirect applications to the new device address.

Access Control Options

Multiple vendor environments, expanding network connectivity, and public networks, such as the Internet, significantly increase accessibility to your business server assets, particularly to your business data. Unfortunately, unauthorized access to your systems is a bigger threat today than ever before. In the era of the new e-business, controlling access to your server is only a beginning. Access to PCs, LANs, workstations, and global networks also must be controlled.

From concept to production, your business is increasingly on-line. Your networks link you to information sources and to production facilities. You must be able to authenticate users to your system, and the system must be able to authenticate its users. Users accessing systems must know that the servers are real and not impostors, and the data and programs they access must be demonstrably reliable and unmodified by unauthorized parties. Competitive advantage in the new era will go to the business that delivers the most cost-effective service while ensuring secure transactions and controlled access to private information.

Challenges to data access security have become more sophisticated in today's business environment. Today's users are more sophisticated, and whether you planned for it or not, your business depends on information sourced from multiple vendors. Threats to the privacy, integrity, and availability of your information systems may come from both internal and external sources and in both centralized and distributed environments. It is quite likely that terrorism will focus on threats of information manipulation, outright destruction, theft and misuse, or alteration and falsification. A good example of that occurred after the bombing of the Chinese embassy in Baghdad or the recent in-air collision of a U.S. surveillance aircraft and a Chinese fighter jet well off the coast of China. The hostility against the United States stirred up in China energized scores of Chinese citizen hackers to attempt to penetrate U.S. military, government, and business servers. That prompted a response from many U.S. citizen hackers on Chinese systems. With the proliferation of the Internet and the access it brings, we should expect unwanted attempts to access by hackers will continue to grow.

Data access control is both a technical and a management challenge. Finding the right degree of protection without imposing constraints that inhibit business growth requires carefully examining your business needs and developing an appropriate security policy. Not all information assets are equally valuable or equally exposed. Degrees of sensitivity can be measured by the effect that the loss, exposure, or modification (corruption) of the data will have on your business. Data requiring the most stringent levels of access control are those that have an immediate negative effect on your business if they are viewed or changed by an unauthorized means, data that cause legal problems for your company if viewed or changed by an unauthorized means, and data that require their origin or authenticity to be verified. Without an effective security policy and a strategy that addresses these data types, your business might be at more risk than you realize.

Securing Data in a Distributed Environment
In a distributed environment, this threat is amplified, because a single unauthorized event can have far-reaching implications. Possible threats in this environment include

- Viruses that infest unsuspecting programs and self-propagate in a difficult-to-detect manner.

- Programs (worms) that replicate themselves to destroy data or to take control of system resources.

- Masqueraders that take control of a workstation by faking the identification of a trusted user or network server. These can propagate in an environment in which trust is based on identification rather than authentication.

- A damaging piece of code (Trojan horse) that executes inside a useful program when the program executes.

- Lapses in a security system (back doors) that allow "hackers" to alter security programs, enabling unauthorized access to programs and data.

- Inconsistent security controls that allow the same data to exist on multiple systems with different levels of access control, allowing access by individuals not authorized for those resources.

Typical distributed systems span multiple domains, each requiring security considerations. The hardware domain covers the physical components of a single system; the operating system domain covers resources on that single standalone system; the network domain covers the network against unauthorized use through features such as link encryption (to protect cabling against passive wiretapping) and gateway authentication (to protect against introduction of unauthorized packets of information). The network operating system domain protects distributed resources, including caches on various machines as well as server disks. The application domain protects resources under the direct control of an application.

Because few distributed systems are homogeneous across all of these domains, the security procedures of each domain are likely to have been designed independently, creating increased opportunity for security breaches. This can result in attacks at the seams between the security domains, misuse of multiple identities and passwords required by the different procedures, and inconsistent audit logs with different formats and interfaces.

To meet the challenges of these potential security exposures, an adequate business solution must address a range of concerns. Users must have access to all authorized resources through a sign-on that authenticates them once to all relevant domains. When users authenticate themselves to the network, encrypted passwords, one-time passwords, or "pass tokens" will reduce the risks incurred with passwords in clear text. Laptop, or mobile user, security requires dealing with physical issues that result from location in public places with portable data and applications.

Security policies must address the registration and enrollment of users and the management of programs, data, and security information, such as encryption/decryption keys. With the advent of public networks, especially connection to the Internet, appropriate protection for network gateways is required before your business can take advantage of electronic commerce. These networks, as well as diskettes and other media introduced from outside the business and by unscrupulous employees, can be the source of viruses, worms, and other self-propagating destructive code. Protecting assets from these agents is essential. Finally, ensuring that your system can prevent circumvention of security, providing a single auditing function for monitoring and reporting security events, and securing the ends of your network as well as all points in between completes your total security solution.

Building Your Total Security Solution
IBM's S/390 security strategy provides end-to-end security for applications and information across multiple hardware and software platforms and networks. It has evolved from a centralized view of enterprise computing to a distributed model of enterprise-wide computing. Security services are provided for each local strategic system platform, allowing your business the flexibility of multiple operating environments. OSF/DCE provides a strategic architecture for securing open distributed environments. DCE provides security services that support distributed applications and enable interoperability and portability across diverse platforms.

A variety of products contribute to the S/390 and zSeries security solution. For example, the Integrated Cryptographic Feature (ICRF) and the Cryptographic Coprocessor feature (PCICC) for encrypting transmitted data were discussed in Chapter 2. The OS/390 and z/OS Firewall Technologies support function, introduced in OS/390 Version 2, Release 4, provides basic firewall capabilities, thereby reducing or eliminating the need for non-OS/390 or z/OS platform firewalls for many OS/390 and z/OS users. Support for the OS/390 or z/OS Security Server includes FTP proxy support, SOCKS daemon support, logging, and configuration/administration. Communications enhancements to the eNetwork Communications Server for OS/390 and z/OS provide IP packet filtering, IP security (tunnels), and network address translation. Firewall Technologies are integrated into OS/390 Version 2, Release 5. Firewall Technologies support requires that a customer have the eNetwork Communications Server for OS/390 and z/OS (TCP/IP) and that the OS/390 or z/OS Security Server be enabled.

The Resource Access Control Facility (RACF), discussed previously in this chapter as a part of the OS/390 and z/OS Security Server, provides identification, authentication, access control, and audit functions for the OS/390 and z/OS system environment. It uses hardware features and software facilities, including the parallel sysplex coupling facility. In combination with other products supporting the IBM security architecture, RACF provides every business using z/OS, z/VM, OS/390, MVS, and VM/ESA operating systems a secure framework for future growth. Since 1990, RACF with other products that compose the Trusted Computing Base have been given the Department of Defense B-1 level of security.

The RACF supports several basic security functions. The RACF user ID allows the RACF to identify users requesting access to the system. The RACF also supports validation using digital certificates. The user password or equivalent authenticates that user ID. Once the user has been authenticated, the RACF and the system resource managers control the interaction between the user and the objects for which access is being attempted. These objects include data sets, minidisks, terminals, commands, tape volumes, and user-defined objects. The RACF allows for centralized or decentralized administra tion, using ISPF panels or Time Sharing Option (TSO) commands. An installation can write its own exit routines to deal with unique security needs.

The RACF supports flexible auditing of access attempts and modifications to security controls. Audit reports are created through either the Data Security Monitor (DSMON) or the Data Base Unload (DBU) utility program. The DSMON allows an authorized user to produce reports on the status of an MVS security environment. The DBU allows the RACF database to be unloaded into a relational database manager for standard or ad hoc queries. To audit access attempts to secured objects, you can use the RACF Report Writer or the RACF System Management Facility (SMF) Data Unload utility program. The Report Writer allows you to build reports on selected SMF records. The SMF Data Unload utility allows you to reformat the audit data for loading into and use in a relational database manager or report generation tool.

When the RACF Sysplex Communication option is enabled, the RACF provides a single image of security across the sysplex. The RACF uses the Cross-System Coupling Facility (XCF) to transmit selected administrative commands to peer RACF systems. These commands can be entered from a single system in a sysplex to take effect on all systems in the sysplex. Also, RACF sysplex data sharing uses coupling facility services to cache data in order to take advantage of high-performance data sharing. With Secured Sign-on, the RACF supports the passticket, an alternative to the RACF password. Secured Sign-on enables the moving of end-user authentication from within the RACF to another authentication service.

The RACF Remote Sharing Facility (RRSF) allows you to maintain and administer RACF databases that are distributed throughout an enterprise. Enterprise protection information, such as password updates and security codes, can be sent to multiple sites from one designated mainframe. With these capabilities, the RACF enables you to establish user ID associations on the same node or on remote nodes and to automatically synchronize passwords between these associated users. RACF support also makes it possible for you to set up hot-backup sites that let one RACF database take over for another in the event of a failure.

Evaluating Vendor Offerings

As dramatic as have been the added functions and improved technologies in the field of computing, the changes in vendor support, services, and pricing are equally dramatic. With increasing numbers of vendors providing basic technologies and system components, computing hardware is increasingly priced as a commodity. To achieve profit and growth targets, many vendors are moving into the service and support arena, creating increased competition and reduced prices. As vendor consortia focus on standards, more vendors are moving into the software application and operating system development field. The movement toward open systems has both stimulated and benefited from this activity.

The net result for your business is an opportunity for gain both from the increased function and technology and from the improvements in vendor offerings. Both sides of your business's cost–benefit analysis must be reassessed to reflect these new opportunities. In prior chapters, we explored technology changes and the benefits resulting from them. In this section, we explore the cost implications and some of the changes made by IBM to provide your business with significant cost improvement.

Cost Justification

All businesses are the same in one respect: Their desire for cost reduction is never ending. Most businesses exist to make profit. Although academic, government, and not-for-profit organizations do not have the profit motive, they still must decide how to invest their limited funds to best meet their objectives. In either case, the only reason for a business to buy a computer is to make the business more efficient. To achieve that objective, the computer system must be cost-justified, usually through a cost–benefit analysis.

Evidence that businesses are taking seriously the need for cost-justified enhancements and that they are benefiting from technology enhancements is found in a mid-1990s industry study (conducted by Nolan, Norton & Co., Boston, MA). In comparing data center spending in 1992–1993 with spending in 1993–1994, survey results (based on 150 data centers at Fortune 1,000 companies) show that total spending was down by 6.3% in 1992–1993 but down by 25% in 1993–1994. In 1994, costs for processors were down by 27%, for disk storage down by 36%, and for tape storage down by 32%, and costs for system software were up by 6%. In this same period, workload increased by 9%. The same trends have continued as we move further into the new Millennium.

The price you pay to a vendor is identified early in the project, but many analyses fail to consider other costs of owning a system. Some costs are a logical corollary to the system purchase. These include costs to modify facilities to accommodate the hardware and communications costs for interconnecting remote workstations or other remote systems. Facilities costs might include running cables between workstations in a campus environment, installing or removing raised floors, modifying power services, and enhancing air conditioning. The cost of operating the system installation after you buy it should also be considered over multiple years.

Costs to consider beyond the price for hardware and software are less technology based and are more a reflection of your business strategy and objectives. Following is a short list of such costs.

- *Hardware and software maintenance* is usually a monthly or annual fee that provides an extended warranty for the hardware or for corrections and updates to software programs. For hardware, there are various alternatives for ensuring the servicing company will come out and effect repairs at no charge if your system breaks down. If you choose not to place your system on a maintenance contract, you typically will pay an hourly fee and parts cost if your system breaks down. Because this parts/labor billing can be extremely expensive, most businesses choose the maintenance contract.

- *Installation services* provide support during the initial installation phase of the new hardware or software to assure that the process runs smoothly.

- *Technical support* ensures the vendor's availability to answer your questions and to resolve any technical problems in either the hardware or software. Some companies charge fees for technical support, but others include some level of support in the price of their products at least for a period of time. The level of support ranges from providing a telephone number to having permanently assigned personnel from the hardware or software company on your premises.

- *Education/training* ensures that the system users become productive and efficient as rapidly as possible. With the frequency of changes in hardware and software, many will need training multiple times. The systems operator(s) will need to understand how to manage the day-to-day operations of the installation; system programmers must understand the hardware and software to ensure an optimum operating environment; the users will have to understand the application programs; and your own development programmer(s) may need to learn new languages and procedures for writing custom application programs for your business.

On the benefits side of the analysis, your system solution is being purchased to solve identified problems and to address known needs. Although it is fairly easy to identify and quantify the costs associated with a system, identifying the benefits is often more difficult. This does not mean that benefits are any less real than costs. It simply means that they require more work to uncover. Some common benefits associated with the use of systems include

- *Improved business cycles* (such as the cycle of buying goods and equipment, taking customer orders for goods or services, making delivery to the customer, and billing the customer), which result in real dollar savings from basic improvements in collecting accounts receivable more quickly or taking better advantage of accounts payable discount terms.

- *Inventory reduction* through proper application of a computer, which can reduce the level of inventory that must be kept on hand, reducing carrying costs related to warehouse space, insurance, taxes, and interest expense.

- *Improved productivity and efficiency*, which allow an organization to get the same amount of work done more quickly or with fewer people. Excess workers can be redirected to perform other tasks, or it may even be possible to allow workforce reductions over time through natural attrition.

- *Improved quality*, which provides information to personnel faster or with better preparation, in turn enabling organizations to improve the quality of their services and products. For example, in manufacturing environments, computers can be applied to everything from design simulations to statistical quality control.

- *Improved customer service* that provides more rapid response or improved accuracy to customer orders, questions, and special requests (for price quotations or for accurately quoting and meeting delivery dates, for example), or perhaps provides direct access to your computer system, which is a significant factor in an organization's ability to attract and retain customers.

- *Competitive advantage*, which is improved through the flexibility provided by a computer system's ability to respond more quickly to changing market demands. Change is inevitable; it represents opportunity for the flexible, doom for the inflexible.

This short list of general benefits is an overview of the areas in which business systems can make a difference. Each organization will be able to add to this list, based on its current situation and objectives.

Identifying benefits, however, is only the first step. The next step is to quantify the benefits in dollars and cents where possible. Unlike the price of hardware and software parts, which you can often look up in a catalog, quantifying benefits is difficult and subjective. They must be calculated based on expected results. However, quantifying benefits will help you focus first on the areas with the largest payoff, and it will also help you compare these investments with any other capital projects you're considering.

For example, if you feel that inventory can be reduced by 10% by installing an inventory management application program, the annual benefit is derived by multiplying 10% of your inventory value times the carrying costs. This is a fairly straightforward example, but other areas are more difficult to quantify accurately. For example, if an engineer's productivity is increased by 15%, you might multiply her annual salary and benefit costs by 15% to yield the annual savings. Since you still must pay the engineer full salary, some would argue that there is no savings. As a counter to this, consider that because the engineer can now spend 15% of paid time developing a product to enter a new market, the actual benefit to the business might be much higher than 15% of the salary. You must decide what a benefit is worth to your organization.

Two other benefits that are typically difficult to quantify when tallying savings are increased sales (resulting from improved customer service) and lower employee turnover (resulting from improved working conditions and pride). The fact that these benefits (and others like them) are difficult to quantify does not make them any less valuable, but it does make it easy for you to overlook them.

After you have quantified the costs and benefits, you can begin to evaluate the proposed computer project against other capital projects. Two often-used rulers with which to compare proposed capital expenditures are payback period and net present value. The payback period is the calculation of the time to recover the investment cost from in-flowing benefits. Net present value is the calculation of the cash flows discounted for inflation based on the cost of money and risk associated with the project.

This type of financial analysis is valuable, but do not overlook other aspects of the capital project such as its strategic value, its effect on customer-perceived quality and professionalism, and so on. Classical accounting techniques are easy to defend, but they may present only a limited picture of a complex, dynamic situation.

Hardware—Lease or Buy?

Just when you think you are through analyzing all the software and hardware alternatives, you face a whole new set of questions concerning the acquisition method you will use. The most obvious alternative is simply to pay cash for the new server system (make an outright purchase). An outright purchase is usually the least expensive way to make an acquisition, but it has a direct and usually substantial impact on your business cash flow and capital position.

The next acquisition alternative is to finance the purchase price over a period of time, just as you would finance a new home. In this case, you simply make a down payment, of 10% for example, and take out a loan for the balance. The loan and interest are repaid through monthly payments, typically over a period of from two to five years. Since you must pay back the interest on the loan, this is a more expensive alternative than a cash purchase, but it can reduce cash flow requirements. In either case, the title of the system passes to your business, as do any tax benefits such as depreciation. The purchaser also has the ability to sell the system, recovering its residual value, a value usually determined by market and technology forces.

Another acquisition alternative is the term lease. In this alternative, the lessor (the owner or manufacturer) grants use of a system to the lessee (the using company), who agrees to make lease payments for a specified period of time or term. Lease terms can be any length but typically run from two to five years. If the lessee wishes to terminate the lease before the end of the term, a termination fee is usually assessed. An advantage offered by the term lease alternative is that it conserves capital and your business lines of credit, allowing the business to use this capital or credit to finance other investments. A consideration with this method, however, must be the expected life cycle for the technology to be installed. None of us wants to have an antiquated system, which given the technology improvement cycles of today can easily occur.

Two common lease types are the capital lease and the operating lease. Capital leases are "rent-to-own" leases; at the end of the term, the lessee can purchase the system for a relatively small fee (for 10% of the original cost, for example). With a capital lease, the lessee is usually considered the owner and receives the tax benefits of ownership. Capital leases are much like a financed purchase, but they do not usually require the user to make a down payment. By contrast, operating leases are more consistent with traditional leasing arrangements, with no discounted purchase option at the end of the lease term. Because the lessor is usually considered to be the owner, retaining the tax benefits of ownership, the lessee typically makes a lower payment than with the capital lease alternative.

One final acquisition alternative is to rent the system month by month. This provides the most flexibility, typically requiring only 1 month's notice to discontinue. Of course, the benefit comes at the cost of higher rental payments. Since the payment is usually not fixed, you are subject to increases.

Software Licensing

Acquiring computer software is a different story. Historically, vendors have preferred to license software, granting the licensee the right to use the software under the conditions specified in a licensing agreement supplied by the software vendor. Typically, these licenses allow the licensee to use the software on a specified computer system for a specified fee.

Three common ways to pay for this license agreement are a one-time charge, a lease, and a monthly charge. With the one-time charge, the licensee pays a set price and retains the right to use the software indefinitely. This charge can be paid in cash or financed. The leasing alternative is another way to finance the one-time charge with no down payment. Finally, the monthly charge is like renting the software month by month indefinitely. As with this way of renting a computer, it provides flexibility. It may also offer a painless way to upgrade to new versions of software as they become available.

Although these basic forms of charging for software are standard, the criteria for establishing the value to charge for software are not. Historically, software value was believed to be directly related to the power of the server on which it ran. Today, vendors are becoming much more creative in measuring the value and are providing alternatives that more closely match the price of the software to the specific value a business receives from the software. These new options focus on user-based and resource-based license charges.

For many years, IBM's charges for system software were based on performance, specifically the throughput (amount of application work) of the server on which the software executed. Several server model groups were defined based on those processing capacities. Initially, a measurement called the Internal Throughput Rate (ITR) was derived for each processor model. Later, the calculations were refined to Million Service Units (MSU) per hour and an MSU value was derived for each server. MSU values range from as low as 3 to over 100 for newer processors, and each MSU represents approximately the same capacity regardless of the processor model and type. Each server continued to be associated with a specific tier or model group.

Software prices, Monthly License Charges (MLCs), were graduated (hence, Graduated Monthly License Charges or GMLCs) based on the processor group in which the software would run. No consideration was given to the number of users or the amount of system resources (number of processors, processor capacity, or memory for example) associated with a particular software package.

As early as 1993, IBM began adjusting its pricing structure for high-end operating systems by eliminating its top two processor groups (Groups 90 and 100), capping its software prices at the Group 80 level. Processors then available in the discontinued groups were placed into Group 80. For businesses with processors in those groups, operating software costs were reduced by up to 36%.

It was not until April 1994, when IBM introduced measured usage as a means of pricing major MVS/ESA subsystems, that software pricing made its first significant move away from processor capacity. With the Measured Usage License Charge (MULC), IBM announced the Parallel Transaction Server and the coupled system version of its Parallel Sysplex Licensing Charge (PSLC), discussed in detail later. (See Chapter 2 for a discussion of sysplex-capable processors.) In September 1994, IBM announced the Parallel Enterprise Server models and with them a variation on the PSLC for "standalone" coupling-capable systems.

In March 1995, IBM expanded its efforts to rebuild the S/390 pricing structure by announcing the Indexed Monthly License Charge (IMLC), capping its GMLC at the performance level of the largest processors then available and positioning larger servers that are not coupling capable on the same pricing scale as noncoupled PSLC servers. These steps positioned PSLC pricing as the replacement for GMLC pricing for all parallel sysplex environments and IMLC pricing for new non-parallel (single) processors exceeding Group 80 MSU.

In 1995, IBM also announced a worldwide Enterprise Agreement for S/390 Software that allowed businesses to use one agreement to manage their S/390 software all over the world. It was a three-year fixed-fee contract offered at the enterprise level that enabled businesses to increase the use of the software at a lower cost than under standard terms. Businesses with sites in multiple countries could request that all of their S/390 software be aggregated into a single agreement.

These changes offer large-system customers a potential reduction in their total cost of computing and more closely align software value and usage with software price. They also provide a means of simplifying the ordering process and improving your business's ability to project software costs. The resource-based and usage-based pricing framework also provide incentive for the business to run applications where they make the most sense for your business. Because these options undergo frequent change and affect their company's cash flow, income statements, balance sheets, and taxes, always consult the proper professionals to determine the best alternative for each situation. A key pricing change is provided for parallel sysplex–capable systems.

Parallel Sysplex License Charge (PLSC)
With the introduction of the parallel sysplex environment in 1994, options for processor granularity increased dramatically. The PSLC was introduced in two stages by IBM to better match the hardware upgrade charges, which were based on the aggregate capacity of the processors regardless of the number of individual processors, with the corresponding increases in software costs.

As of April 1994, businesses already owning two or more coupling-capable processors benefited from the PSLC announcement. To qualify for the PSLC, a business had to operate one or more explicitly defined parallel sysplex processors either as a standalone processor in a parallel sysplex environment or in an actively coupled sysplex. The parallel sysplex environment was defined as a specific set of S/390 software programs operating on one or all specifically identified processors. An actively coupled sysplex required that the processors use the appropriate set of coupling links. The requirement for the licensing charge was simply that certain parallel sysplex hardware was installed, but not that it was exploited, which was a "loophole" that drove many to install the hardware before they were ready to exploit it. The PSLC became an element of the Growth Opportunity License Charge (GOLC) introduced with the S/390 Multiprise 3000 offering in 1999 and is discussed later in this chapter.

Three configuration options were defined to meet the parallel sysplex requirement:

- The Coupling Facility (9674), together with coupling links, physically interconnecting any PSLC qualifying processor (ES/9021 711-based models, ES/9121 511-based models, and 9672 models).

- Any 9672 model with one or more Central Electronic Complexes (CECs), or Logical Partitions (LPARs), running the Coupling Facility control code. The 9672 can run as a standalone unit or be interconnected with other coupling-capable processors.

- An ES/9021 711-based model fitted with a specially designed engineering change, enabling it to run the Coupling Facility control code in a logical partition. This processor can then be connected to any other coupling capable processor.

In September 1994, IBM extended the benefits of the PSLC to any business owning or purchasing a single processor meeting the hardware and software requirements to operate in a parallel sysplex environment. This includes installing MVS/ESA Version 5, Release 2 (containing full software support for the parallel sysplex). The reduced system software costs provided through the PSLC were now available across the entire S/390 server range, from a single CPU Parallel Enterprise Server (9672) to the 10-way ES/9021 Model 9X2. In 1996, IBM made additional minor modifications to PSLC pricing.

Under the GMLC, the capacity of each processor running an operating system was evaluated individually. The total license charge for multiple processors was the sum of the group-priced systems. Under the PSLC, two major business benefits were accrued. Prices were positioned along a sloped line (reflecting the increased granularity of processor options under parallel sysplex) that was placed entirely below the steps of the GMLC pricing structure. This reflects an across-the-board price reduction for businesses running, or planning to run, in a parallel sysplex environment.

The second benefit applied to businesses running two or more servers in an actively coupled environment. This benefit comes through the aggregation of MSU values associated with each server. PSLC continues to use MSU as the base for price calculations. Now, however, the MSU value for all of the coupled servers in the parallel sysplex is added into a single total that determines the final PSLC charge. Adjustments to the size of the parallel sysplex configuration result in adjustments to the PSLC charge based on movement up or down the configuration scale. You pay for what you use, and you use only what you need. Businesses participating in a parallel sysplex environment receive a distinct software price advantage over those continuing to operate in large uniprocessor or multiprocessor environments.

In early 1998, IBM removed the "loophole" that some users had employed to receive the PSLC. IBM clarified that PSLCs require that the user's machines be operating in an "actively coupled" environment to qualify for aggregated PSLC pricing. To be considered "actively coupled" and therefore qualify for PSLC, the user had to comply with the following conditions:

1. All processors in the parallel sysplex must be physically attached via coupling links to a common Coupling Facility from Group B of the PSLC Exhibits and via timer links to a common Sysplex Timer.

2. All OS/390 and MVS/ESA Version 5 images that comprise the parallel sysplex environment must have at least one common systems enablement function activated to use the Coupling Facility across all images in the sysplex.

3. The OS/390 and MVS Images participating in the sysplex functions must account for at least 50% of the total OS/390 and MVS workload on each machine.

Indexed Monthly License Charge (IMLC)

New servers, announced after March 1995, that run MVS, that do not perform in a coupled parallel sysplex environment, and that are measured with MSU values that exceed the upper bound of Group 80 are placed in the IMLC category. The IMLC is a sloped pricing structure that tracks the slope of the PSLC and indexes prices based on the total capacity of the server, measured in MSU. The significant difference is that software prices apply to the single system and cannot be aggregated with any other system. (For those systems that were running under VM or VSE, a special bid price is required.)

Two additional changes were made with the introduction of the IMLC. The Distributed System License Option (DSLO) was discontinued for systems covered under IMLC but continued for systems covered by the GMLC. The DSLO offers a 25% discount on software licenses running on System/370 or S/390 servers, other than the first one purchased by a business. For businesses benefiting from the DSLO, it was the responsibility of the lead site to distribute the software and system changes to the "discounted" systems.

Workload License Charges

This is the newest IBM software pricing strategy, designed to support e-business reality and applicable to z/OS installed on z900 servers running in z/Architecture mode. It was scheduled to be available at 100% capacity on March 30, 2001, with a transition program available to facilitate migration to Workload Licensing Charges (WLC). Middleware from IBM such as DB2, CICS, IMS, and MQSeries are included in the new variable WLC. Most software products including VM/ESA and VSE/ESA are flat WLC priced. IBM Cross Platform products such as WebSphere and Linux-based products are only priced as One Time Charge (OTC). With Workload License Charges users pay only for the software capacity that they need, defined for one or more LPARs, and the new pricing structure is designed around leading-edge technology and the concept of paying for what you need. It also provides common pricing for many cross-platform products. This changes the software pricing metric from machine capacity to sub–machine capacity and therefore provides enhanced price performance. It allows the user to grow one workload at a time and have excess hardware capacity installed without incurring software charges. Users define and pay for the software on their four-hour rolling average usage rather than peak usage. Workload License Charges for z/OS are up to 42% less expensive than those for OS/390 Version 2. It should be noted that WLC at less than 100% capacity will only be available coincident with the production-ready IBM License Manager, scheduled for September 30, 2001.

Example of Software Pricing Offerings
To better understand the value of several of the software pricing offerings described earlier, we can look at an example of a business that has two S/390 Generation 5 Model R56 servers uncoupled and running OS/390 with CICS TS Version 1 and DB2 Version 6. The total number of MSUs in this example is 186. The business financed the software OTC (One-Time Charge) over a period of 36 months so that the example comparisons that follow will be made on a monthly software GMLC cost basis. The business pays $81,540 × 2 for a total of $163,080 per month or $877/MSU/month.

In Step 1 of this example, the business couples the two R56 models to now run in a single parallel sysplex environment for a total of 186 MSU but qualifying for the PSLC. The Step 1 monthly software costs are

- Total monthly software costs: $119,620 ($643/MSU)

- The PSLC aggregation delivers 37% price performance improvement ($643/MSU versus $877/MSU)

In Step 2 the business consolidates the two S/390 G5 servers on to one z900 Model 108 (245 MSUs), with the same software, to accommodate a 32% capacity growth. The Step 2 costs are

- Total monthly cost: $138,264 ($564/MSU)

- The PSLC aggregation and 32% capacity growth delivers price performance improvement of 15% ($564/MSU versus $643/MSU)

In Step 3 the business upgrades to a z900 Model 1C9 (302 MSU) to accommodate an additional 20% capacity growth and CICS TS Version 1, DB2 Version 6, and z/OS. The business now qualifies for Workload License Charges (WLC), but depending on the configuration there could be a range of prices for the software. The following three scenarios illustrate the configuration effect on software prices under WLC.

- *Scenario A:* 100% defined capacity, all software runs in all LPARs:

  - Workload License Charges: $151,155 ($501/MSU)

  - Price performance improvement of 11% ($501/MSU versus $564/MSU)

- *Scenario B (most likely):* 90% defined capacity, most software runs in all LPARs

  - LPAR 1 = 211 MSUs for CICS, DB2. and z/OS

  - LPAR 2 = 60 MSUs for DB2 and z/OS

  - Workload License Charges: $139,147 ($461/MSU)

  - Price performance improvement of 18% ($461/MSU versus $564/MSU)

- *Scenario C:* 80% defined capacity, varying software runs in all LPARs:

  - LPAR 1 = 121 MSUs running CICS, DB2, and z/OS

- LPAR 2 = 121 MSUs running only z/OS

- Workload License Charges: $117,093 ($388/MSU)

- Price performance improvement of 31% ($388/MSU versus $564/MSU)

In summary, qualifying for the PSLC and WLC has a big impact on software license charges. It is not a simple equation, and it is well worth a business's time to discuss all the options with an IBM representative to find the best financial solution fitting immediate and longer-term needs.

Linux Integrated Facility Example
The Integrated Facility for Linux (IFL) is described in Chapter 4, and the technical description of the Linux IFL design implementation for the S/390 and z900 was covered in Chapter 2. The financial considerations are important to understand because the software pricing allows for extremely price competitive Linux images running on a single engine of S/390 G5/G6 or z900. In this example there are some basic assumptions to be defined. The example is based on one IFL running WebSphere Application Server for Linux at a cost of $361/month, DB2 UDB for Linux is $17,600/engine plus $1,700/year for support, equaling $631/month spread over 36 months. Although the code will be provided free from SuSE, the support desired by most users varies depending on the number of server engines running Linux. One-engine support is $24,000 (maximum of 15 Linux instances) annually for a G5/G6, and as a simplifying assumption also for the z900, resulting in $2,000/month. The resultant stack total is $2,992/month. The Linux single-engine price per these assumptions would be equivalent to $136/MSU on a G5, $100/MSU on a G6, and $73/MSU on a z900, which is a very competitive price. In addition, an engine will accommodate multiple Linux images, thus making it exceptionally attractive for a business to run Linux on a S/390 G5/G6 or z900 server.

IBM License Manager (ILM) for z/OS
The new IBM License Manager technology facilitates easy, granular, user-managed growth. The ILM was developed around an industry standard for license management, XOpen Software License Management (XSLM). It is a base element of z/OS, and for each product running on z/OS the business is given an electronic certificate.

The business can modify the licensing terms in its certificates as often as it wants and can control its software bill on a monthly basis with nearly any granularity. This requires no phone call to IBM and no need to immerse itself in the procurement process. If, for example, additional DB2 capacity is required, the business simply utilizes the Windows-based License Manager Administration Tool to increase the defined capacity for DB2. The new technology ensures that the business stays within the bounds of its licensed software, and the process is protected by S/390's existing industrial-strength security and password protection facilities.

IBM Global Finance

Whether the business need is to finance the acquisition of a new z900, a used S/390 server or PCs, peripheral hardware, new software financed over thirty-six months rather than One Time Charge(OTC) or Services, it is worthwhile to discuss the options with IBM Global Finance. IBM Global Finance does business in more than 40 countries, providing a broad range of Offerings. A business will find these services provide them with significant financial savings and flexibility while protecting themselves from product obsolescence. Small or medium businesses will find that acquisition of IBM Certified Used Equipment or Lease of equipment may be a good solution to their IT costs and business cash flow.

Integrated Offerings

Installing new powerful z900 or S/390 platforms, such as those required to support an OS/390, z/OS, MVS/ESA, VM/ESA, z/VM, or VSE/ESA operating system environment smoothly and successfully, with minimal or no disruption to current business operations, requires up-front planning, careful analysis, and skilled personnel. To assist in these efforts, IBM provides a variety of "customized" solutions and "integrated" offerings that include sets of services provided with the purchase of combined server hardware and software.

Parallel Server Offerings

In 1994, with the availability of the S/390 microprocessor parallel servers, IBM introduced a package called "S/390 Customized Solutions" as a fee-based service that loads, configures, customizes, and tests system application software with selected new IBM hardware and operating systems. With this package, all the necessary hardware and software components can be preconfigured, preloaded, customized, and tested to meet individual business needs. Obvious benefits include shortened installation time, getting into production more quickly, and minimized risk to operations.

Ordering this new solution requires nothing more than sitting down with the IBM representative to complete a questionnaire covering the current system, the new system, and products the business intends to install. The customization services requested are analyzed and performed by trained personnel at IBM. Clearly, the impact to personnel and operations is minimized.

Specific elements included in the S/390 Customized Solutions span both software and hardware customization. Software customization preloads fully configured system and application software directly onto the new S/390 solution. This includes preloading new IBM DASDs with all necessary software; preloading related workstation software; creating a Logical Partition (LPAR) in which your existing operating system can be restored; preloading Input/Output Configuration Data Sets (IOCDSs); and creating customized tapes. The operating systems supported are MVS, VM, VSE, and VM/VSE.

The hardware customization includes configuring and attaching new IBM peripherals and devices, installing cards and adapters in IBM workstations that support the S/390 solution, and reconfiguring Hardware Management Consoles (HMCs) to match processor relocation and/or upgrades. The S/390 processors supported are the S/390 Parallel Enterprise Server (9672 R models) and the S/390 Parallel Transaction Server models.

An optional enhancement, Single Point of Contact (SPOC) for problems encountered during the migration to a parallel environment, is also available. SPOC is a support team consisting of individuals with broad technical skills and diagnostic expertise. For a subset of software problems relating to vendor products that are a part of the Enterprise Server, IBM will initiate a smooth transfer of problem ownership to participating vendor organizations without customer involvement.

IBM e-Business Start Now Program

There are users running their mission-critical applications on small early generation S/390 servers or even S/370 servers. The growth outlook for these applications will surpass the capacity of their installed system. In addition, they want to test and implement new e-business applications. Because their capacity requirements are less than those of an S/390 G5/G6 or a z900 and upgrades for their current system are no longer available, they were provided a unique growth offering in September 1999. The Multiprise 3000 server is based on proven S/390 technology with G5 chip technology and has nearly all G5/G6 generation function but in a small prepackaged offering. Because of their current platform, users needed growth options that would not add costs to their IT infrastructure (e.g., hardware, operating system, and maintenance), but would still provide new business and especially e-business capabilities. The S/390 Multiprise 3000 was packaged in the IBM e-business Start Now Program comprising varied packages of pre-tested hardware solutions, software designed to reduce user complexities, sample applications, and services provided by Business Partners. The hardware is supported by OS/390, VM/ESA, and VSE/ESA.

The e-business Start Now Program is provided in four solution areas: Net.Commerce, WebSphere, Lotus Domino R5 for OS/390, and Business Intelligence. With the introduction of the Multiprise 3000, IBM introduced the Growth Opportunity License Charge (GOLC), enabling businesses interested in the Multiprise 3000 a more affordable path for capacity and application growth. The GOLC is composed of the Parallel Sysplex License Charge (PLSC), described earlier in this chapter, and the New Application License Charge (NALC). The NALC can provide the user a reduced software charge on a dedicated new processor and a reduced software charge on a number of CPs in a dedicated LPAR. The GOLC enables Multiprise 3000 and S/390 users the ability to increase the size of their existing workloads and more affordably introduce new application workloads.

The hardware is based on the Multiprise 3000, machine type 7060, which is a member of the S/390 family and the logical successor to the Multiprise 2000 server. The 7060 is based on G5 processor chip technology and repackaged on a Processor Memory I/O (PMI) card. The base configuration fits in a desk-high frame with a footprint much smaller than one square meter. There are three models; the H30 is a subuniprocessor, where the processor has been slowed down to less than a uniprocessor with a fixed 1 GB of processor memory. The H50 is a uniprocessor with a fixed memory of 2 GB. The third model is the H70, which is a 2-way system with a fixed memory of 4 GB. The H30 is upgradable to the H50, which in turn is upgradable to the H70. The H70 is not upgradable. All three models contain an additional processor used as the System Assist Processor (SAP) to manage the I/O subsystem. As with the S/390 G5/G6, it is possible to define up to 15 Logical

PARtitions (LPARs), enabling production work and test and development to run alongside each other in a totally separate environment.

There are many configuration options available, and depending on the configuration chosen up to two expansion frames may be added.

Configuration Options—S/390 Multiprise 3000

The S/390 Multiprise 3000 can be configured with up to 56 parallel or ESCON channels. Up to 24 channels can be installed in the base frame, and up to 32 additional channels would be located in the first expansion frame.

In the e-commerce, networking, and Internet environment, the concern for end-to-end security is imperative. Data privacy, integrity, authentication, and nonrepudiation are becoming increasingly important, and the Multiprise 3000 has the ability to optionally add the IBM Cryptographic Coprocessor feature.

The Multiprise 3000 offers several network connectivity options. LAN connectivity is provided by token-ring or Ethernet adapter cards up to a maximum of four adapters. WAN connectivity can be achieved by using standard S/390 channel-attached communication devices (e.g., the 3745) or by using WAN emulation functions. ICA emulation is particularly important for VM/ESA and VSE/ESA users who may be currently using this function on, for example, a 9221. There is no OSA-2 or OSA-3 support on this server.

The Multiprise 3000 has Integrated Coupling Migration Facility (ICMF) support, allowing test of a parallel sysplex environment without the need of an internal or external Coupling Facility or Sysplex Timer. VM/ESA Version 2, Release 3 or later supports OS/390 guest virtual parallel sysplex environment. The Multiprise 3000 also supports an optional Hardware Management Console (HMC).

The Multiprise 3000 server supports a high-performance internal disk subsystem as well as traditional external channel-attached peripheral subsystems. The internal disk subsystem uses SSA RAID architecture based on 18.2 GB HDDs (Hard Disk Drive), operating at up to 40 MB/s, with Fast Write implemented in the SSA RAID adapters and its own internal rechargeable battery backup. The S/390 volumes are mapped onto the RAID-5 internal disk arrays. All internal disk RAID arrays are connected in a single SSA loop, described in Chapter 3. If an internal disk is installed, a minimum of 72 GB up to a maximum of 216 GB of usable disk capacity must be installed in the base frame. The minimum permits space in the base frame for a maximum of 12 parallel or ESCON channel adapters, each supporting two S/390 channel interfaces. Each of the two expansion frames can accommodate up to 288 GB of usable internal disk capacity for a system total of 56 HDDs. The first expansion frame can contain up to 32 parallel or ESCON channels. The second expansion frame cannot contain channel cards.

IBM Global Services

IBM has significantly expanded the role of services within the corporation. IBM Global Services is a group of more than 120,000 professionals in 164 countries, working to deliver strategic technology solutions. The services focus includes professional services, product support services, and networking services. Further information can be found on the World Wide Web at *www.ibm.com/services*. Professional services include

- Application Enabling Services

- Consulting

- e-Business Services

- Education and Training Services

- Strategic Outsourcing Services

- Systems Integration Services

Product support services include

- Hardware and Software Support Services

- Systems Management and Networking Services

- Site and Connectivity Services

- Business Recovery Services

Networking services include

- Managed Data Network Services

- Managed Electronic Transaction Services

- Managed Messaging and Collaborative Services

- Managed Internet and Intranet Services

- Network Outsourcing Services

Education

No matter what server hardware and software a business selects, its staff will have to operate them. To maximize their efficiency and morale, they must be educated in the use of the server system itself and in the use of its software. Proper education is critical to the success of any server automation project. Inadequate education may preclude productivity benefits afforded by moving a task to the server. The goal of the education is to make the users proficient at using the system hardware and software and to make their interaction with the system enjoyable. When operating a system is enjoyable, a user is more highly motivated. If, on the other hand, using the system represents a frustrating struggle due to inadequate education, the user is less productive and may avoid it altogether.

Most S/390 and z900 users will be accessing the system using workstations and displays with which they should be familiar. Although training in the use of these items should not be overlooked, it can usually be handled easily on an informal basis. For system operators, system programmers, and others who have to deal with tape drives, communications controllers, workstation controllers, and other peripherals, more formal hardware and systems software training is necessary.

After the users are familiar with the hardware elements with which they will interact, they must be trained to use the software with which they will be working. For users, much of the complexity of operating system components is handled by the application. In-depth and formal training for system operators, system programmers, and application developers is a good investment. Traditional classroom education is available from IBM and others when more detailed knowledge of S/390 operating systems is needed.

Everyone using application programs of any complexity should receive formal education on their use. Since users spend most or all of their computing time working with the application programs, this is the most important component of a good user education plan. The content of this education depends on the particular application program selected. Typically, manuals provided with the application program contain step-by-step tutorials designed to train the user. Depending on how complex the application program is, how much experience the user has, and the quality of the tutorial, this education method achieves varying levels of success. It is important to separate the education into categories that are appropriate to the user category. For example, the information needed by the application support person would vary widely from that needed by the end user.

There are other ways of getting application program education. Software companies offer classes tailored to using their application programs. Businesses will usually send one person to a class of this type and then have the person teach other users upon returning. IBM, other software publishers, and consultants can provide information about various classes, books, videotapes, and other media that are available for training new users.

IBM Teach is one source, in the United States, of education for S/390-related topics. Courses are available for end users, application programmers, and system programmers. Courses in the curriculum cover such things as computer concepts (including the latest material on parallel sysplex environments); S/390 operations; OS/390, MVS, VM, z/OS, z/VM, and VSE services; CMS; TSO; REXX; ISPF; RACF; performance and tuning; and software installation and maintenance. In addition to the major operating systems, courses are offered in storage subsystems, personal and application systems, communication systems, database, and data communications. Business and personal development courses for technical users are also included. Courses are taught in many major cities; with special arrangement, they may be taught at your location.

The World Wide Web is now a major source of educational material. IBM offers vast amounts of information accessible through its Web site. There are many specific sites on hardware and software, but a good starting point for all is *www.ibm.com*.

Servicing A System

Despite all the precautions taken to make S/390 and zSeries servers as reliable as possible, unlikely as it is, they might fail. If one does, there must be a way of getting it fixed. All of these servers come with a warranty that provides free on-site repairs from IBM's service division, 7 days a week, 24 hours a day. The various displays and printers associated with S/390 computers have their own warranty terms and periods.

After the warranty period, the business becomes responsible for maintenance of the system. IBM and others offer service agreements that, for a fee, provide postwarranty on-site service just like that provided during the warranty. Various maintenance discounts are available, depending on the level of systems management procedures a business is willing to implement in its organization. If a system fails and the business does not have any type of service contract, it will have to pay for parts and labor, which can be extremely expensive. For this reason, most people choose to keep their systems on maintenance after warranty as a type of insurance policy.

No matter what server system a business chooses, it will require ongoing support: Questions will need answering, hardware problems must be addressed, software updates must be installed, and so forth. This support can be delivered in many different ways. Personnel from the manufacturer, the software company, and the business's own staff are generally involved in supporting the server system and its users. In an effort to make this support more effective and convenient, IBM offers IBMLink.

With IBMLink, support is delivered electronically, which improves access to technical and product information and simplifies communications between IBM personnel and users. Just as electronic mail and on-line business information streamline a business's operation, IBMLink streamlines the support provided to business operations. Access to IBMLink is provided through the IBM Global Services (IGS) Network or through the Internet. The services include the following:

- InfoLink provides many of the same tools used by IBM personnel to support users. From InfoLink, customers can view IBM product announcement letters, hardware and software product catalogs, product prices, volume discount schedules, publication information, lists of local dealers, and so forth. They can also use hardware and software configuration planning tools to define and price workable computer systems with their various options.

- OrderLink allows customers to look at the equipment they currently have on order.

- SupportLink provides a national database of technical questions and answers. This database can be searched by keywords to locate previously answered questions on a variety of technical topics. A user can enter new questions, which will be answered by IBM support personnel and then added to the national question/answer database for others to view. Through SupportLink, users also can view Technical Bulletins and FLASHes posted by IBM. The "copy screen" function of SupportLink allows IBM personnel to interact directly with the user's computer system. Both the user and the IBM representative can see the same screen image on their respective workstations. This common image helps resolve user questions and helps users learn the system.

- ServiceLink allows customers to communicate electronically with IBM service personnel to report problems. Further, customers (or IBM service personnel) can electronically search through IBM's software updates, called Program Temporary Fixes (PTFs); receive the software update electronically; and apply the fix. Problems detected by the S/390 computer generate alert messages that can be automatically sent to IBM service without any user intervention.

- TalkLink provides a conference service supporting customers and developers (such as independent software vendors) with technical support. An entry, S/390 Developers Association, in the TalkLink panel provides access to services for OS/390, MVS, VM, and VSE. Features available include fast paths for performance, panel news, and download and forum services.

- User functions reduce "telephone tag" by providing some simple electronic mail functions between IBM personnel and the users. Users can send comments back to IBMLink through these user functions.

Summary

The S/390 has evolved into an increasingly powerful and manageable large-scale server and is the basis for the new z/Architecture zSeries 900, on which new and improved function and features have been added with unknown new function yet to come. Whether a business is relatively small, medium, or large, either of these server families deserves serious consideration in supporting business goals and objectives for the next decade and beyond.

Although more function and power have been added to these servers, the real cost of operation has been dramatically reduced and the ease of using the system has increased. Users of other systems can argue that one element or another is superior to S/390's capability, but many believe that S/390 and the zSeries 900, as an integrated server system environment, has no equal for solving complex business problems. Any business seeking to improve the business value of its server platform solution, especially those pursuing an enterprise-wide network computing e-business perspective, owes itself a close look at S/390 and zSeries in this new e-business era.

Appendix A: Upgrade Paths

Original Model	Upgrade Model
101	1C1-1C9*, 102-116
102	1C2-1C9*, 103-116
103	1C3-1C9*, 104-116
104	1C4-1C9*, 105-116
105	1C5-1C9*, 106-116
106	1C6-1C9*, 107-116
107	1C7-1C9*, 108-116
108	1C8-1C9*, 109-116
109	1C9-1C9*, 110-116
1C1	1C2-1C9*, 110-116
1C2	1C3-1C9*, 110-116
1C3	1C4-1C9*, 110-116
1C4	1C5-1C9*, 110-116
1C5	1C6-1C9*, 110-116
1C6	1C7-1C9*, 110-116
1C7	1C8-1C9*, 110-116
1C8	1C9*, 110-116
1C9	110-116
110	111-116
111	112-116
112	113-116
113	114-116
114	115-116
115	116

Notes:

Installed Internal Coupling Facilities (ICFs) and Integrated Facilities for Linux (IFLs) are carried forward (converted) to the new model.

ICF and IFL are not available on Model 109 and Model 116.

*All 1Cn models are Capacity models which are only available with CBU features.

Figure A.1.   Vertical upgrade paths within z900.

Original Model	Upgrade Model
RA6	1C1-1C9*, 101-116
R16	1C1-1C9*, 101-116
RB6	1C1-1C9*, 101-116
R26	1C2-1C9*, 102-116
RC6	1C2-1C9*, 102-116
RD6	1C3-1C9*, 103-116
T16	1C1-1C9*, 101-116
T26	1C2-1C9*, 102-116
R36	1C2-1C9*, 102-116
R46	1C3-1C9*, 103-116
R56	1C3-1C9*, 103-116
R66	1C4-1C9*, 104-116
R76	1C4-1C9*, 105-116
R86	1C5-1C9*, 105-116
R96	1C5-1C9*, 105-116
RX6	1C6-1C9*, 106-116
Y16	1C1-1C9*, 101-116
Y26	1C2-1C9*, 102-116
Y36	1C2-1C9*, 103-116
Y46	1C3-1C9*, 103-116
Y56	1C4-1C9*, 104-116
Y66	1C5-1C9*, 105-116

Original Model	Upgrade Model
Y76	1C5-1C9*, 105-116
Y86	1C6-1C9*, 106-116
Y96	1C6-1C9*, 107-116
YX6	1C7-1C9*, 107-116
X17	1C1-1C9*, 101-116
X27	1C2-1C9*, 102-116
X37	1C3-1C9*, 103-116
X47	1C4-1C9*, 104-116
X57	1C4-1C9*, 104-116
X67	1C5-1C9*, 105-116
X77	1C6-1C9*, 106-116
X87	1C7-1C9*, 107-116
X97	1C8-1C9*, 108-116
XX7	1C8-1C9*, 108-116
XY7	1C9*, 109-116
XZ7	1C9*, 109-116
Z17	1C1-1C9*, 101-116
Z27	1C2-1C9*, 102-116
Z37	1C3-1C9*, 103-116
Z47	1C4-1C9*, 104-116
Z57	1C5-1C9*, 105-116
Z67	1C6-1C9*, 106-116
Z77	1C7-1C9*, 107-116
Z87	1C8-1C9*, 108-116
Z97	1C8-1C9*, 108-116
ZX7	1C9*, 109-116
ZY7	110-116
ZZ7	110-116

Notes:

Installed Internal Coupling Facilities (ICFs) and Integrated Facilities for Linux (IFLs) are carried forward (converted) to the new model.

ICF and IFL are not available on Model 109 and Model 116.

*All 1Cn models are Capacity models which are only available with CBU features.

Figure A.2. Horizontal upgrade paths from S390 G5/G6 to z900.

Original Model	Upgrade Model
100 with 1 ICF	100 with 2-9 ICFs
100 with 2 ICF	100 with 3-9 ICFs
100 with 3 ICF	100 with 4-9 ICFs
100 with 4 ICF	100 with 5-9 ICFs
100 with 5 ICF	100 with 6-9 ICFs
100 with 6 ICF	100 with 7-9 ICFs
100 with 7 ICF	100 with 8-9 ICFs
100 with 8 ICF	100 with 9 ICFs

Figure A.3. Vertical upgrade paths for z900 Coupling Facility Model 100.

Original Model	Upgrade Model
100 with 1 ICF	1C1-1C9*, 101-116
100 with 2 ICFs	1C2-1C9*, 103-116
100 with 3 ICFs	1C3-1C9*, 104-116
100 with 4 ICFs	1C4-1C9*, 105-116
100 with 5 ICFs	1C5-1C9*, 106-116
100 with 6 ICFs	1C6-1C9*, 107-116`
100 with 7 ICFs	1C7-1C9*, 108-116
100 with 8 ICFs	1C8-1C9*, 109-116
100 with 9 ICFs	1C9*, 110-116

Notes:

You can upgrade the z900 Coupling Facility model to general purpose or Capacity models by adding Central Processors (CPs), ICFs or IFLs. Additional CPs/ICFs/IFLs are available as optional features.

All 1Cn models are Capacity models which are only available with CBU features.

Figure A.4. Upgrade paths from z900 CF Model 100 to general purpose/CBU model.

Original Model	Upgrade Model
9672 R06	z900 100 (with 1-9 ICFs), 1C1-1C9*, 101-116

Note: **All 1Cn models are Capacity models which are only available with CBU features.*

Figure A.5. Upgrade paths from Coupling Facility Model R06 to z900.

Appendix B: S/390 G5/G6 and z900 Relative Performance

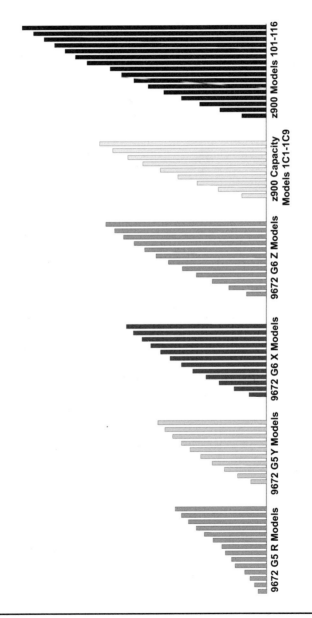

Figure B.1. S390 Generation 5/Generation 6—z900 relative performance.

Index

24-bit addressing, 211, 213, 274
30XX series, 18–19
31-bit addressing, 213, 272, 273
43XX series, 18
64-bit architecture
    Virtual Machine/Enterprise System
        Architecture (VM/ESA), 263–264
    z900, 25, 34–35, 36
    z/OS, 238–239, 242
155 ATM feature, I/O subsystem, 31
3270 display, 148
3490 Magnetic Tape Subsystems,
    146–147
3494 Automated Tape Library (ATL)
    Dataserver, 144–146
3590 High-Performance Tape Subsystem,
    140–144
3745 Communications Controller, 311–314
3746 Model 900 Extension Unit,
    314–316
3746 N-way Multinetwork Controller
    Model 950, 316–317
3990 Storage Control, 131–134
3995 Optical Library, 138–139
9729 Optical Wavelength Division Multi-
    plexor (Muxmaster), 119–120

A
access control, 344–349. See also data
    preservation
    audit reports, 348
    back doors, 346
    Cryptographic Coprocessor (PCICC),
        347
    Data Base Unload (DBU), 348
    Data Security Monitor (DSMON), 348
    digital certificates, 333, 348
    Distributed Computing Environment
        (DCE), 347
    distributed environment and, 345–347
    eNetwork Communications Servers, 347
    firewalls, 347
    gateway protection, 346, 347
    hackers, 346
    Integrated Cryptographic Feature
        (ICRF), 24, 333, 347
    link encryption, 346
    masqueraders, 345–346
    overview, 344–345
    passwords, 346, 348, 349
    RACF Remote Sharing Facility (RRSF),
        349
    RACF Sysplex Communication option,
        348
    Resource Access Control Facility
        (RACF), 348–349
    security policies, 346, 347
    Security Servers, 235, 332, 347
    Trojan horse, 346
    viruses, 345
    worms, 345
accessor service area, tape storage, 145
access-register addressing, 215, 254–255,
    272, 273
access registers, 20
ACF (Automatic Cartridge Facility), 141
ACF/NCP (Advanced Communications
    Function/Network Control
    Program), 311, 313, 314, 315
ACF/VTAM (Advanced Communications
    Function/Virtual Telecommunica-
    tions Access Method), 252, 258,
    277–278
ACL (Automatic Cartridge Loader), 141
ACS (Automated Cartridge System), 142
"active wait" mode, 66
AD (Application Development), 184
ADMF (Asynchronous Data Mover
    Facility), 24, 256
ADP (Advanced Function Presentation)
    data, 184, 330
ADSTAR Distributed Storage Manager
    (ADSM), 225, 227, 328–329
Advanced Communications Function/
    Network Control Program (ACF/
    NCP), 311, 313, 314, 315
Advanced Communications Function/
    Virtual Telecommunications
    Access Method (ACF/VTAM),
    252, 258, 277–278
Advanced Function Common Control Unit
    (AFCCU), 153

Advanced Function Presentation (AFP)
    data, 184, 330
Advanced Interactive eXecutive/Enterprise
    Systems Architecture (AIX/ESA),
    278
Advanced Peer-to-Peer Networking
    (APPN), 87, 94, 278, 304–305
Advanced Peer-to-Peer Networking
    (APPN)/High-Performance
    Routing (HPR), 313, 316
Advanced Program-to-Program Communi-
    cations (APPC), 198, 252, 300
Advanced Program-to-Program Communi-
    cations/MVS (APPC/MVS),
    217–218
Advanced Transistor Technology (ATX), 37
AFCCU (Advanced Function Common
    Control Unit), 153
AirLine Control System (ALCS),
    280–281
AIW (APPN Implementor's Workshop),
    304–305
AIX/ESA (Advanced Interactive eXecutive/
    Enterprise Systems Architecture),
    278
ALCS (AirLine Control System),
    280–281
All-Points-Addressable (APA) mode,
    printers, 149
alphanumeric mode, printers, 149
American Airlines, 4
AnyNet products, 303, 305–306
AON/MVS (Automated Operations
    Network/MVS), 326–327, 328
AORs (Application Owning Regions),
    67–68
APA (All-Points-Addressable) mode,
    printers, 149
API (Application Programming Interface)
    application enablers for extending, 190,
    191, 192, 194
    operating systems and, 78, 79, 81
    POSIX-compliant, 219
    software and, 78, 79, 81, 162, 163, 164
APPC (Advanced Program-to-Program
    Communications), 198, 252, 300
APPC/MVS (Advanced Program-to-
    Program Communications/MVS),
    217–218
APPC/VM Virtual Telecommunications
    Access Method Support (AVS), 252
Application Development (AD), 184

application enablers, 190–200. *See also*
    application program development
Advanced Program-to-Program Commu-
    nications (APPC), 198
Application Programming Interface
    (API), extending, 190, 191, 192,
    194
Business Application Services (BAS)
    facility, 195
Central Processor Complex (CPC) and,
    199
CICSPlex System Manager (CPSM), 195
Coupling Facility (CF) and, 199
Cross System Extended Services (XES),
    199
Customer Information Control System
    (CICS), 193–195
Database 2 (DB2) and, 194, 195–197
database application enablers,
    195–197
Data Language/1 (DL/1), 197–198
Distributed Relational Database
    Architecture (DRDA), 196
Enterprise Document Management Suite
    (EDMSuite), 206
FlowMark, 206
Hierarchical Database Enablers,
    197–200
ImagePlus, 177–179, 206
IMS Client for Java, 200
IMS Connectors, 199–200
IMS/ESA Database Manager (IMS/ESA
    DB), 198
IMS/ESA Transaction Manager (IMS/ESA
    TM), 198–199
IMS Resource Lock Manager (IRLM),
    67, 68, 198
IMS Shared Message Queue (SMQ),
    199
IMS TOC (TCP/IP OTMA Connection),
    198, 199–200
IMS WWW Templates, 199
Information Management System/
    Enterprise System Architecture
    (IMS/ESA), 197–200
MultiNode Persistent Sessions (MNPS),
    194–195
non-parallel sysplex configuration, 194
N-way data sharing, 198
overview, 190
Parallel Sysplex Coupling Facility, 199
parallel sysplex support, 194

Relational Database Enablers: DB2 and
  SQL, 195–197
Remote Site Recovery (RSR), 75, 198
Resource Definition On-line (RDO),
  194
single-system sysplex configuration, 194
Structured Query Language (SQL), 196
transaction-processing application
  enablers, 190, 193–195
Web connectivity, 199–200
WorkLoad Manager (WLM), 199
application frame, SSA, 158
Application Owning Regions (AORs),
  67–68
application program development, 183–205.
  See also application enablers;
  application programs on S/390;
  data warehouses; front-ending
  existing applications; procedural
  application development; software
atomic database theory, 200
business information, developing usable,
  200–204
Common Gateway Interface (CGI),
  189
Common Object Request Broker
  Architecture (CORBA), 189
compatibility, 78, 162–163
Component Broker Series (CBS), 189
Database 2 (DB2) relational data access
  and, 189
data mining, 204–205
Enterprise JavaBeans (EJB), 171,
  188–189
flexibility of eservers, 8
IBM Solution Developer Program, 189
Internet Connection Application Programming Interface (ICAPI), 189
Java and, 8, 95, 172, 188–189
Just-In-Time (JIT) compiler, 188
Object-Oriented (OO) Programming
  (OOP), 188–189
On-Line Transaction Processing (OLTP),
  73, 188
operating systems and, 81
parallel processing and, 59
SmoothStart for Domino, 190
support services, 189–190
VisualAge Object Connection program,
  189–190
VisualGen, 188
application program layer, 77–79, 167, 168

Application Programming Interface. *See* API
application programs on S/390,
  167–206. *See also* application
  program development; cross-
  industry application programs;
  industry-specific application
  programs
application program layer, 77–79, 167,
  168
batch processing, 82–83, 167
custom application programs, 168,
  182–183
parallel processing, 167
prewritten application programs, 168,
  169–181
sequential processing, 167
throughput, 100–101, 167, 355
transaction processing, 167
application support of OS/390, 234, 235,
  237
Application System (AS), 176, 203
application workloads, e-business, 5
APPN (Advanced Peer-to-Peer Networking),
  87, 94, 278, 304–305
APPN/HPR (Advanced Peer-to-Peer
  Networking/High-Performance
  Routing), 313, 316
APPN Implementor's Workshop (AIW),
  304–305
architecture, software, 162–163
architecture definition step, 15–16
archiving data, 340–341
Ariba, 8, 172
AS/400 systems and distributed computer
  communications,
  295–296, 297
AS (Application System), 176, 203
ASCII terminal support, 220, 231–232
asset protection. *See* access control; data
  preservation
Association Detection Algorithm, 204
Asynchronous (Async) protocol, 89
Asynchronous Data Mover Facility
  (ADMF), 24, 256
Asynchronous Pageout Facility, 218, 256
Asynchronous Transfer Mode (ATM)
  networks, 93–94, 305,
  306–308, 317
ATM connectivity of OS/390, 234
ATM LAN Emulation (LANE), 94
ATM support of OS/390, 237
atomic database theory, 200

ATX (Advanced Transistor Technology), 37
audit reports, 348
Automated Cartridge System (ACS), 142
Automated Operations Network/MVS
     (AON/MVS), 326–327, 328
Automatic Cartridge Facility (ACF), 141
Automatic Cartridge Loader (ACL), 141
availability and fault tolerance, 72–77
     Capacity BackUp (CBU), 22, 71, 77
     Capacity Upgrade on Demand (CUoD),
          6, 22, 28, 76–77
     Central Electronic Complex (CEC), 73
     Central Processor (CP) failure, 73–74
     channel maintenance, 75
     concurrent channel maintenance, 75
     concurrent patch maintenance, 75
     Coupling Facility (CF) and, 73
     coupling for, 66–67
     Dynamic Coupling Facility Dispatching
          function, 74
     dynamic reconfiguration management,
          75
     ESCON/FICON cables, 76
     eservers, 7
     Fault Tolerant Dynamic Memory Arrays
          Facility, 75
     Graphical User Interface (GUI), 76
     Hardware Configuration Definition
          (HCD), 75–76, 236, 237
     Hardware Configuration Manager
          (HCM), 76, 236
     Internal Coupling Facility (ICF) failure, 74
     Licensed Internal Code Configuration
          Control (LICCC), 76–77
     Licensed Internal Code (LIC), 75, 77,
          78, 80
     MVS/ESA SP Version 4, 217
     On-Line Transaction Processing (OLTP),
          73, 188
     patch maintenance, 75
     "power save state," 73
     power supply, 73
     Processing Units (PUs) and, 45, 46, 73
     RAMAC array architecture, 124–125,
          127–128
     reconfiguration management, 75
     Remote Site Recovery (RSR), 75, 198
     software cloning, 73
     Subspace Group Facilities, 74–75, 256
     subsystem storage protection, 74
     System Assist Processor (SAP) failure,
          28, 41, 74
     Uninterruptible Power System (UPS), 73

average latency, DASDs, 121
average seek time, DASDs, 120, 121
AVS (APPC/VM Virtual Telecommunica-
     tions Access Method Support), 252

B
back doors, 346
backing up data, 339–340
backup capability
     ESCON channels, 111–112
     parallel processing, 62–63
balancing workload of MVS/ESA Version
     5, 220
band-matrix printing, 150–151
bandwidth increase, SSA, 156–157
BAS (Business Application Services) facility,
     195
base package ("book and cage"), CMOS,
     41–42
Basic Sequential Access Method (BSAM)
     and MVS/ESA Version 5, 221, 223
Batch Local Shared Resources (BLSR), 223
BatchPipes/MVS, 221–222, 223
batch vs. interactive processing, 82–83, 167
benchmark testing, 99–100
benefits qualification, 351–353
BFS (Byte File System), 260
BI (Business Intelligence) applications and
     I/O subsystem, 32
binary-compatible application class
     libraries, 232–233
Binary Synchronous Communications
     (BSC, Bisync), 89–90
bipolar technology, 38–40, 40, 41
Block, Erich, 20
block multiplex mode, 108, 117
block paging, 218
blocks of data, DASDs, 54
BLSR (Batch Local Shared Resources), 223
BonusPak II, OS/390, 235
"book and cage" (base package), CMOS,
     41–42
bridges, 285, 302
Brooks, Fred, 20
BSAM (Basic Sequential Access Method)
     and MVS/ESA Version 5, 221, 223
BSC (Binary Synchronous Communica-
     tions), 89–90
bus cable, 108, 110
business and zSeries and S/390 families. See
     managing complexity; "Open
     Business" Policy; vendor offering
     evaluation

Business Application Services (BAS) facility, 195
business cycle improvements, 351
business information, developing usable, 200–204
Business Intelligence (BI) applications and I/O subsystem, 32
buying vs. leasing, 353–355
Byte File System (BFS), 260
byte multiplex mode, 108, 117, 118

C
C4 (Controlled Collapse Chip Connection), 43
cables, LANs, 285
cache
    hits and misses, RAMAC array architecture, 126
    storage hierarchy, 44, 45, 50–51
    structures, coupling, 66
    tape storage advantages, 144–145
caching, VM/ESA, 256
Cambridge Scientific Center, 248
Capacity BackUp (CBU), 22, 71, 77
capacity of eservers, 6
capacity server models (Models 1C1-1C9), z900, 27, 28
Capacity Upgrade on Demand (CUoD), 6, 22, 28, 76–77
capital leases, 354
Carrier Sense Multiple Access/Collision Detect (CSMA/CD), 92–93
CAU (Controller Access Unit), 285
CBS (Component Broker Series), 189
CBU (Capacity BackUp), 22, 71, 77
CCUs (Central Control Units), 313
CCW (Continuous Composite Write-Once), 137
CCWs (Channel Command Words), 107
CDMF (Commercial Data Masking Facility), 235
CDS (Cell Directory Service), 262
CEC (Central Electronic Complex)
    availability and fault tolerance, 73
    Complementary Metal Oxide Semiconductor (CMOS) and, 43, 45
    S/390 family evolution, 21
    Virtual Storage Extended/Enterprise System Architecture (VSE/ESA), 275
CE (Cryptographic Element), 46
Cell Directory Service (CDS), 262
cells within ATM, 94, 308

Central Control Units (CCUs), 313
Central Electronic Complex. *See* CEC
centralized support, xv
Central Processor. *See* CP
Central Processor Complex (CPC), 29, 46, 199
central storage (main memory)
    Complementary Metal Oxide Semiconductor (CMOS) and, 44
    Multiple Virtual Storage/Enterprise System Architecture (MVS/ESA), 213, 214, 215
    storage hierarchy, 50, 51
    zSeries and S/390 families, 35
CFCC (Coupling Facility Control Code), 64, 66
CF (Coupling Facility)
    application enablers and, 199
    availability and fault tolerance, 73
    MVS/ESA Version 5, 219
    overview, 63, 64, 65–66
    parallel processing, 60
    S/390 family evolution, 21, 22
CF (Coupling Facility) Model 100, 27, 28
CGI (Common Gateway Interface), 189
changed data, data warehouses, 202
Channel Command Words (CCWs), 107
channel maintenance, 75
Channel Status Words (CSWs), 107
Channel Subsystem Priority Queuing, z/OS, 240
Channel-to-Channel (CTC), 110, 111, 216
character printers, 149–150
character sets, 149
Chilisoft, 8
chip technology, 36–40
choosing server configurations, 323
CICS (Customer Information Control System), 193–195, 219, 288, 290
CICS Gateway for Java, 185
CICSPlex System Manager. *See* CPSM
CICS Transaction Server, 277
circuit cards, 38
CKD (Count-Key-Data) format, 54
CLA (Communication Line Adapter), 314
C language, 228, 229, 231, 234, 236–237
classifiers, data mining, 204–205
client/server support, 180–181, 246
CLP (Communication Line Processor), 314–315
clustering, data mining, 205

CMIP (Common Management Information Protocol), 309
CMOS (Complementary Metal Oxide Semiconductor), 40–47. *See also* processor technology
base package ("book and cage"), 41–42
bipolar technology and, 38–40, 41
Central Electronic Complex (CEC), 43, 45
Central Processor (CP), 41
central storage (main memory), 44
CMOS II, 37, 38
Controlled Collapse Chip Connection (C4), 43
Control Store (CS), 41
cycle time and, 40
External Time Reference (ETR) card, 45, 46
Floating-Point (FP) assist processor, 41
footprint, 46–47
"hot plugging" cards, 45
Level 1 (L1) cache, 41, 45
Level 2 (L2) cache, 44, 45
MultiChip Module (MCM), 22, 40, 41, 42, 45, 47
planar board, 45
Processing Units (PUs) and, 45, 46, 73
processor technology, 20–21, 22, 37, 38
R1 models, 44
R2 models, 43, 44
R3 models, 41, 44, 45
S/390 evolution and, 20–21, 22, 40, 45
substrates, 38, 43–44
System Assist Processor (SAP), 28, 41, 74
Universal Processor Controller (UPC), 45
CMOS II, 37, 38
CMS (Conversational Monitor System), 248, 251, 255, 257, 260–261
CMS Pipelines, 252
CNN (Composite Network Node), 313
coaxial cable, 92, 93
coexistence, z/OS, 244, 245
COLD (Computer Output to Laser Disk) functions, 184
collisions, 93
Commercial Data Masking Facility (CDMF), 235
common access tool (VMLINK), 256
common area approach of MVS/ESA, 210, 211, 213
Common Gateway Interface (CGI), 189
Common Management Information Protocol (CMIP), 309

Common Object Request Broker Architecture (CORBA), 189
Common Programming Interface for Communications (CPI-C), 298
Common Storage Tracker, 219
Common Transport Semantics (CTS), 302–306
Common User Access (CUA) constructs, 184
Communication Line Adapter (CLA), 314
Communication Line Processor (CLP), 314–315
communications, 84–94, 283–321. *See also* communications options; distributed computer communications; LANs (Local Area Networks); TCP/IP (Transmission Control Protocol/Internet Protocol)
Advanced Peer-to-Peer Networking (APPN), 87, 94, 278, 304–305
Asynchronous (Async) protocol, 89
Asynchronous Transfer Mode (ATM) networks, 93–94, 305, 306–308, 317
ATM LAN Emulation (LANE), 94
Binary Synchronous Communications (BSC, Bisync), 89–90
Carrier Sense Multiple Access/Collision Detect (CSMA/CD), 92–93
cells within ATM, 94, 308
coaxial cable, 92, 93
collisions, 93
distributed servers, 85–87
Electronic Data Interchange (EDI), 85–86
Ethernet LAN, 92–93, 94
Fiber Distributed Data Interface (FDDI), 93, 94
fiber-optic links, 92
High-Performance Routing (HPR), 87, 94
Integrated Services Digital Network (ISDN), 90, 308, 317
interfaces, 88
Internet impact on, 283–284
local workstation controller, 85, 86
message frames, 90–92
modems, 85, 86, 320
multiplexed data traffic, 93–94
MVS/ESA SP Version 4 and, 217–218
network computing, 234, 235, 237, 262, 283
Open Systems Adapter (OSA), 87–88, 94, 287, 292
overview, 84–88

protocols, 85, 88–94
remote workstation controller, 85, 86
server systems, 85–87
size of business and difficulties of, 85
Synchronous Data Link Control
    (SDLC), 90
Systems Network Architecture (SNA),
    85, 86, 87, 90, 94, 313, 316
token-ring networks, 90–92,
    285–289
twisted-pair (two-wire) cable, 92, 285
X.25 protocol, 90, 317
Communications Controllers, 292, 304,
    311–316
communications options, 309–320. *See also*
    communications
    3745 Communications Controller,
        311–314
    3746 Model 900 Extension Unit,
        314–316
    3746 N-way Multinetwork Controller
        Model 950, 316–317
    Advanced Communications Function/
        Network Control Program (ACF/
        NCP), 311, 313, 314, 315
    Advanced Peer-to-Peer Networking
        (APPN)/High-Performance
        Routing (HPR), 313, 316
    Central Control Units (CCUs), 313
    Communication Line Adapter (CLA),
        314
    Communication Line Processor (CLP),
        314–315
    Communications Controllers, 292, 304,
        311–316
    Composite Network Node (CNN), 313
    Dependent Logical Unit Requester
        (DLUR), 305, 316–317
    eNetwork Communications Servers,
        319–320
    eNetwork Host on Demand, 320
    ESCON channel adapter, 315, 316
    ESCON Director, 315
    ESCON Multiple Image Facility (EMIF),
        315
    HiperSockets ("Network in the Box"),
        30, 310, 319
    I/O channel controllers and connectivity,
        310–319
    Maintenance and Operator Subsystem
        (MOSS-E), 311, 317
    modems, 85, 86, 320
    Multiaccess Connector, 311
    Open Systems Adapter (OSA)-Express,
        31, 309–310, 317–319
    Open Systems Adapter (OSA)-Express
        Fast EtherNET (OSA-E FENET),
        31, 317, 319
    overview, 309–310
    Secure Sockets Layer (SSL), 171, 320
    Token-Ring Processor (TRP), 315, 316
communications server of OS/390,
    235–236
Communications Services, 298–302
compatibility
    migration of S/390 and, 15
    optical storage, 137
    software, 78, 162–163
    tape storage, 143
competitive advantage, 352
Complementary Metal Oxide Semiconduc-
    tor. *See* CMOS
Component Broker for OS/390 Application
    Enabling Technology, 237
Component Broker Series (CBS), 189
component redundancy, RAMAC, 120
Composite Network Node (CNN), 313
compression of data, VM/ESA, 257
Computer Output to Laser Disk (COLD)
    functions, 184
computing power, today's vs. yesterday's,
    xvi
concurrent channel maintenance, 75
concurrent copy, 127, 131, 136
concurrent patch maintenance, 75
configuration options, 366–367
connectivity options, z900, 69–70
"connector" services, 167
console services of MVS/ESA SP Version 4,
    216–217
Continuous Composite Write-Once (CCW),
    137
control frame, SSA, 158
Controlled Collapse Chip Connection (C4),
    43
Controller Access Unit (CAU), 285
Control Program-40 (CP-40), 249–250
Control Program (CP), 248, 249, 251, 253,
    257
Control Store (CS), 41
control unit (controller), 106
Conversational Monitor System (CMS),
    248, 251, 255, 257, 260–261
conversations, 298, 300
cooperative processing, LANs, 288,
    290–291

CORBA (Common Object Request Broker Architecture), 189
cost effectiveness of optical storage, 137
cost justification, 349–353. *See also* vendor offering evaluation
    benefits qualification, 351–353
    business cycle improvements, 351
    competitive advantage, 352
    customer service improvements, 352
    education costs, 351
    efficiency improvements, 352
    employee turnover, 353
    hardware maintenance costs, 350
    installation services costs, 351
    inventory reduction, 352
    net present value, 353
    payback period, 353
    productivity improvements, 352
    quality improvements, 352
    sales increase, 353
    software maintenance costs, 350
    technical support costs, 351
    training costs, 351, 368–369
cost per transaction per unit of time, 102
Count-Key-Data (CKD) format, 54
coupling, 64–70. *See also* parallel processing
    "active wait" mode, 66
    Application Owning Regions (AORs), 67–68
    availability achievement by, 66–67
    cache structures, 66
    CICSPlex System Manager (CPSM), 67
    Coupling Facility (CF), 63, 64, 65–66
    Coupling Facility Control Code (CFCC), 64, 66
    coupling links, 64, 69–70
    Database 2 (DB2), 68
    Dynamic CF Dispatch, 66
    Dynamic ICF Expansion, 66
    HiPerLinks, 70
    IMS Resource Lock Manager (IRLM), 67, 68, 198
    Information Management System Database Manager (IMS DB), 67
    Integrated Cluster Bus (ICB), 36, 69
    Integrated Coupling Facility (ICF), 28, 66, 74
    Internal Coupling (IC) channels, 69
    Job Entry Subsystem 2 (JES2), 68
    list structures, 66
    lock structures, 66
    MultiNode Persistent Sessions (MNPS), 68

MultiSystem Coupling (MSC) feature, 67
    Overflow Sequential Access Method (OSAM), 67
    reliability achievement by, 9, 66–67
    Resource Access Control Facility (RACF), 68
    serviceability achievement by, 66–67
    Shared Queue Support, 67
    "sleep" mode, 66
    Standalone Coupling Facility, 64, 65–66
    Structured Query Language (SQL), 68
    structures, 66
    subsystems and, 65, 67–69
    Sysplex Timer, 65, 71–72, 216
    Terminal Owning Regions (TORs), 67
    Transmission Control Protocol/Internet Protocol (TCP/IP) support, 69
    Virtual Storage Access Method (VSAM), 67, 68, 257
    Virtual Telecommunications Access Method (VTAM), 68, 289
    WorkLoad Manager (WLM), 67
Coupling Facility. *See* CF
Coupling Facility (CF) model (Model 100), 27, 28
Coupling Facility Control Code (CFCC), 64, 66
Coupling Facility mode, 35, 52
coupling links, 64, 69–70
CP-40 (Control Program-40), 249–250
CPC (Central Processor Complex), 29, 46, 199
CP (Central Processor)
    availability and fault tolerance, 73–74
    Complementary Metal Oxide Semiconductor (CMOS) and, 41
    input/output (I/O) channel architecture and, 107
    S/390 family evolution, 22
    storage hierarchy, 49
    z900 family, 28
CP (Control Program), 248, 249, 251, 253, 257
CPI-C (Common Programming Interface for Communications), 298
CPSM (CICSPlex System Manager)
    application enablers, 195
    coupling, 67
    managing complexity, 67, 195, 220, 331
    MVS/ESA Version 5, 220
CRM (Customer Relationship Management) applications, 181

cross-industry application programs, 169–179. *See also* application programs on S/390
Application System (AS), 176, 203
Database 2 (DB2) relational database management family, 174
databases and, 173–176
Decision Support System (DSS), 176
Enterprise JavaBeans (EJB), 171, 188–189
eXtensible MarkUp Language (XML) and, 8, 172
HyperText Markup Language (HTML), 172
IBM WebSphere Software Platform, 170–173
image manipulation, 177–179
ImagePlus, 177–179, 206
Interactive Network Dispatcher, 172
Java and, 172
Lightweight Directory Access Protocol (LDAP) and, 172
Lotus Approach, 175–176
Lotus Domino, 170
Lotus SmartSuite 97 and, 175
open industry standards and, 172
OS/390 proxy servers, 172
overview, 169
QMF HPO/Shuttle feature, 174–175
Query Management Facility (QMF), 173–176, 203
Secure Sockets Layer (SSL), 171, 320
WebSphere Application Server for OS/390 and z/OS, 170–171, 235, 237, 238
Wireless Application Protocol (WAP) and, 172
Cross Memory Facility (Dual-Address-Space Facility), 210–211, 213
Cross-Partition Communication Control (XPCC), 269, 270, 272
Cross Platform Extension (XPE), 131
Cross System Coupling Facility (XCF), 63, 217, 304
Cross System Extended Services (XES), 199
cryptographic coprocessor, eservers, 9, 33–34
Cryptographic Coprocessor (PCICC), 347
Cryptographic Element (CE), 46
cryptography, xvi
CS (Control Store), 41
CSMA/CD (Carrier Sense Multiple Access/Collision Detect), 92–93
CSWs (Channel Status Words), 107

CTC (Channel-to-Channel), 110, 111, 216
CTS (Common Transport Semantics), 302–306
CUA (Common User Access) constructs, 184
CUoD (Capacity Upgrade on Demand), 6, 22, 28, 76–77
custom application programs, 168, 182–183
customer care and eservers, 7
Customer Information Control System (CICS), 193–195, 219, 288, 290
Customer Relationship Management (CRM) applications, 181
customer service improvements, 352
cycle time of processors, 38–39, 40

D
DAE (Dump Analysis and Elimination), 217
DASD Fast Write, 125–126
DASDs (Direct Access Storage Devices), 128–134
    3990 Storage Control, 131–134
    average latency, 121
    average seek time, 120, 121
    blocks of data, 54
    Count-Key-Data (CKD) format, 54
    data transfer rate, 121
    First Failure Support Technology (FFST), 134
    Fixed Block Architecture (FBA), 54, 251
    Head-Disk Assembly (HDA), 53
    overview, 50, 52–54
    performance of, 120–121
    Periodic Resident Testing (PRT), 134
    Service Information Messages (SIMs), 134
Database 2. *See* DB2
databases and cross-industry applications, 173–176
Data Base Unload (DBU), 348
data distribution with LANRES, 225
Data Encryption Standard (DES), 33, 333
Data Facility Program (DFP), 127
Data Facility Sort (DFSORT), 234
Data Facility Storage Management Subsystem (DFSMS), 138, 328, 343–344
DataGuide, 202
data integration, data mining, 205
Data Language/1 (DL/1), 197–198
data management alternatives, 96–97. *See also* data preservation

data manipulation and evaluation, 336–337
data mining, 204–205
    Association Detection Algorithm, 204
    classifiers, 204–205
    clustering, 205
    data integration, 205
    data preparation, 205
    data selection and preanalysis, 205
    information discovery, 205
    Intelligent Miner, 205
    MediaMiner, 205
    sequential patterns, 204
data mirroring (RAID-1), 122
data perception, changes in, 105
data preparation, data mining, 205
data preservation, 339–344. *See also* access
    control
    archiving data, 340–341
    backing up data, 339–340
    Data Facility Storage Management
        Subsystem (DFSMS), 138, 328,
        343–344
    disaster recovery, 341–342
    Error Recovery Procedure (ERP), 343
    eXtended Remote Copy (XRC), 71, 134,
        136, 343–344
    overview, 339
    Peer-to-Peer Remote Copy (PPRC),
        70–71, 134, 135, 343
    real-time data recovery, 342–344
    restoring data, 339–340
    System Data Mover (SDM), 343–344
Data Processing (DP) mode, printers, 149
Data Processing text (DP text) mode,
    printers, 149
Data Propagator, 203
Data Security Monitor (DSMON), 348
data selection and preanalysis, data mining,
    205
data sharing
    Local Area Networks (LANs),
        286–287, 289
    Multiple Virtual Storage/Enterprise
        System Architecture (MVS/ESA),
        215
    N-way data sharing, 198
    parallel processing, 59–64
    Virtual Machine/Enterprise System
        Architecture (VM/ESA), 254–255
    Virtual Storage Extended/Enterprise
        System Architecture (VSE/ESA),
        266, 267, 269, 272, 274

data spaces
    Multiple Virtual Storage/Enterprise
        System Architecture (MVS/ESA),
        214, 215
    S/390 family evolution, 20
    Virtual Machine/Enterprise System
        Architecture (VM/ESA), 254, 255
    Virtual Storage Extended/Enterprise
        System Architecture (VSE/ESA),
        272, 273, 274
data striping (RAID-0), 122
data transaction workloads, e-business, 5
data transfer rates
    Direct Access Storage Devices (DASDs),
        121
    ESCON channels, 110, 112
    I/O channel, 110, 112, 118
data warehouses, 200–204
    Application System (AS), 176, 203
    changed data, 202
    DataGuide, 202
    Data Propagator, 203
    Decision Support System (DSS) and,
        200, 203–204
    derived data, 202
    Domino Web Server, 203
    Information Warehouse Solution,
        200–204
    Intelligent Decision Server (IDS), 203
    Lotus Approach, 203
    metadata, 202
    Query Management Facility (QMF),
        173–176, 203
    real-time data, 200–201
    reconciled data, 202
    TeamConnection DataAtlas, 202
    Ultimedia Manager, 203–204
    Visualizer, 203
    Visual Warehouse, 202
    WebSphere Application Server, 203
DB2 (Database 2)
    application enablers and, 194, 195–197
    application program development, 189
    coupling and, 68
    relational database management, 174
DB2/Performance Manager (DB2PM), 331
DB2 Sort Enhancement, 24
DB2 Universal Database, 181
DBU (Data Base Unload), 348
DCE Application Support, 236
DCE (Distributed Computing Environment)
    access control, 347

Open Blueprint Network Services, 300
UNIX Services, 229, 230
Virtual Machine/Enterprise System
    Architecture (VM/ESA), 259,
    261–262
DCS (Differential Current Switch) technol-
    ogy, 38
DDLs (Dynamic Link Libraries), 187
Decision Support System (DSS), 176, 200,
    203–204
dedicated connections, ESCON channels,
    115
Dependent Logical Unit Requester (DLUR),
    305, 316–317
derived data, data warehouses, 202
DES (Data Encryption Standard), 33, 333
device attachments, ESCON channels,
    110–111
DFP (Data Facility Program), 127
DFS (Distributed File Service), 235
DFSMS (Data Facility Storage Management
    Subsystem), 138, 328, 343–344
DFSORT (Data Facility Sort), 234
Differential Current Switch (DCS) technol-
    ogy, 38
digital certificates, 333, 348
digital printing, 330
Direct Access Storage Devices. *See* DASDs
Directory Maintenance (DirMaint), 259
Directory Service, UNIX, 230
direct retailing and multimedia, 97
DirMaint (Directory Maintenance), 259
disaster recovery, 341–342
Disk Operating System (DOS) and VSE/ESA,
    264–267
disk serving with LANRES, 223
disk storage, 120–136. *See also* RAMAC
    array architecture
  concurrent copy, 127, 131, 136
  TO copy, 135, 136
  data mirroring (RAID-1), 122
  data striping (RAID-0), 122
  Enterprise Storage Server (ESS)
    ("Shark"), 135–136
  ESS EX Performance Package, 136
  eXtended Remote Copy (XRC), 71, 134,
    136, 343–344
  Flash Copy, 135, 264
  I/O Priority Queuing, 136
  Logical UNit (LUN), 135
  Logic Structured File (LSF), 135
  Multiple Allegiance (MA), 136

Parallel Access Volumes (PAV), 136, 264
parity concept, 122
Peer-to-Peer Remote Copy (PPRC),
    70–71, 134, 135, 343
Reduced Instruction Set Computing
    (RISC), 135
Redundant Arrays of Independent Disks
    (RAIDs), 54, 120, 121–122
"write penalty," 122
display stations ("dumb heads"), 147–148
distances supported by I/O channel, 110,
    112, 118
distributed computer communications,
    291–309. *See also* communica-
    tions; Open Blueprint Network
    Services
  advantages of, 291
  AS/400 systems and, 295–296, 297
  Communications Controllers, 292, 304,
    311–316
  disadvantages of, 291–292
  Initialization/Recovery Path, 293, 294,
    295, 296
  network management, 294–295
  Open Systems Adapter (OSA), 87–88,
    94, 287, 292
  overview, 292, 293
  Remote operator Facility, 294, 295
  TME 10 NetView (NetView),
    294–295, 296, 324–327
  zSeries and S/390 with, 295–296, 297
Distributed Computing Environment. *See*
    DCE
distributed computing of OS/390, 236
distributed data systems, parallel process-
    ing, 60, 61, 62
distributed environment and access control,
    345–347
Distributed File Service (DFS), 235
Distributed Processing Programming
    eXecutive/370 (DPPX/370), 281
Distributed Relational Database Architec-
    ture (DRDA), 196
distributed servers, 85–87
Distributed SOM (DSOM), 233
distributed support, xv
Distributed System License Option (DSLO),
    359
"Distributed VM" capability, 256
DL/1 (Data Language/1), 197–198
DLUR (Dependent Logical Unit Requester),
    305, 316–317

DNS (Domain Name Server), 236
Document on Demand function, 150
Domain Name Server (DNS), 236
Domino Go Webserver. *See* WebSphere
    Application Server
Domino Web Server, 203
DOS (Disk Operating System) and VSE/ESA,
    264–267
dot-matrix printing, 149–150
DP (Data Processing) mode, printers, 149
DPPX/370 (Distributed Processing Pro-
    gramming eXecutive/370), 281
DP text (Data Processing text) mode,
    printers, 149
drawer, RAMAC, 124, 130
DRDA (Distributed Relational Database
    Architecture), 196
DSLO (Distributed System License Option),
    359
DSMON (Data Security Monitor), 348
DSOM (Distributed SOM), 233
DSR (Dynamic Storage Reconfiguration), 35
DSS (Decision Support System), 176, 200,
    203–204
Dual-Address-Space Facility (Cross
    Memory Facility), 210–211, 213
Dual Peripheral Component Interconnect
    Cryptographic Coprocessor (Dual
    PCICC), 34
dual-port architecture, SSA, 156–157
dual-purpose paper module, 150
"dumb heads" (display stations), 147–148
Dump Analysis and Elimination (DAE),
    217
Dump Viewing Facility, 253
Dynamic CF Dispatch, 66
Dynamic Channel Path Management,
    z/OS, 240
Dynamic Channel Subsystem, 272
Dynamic Coupling Facility Dispatching
    function, 74
dynamic disk reconstruction, 127–128
Dynamic ICF Expansion, 66
Dynamic IP support of OS/390, 237
Dynamic Link Libraries (DDLs), 187
dynamic partitions, 257, 269–271, 273,
    274
dynamic reconfiguration management, 75
dynamic sparing, RAMAC, 128
Dynamic Storage Reconfiguration (DSR),
    35
dynamic switching, ESCON channels,
    113–114

E
ease-of-manageability, z/OS, 240–241
e-business, 1–12. *See also* eserver Advan-
    tages; zSeries and S/390 families
    application workloads, 5
    data transaction workloads, 5
    evolution of, 2–4
    infrastructure for, 4–6
    Internet impact on, 1–2, 3–4, 105, 161,
        283–284
    personal computers (PCs) and, 3
    VNET, 2–3
    Web application workloads, 5
    workload categories, 5–6
e-Business Start New Program, 364–367
ECC (Error Correction Code), 144
EC (Extended Control), 17
ECL (Emitter-Coupled Logic) technology,
    37, 38
EDI (Electronic Data Interchange), 85–86
EDMSuite (Enterprise Document Manage-
    ment Suite), 206
education costs, 351, 368–369
efficiency improvements, 352
EJB (Enterprise JavaBeans), 171, 188–189
ElectroMagnetic Interference (EMI), 109
Electronic Data Interchange (EDI), 85–86
electronic mail of IBMLink, 371
ElectroPhotographic (EP) printing, 152
EMI (ElectroMagnetic Interference), 109
EMIF (ESCON Multiple Image Facility)
    communications options, 315
    ESCON (Enterprise Systems
        CONnection) channels, 112, 113
    S/390 family evolution, 25
    Virtual Machine/Enterprise System
        Architecture (VM/ESA), 255–256
Emitter-Coupled Logic (ECL) technology,
    37, 38
employee turnover, 353
ENCINA Toolkit, 236
eNetwork Communications Servers
    access control, 347
    communications options, 319–320
    Local Area Networks (LANs), 287, 289
    MVS/ESA Version 5, 223
    Open Blueprint Network Services,
        303–305
    "Open Business" policy, 347
    operating S/390 (OS/390), 237, 238
eNetwork Host on Demand, 320
eNetwork Personal Communications
    (PCOMM), 289, 290

Enterprise Agreement, 356
Enterprise Document Management Suite (EDMSuite), 206
Enterprise Extender, 305
Enterprise JavaBeans (EJB), 171, 188–189
enterprise multimedia capability, 97–98
Enterprise Performance Data Manager/MVS (EPDM/MVS), 330, 331
Enterprise Server Offering (ESO) solutions, 21
Enterprise Storage Server (ESS, "Shark"), 135–136
Enterprise System Architecture (ESA/370), 20, 213
Enterprise System Architecture (ESA/390), 20
Enterprise Systems Architecture/eXtended Configuration (ESA/XC), 254, 255
Enterprise Systems CONnection channels. *See* ESCON
EPDM/MVS (Enterprise Performance Data Manager/MVS), 330, 331
EP (ElectroPhotographic) printing, 152
Ernst & Young, 172
ERP (Error Recovery Procedure), 343
Error Correction Code (ECC), 144
Error Recovery Procedure (ERP), 343
ES/9000, 20. *See also* S/390
ESA/370 (Enterprise System Architecture), 20, 213
ESA/390 architecture, 162–163
ESA/390 architecture mode, 35
ESA/390 (Enterprise System Architecture), 20
ESA/900 mode, ESCON channels, 112
ESA/XC (Enterprise Systems Architecture/ eXtended Configuration), 254, 255
ESCON (Enterprise Systems CONnection) architecture, 23–24
ESCON (Enterprise Systems CONnection) channels, 109–118. *See also* I/O (input/ output) channel architecture
adapter, 315, 316
backup capability, 111–112
block multiplex mode, 117
byte multiplex mode, 117, 118
Channel-to-Channel (CTC), 110, 111
data transfer rates, 110, 112
dedicated connections, 115

device attachments, 110–111
distances supported, 110, 112
dynamic switching, 113–114
ElectroMagnetic Interference (EMI), 109
ESA/900 mode, 112
ESCON Converters, 113, 114, 115, 116–118
ESCON Directors, 111–112, 113–116, 119, 315
ESCON Manager, 116
ESCON Multiple Image Facility (EMIF), 112, 113
eXtended Distance Feature (XDF), 110
fiber-optic cables, 109–110
ground shifts, 109
Logical PARtition (LPAR) mode, 112
multimode fiber, 110
non-ESCON control units, 113, 114, 115, 116
parallel to fiber-optic protocols, 116
performance and, 112
Radio-Frequency Interference (RFI), 109
serial channels, 112
switching functions, 113–114
Virtual Machine/Enterprise System Architecture (VM/ESA) and, 255–256
workload balance, 112
z900 and, 112
ESCON (Enterprise Systems CONnection) environment, 30, 31, 33
ESCON/FICON cables, 76
ESCON Multiple Image Facility. *See* EMIF
eserver Advantages, 6–12. *See also* e-business; zSeries and S/390 families
application flexibility, 8
availability, 7
capacity, 6
Capacity Upgrade on Demand (CUoD), 6, 22, 28, 76–77
cryptographic coprocessor, 9, 33–34
customer care, 7
financial options, 7
Horizontal Capacity Upgrade on Demand, 6
integrated solutions, 8
iSeries, 11
Linux support, 8, 28–29, 278–280
management tools, 6–8
open system industry standards, 8
performance, 9
pSeries, 10–11

reliability technology, 9, 66–67
scalability, xviii, 9
software technology, 9
solution assurance, 7
system management, 7–8
WebSphere Application Server, 8
Workload Licensing Charges (WLC), 6,
        241, 359–360, 361–362
xSeries, 11–12
zSeries, 10
ESO (Enterprise Server Offering) solutions,
        21
ESS (Enterprise Storage Server, "Shark"),
        135–136
ESS EX Performance Package, 136
Ethernet LAN, 92–93, 94
ETR (External Time Reference) card, 45,
        46
Evans, Bob, 20
evolution
        of e-business, 2–4
        of Multiple Virtual Storage/Enterprise
                System Architecture (MVS/ESA),
                208–213
        of peripherals, 160
        of printers, 149
        of Virtual Machine/Enterprise System
                Architecture (VM/ESA), 248–251
        of Virtual Storage Extended/Enterprise
                System Architecture (VSE/ESA),
                264–269
expanded storage, 35, 50, 51–52, 213–215
expanded virtual storage, VM/ESA,
        253–254
eXtended Architecture (XA), 250–251
Extended Control (EC), 17
eXtended Distance Feature (XDF), 110
Extended Real Addressing enhancement,
        MVS/ESA, 209–210
eXtended Remote Copy (XRC), 71, 134,
        136, 343–344
eXtensible Mark-Up Language (XML), 8,
        172
external storage, 52–55. See also DASDs
        (Direct Access Storage Devices);
        RAMAC array architecture;
        storage hierarchy
        optical storage, 50, 54–55, 136–139
        overview, 50
        Redundant Arrays of Independent Disks
                (RAIDs), 54, 120,
                121–122

rewritable optical storage, 55
tape storage, 50, 55, 139–147
write-once optical storage, 55
External Time Reference (ETR) card, 45, 46
Extricity, 172

F
Fast Draft Mode, printers, 149, 150
Fast Service Upgrade (FSU) feature, VSE/
        ESA, 268, 276
fault-tolerant availability, RAMAC, 124
Fault Tolerant Dynamic Memory Arrays
        Facility, 75
FBA (Fixed Block Architecture), 54, 251
FC-PH (Fiber Channel PHysical) signaling
        standard, 118
FDDI (Fiber Distributed Data Interface), 93,
        94, 154
Federal Information Processing Standard
        (FIPS), 33
FedEx, 4
FFST (First Failure Support Technology),
        134
fiber cable, 32–33
Fiber Channel PHysical (FC-PH) signaling
        standard, 118
FIber CONnection (FICON) architecture,
        22–23, 24, 30, 31–32, 118–119
Fiber Distributed Data Interface (FDDI),
        93, 94, 154
fiber-optic cables, 109–110
Fiber Optic Extender Link, 108
fiber-optic links, 92
Fiber Optic Sub Assembly (FOSA) technol-
        ogy, 32–33
Fiber Saver (2029), 72
FICON (FIber CONnection) architecture,
        22–23, 24, 30, 31–32, 118–119
financial justification. See cost justification
financial options of eservers, 7
financing purchases, 354
FIPS (Federal Information Processing
        Standard), 33
firewalls, 347
First Failure Support Technology (FFST),
        134
Fixed Block Architecture (FBA), 54, 251
Flash Copy, 135, 264
Floating-Point (FP) assist processor, 41
FlowMark, 206
folder management and multimedia, 97
footprint, 46–47

fork() function, 260, 263
forms printing, 150, 152
FOSA (Fiber Optic Sub Assembly) technology, 32–33
FP (Floating-Point) assist processor, 41
frame routing, SSA, 157, 159–160
frameworks, software, 163–167
front-ending existing applications, 183–186.
    See also application program development
    Advanced Function Presentation (AFP) data, 184
    Application Development (AD), 184
    CICS Gateway for Java, 185
    Common User Access (CUA) constructs, 184
    Computer Output to Laser Disk (COLD) functions, 184
    Interactive System Productivity Facility (ISPF), 184–185
    MQSeries Client for Java, 185–186
    Net.Data, 186
    OnDemand for OS/390, 184
    overview, 183–184
    VisualAge, 184
FSU (Fast Service Upgrade) feature, VSE/ESA, 268, 276
full-duplex architecture, SSA, 157

G
Gates, Bill, xvi
gateway protection, 346, 347
GCS (Group Control System), 251, 257
GDDM-PGF (Graphical Data Display Manager - Presentation Graphic Feature), 234
GDPS (Geographically Dispersed Parallel Sysplex), 70–71
GEM (Global Enterprise Management), 337–338
general-purpose models (Models 101-116), z900, 27, 28
Generation 3 (G3) processor, 21
Generation 4 (G4) processor, 22
Generation 5 (G5) processor, 22, 31
Generation 6 (G6) processor, 22–23, 31
Geographically Dispersed Parallel Sysplex (GDPS), 70–71
Global Enterprise Management (GEM), 337–338
global interconnected society demands, xv–xvii

Global Resource Serialization (GRS) function, 217
GMLC (Graduated Monthly License Charge), 356, 358
GOLC (Growth Opportunity License Charge), 357, 365
Graduated Monthly License Charge (GMLC), 356, 358
Graphical Data Display Manager - Presentation Graphic Feature (GDDM-PGF), 234
Graphical Enterprise Option of NetView, 325
Graphical User Interface (GUI), 76, 257–258
ground shifts and ESCON channels, 109
Group Control System (GCS), 251, 257
Growth Opportunity License Charge (GOLC), 357, 365
GRS (Global Resource Serialization) function, 217
guest operating system support, VM/ESA, 247–248, 256
GUI (Graphical User Interface), 76, 257–258

H
hackers, 346
hardware, leasing or buying, 353–355
hardware compression, VSE/ESA, 276
Hardware Configuration Definition (HCD), 75–76, 236, 237
Hardware Configuration Manager (HCM), 76, 236
hardware maintenance costs, 350
Hardware Management Console (HMC), 56–57, 58
HCD (Hardware Configuration Definition), 75–76, 236, 237
HCM (Hardware Configuration Manager), 76, 236
HDA (Head-Disk Assembly), 53
Head-Disk Assembly (HDA), 53
HFS (Hierarchical File System), 229, 231
Hierarchical Database Enablers, 197–200
Hierarchical File System (HFS), 229, 231
High-Performance Data Transport (HPDT), 305
High-Performance Routing (HPR), 87, 94, 304–305
Hiperbatch, 222–223
HiPerLinks, 70
HiperSockets ("Network in the Box"), 30, 310, 319

hiperspaces, 214, 216
historical background of zSeries and S/390, xv–xx
HMC (Hardware Management Console), 56–57, 58
Horizontal Capacity Upgrade on Demand, 6
"hot plugging," 45, 127–128, 157–158
hot spots, 61
HPDT (High-Performance Data Transport), 305
HPR (High-Performance Routing), 87, 94, 304–305
HTML (HyperText Markup Language), 172
HTTP support, 166
hubs, LANs, 285
Hyperion, 8
HyperText Markup Language (HTML), 172

I
i2, 172
IBM COBOL, 187
IBM eXtended Facilities Product (IXFP), 131
IBM Global Services (IGS), 181, 367–368
IBM License Manager (ILM), 241, 362–363
IBMLink, 370–371
IBM Network Station, 237
IBM Open Blueprint. *See* Open Blueprint Network Services
IBM—Siebel Global Strategic Alliance, 181
IBM Solution Developer Program, 189
IBM Teach, 369
IBM WebSphere Software Platform, 170–173
ICAPI (Internet Connection Application Programming Interface), 189
ICB (Integrated Cluster Bus), 36, 69
ICF (Integrated Coupling Facility), 28, 66, 74
IC (Internal Coupling) channels, 69
ICL (Integrated Cartridge Loader), 141
ICRF (Integrated Cryptographic Feature), 24, 333, 347
ICSF (Integrated Cryptographic Service Facility), 235
ICSS (Internet Connection Secure Server), 235. *See also* WebSphere Application Server
IDRC (Improved Data Recording Capability), 146–147
IDS (Intelligent Decision Server), 203
IFL (Integrated Facility for Linux), 28, 29, 362

IGS (IBM Global Services), 181, 367–368
IIOP support, 166
ILM (IBM License Manager), 241, 362–363
image manipulation, 177–179
ImagePlus, 177–179, 206
IMLC (Indexed Monthly License Charge), 356, 359
Improved Data Recording Capability (IDRC), 146–147
IMS Client for Java, 200
IMS Connectors, 199–200
IMS DB (Information Management System Database Manager), 67
IMS/ESA Database Manager (IMS/ESA DB), 198
IMS/ESA (Information Management System/Enterprise System Architecture), 197–200
IMS/ESA Transaction Manager (IMS/ESA TM), 198–199
IMS Resource Lock Manager (IRLM), 67, 68, 198
IMS Shared Message Queue (SMQ), 199
IMS TOC (TCP/IP OTMA Connection), 198, 199–200
IMS WWW Templates, 199
independent commercial benchmarks, 99
Independent Software Vendors (ISVs), 162, 172
Indexed Monthly License Charge (IMLC), 356, 359
industry-specific application programs, 179–181. *See also* application programs on S/390
  client/server data processing, 180–181
  Customer Relationship Management (CRM) applications, 181
  DB2 Universal Database, 181
  IBM Global Services and, 181, 367–368
  IBM—Siebel Global Strategic Alliance, 181
  overview, 179–180
  SAP R/3, 180–181
  three-tier client/server implementation, 180
industry-standard benchmarks, 99
InfoLink, 370
InfoPrint Manager, 330
information discovery, data mining, 205
information flow, I/O channel, 106, 107
Information Management System Database Manager (IMS DB), 67

Information Management System/Enterprise System Architecture (IMS/ESA), 197–200

information vs. technology, xvii–xviii

Information Warehouse Solution, 200–204

infrastructure for e-business, 4–6

Initialization/Recovery Path, 293, 294, 295, 296

initiator nodes, SSA, 159

Inmon, William H., 200

input/output channel architecture. *See* I/O

INRANGE, 33

Installation Productivity Option (IPO), VSE/ESA, 267

installation services costs, 351

instruction set, 162–163

insurance claims handling and multimedia, 97–98

Integrated Cartridge Loader (ICL), 141

Integrated Cluster Bus (ICB), 36, 69

Integrated Coupling Facility (ICF), 28, 66, 74

Integrated Cryptographic Feature (ICRF), 24, 333, 347

Integrated Cryptographic Service Facility (ICSF), 235

Integrated Facility for Linux (IFL), 28, 29, 362

integrated functions, 94–97

   data management alternatives, 96–97

   MVS/ESA, 95

   object technology, 95–96

   Portable Operating System Interface (POSIX) standards, 95

   UNIX Services (OpenEdition MVS), 94–95

integrated offerings, 363–367

Integrated Services Digital Network (ISDN), 90, 308, 317

integrated sockets, 230, 231

integrated solutions and eservers, 8

Intelligent Decision Server (IDS), 203

Intelligent Miner, 205

Intelligent Printer Data Stream (IPDS), 150

Intelligent Resource Director (IRD), 239–240

interactive computing support, VM/ESA, 246

Interactive Network Dispatcher, 172

interactive processing vs. batch, 82–83, 167

Interactive System Productivity Facility (ISPF), 184–185

interfaces, communications, 88

interleaved longitudinal recording, 143–144

Internal Coupling (IC) channels, 69

Internal Throughput Rate (ITR), 100, 101, 355

International Technical Union—Telecommunications Standardization Sector (ITU-T), 308

Internet Connection Application Programming Interface (ICAPI), 189

Internet Connection Secure Server (ICSS), 235. *See also* WebSphere Application Server

Internet impact on e-business, 1–2, 3–4, 105, 161, 283–284

Internet Packet eXchange (IPX, Novell), 306

interoperability, UNIX, 228

inventory reduction, 352

I/O cage, 31, 32

I/O channel controllers and connectivity, 310–319

I/O Configuration Program (IOCP), 108

IOCP (I/O Configuration Program), 108

I/O (input/output) channel architecture, 106–119. *See also* ESCON (Enterprise Systems CONnection) channels

   block multiplex mode, 108, 117

   bus cable, 108, 110

   byte multiplex mode, 108, 117, 118

   Central Processor (CP) and, 107

   Channel Command Words (CCWs), 107

   Channel Status Words (CSWs), 107

   control unit (controller), 106

   data transfer rates, 110, 112, 118

   distances supported, 110, 112, 118

   Fiber Channel PHysical (FC-PH) signaling standard, 118

   FIber CONnection (FICON) channels, 22–23, 24, 30, 31–32, 118–119

   Fiber Optic Extender Link, 108

   information flow, 106, 107

   I/O Configuration Program (IOCP), 108

   mode of operation, 108

   packets of information, 107

   parallel channels, 108–109

   performance and, 107–108

   storage hierarchy and, 107–108

   tag cable, 108, 110

I/O Priority Queuing, 136

I/O subsystem channels and adapters, 29–33. *See also* z900 family
155 ATM feature, 31

Business Intelligence (BI) applications
and, 32
Central Processor Complex (CPC), 29,
46
Enterprise Systems CONnection
(ESCON) environment, 30, 31, 33
fiber cable, 32–33
FIber CONnection (FICON) architec-
ture, 22–23, 24, 30, 31–32,
118–119
Fiber Optic Sub Assembly (FOSA)
technology, 32–33
Generation 5/6 (G5/6) cards and, 31
HiperSockets ("Network in the Box"),
30, 310, 319
I/O cage, 31, 32
ISC-3 card, 31
Long Wave Card, 32
Mode Conditioner Patch (MCP) cable,
32
Modular Cooling Units (MCUs), 22, 29,
46
Open Systems Adapter (OSA)-Express,
31, 309–310, 317–319
Open Systems Adapter (OSA)-Express
Fast EtherNET (OSA-E FENET),
31, 317, 319
Short Wave Card, 33
Z-Frame, 31
IPDS (Intelligent Printer Data Stream), 150
IPO (Installation Productivity Option),
VSE/ESA, 267
IPX (Internet Packet eXchange) (Novell), 306
IRD (Intelligent Resource Director),
239–240
IRLM (IMS Resource Lock Manager), 67,
68, 198
ISC-3 card, 31
ISDN (Integrated Services Digital Network),
90, 308, 317
iSeries, 11
ISPF (Interactive System Productivity
Facility), 184–185
ISVs (Independent Software Vendors), 162,
172
ITR (Internal Throughput Rate), 100, 101,
355
ITU-T (International Technical Union—
Telecommunications Standardiza-
tion Sector), 308
IXFP (IBM eXtended Facilities Product),
131

J
Java, 8, 95, 172, 188–189
JavaBeans, 95, 166
Java DataBase Connect (JDBC), 189
Java Development Kit (JDK), 188
Java for OS/390, 188–189
JCL (Job Control Language), 221
JDBC (Java DataBase Connect), 189
JDK (Java Development Kit), 188
JES2 (Job Entry Subsystem 2)
coupling, 68
managing complexity, 334, 336
Multiple Virtual Storage/Enterprise
System Architecture, System
Product Version 4 (MVS/ESA SP
Version 4), 217
MVS/ESA Version 5, 221
JIT (Just-In-Time) compiler, 188
Job Control Language (JCL), 221
Job Entry Subsystem 2. *See* JES2
"just-in-time" delivery of components, 166
Just-In-Time (JIT) compiler, 188

L
LAN administration with LANRES, 225
LANE (ATM LAN Emulation), 94
LAN File Services/ESA, 225, 258
Language Environment, 186–187, 237
LAN Resource Extension and Services
(LANRES), 223–225, 258, 289
LAN Server for MVS, 225–227
LANs (Local Area Networks), 284–291.
See also communications
bridges, 285
cables, 285
Controller Access Unit (CAU), 285
cooperative processing, 288, 290–291
Customer Information Control System
(CICS), 288, 290
data sharing, 286–287, 289
eNetwork Communications Servers,
287, 289
eNetwork Personal Communications
(PCOMM), 289, 290
hubs, 285
LAN Resource Extension and Services
(LANRES), 223–225, 258, 289
NetWare Server (Novell), 289
network stations, 285
Open Systems Adapter (OSA), 87–88,
94, 287, 292
overview, 90–93

personal computers (PCs) as front end, 288, 290–291
printer sharing, 286–287, 289
routers, 285
switches, 285
Systems Network Architecture (SNA), 284
token-ring networks, 90–92, 285–289
twisted-pair (two-wire) cable, 92, 285
Virtual Telecommunications Access Method (VTAM), 68, 289
workstations on, 286–287, 289
Large System Performance Reference (LSPR) ratios, 100–102
laser/ElectroPhotographic (EP) printing, 152
LDAP (Lightweight Directory Access Protocol), 172, 236
leases vs. buying, 353–355
Level 1 (L1) cache, 41, 45, 50–51
Level 2 (L2) cache, 44, 45, 51
LICCC (Licensed Internal Code Configuration Control), 76–77
Licensed Internal Code Configuration Control (LICCC), 76–77
Licensed Internal Code (LIC), 75, 77, 78, 80
LIC (Licensed Internal Code), 75, 77, 78, 80
Lightweight Directory Access Protocol (LDAP), 172, 236
line printers, 150–151
link encryption, 346
links, SSA, 156, 158, 159, 160
Linux Operating System, 8, 28–29, 278–280
list structures, 66
Local Area Networks. *See* LANs
local workstation controller, 85, 86
lock structures, 66
Logger, 234
logical integration of software, 268
logical operations and processors, 39
logical partitioning, 47–48
Logical PARtition (LPAR), 25, 35, 112
Logical UNit (LUN), 135
Logical Units (LUs), SSA, 159
Logic Structured File (LSF), 135
Logilon, 8
LOGON BY function, 256
Long Wave Card, 32
loop-based interface, SSA, 155–156, 157
Lotus Approach, 175–176, 203

Lotus Corp., 3
Lotus Domino, 170
Lotus SmartSuite 97 and cross-industry applications, 175
LPAR coexistence, z/OS, 244, 245
LPAR CPU Management, 239–240
LPAR (Logical PARtition), 25, 35, 112
LSF (Logic Structured File), 135
LSPR (Large System Performance Reference) ratios, 100–102
LUN (Logical UNit), 135
LUs (Logical Units), SSA, 159

M
machine cycle, processors, 38
Macromedia, 172
Magneto-Optical (MO) rewritable, 137, 138
MagnetoResistive (MR) head technology, 123, 144
mainframe computers, xv
main memory. *See* central storage
Maintenance and Operator Subsystem (MOSS-E), 311, 317
maintenance and vendors, 370
MA (Multiple Allegiance), 136
management tools of eservers, 6–8
managing complexity, 323–338
    ADSTAR Distributed Storage Manager (ADSM), 225, 227, 328–329
    Advanced Function Presentation (AFP) data, 184, 330
    Automated Operations Network/MVS (AON/MVS), 326–327, 328
    CICSPlex System Manager (CPSM), 67, 195, 220, 331
    Data Encryption Standard (DES), 33, 333
    Data Facility Storage Management Subsystem (DFSMS), 138, 328, 343–344
    data manipulation and evaluation, 336–337
    DB2/Performance Manager (DB2PM), 331
    digital certificates, 333, 348
    digital printing, 330
    Enterprise Performance Data Manager/MVS (EPDM/MVS), 330, 331
    Global Enterprise Management (GEM), 337–338
    Graphical Enterprise Option of NetView, 325
    InfoPrint Manager, 330

Integrated Cryptographic Service Feature (ICRF), 24, 333, 347
Job Entry Subsystem 2 (JES2), 334, 336
MultiSystem Manager of NetView, 326
NetView Access Services (NVAS), 333
NetView Graphic Monitor Facility (NGMF), 326, 327, 331
NetView Performance Monitor (NPM), 330–331
Network File System (NFS), 328
Open Topology Interface, 326
Operations Planning and Control/ESA (OPC/ESA), 333–334, 335
overview, 323–324
performance management, 330–331
Personal Security Card, 333
problem management, 331–332
Procedural Option of NetView, 325
Resource Access Control Facility (RACF), 332–333
Resource Management Facility (RMF), 330, 336–337
Resource Object Data Manager (RODM), 324, 325, 326, 327, 334
RMF Sysplex Data Server, 337
SecureWay Security Server, 235, 332, 347
Security Access Facility (SAF), 324
security management, 332–333
System Automation, 327
System Display and Search Facility (SDSF), 234, 334, 336
Systems Network Architecture (SNA), 324, 325
Tivoli Storage Manager, 328–329
TME 10 Enterprise Console (TEC), 332
TME 10 GEM Application Policy Manager (APM), 331–332
TME 10 Global Enterprise Manager (GEM), 331
TME 10 Information/Management, 331–332
TME 10 NetView (NetView), 294–295, 296, 324–327
Transaction Security System, 333
Unattended Option of NetView, 325
workload management, 333–334, 335
manuals on CD-ROM, 24
MAS (MultiAccess Spool), 217
masqueraders, 345–346
Massively Parallel Processing (MPP), 58–59
master node, SSA, 159
Maximum Press Web site, xx

MCCU (Multisystem Channel Communication Unit), 216
McDATA, 33
MCM (MultiChip Module), 22, 40, 41, 42, 45, 47
MCP (Mode Conditioner Patch) cable, 32
MCUs (Modular Cooling Units), 22, 29, 46
Measured Usage License Charge (MULC), 356
media inventory and multimedia, 98
MediaMiner, 205
"Members Only" Web site, xx
Message and Queue Interface (MQI), 298, 300–302
message frames, 90–92
message passing, 63–64
metadata, 202
metal particle medium, 143
Microsoft Corp., xvi
migration considerations, z/OS, 242–244
Million Service Units (MSUs) for pricing, 355
MLC (MonoLithic Circuit) technology, 16
MNPS (MultiNode Persistent Sessions), 68, 235
Mode Conditioner Patch (MCP) cable, 32
modems, 85, 86, 320
mode of operation, I/O channel, 108
Modular Cooling Units (MCUs), 22, 29, 46
MO (Magneto-Optical) rewritable, 137, 138
MonoLithic Circuit (MLC) technology, 16
monthly charge for software, 355
MOSS-E (Maintenance and Operator Subsystem), 311, 337
motor insurance claims handling and multimedia, 97–98
Move Page enhancement, MVS/ESA, 216
MPP (Massively Parallel Processing), 58–59
MPTN (MultiProtocol Transport Networking), 303
MQI (Message and Queue Interface), 298, 300–302
MQSeries, 81, 300–302
MQSeries Client for Java, 185–186
MR (MagnetoResistive) head technology, 123, 144
MSC (MultiSystem Coupling) feature, 67
MSUs (Million Service Units) for pricing, 355
msys for Setup, 240–241
MULC (Measured Usage License Charge), 356

Multiaccess Connector, 311
MultiAccess Spool (MAS), 217
MultiChip Module (MCM), 22, 40, 41, 42, 45, 47
multilevel cache, 126
multimedia, 97–98, 307–308
multimode fiber, 110
MultiNode Persistent Sessions, 194–195
MultiNode Persistent Sessions (MNPS), 68, 235
Multiple Allegiance (MA), 136
Multiple Virtual Storage/370 (MVS/370), 209–211
Multiple Virtual Storage/Enterprise System Architecture. *See* MVS/ESA
Multiple Virtual Storage/Enterprise System Architecture, System Product Version 4. *See* MVS/ESA SP Version 4
Multiple Virtual Storage/eXtended Architecture (MVS/XA), 211–213
multiplexed data traffic, 93–94
multiprocessing configuration, S/390, 18
multiprocessors, 58
multiprogramming support of operating systems, 58, 83–84
MultiProtocol Transport Networking (MPTN), 303
Multisystem Channel Communication Unit (MCCU), 216
MultiSystem Coupling (MSC) feature, 67
MultiSystem Manager of NetView, 326
multiuser support of operating systems, 83
Muxmaster (9729 Optical Wavelength Division Multiplexor), 119–120
MVS/370 (Multiple Virtual Storage/370), 209–211
MVS/ESA (Multiple Virtual Storage/ Enterprise System Architecture), 208–233. *See also* MVS/ESA SP Version 4 (Multiple Virtual Storage/Enterprise System Architecture, System Product Version 4); MVS/ESA Version 5; OS/390 (Operating S/390); UNIX services
   24-bit mode of operation, 211, 213
   31-bit mode of operation, 213
   access-register addressing, 215
   binary-compatible application class libraries, 232–233
   central storage of, 213, 214, 215

   common area approach, 210, 211, 213
   Cross Memory Facility (Dual-Address-Space Facility), 210–211, 213
   data sharing, 215
   data spaces, 214, 215
   Distributed SOM (DSOM), 233
   Enterprise System Architecture (ESA/370) and, 213
   evolution of, 208–213
   expanded storage and, 213–215
   Extended Real Addressing enhancement, 209–210
   hiperspaces, 214, 216
   Move Page enhancement, 216
   Multiple Virtual Storage/370 (MVS/370), 209–211
   Multiple Virtual Storage/eXtended Architecture (MVS/XA), 211–213
   Operating System/Multiprogramming with Fixed number of Tasks (OS/MFT), 209
   Operating System/Multiprogramming with Variable Tasks (OS/MVT), 208–209
   Operating System/Virtual Storage 2 (OS/VS2), 209
   overview, 95
   partitions, 208–209
   processor storage, 215
   System Object Model (SOM) objects for MVS (SOMobjects for MVS), 232–233
   virtual storage support, 209
MVS/ESA SP Version 4 (Multiple Virtual Storage/Enterprise System Architecture, System Product Version 4), 216–219. *See also* MVS/ESA (Multiple Virtual Storage/Enterprise System Architecture); MVS/ESA Version 5
   Advanced Program-to-Program Communications/MVS (APPC/MVS), 217–218
   Asynchronous Pageout Facility, 218
   availability, 217
   block paging, 218
   Channel-to-Channel (CTC) connections, 216
   Common Storage Tracker, 219
   communications, 217–218
   console services, 216–217
   Cross System Coupling Facility (XCF), 217

Customer Information Control System (CICS), 219
Dump Analysis and Elimination (DAE), 217
Global Resource Serialization (GRS) function, 217
Job Entry Subsystem 2 (JES2), 217
MultiAccess Spool (MAS), 217
Multisystem Channel Communication Unit (MCCU), 216
numerically intensive applications and, 218–219
open system environment, 219
Partitioned Data Set Extended (PDSE), 217
POSIX-compliant Application Programming Interface (API), 219
Server Facilities, 218
subsystem storage protection, 219
Switched Virtual Circuits (SVC) dumps, 217
SYSMDUMPs, 217
sysplex support, 216–217
Sysplex Timer, 216
System Application Architecture (SSA) Common Programming Interface for Communications (CPI-C), 218
Vector Facility enhancements, 219
Virtual Lookaside Facility (VLF) NOTE command (VLFNOTE), 217
working set management, 218
MVS/ESA System Product (SP) Base Control Program (BCP), 221
MVS/ESA Version 5, 219–227. *See also* MVS/ESA (Multiple Virtual Storage/Enterprise System Architecture); MVS/ESA SP Version 4 (Multiple Virtual Storage/Enterprise System Architecture, System Product Version 4)
ADSTAR Distributed Storage Manager (ADSM), 225, 227
ASCII terminal support, 220
balancing workload, 220
Basic Sequential Access Method (BSAM) and, 221, 223
Batch Local Shared Resources (BLSR), 223
BatchPipes/MVS, 221–222, 223
CICSPlex System Manager (CPSM), 220
Coupling Facility (CF), 219
data distribution with LANRES, 225
disk serving with LANRES, 223

eNetwork Communications Servers, 223
Hiperbatch, 222–223
Job Control Language (JCL), 221
Job Entry Subsystem 2 (JES2), 221
LAN administration with LANRES, 225
LAN File Services/ESA, 225
LAN Resource Extension and Services (LANRES), 223–225
LAN Server for MVS, 225–227
MVS/ESA System Product (SP) Base Control Program (BCP), 221
NetWare (Novell) workstation users and, 223–225
Network File System (NFS) file serving capabilities, 227
parallel sysplex services support, 219
performance data, 220
print serving with LANRES, 224
Queued Sequential Access Method (QSAM) and, 221, 223
Resource Management Facility (RMF), 220
Sequential Data Striping, 223
Systems Network Architecture (SNA), 223
Systems Resource Manager (SRM) interfaces, simplified, 220
Time Sharing Option/Extensions (TSO/E), 223
Tivoli Storage Manager, 225, 227
Transmission Control Protocol/Internet Protocol (TCP/IP) support, 223
Virtual I/O (VIO), 221
WorkLoad Manager (WLM), 219–220
X/Open Single UNIX Specification support, 220–221
XPG4 Base Specification support, 220, 231

N
NALC (New Application License Charge), 365
National Medal of Technology, 20
NCF (Network Computing Framework), 165–167
Near-Letter-Quality (NLQ) mode, printers, 149
NetBIOS support, 306
Net.Data, 186
net present value, 353
NetQuestion, 235
NetView Access Services (NVAS), 333
NetView Graphic Monitor Facility (NGMF), 326, 327, 331

NetView Performance Monitor (NPM), 330–331
NetView (TME 10 NetView), 294–295, 296, 324–327
NetWare (Novell) workstation users and MVS/ESA Version 5, 223–225
NetWare Server (Novell), 289
network characteristics, SSA, 158–159
network computing, 234, 235, 237, 262, 283. *See also* distributed computer communications
Network Computing Framework (NCF), 165–167
Network File System. *See* NFS
networking IBM Global Services, 367–368
"Network in the Box" (HiperSockets), 30, 310, 319
network management, 294–295
Network Queuing System/MVS (NQS/MVS), 231
Network Services, 299, 302–308
network stations, 285
New Application License Charge (NALC), 365
NFS (Network File System)
   managing complexity, 328
   MVS/ESA Version 5, 227
   Operating S/390 (OS/390), 234
   optical storage, 138
   UNIX Services, 229–230
NGMF (NetView Graphic Monitor Facility), 326, 327, 331
NLQ (Near-Letter-Quality) mode, printers, 149
nodes, SSA, 156, 158–159
non-ESCON control units, 113, 114, 115, 116
non-parallel sysplex configuration, 194
nonparallel work units, 276
NonVolatile Storage (NVS), 125–126, 128, 131–132
Novell, 172
NPM (NetView Performance Monitor), 330–331
NQS/MVS (Network Queuing System/MVS), 231
numerically intensive applications and MVS/ESA SP Version 4, 218–219
NVAS (NetView Access Services), 333
NVS (NonVolatile Storage), 125–126, 128, 131–132
N-way data sharing, 198

O
OAM (Object Access Method), 138
Object Access Method (OAM), 138
Object-Oriented Programming (OOP), 188–189
object technology, 95–96
OLTP (On-Line Transaction Processing), 73, 188
OnDemand for OS/390, 184
One-Time Charge (OTC), 355, 360
On-Line Transaction Processing (OLTP), 73, 188
OOP (Object-Oriented Programming), 188–189
OPC/ESA (Operations Planning and Control/ESA), 333–334, 335
Open Blueprint Network Services, 296–309. *See also* distributed computer communications
   Advanced Peer-to-Peer Networking (APPN), 304–305
   Advanced Program-to-Program Communications (APPC), 300
   AnyNet products, 303, 305–306
   APPN Implementor's Workshop (AIW), 304–305
   Asynchronous Transfer Mode (ATM), 305, 306–308
   bridges, 302
   cells within ATM, 94, 308
   Common Management Information Protocol (CMIP), 309
   Common Programming Interface for Communications (CPI-C), 298
   Common Transport Semantics (CTS), 302–306
   Communications Controllers, 304
   Communications Services, 298–302
   conversations, 298, 300
   Cross System Coupling Facility (XCF), 304
   Dependent LU Server/Requester, 305, 316–317
   Distributed Computing Environment (DCE), 300
   eNetwork Communications Servers, 303–305
   Enterprise Extender, 305
   High-Performance Data Transport (HPDT), 305
   High-Performance Routing (HPR), 87, 94, 304–305

Integrated Services Digital Network (ISDN), 90, 308, 317
Internet Packet eXchange (IPX) (Novell) support, 306
Message and Queue Interface (MQI), 298, 300–302
MQSeries, 81, 300–302
multimedia communications, 307–308
MultiProtocol Transport Networking (MPTN), 303
NetBIOS support, 306
Network Services, 299, 302–308
Open System Foundation (OSF), 300
Open System Interconnection (OSI) support, 306
overview, 298, 299
parallel sysplex and networking, 309, 310
Remote Procedure Call (RPC), 298, 300
Signaling and Control Pane, 308
Sockets, 305–206
subnetworking, 306–308
Synchronous Optical NETwork (SONET), 306
Systems Management, 299, 309, 310
Systems Network Architecture (SNA), 305, 309
Transmission Control Protocol/Internet Protocol (TCP/IP) support, 305, 306, 309
Transport Services, 299, 306–309
UNIX Services, 228, 232, 305–306
Virtual Machine/Enterprise System Architecture (VM/ESA), 261
Virtual Storage Extended/Enterprise System Architecture (VSE/ESA), 276
Wide Area Networks (WANs), 306, 309
"Open Business" policy, 338–349
access control options, 344–349
archiving data, 340–341
audit reports, 348
back doors, 346
backing up data, 339–340
Cryptographic Coprocessor (PCICC), 347
Data Base Unload (DBU), 348
Data Facility Storage Management Subsystem (DFSMS), 138, 328, 343–344
data preservation options, 339–344
Data Security Monitor (DSMON), 348
digital certificates, 333, 348

disaster recovery, 341–342
Distributed Computing Environment (DCE), 347
distributed environment and securing data, 345–347
eNetwork Communications Servers, 347
Error Recovery Procedure (ERP), 343
eXtended Remote Copy (XRC), 71, 134, 136, 343–344
firewalls, 347
gateway protection, 346, 347
hackers, 346
Integrated Cryptographic Feature (ICRF), 24, 333, 347
link encryption, 346
masqueraders, 345–346
overview, 338–339
passwords, 346, 348, 349
Peer-to-Peer Remote Copy (PPRC), 70–71, 134, 135, 343
RACF Remote Sharing Facility (RRSF), 349
RACF Sysplex Communication option, 348
real-time data recovery, 342–344
Resource Access Control Facility (RACF), 348–349
restoring data, 339–340
security policies, 346, 347
Security Servers, 235, 332, 347
System Data Mover (SDM), 343–344
Trojan horse, 346
viruses, 345
worms, 345
OpenEdition DCE Distributed File Service, 235
OpenEdition for VM/ESA, 259–262
OpenEdition MVS (UNIX Services), 94–95
Open Software Foundation (OSF) standards, S/390, 25
Open Software Foundation's Distributed Computing Environment (OSF/DCE), 230
open system environment and MVS/ESA SP Version 4, 219
Open System Foundation (OSF), 300
open system industry standards, 8, 172
Open System Interconnection (OSI), 306
Open Systems Adapter (OSA), 87–88, 94, 256–257, 287, 292
Open Systems Adapter (OSA)-Express, 31, 309–310, 317–319

Open Systems Adapter (OSA)-Express Fast EtherNET (OSA-E FENET), 31, 317, 319
open systems importance and UNIX, 227–228
Open Topology Interface, 326
operating modes, 35–36, 52
operating ("rent-to-own") leases, 354
Operating S/390. *See* OS/390
operating system layer, 77, 78, 79, 163, 164
Operating System/Multiprogramming with Fixed number of Tasks (OS/MFT), 209
Operating System/Multiprogramming with Variable Tasks (OS/MVT), 208–209
operating systems, 80–84, 207–282. *See also* MVS/ESA (Multiple Virtual Storage/Enterprise System Architecture); OS/390 (Operating S/390); VM/ESA (Virtual Machine/Enterprise System Architecture); VSE/ESA (Virtual Storage Extended/Enterprise System Architecture); z/OS
    Advanced Interactive eXecutive/Enterprise Systems Architecture (AIX/ESA), 278
    Application Programming Interface (API) and, 78, 79, 81
    applications and, 81
    batch vs. interactive processing, 82–83, 167
    compatibility with software, 163, 165
    Distributed Processing Programming eXecutive/370 (DPPX/370), 281
    interactive processing vs. batch, 82–83, 167
    Linux Operating System, 8, 28–29, 278–280
    MQSeries, 81, 300–302
    multiprogramming support, 58, 83–84
    multiuser support, 83
    overview, 207–208
    time sharing (slicing), 84
    Transaction Processing Facility (TPF), 280–281
Operating System/Virtual Storage 2 (OS/VS2), 209
Operations Planning and Control/ESA (OPC/ESA), 333–334, 335
optical storage, 136–139
    3995 Optical Library, 138–139
    compatibility, 137
    Continuous Composite Write-Once (CCW), 137
    cost effectiveness of, 137
    Data Facility Storage Management Subsystem (DFSMS), 138, 328, 343–344
    Magneto-Optical (MO) rewritable, 137, 138
    Network File System (NFS), 138
    Object Access Method (OAM), 138
    overview, 50, 54–55
    permanency of, 137
    Write-Once, Read-Many (WORM), 137
Optical Wavelength Division Multiplexor (Muxmaster), 119–120
OrderLink, 370
OS/390 BonusPak II, 235
OS/390 (Operating S/390), 208–238. *See also* MVS/ESA (Multiple Virtual Storage/Enterprise System Architecture); operating systems; UNIX services; z/OS Version 1, Release 1 (OS/390 Version 2, Release 10)
    application support, 234, 235, 237
    ATM connectivity, 234
    ATM support, 237
    base services, 233–234
    BonusPak II, 235
    C language support, 228, 229, 231, 234, 236–237
    Commercial Data Masking Facility (CDMF) support, 235
    communications server, 235–236
    Component Broker for OS/390 Application Enabling Technology, 237
    Data Facility Sort (DFSORT), 234
    DCE Application Support, 236
    distributed computing, 236
    Distributed File Service (DFS), 235
    Domain Name Server (DNS), 236
    Dynamic IP support, 237
    ENCINA Toolkit, 236
    eNetwork Communications Servers, 237, 238
    FICON channel support, 237
    Graphical Data Display Manager - Presentation Graphic Feature (GDDM-PGF), 234
    Hardware Configuration Definition (HCD), 75–76, 236, 237

Hardware Configuration Manager (HCM), 76, 236
IBM Network Station, 237
Integrated Cryptographic Service Facility (ICSF), 235
Internet Connection Secure Server (ICSS), 235
Language Environment, 237
Lightweight Directory Access Protocol (LDAP), 236
Logger, 234
migration, 242–243
Multinode Persistent Sessions, 235
NetQuestion, 235
network computing, 234, 235, 237
Network File System (NFS), 234
OpenEdition DCE Distributed File Service, 235
optional features, 233, 234
OS/390 BonusPak II, 235
overview, 233
Parallel Sysplex Technology, 237, 238
PCI Cryptographic support, 238
proxy servers, 172
Public Key API (PKA) support, 235
Release 1, 234
Release 2, 234
Release 3, 234–235
Release 4 (Version 2), 235–237
Release 5-9 (Version 2), 237–238
Resource Access Control Facility (RACF), 235, 238
Resource Management Facility (RMF), 234, 237
Secure Network Server, 235
SecureWay Communications Server, 238
security, 235
Security Servers, 235, 332, 347
ServerPac, 234
SMP/E enhancements, 234
System Display and Search Facility (SDSF), 234
System Object Model (SOM)/Distributed SOM (DSOM) support, 234
system services, 236
systems management, 236
Systems Network Architecture (SNA), 235
Telnet support, 237
Tivoli Management Agent, 238
Tivoli TME 10 Framework, 236
Transmission Control Protocol/Internet Protocol (TCP/IP) support, 235–236, 237

Trusted Key Entry (TKE) support, 235
UNIX Services, 234–235, 238
UNIX support, 236–237
Version 2, 235–238
Version 2 Release 10, 13–14
VisualLift, 234
WebSphere Application Server, 170–171, 235, 237, 238
Web Usage Mining, 235
WorkLoad Manager (WLM), 234, 236, 237
OSA-E FENET (Open Systems Adapter (OSA)-Express Fast EtherNET), 31, 317, 319
OSA-Express (Open Systems Adapter-Express), 31, 309–310, 317–319
OSAM (Overflow Sequential Access Method), 67
OSA (Open Systems Adapter), 87–88, 94, 256–257, 287, 292
OSF/DCE (Open Software Foundation's Distributed Computing Environment), 230
OSF (Open Software Foundation) standards, S/390, 25
OSF (Open System Foundation), 300
OSI (Open System Interconnection), 306
OS/MFT (Operating System/Multiprogramming with Fixed number of Tasks), 209
OS/MVT (Operating System/Multiprogramming with Variable Tasks), 208–209
OS/VS2 (Operating System/Virtual Storage 2), 209
OTC (One-Time Charge), 355, 360
Overflow Sequential Access Method (OSAM), 67
overhead reduction, SSA, 157

P
packets of information, I/O channel, 107
page printers, 151–154
Parallel Access Volumes (PAV), 136, 264
parallel channels, 108–109
parallel processing, 57–72. *See also* availability and fault tolerance; coupling
application programs and, 167
applications and, 59
backup capability, 62–63
Capacity BackUp (CBU) feature, 22, 71, 77

Coupling Facility (CF), 60
Cross-System Coupling Facility (XCF), 63
data sharing environment, 59–64
distributed data systems, 60, 61, 62
eXtended Remote Copy (XRC), 71, 134, 136, 343–344
Geographically Dispersed Parallel Sysplex (GDPS), 70–71
hot spots, 61
Massively Parallel Processing (MPP), 58–59
message passing, 63–64
multiprocessors, 58
parallel sysplex, 59–60, 63–64, 71–72
partitioned data systems, 60–61, 62
Peer-to-Peer Remote Copy (PPRC), 70–71, 134, 135, 343
Recovery Point Objective (RPO), 71
remote copy, 70–71, 134
RS/6000 platform, 59
S/390, 21
server, loss of, 61–62
shared data environment, 59–64
"shares nothing" design, 58–59
"single-system" image of, 62
Symmetric MultiProcessing (SMP), 27, 58
Sysplex Timer (9037), 65, 71–72, 216
Time-Of-Day (TOD) clocks, 65, 71
UNIX environment, 59
workload balancing, 61–62, 112
WorkLoad Manager (WLM), 62
parallel server offerings, 363–364
parallel sysplex
application enablers, 194
MVS/ESA Version 5, 219
Open Blueprint Network Services, 309, 310
Operating S/390 (OS/390), 237, 238
overview, 59–60, 63–64, 71–72
S/390 family evolution, 20
virtual Machine/Enterprise System Architecture (VM/ESA), 262
Parallel Sysplex Coupling Facility, 199
Parallel Sysplex Licensing Charge (PSLC), 356, 357–359, 360–361
parallel to fiber-optic protocols, 116
Parallel Transaction Server, 356
parallel work units, 276
parity concept, 122
parking area of tape storage, 145
Partitioned Data Set Extended (PDSE), 217

partitioned data systems, 60–61, 62
partitions
Multiple Virtual Storage/Enterprise System Architecture (MVS/ESA), 208–209
processor technology, 47–48
Virtual Storage Extended/Enterprise System Architecture (VSE/ESA), 267, 269–270, 272–273, 277
passwords, 346, 348, 349
patch maintenance, 75
PAV (Parallel Access Volumes), 136, 264
payback period, 353
PCICC (Cryptographic Coprocessor), 347
PCI Cryptographic support, 238
PCOMM (eNetwork Personal Communications), 289, 290
PCs (personal computers)
e-business and, 3
front end for Local Area Networks (LANs), 288, 290–291
zSeries and S/390 families and, xv
PDSE (Partitioned Data Set Extended), 217
Peer-to-Peer Remote Copy (PPRC), 70–71, 134, 135, 343
performance, 98–102
benchmark testing, 99–100
cost per transaction per unit of time, 102
DASDs, 120–121
ESCON channels and, 112
eservers, 9
independent commercial benchmarks, 99
industry-standard benchmarks, 99
Internal Throughput Rate (ITR), 100, 101, 355
I/O channel and, 107–108
Large System Performance Reference (LSPR) ratios, 100–102
management, 330–331
MVS/ESA Version 5, 220
RAMAC array architecture, 123, 124–127
S/390, 377
storage hierarchy and, 49
throughput, 100–101, 167, 355
Transaction Processing Performance Council (TPC), 99, 102
transactions per second/minute (tps/m), 102
workload environments, 101, 102
z900, 25, 27, 377

zSeries and S/390, 377
Periodic Resident Testing (PRT), 134
peripherals, 104–160. *See also* disk storage;
    I/O (input/output) channel
    architecture; optical storage;
    printers; SSA (Serial Storage
    Architecture); tape storage
    9729 Optical Wavelength Division
      Multiplexor (Muxmaster), 119–120
    data perception, changes in, 105
    display stations ("dumb heads"), 147–148
    evolution of, 160
    Optical Wavelength Division Multi-
      plexor (Muxmaster), 119–120
permanency of optical storage, 137
personal computers. *See* PCs
Personal Security Card, 333
physical integration of software, 267
pipelines, 252
PKA (Public Key API) support of OS/390,
    235
PL/1 multitasking support, 187
planar board, 45
POR (Power-On-Reset), 35
portability of UNIX, 228
Portable Operating System Interface
    (POSIX) standards, 95, 228–231,
    260–261
POSIX-compliant Application Program-
    ming Interface (API), 219
POSIX (Portable Operating System
    Interface) standards, 95, 228–231,
    260–261
POWEROFF option, 256
Power-On-Reset (POR), 35
"power save state," 73
Power Service and Control Network
    (PSCN), 56
power supply, 73
PPRC (Peer-to-Peer Remote Copy), 70–71,
    134, 135, 343
prewritten application programs, 168,
    169–181. *See also* application
    programs on S/390; cross-industry
    application programs; industry-
    specific application programs
pricing strategies for software, 355–363
printers, 148–154
    Advanced Function Common Control
      Unit (AFCCU), 153
    All-Points-Addressable (APA) mode, 149
    alphanumeric mode, 149
    band-matrix printing, 150–151

    character printers, 149–150
    character sets, 149
    Data Processing (DP) mode, 149
    Data Processing text (DP text) mode,
      149
    Document on Demand function, 150
    dot-matrix printing, 149–150
    dual-purpose paper module, 150
    evolution of, 149
    Fast Draft Mode, 149, 150
    Fiber Distributed Data Interface (FDDI),
      154
    forms printing, 150, 152
    Intelligent Printer Data Stream (IPDS),
      150
    laser/ElectroPhotographic (EP) printing,
      152
    line printers, 150–151
    Near-Letter-Quality (NLQ) mode, 149
    page printers, 151–154
    sharing, Local Area Networks (LANs),
      286–287, 289
print serving with LANRES, 224
privileged frame, SSA, 158
problem management, 331–332
procedural application development, 186–
    187. *See also* application program
    development
    Dynamic Link Libraries (DDLs), 187
    IBM COBOL for OS/390 and VM, 187
    IBM COBOL for VSE, 187
    Language Environment for MVS and
      VM, Release 5, 186–187
    overview, 186
    PL/1 multitasking support, 187
    System Object Model (SOM), 187
    Workstation Interactive Test Tool
      (WITT and X/WITT), 187
Procedural Option of NetView, 325
Processing Units (PUs), 45, 46, 73
processor capacity for pricing software,
    355–356
processor controller, 56–57
Processor Resource/Systems Manager
    (PR/SM), 48
processor storage, MVS/ESA, 215
processor technology, 36–48. *See also*
    CMOS (Complementary Metal
    Oxide Semiconductor)
    Advanced Transistor Technology (ATX),
      37
    bipolar technology, 38–40, 41
    chip technology, 36–40

circuit cards, 38
Complementary Metal Oxide Semiconductor (CMOS) technology, 20–21, 22, 37, 38, 40–47
cycle time, 38–39, 40
Differential Current Switch (DCS) technology, 38
Emitter-Coupled Logic (ECL) technology, 37, 38
logical operations, 39
logical partitioning, 47–48
machine cycle, 38
partitions, 47–48
Processor Resource/Systems Manager (PR/SM), 48
Static Random Access Memory (SRAM), 37–38
substrates, 38, 43–44
Thermal Conduction Module (TCM), 38, 39, 40
Processor Unit (PU) MCM, 25, 26, 28
productivity improvements, 352
product support IBM Global Services, 367
professional IBM Global Services, 367
protocols, 85, 88–94
PR/SM (Processor Resource/Systems Manager), 48
PRT (Periodic Resident Testing), 134
PSCN (Power Service and Control Network), 56
pSeries, 10–11
PSLC (Parallel Sysplex Licensing Charge), 356, 357–359, 360–361
PS/SM facility, 24
publication. *See* software for business
Public Key API (PKA) support of OS/390, 235
PU (Processor Unit) MCM, 25, 26, 28
PUs (Processing Units), 45, 46, 73

Q
QDIO (Queued Direct I/O), 264
QMF HPO/Shuttle feature, 174–175
QMF (Query Management Facility), 173–176, 203
QSAM (Queued Sequential Access Method) and MVS/ESA Version 5, 221, 223
quality improvements, 352
Query Management Facility (QMF), 173–176, 203
Queued Direct I/O (QDIO), 264
Queued Sequential Access Method (QSAM) and MVS/ESA Version 5, 221, 223

R
R1-R3 models, CMOS, 41, 43, 44, 45
RACF Remote Sharing Facility (RRSF), 349
RACF (Resource Access Control Facility)
access control, 348–349
coupling, 68
managing complexity, 332–333
"Open Business" policy, 348–349
Operating S/390 (OS/390), 235, 238
RACF Sysplex Communication option, 348
rack, RAMAC, 124, 125
Radio-Frequency Interference (RFI), 109
RAID-0 (data striping), 122
RAID-1 (data mirroring), 122
RAIDs (Redundant Arrays of Independent Disks), 54, 120, 121–122
RAMAC array architecture, 123–131
3990 Storage Control, 131–134
availability of, 124–125, 127–128
cache hits and misses, 126
component redundancy, 120
concurrent copy, 127, 131, 136
Cross Platform Extension (XPE), 131
DASD Fast Write, 125–126
Data Facility Program (DFP), 127
drawer, 124, 130
dynamic disk reconstruction, 127–128
dynamic sparing, 128
fault-tolerant availability, 124
"hot plugging," 127–128
IBM eXtended Facilities Product (IXFP), 131
MagnetoResistive (MR) head technology, 123, 144
multilevel cache, 126
NonVolatile Storage (NVS), 125–126, 128, 131–132
overview, 14, 54
performance of, 123, 124–127
rack, 124, 125
RAMAC 2, 123
RAMAC 2 Scalable Array 2, 128–130
RAMAC 3, 123
RAMAC 3 Storage Frame and Drawer, 130
record caching, 127
RVA 2 Turbo devices, 127, 130–131, 135
Sequential Data Striping, 125
SnapShot, 127, 131
storage frames, 123, 130
track caching, 126
Ultrastar 2XP disk drive, 123, 130

Rational, 172
Razorfish, 172
RDO (Resource Definition On-line), 194
real-time data, data warehouses, 200–201
real-time data recovery, 342–344
Real-Time Monitor (RTM) VM/ESA, 264
reconciled data, data warehouses, 202
reconfiguration management, 75
record caching, RAMAC, 127
Recovery Point Objective (RPO), 71
Red Hat, 172
Reduced Instruction Set Computing (RISC), 135
Redundant Arrays of Independent Disks (RAIDs), 54, 120, 121–122
registers, 49–50
Relational Database Enablers: DB2 and SQL, 195–197
reliability, 9, 66–67
remote copy, 70–71, 134
Remote operator Facility, 294, 295
Remote Procedure Call. *See* RPC
Remote Site Recovery (RSR), 75, 198
Remote Spooling Communications Subsystem (RSCS), 258–259
Remote Support Facility, 56
remote workstation controller, 85, 86
renting, 354–355
"rent-to-own" (operating) leases, 354
Resource Access Control Facility. *See* RACF
Resource Definition On-line (RDO), 194
Resource Management Facility. *See* RMF
resource management of VM/ESA, 246
Resource Object Data Manager (RODM), 324, 325, 326, 327, 334
restoring data, 339–340
REstructured eXtended eXecutor (REXX/VSE) language, 252, 278
retailing and multimedia, 97
rewritable optical storage, 55
REXX/VSE (REstructured eXtended eXecutor) language, 252, 278
RFI (Radio-Frequency Interference), 109
RISC (Reduced Instruction Set Computing), 135
RMF (Resource Management Facility)
managing complexity, 330, 336–337
MVS/ESA Version 5, 220
Operating S/390 (OS/390), 234, 237
RMF Sysplex Data Server, 337
RODM (Resource Object Data Manager), 324, 325, 326, 327, 334

routers, LANs, 285
RPC (Remote Procedure Call)
Open Blueprint Network Services, 298, 300
UNIX Services, 230, 236
Virtual Machine/Enterprise System Architecture (VM/ESA), 261–262
RPO (Recovery Point Objective), 71
RRSF (RACF Remote Sharing Facility), 349
RS/6000 platform, 59
RSCS (Remote Spooling Communications Subsystem), 258–259
RSR (Remote Site Recovery), 75, 198
RTM (Real-Time Monitor) VM/ESA, 264
RVA 2 Turbo devices, 127, 130–131, 135

S
S/360 family, 16
S/370 family, 16–20, 23
S/390 family evolution, 13–25. *See also* application programs on S/390; z900 family; zSeries and S/390 families
30XX series, 18–19
43XX series, 18
3270 display, 148
access registers, 20
architecture definition step, 15–16
Asynchronous Data Mover Facility (ADMF), 24
Capacity BackUp (CBU), 22, 71, 77
Capacity Upgrade on Demand (CUoD), 6, 22, 28, 76–77
Central Electronic Complex (CEC), 21
Central Processors (CPs), 22
CMOS and, 20–21, 22, 40, 45
compatibility and migration, 15
Complementary Metal Oxide Semiconductor (CMOS) and, 20–21, 22, 40, 45
Coupling Facility (CF), 21, 22
data spaces, 20
DB2 Sort Enhancement, 24
Enterprise Server Offering (ESO) solutions, 21
Enterprise System Architecture (ESA/370), 20, 213
Enterprise System Architecture (ESA/390), 20
Enterprise Systems CONnection (ESCON) Architecture, 23–24
ES/9000, 20

ESCON Multiple Image Facility (EMIF), 25
Extended Control (EC), 17
FIber CONnection (FICON) channels, 22–23, 24, 30, 31–32, 118–119
Generation 3 (G3) processor, 21
Generation 4 (G4) processor, 22
Generation 5 (G5) processor, 22, 31
Generation 6 (G6) processor, 22–23, 31
Integrated Cryptographic Feature (ICRF), 24, 333, 347
I/O Priority Queuing, 136
Logical PARtition (LPAR), 25
manuals on CD-ROM, 24
Modular Cooling Units (MCUs), 22, 29, 46
MonoLithic Circuit (MLC) technology, 16
MultiChip Module (MCM), 22, 40, 41, 42, 45, 47
Multiple Allegiance (MA), 136
multiprocessing configuration, 18
Open Software Foundation (OSF) standards, 25
overview, xv
Parallel Access Volumes (PAV), 136, 264
parallel processing, 21
parallel sysplex technology, 20
performance, 377
PS/SM facility, 24
RAMAC, 14, 123–131
roles for, 23
S/370 family, 16–20, 23
S/390 Cryptographic Facility, 24
S/390 Data Compression, 24
S/390 Multiprise 2000, 21, 22
S/390 Multiprise 3000, 366–367
S/390 Parallel Enterprise Server, 20–22
S/390 Parallel Query Server, 21
S/390 Parallel Transaction Server, 21
Solid Logic Technology (SLT), 16
SPREAD task force, 15–16
subsystem storage protection, 24
System/360 family, 16
vacuum tube technology, 14
virtual memory, 17
VM Data Spaces architecture, 24
z900 vs., 46, 48
SAF (Security Access Facility), 324
sales increase, 353
SAP, 8
SAP R/3, 180–181
SAP (System Assist Processor), 28, 41, 74

scalability of eservers, xviii, 9
SCM (Single Chip Module), 46
SCSI (Small Computer System Interface), 141, 155–156
SDLC (Synchronous Data Link Control), 90
SDM (System Data Mover), 343–344
SDSF (System Display and Search Facility), 234, 334, 336
Seascape technology, 141, 142
secure file access, VM/ESA, 260–261
Secure Network Server, 235
Secure Sockets Layer (SSL), 171, 320
SecureWay Communications Server, 238
SecureWay Security Server, 332
security
    management, 332–333
    OS/390, 235
    policies, 346, 347
    z900, 33–34
Security Access Facility (SAF), 324
Security Servers, 235, 347
Security Service, 230
Sequential Data Striping, 125, 223
sequential patterns, data mining, 204
sequential processing, 167
serial channels, 112
Serial Storage Architecture. *See* SSA
server, loss of, 61–62
server configurations, choosing, 323
Server Facilities, 218
ServerPac, 234
server systems, 85–87
serviceability achievement by coupling, 66–67
Service Information Messages (SIMs), 134
ServiceLink, 371
servicing a system, 369–371
SEs (Support Elements), 56, 57, 58
SFS (Shared File System), 255, 260
shared area of virtual storage, VSE/ESA, 266, 267, 269, 272
shared data environment, parallel processing, 59–64
Shared File System (SFS), 255, 260
Shared Queue Support, 67
"shares nothing" design, 58–59
"Shark" (Enterprise Storage Server, ESS), 135–136
shell, 260, 261
Short Wave Card, 33
SHUTDOWN command, 256
Siebel, 8, 172, 181

Signaling and Control Pane, 308
SIMs (Service Information Messages), 134
Single Chip Module (SCM), 46
Single Point of Contact (SPOC), 364
"single-system" image of parallel processing, 62
single-system sysplex configuration, 194
Single UNIX Specification, 231, 236
Single Virtual Storage (SVS). *See* Operating
    System/Virtual Storage 2 (OS/VS2)
SIPO (System Installation Productivity
    Option), VSE/ESA, 267
size of business and difficulties of, 85
"sleep" mode, 66
slicing (time sharing), 84
SLT (Solid Logic Technology), 16
Small Computer System Interface (SCSI),
    141, 155–156
SmoothStart for Domino, 190
SMP/E enhancements of OS/390, 234
SMP (Symmetric MultiProcessing), 27, 58
SMQ (IMS Shared Message Queue), 199
SnapShot, 127, 131
SNA (Systems Network Architecture)
    communications, 85, 86, 87, 90, 94,
        313, 316
    Local Area Networks (LANs), 284
    managing complexity, 324, 325
    MVS/ESA Version 5, 223
    Open Blueprint Network Services, 305,
        309
    Operating S/390 (OS/390), 235
Sockets, 261, 305–206
software, 161–282. *See also* application
    program development; application
    programs on S/390; operating
    systems; software for business;
    software licensing
    application program compatibility,
        162–163
    Application Programming Interface
        (API), 78, 79, 81, 162, 163, 164
    architecture, 162–163
    compatibility, 78, 162–163
    "connector" services, 167
    ESA/390 architecture, 162–163
    eservers and, 9
    frameworks, 163–167
    HTTP support, 166
    IIOP support, 166
    Independent Software Vendors (ISVs),
        162, 172
    instruction set, 162–163

JavaBeans, 95, 166
"just-in-time" delivery of components,
    166
maintenance costs, 350
Network Computing Framework (NCF),
    165–167
operating system compatibility, 163, 165
operating system layer, 77, 78, 79, 163,
    164
software cloning, 73
software for business, 77–80. *See also*
    application program development;
    application programs on S/390;
    operating systems; software;
    software licensing
application program layer, 77–79, 167,
    168
Application Programming Interface
    (API), 78, 79, 81, 162, 163, 164
compatibility, 78
Licensed Internal Code (LIC) layer, 75,
    77, 78, 80
operating system layer, 77, 78, 79, 163,
    164
"User's View," 77–78
software licensing, 355–363. *See also*
    vendor offering evaluation
Distributed System License Option
    (DSLO), 359
Enterprise Agreement, 356
Graduated Monthly License Charge
    (GMLC), 356, 358
Growth Opportunity License Charge
    (GOLC), 357, 365
IBM License Manager (ILM), 241,
    362–363
Indexed Monthly License Charge
    (IMLC), 356, 359
Integrated Facility for Linux (IFL), 28,
    29, 362
Internal Throughput Rate (ITR) for
    pricing, 100, 101, 355
leasing, 355
Measured Usage License Charge
    (MULC), 356
Million Service Units (MSUs) for
    pricing, 355
monthly charge for, 355
New Application License Charge
    (NALC), 365
One-Time Charge (OTC), 355, 360
Parallel Sysplex Licensing Charge
    (PSLC), 356, 357–359, 360–361

Parallel Transaction Server, 356
pricing strategies, 355–363
processor capacity for pricing, 355–356
throughput for pricing, 100–101, 167, 355
Workload Licensing Charges (WLC), 6, 241, 359–360, 361–362
Solid Logic Technology (SLT), 16
solution assurance of eservers, 7
SOM/DSOM (System Object Model/ Distributed SOM), 234
SOMobjects for MVS (System Object Model (SOM) objects for MVS), 232–233
SOM (System Object Model), 187
SONET (Synchronous Optical NETwork), 306
spatial reuse, SSA, 156–157, 160
Spec 1170, 231
SPOC (Single Point of Contact), 364
SPREAD task force, 15–16
SPXTAPE command, 256
SQL (Structured Query Language), 68, 196
SRAM (Static Random Access Memory), 37–38
SRM (Systems Resource Manager) inter- faces, simplified, 220
SSA (Serial Storage Architecture), 155–160
    application frame, 158
    bandwidth increase, 156–157
    control frame, 158
    dual-port architecture, 156–157
    frame routing, 157, 159–160
    full-duplex architecture, 157
    "hot plugging," 157–158
    initiator nodes, 159
    links, 156, 158, 159, 160
    Logical Units (LUs), 159
    loop-based interface, 155–156, 157
    master node, 159
    network characteristics, 158–159
    nodes, 156, 158–159
    overhead reduction, 157
    privileged frame, 158
    Small Computer System Interface (SCSI) vs., 141, 155–156
    spatial reuse, 156–157, 160
    string topology, 156
    switch topology, 156
    target nodes, 159
SSA (System Application Architecture) Common Programming Interface for Communications (CPI-C), 218

SSL (Secure Sockets Layer), 171, 320
Standalone Coupling Facility, 64, 65–66
static partitions, VSE/ESA, 270, 272–273, 274
Static Random Access Memory (SRAM), 37–38
storage frames, RAMAC, 123, 130
storage hierarchy, 49–55. *See also* External storage
    cache, 44, 45, 50–51
    central processors (CPs) and, 49
    central storage (main memory), 50, 51
    expanded storage, 35, 50, 51–52, 213–215
    I/O channel and, 107–108
    Level 1 (L1) cache, 41, 45, 50–51
    Level 2 (L2) cache, 44, 45, 51
    performance and, 49
    registers, 49–50
string topology, SSA, 156
Structured Query Language (SQL), 68, 196
structures, 66
subnetworking, Open Blueprint Network Services, 306–308
Subspace Group Facilities, 74–75, 256
substrates, 38, 43–44
subsystems and coupling, 65, 67–69
subsystem storage protection, 24, 74, 219, 256
Sun Microsystems, 188
Support Elements (SEs), 56, 57, 58
SupportLink, 371
support services, 189–190
SVC (Switched Virtual Circuits) dumps, 217
SVS (Single Virtual Storage). *See* Operating System/Virtual Storage 2 (OS/VS2)
Switched Virtual Circuits (SVC) dumps, 217
switches, LANs, 285
switching functions, ESCON channels, 113–114
switch topology, SSA, 156
Symmetric MultiProcessing (SMP), 27, 58
Synchronous Data Link Control (SDLC), 90
Synchronous Optical NETwork (SONET), 306
SYSMDUMPs, 217
Sysplex Distributor, 241, 242
sysplex support, MVS/ESA SP Version 4, 216–217
Sysplex Timer, 65, 71–72, 216

System Application Architecture (SSA)
Common Programming Interface
for Communications (CPI-C), 218
System Assist Processor (SAP), 28, 41, 74
System Automation, 327
System Data Mover (SDM), 343–344
System Display and Search Facility (SDSF),
234, 334, 336
System Installation Productivity Option
(SIPO), VSE/ESA, 267
system management, VM/ESA, 256
system management of eservers, 7–8
System Object Model (SOM), 187
System Object Model (SOM)/Distributed
SOM (DSOM), 234
System Object Model (SOM) objects for
MVS (SOMobjects for MVS),
232–233
system services of OS/390, 236
Systems Management, 299, 309, 310
systems management of OS/390, 236
Systems Network Architecture. *See* SNA
Systems Resource Manager (SRM) inter-
faces, simplified, 220

T
tag cable, 108, 110
TalkLink, 371
tape storage, 139–147
3490 Magnetic Tape Subsystems,
146–147
3494 Automated Tape Library (ATL)
Dataserver, 144–146
3590 High-Performance Tape Subsystem, 140–144
accessor service area, 145
Automated Cartridge System (ACS), 142
Automatic Cartridge Facility (ACF), 141
Automatic Cartridge Loader (ACL), 141
cache advantages, 144–145
compatibility, 143
Error Correction Code (ECC), 144
Improved Data Recording Capability
(IDRC), 146–147
Integrated Cartridge Loader (ICL), 141
interleaved longitudinal recording,
143–144
MagnetoResistive (MR) head technology, 123, 144
metal particle medium, 143
overview, 50, 55
parking area, 145
tape technology, 141, 142

Small Computer System Interface (SCSI),
141, 155–156
target nodes, SSA, 159
TCM (Thermal Conduction Module), 38,
39, 40
TCP/IP OTMA Connection (IMS TOC),
198, 199–200
TCP/IP (Transmission Control Protocol/
Internet Protocol)
communications, 87, 90, 94, 313
coupling, 69
MVS/ESA Version 5, 223
Open Blueprint Network Services, 305,
306, 309
Operating S/390 (OS/390), 235–236,
237
Virtual Machine/Enterprise System
Architecture (VM/ESA), 258, 264
Virtual Storage Extended/Enterprise
System Architecture (VSE/ESA),
276
z/OS Version 1, Release 1 (OS/390
Version 2, Release 10), 241–242
TeamConnection DataAtlas, 202
technical support costs, 351
technology vs. information, xvii–xviii
TEC (TME 10 Enterprise Console), 332
Telnet support of OS/390, 237
Terminal Owning Regions (TORs), 67
term leases, 354
Thermal Conduction Module (TCM), 38,
39, 40
three-tier client/server implementation, 180
throughput, 100–101, 167, 355
Time-Of-Day (TOD) clocks, 65, 71
Time Service, 230
Time Sharing Option/Extensions (TSO/E),
223
time sharing (slicing), 84
Tivoli. *See* TME 10
Tivoli Management Agent, 238
Tivoli Storage Manager, 225, 227, 328–329
Tivoli TME 10 Framework, 236
TKE (Trusted Key Entry) support of OS/390,
235
TME 10 Enterprise Console (TEC), 332
TME 10 GEM Application Policy Manager
(APM), 331–332
TME 10 Global Enterprise Manager
(GEM), 331
TME 10 Information/Management, 331–332
TME 10 NetView (NetView), 294–295,
296, 324–327

TO copy, 135, 136
TOD (Time-Of-Day) clocks, 65, 71
token-ring networks, 90–92, 285–289
Token-Ring Processor (TRP), 315, 316
TORs (Terminal Owning Regions), 67
Torvalds, Linus, 278–279
TPC (Transaction Processing Performance
    Council), 99, 102
TPF (Transaction Processing Facility),
    280–281
tps/m (transactions per second/minute), 102
track caching, RAMAC, 126
training costs, 351, 368–369
transaction processing, 167
transaction-processing application enablers,
    190, 193–195
Transaction Processing Facility (TPF),
    280–281
Transaction Processing Performance
    Council (TPC), 99, 102
Transaction Security System, 333
transactions per second/minute (tps/m),
    102
Transmission Control Protocol/Internet
    Protocol. *See* TCP/IP
Transparent Services Access Facility
    (TSAF), 252
Transport Services, Open Blueprint
    Network Services, 299, 306–309
trimodel addressing, z900, 34–35
Trojan horse, 346
TRP (Token-Ring Processor), 315, 316
Trusted Key Entry (TKE) support of OS/390,
    235
TSAF (Transparent Services Access Facility),
    252
TSO/E (Time Sharing Option/Extensions),
    223
Turbo Dispatcher, 275–276
twisted-pair (two-wire) cable, 92, 285

U
Ultimedia Manager, 203–204
Ultrastar 2XP disk drive, 123, 130
Unattended Option of NetView, 325
Uninterruptible Power System (UPS), 73
Universal Processor Controller (UPC), 45
University of California at Berkeley, 121
UNIX application support
    OS/390, 236–237
    parallel processing and, 59
    Virtual Machine/Enterprise System
        Architecture (VM/ESA), 263

UNIX Services, 227–232. *See also* MVS/
    ESA (Multiple Virtual Storage/
    Enterprise System Architecture)
ASCII terminal support, 231–232
C language and, 228, 229, 231, 234,
    236–237
Directory Service, 230
Distributed Computing Environment
    (DCE), 229, 230
Hierarchical File System (HFS), 229,
    231
IBM Networking Blueprint, 228
integrated sockets, 230, 231
interoperability, 228
Network File System (NFS), 229–230
Network Queuing System/MVS
    (NQS/MVS), 231
Open Blueprint Network Services, 228,
    232, 305–306
Open Software Foundation's Distributed
    Computing Environment
    (OSF/DCE), 230
open systems importance, 227–228
OS/390 and, 234–235, 238
portability, 228
Portable Operating System Interface
    (POSIX) standards, 228–231
Remote Procedure Call (RPC), 230,
    236
Security Service, 230
Single UNIX Specification, 231, 236
Spec 1170, 231
Time Service, 230
X/Open Distributed Computing
    Services, 228
X/Open Portability Guides (XPG), 228,
    263
XPG4 Base Specification support, 220,
    231, 263
UNIX Services (OpenEdition MVS), 94–95
UPC (Universal Processor Controller), 45
upgrade paths, 373–375
UPS, 4
UPS (Uninterruptible Power System), 73
U.S. Postal Service, 4
"User's View," 77–78

V
vacuum tube technology, 14
VAE (Virtual Addressability Extensions)
    feature, 268–269, 270
Vector Facility enhancements, MVS/ESA SP
    Version 4, 219

vendor offering evaluation, 349–372. *See also* cost justification; software licensing
  buying vs. leasing, 353–355
  capital leases, 354
  configuration options, 366–367
  e-Business Start New Program, 364–367
  education, 351, 368–369
  electronic mail of IBMLink, 371
  financing purchases, 354
  Growth Opportunity License Charge (GOLC), 357, 365
  hardware, leasing or buying, 353–355
  IBM Global Services (IGS), 181, 367–368
  IBMLink, 370–371
  IBM Teach, 369
  InfoLink, 370
  integrated offerings, 363–367
  leases vs. buying, 353–355
  maintenance, 370
  networking IBM Global Services, 367–368
  New Application License Charge (NALC), 365
  operating ("rent-to-own") leases, 354
  OrderLink, 370
  overview, 349
  parallel server offerings, 363–364
  product support IBM Global Services, 367
  professional IBM Global Services, 367
  renting, 354–355
  S/390 Customized Solutions, 363–364
  S/390 Multiprise 3000, 366–367
  ServiceLink, 371
  servicing a system, 369–371
  Single Point of Contact (SPOC), 364
  SupportLink, 371
  TalkLink, 371
  term leases, 354
  training, 351, 368–369
  warranties, 370
VES/VSAM for VM, 259
VIF (Virtual Image Facility), 28, 29
VIO (Virtual I/O), 221
VIPA (Virtual Internet Protocol Addressing), 241–242
Virtual Addressability Extensions (VAE) feature, 268–269, 270
Virtual Image Facility (VIF), 28, 29
Virtual Internet Protocol Addressing (VIPA), 241–242
  '/O (VIO), 221

Virtual Lookaside Facility (VLF) NOTE command (VLFNOTE), 217
Virtual Machine/Enterprise System Architecture. *See* VM/ESA
Virtual Machine Serviceability Enhancements Staged/Extended (VMSES/E), 253
virtual memory, 17
virtual storage, 209
Virtual Storage Access Method (VSAM), 67, 68, 257
Virtual Storage Extended/Enterprise System Architecture. *See* VSE/ESA
Virtual Storage Extended/System Package (VSE/SP), 267–269
Virtual Telecommunications Access Method (VTAM), 68, 289
viruses, 345
VisualAge, 184
VisualAge Object Connection program, 189–190
VisualGen, 188
Visualizer, 203
VisualLift, 234
Visual Warehouse, 202
VLFNOTE (Virtual Lookaside Facility NOTE command), 217
VM Data Spaces architecture, 24
VM/ESA (Virtual Machine/Enterprise System Architecture), 246–264. *See also* operating systems
  64-bit architecture support, 263–264
  access-register addressing, 254–255
  Advanced Communications Function/ Virtual Telecommunications Access Method (ACF/VTAM), 252, 258, 277–278
  Advanced Program-to-Program Communications (APPC), 252
  APPC/VM Virtual Telecommunications Access Method Support (AVS), 252
  Asynchronous Data Mover Facility (ADMF), 256
  Asynchronous Pageout Facility support, 256
  Byte File System (BFS), 260
  caching, 256
  Cell Directory Service (CDS), 262
  client/server computing support, 246
  CMS Pipelines, 252
  common access tool (VMLINK), 256
  compression of data, 257
  Control Program-40 (CP-40), 249–250

Control Program (CP), 248, 249, 251, 253, 257
Conversational Monitor System (CMS), 248, 251, 255, 257, 260–261
data sharing, 254–255
data spaces, 254, 255
Directory Maintenance (DirMaint), 259
Distributed Computing Environment (DCE) support, 259, 261–262
"Distributed VM" capability, 256
Dump Viewing Facility, 253
dynamic partitioning, 257
Enterprise Systems Architecture/ eXtended Configuration (ESA/XC), 254, 255
ESCON channel support, 255–256
ESCON Multiple Image Facility (EMIF) support, 255–256
evolution of, 248–251
expanded virtual storage, 253–254
eXtended Architecture (XA), 250–251
Fixed Block Architecture (FBA), 251
Flash Copy support, 264
fork() function, 260, 263
Graphical User Interface (GUI), 257–258
Group Control System (GCS), 251, 257
guest operating system support, 247–248, 256
interactive computing support, 246
LAN File Services/ESA, 258
LAN Resource Extension and Services (LANRES), 258
LOGON BY function, 256
migration, 243–244
network computing support, 262
Open Blueprint Network Services, 261
OpenEdition for VM/ESA, 259–262
Open Systems Adapter (OSA) support, 256–257
overview, 246, 247
Parallel Access Volumes (PAV) support, 264
parallel sysplex testing support, 262
pipelines, 252
Portable Operating System Interface (POSIX) standards, 260–261
POWEROFF option, 256
Queued Direct I/O (QDIO), 264
Real-Time Monitor (RTM) VM/ESA, 264
Remote Procedure Call (RPC), 261–262
Remote Spooling Communications Subsystem (RSCS), 258–259

resource management of, 246
REstructured eXtended eXecutor (REXX/VSE) language, 252, 278
secure file access, 260–261
Shared File System (SFS), 255, 260
shell, 260, 261
SHUTDOWN command, 256
Sockets support, 261
SPXTAPE command, 256
Subspace Group Facilities, 256
Subsystem Storage Protection support, 256
system management, 256
Transmission Control Protocol/Internet Protocol (TCP/IP), 258, 264
Transparent Services Access Facility (TSAF), 252
UNIX application support, 263
Version 1, 251–253, 256
Version 2, 252, 256–259
Version 2, Release 1, 259–262
Version 2, Release 3.0, 262–263
VES/VSAM for VM, 259
Virtual Machine Serviceability Enhancements Staged/Extended (VMSES/E), 253
Virtual Storage Access Method (VSAM), 67, 68, 257
VM Performance Reporting Facility (VM PRF), 264
VM/SP, 250, 251
VM/SP High-Performance Option (HPO), 250, 251
VM Workstation Agent, 257–258
VM/XA, 251
z/Architecture support, 263–264
z/VM Version 3, Release 1, 263–264
VMLINK (common access tool), 256
VM Performance Reporting Facility (VM PRF), 264
VM PRF (VM Performance Reporting Facility), 264
VMSES/E (Virtual Machine Serviceability Enhancements Staged/Extended), 253
VM/SP, 250, 251
VM/SP High-Performance Option (HPO), 250, 251
VM Workstation Agent, 257–258
VM/XA, 251
VNET, 2–3
VSAM (Virtual Storage Access Method), 67, 68, 257

VSE/Advanced Functions (VSE/AF), 277
VSE/ESA (Virtual Storage Extended/
    Enterprise System Architecture),
    264–278. *See also* operating
    systems
  24-bit addressing, 274
  31-bit addressing, 272, 273
  access-register addressing, 272, 273
  Advanced Peer-to-Peer Networking
      (APPN) support, 278
  Central Electronic Complex (CEC), 275
  CICS Transaction Server, 277
  Cross-Partition Communication Control
      (XPCC), 269, 270, 272
  data sharing, 266, 267, 269, 272, 274
  data spaces, 272, 273, 274
  Disk Operating System (DOS) and,
      264–267
  Dynamic Channel Subsystem, 272
  dynamic partitions, 269–271, 273, 274
  ESCON Director support, 274
  evolution of, 264–269
  Fast Service Upgrade (FSU) feature, 268,
      276
  hardware compression, 276
  Installation Productivity Option (IPO),
      267
  logical integration of software, 268
  nonparallel work units, 276
  Open Blueprint Network Services, 276
  parallel work units, 276
  partitions, 267, 269–270, 272–273, 277
  physical integration of software, 267
  shared area of virtual storage, 266, 267,
      269, 272
  static partitions, 270, 272–273, 274
  System Installation Productivity Option
      (SIPO), 267
  Systems Network Architecture (SNA),
      277
  Transmission Control Protocol/Internet
      Protocol (TCP/IP), 276
  Turbo Dispatcher, 275–276
  Version 1, 269–275
  Version 2, 275–277
  Virtual Addressability Extensions (VAE)
      feature, 268–269, 270
  Virtual Storage Extended/System
      Package (VSE/SP) and, 267–269
  VSE/Advanced Functions (VSE/AF), 277
  Interactive Compute and Control
      Facility (VSE/ICCF), 278
  POWER, 277

VSE/System Product, 277
VSE/Virtual Storage Access Method
    (VSE/VSAM), 277
VSE Workdesk, 276
VSE/ICCF (VSE/Interactive Compute and
    Control Facility), 278
VSE/Interactive Compute and Control
    Facility (VSE/ICCF), 278
VSE/POWER, 277
VSE/SP (Virtual Storage Extended/System
    Package), 267–269
VSE/System Product, 277
VSE/Virtual Storage Access Method
    (VSE/VSAM), 277
VSE/VSAM (VSE/Virtual Storage Access
    Method), 277
VSE Workdesk, 276
VTAM (Virtual Telecommunications Access
    Method), 68, 289

W
WANs (Wide Area Networks), 306, 309
WAP (Wireless Application Protocol), 172
warranties, 370
Watson, Thomas J., Sr., xvi
Web application workloads, e-business, 5
Web connectivity, 199–200
Web site for zSeries and S/390, xx
WebSphere Application Server
    cross-industry application programs,
        170–171, 235, 237, 238
    data warehouses, 203
    eserver Advantages, 8
    Operating S/390 (OS/390), 170–171,
        235, 237, 238
Web Usage Mining, 235
Wide Area Networks (WANs), 306, 309
Wireless Application Protocol (WAP), 172
WITT (Workstation Interactive Test Tool),
    187
WLC (Workload Licensing Charges), 6,
    241, 359–360, 361–362
WLM (WorkLoad Manager)
    application enablers, 199
    coupling, 67
    MVS/ESA Version 5, 219–220
    Operating S/390 (OS/390), 234, 236,
        237
    parallel processing, 62
    z/OS Version 1, Release 1 (OS/390
        Version 2, Release 10), 239–240
working set management, MVS/ESA SP
    Version 4, 218

workload
>balancing, 61–62, 112
>categories of e-business, 5–6
>environments and performance, 101, 102
>management, 333–334, 335
Workload Licensing Charges (WLC), 6,
>241, 359–360, 361–362
WorkLoad Manager. *See* WLM
Workstation Interactive Test Tool (WITT
>and X/WITT), 187
workstations on LANs, 286–287, 289
worms, 345
Write-Once, Read-Many (WORM), 137
write-once optical storage, 55
"write penalty," 122

X
X.25 protocol, 90, 317
XA (eXtended Architecture), 250–251
XCF (Cross System Coupling Facility), 63,
>217, 304
XDF (eXtended Distance Feature), 110
XES (Cross System Extended Services), 199
XML (eXtensible Mark-Up Language), 8,
>172
X/Open Corporation, Ltd., 231
X/Open Distributed Computing Services,
>228
X/Open Portability Guides (XPG), 228, 263
X/Open Single UNIX Specification support,
>MVS/ESA Version 5, 220–221
XPCC (Cross-Partition Communication
>Control), 269, 270, 272
XPE (Cross Platform Extension), 131
XPG4 Base Specification support, 220, 231,
>263
XPG (X/Open Portability Guides), 228, 263
XRC (eXtended Remote Copy), 71, 134,
>136, 343–344
xSeries, 11–12

Z
z900 family, 25–35. *See also* I/O subsystem
>channels and adapters; zSeries and
>S/390 families
>64-bit operating system support, 25,
>>34–35, 36
>capacity server models (Models 1C1-
>>1C9), 27, 28
>Capacity Upgrade on Demand (CUoD),
>>6, 22, 28, 76–77
>Central Processor (CP), 28
>connectivity options, 69–70

Coupling Facility (CF), 65–66
Coupling Facility (CF) model (Model
>100), 27, 28
Cryptographic Coprocessors, 9, 33–34
Cryptographic Element (CE), 46
Data Encryption Standard (DES), 33,
>333
Dual Peripheral Component Intercon-
>nect Cryptographic Coprocessor
>(Dual PCICC), 34
ESCON channels and, 112
Federal Information Processing Standard
>(FIPS), 33
general-purpose models (Models
>101-116), 27, 28
HiPerLinks, 70
Integrated Coupling Facility (ICF), 28
Integrated Facility for Linux (IFL), 28,
>29, 362
Linux operating system support, 8,
>28–29, 278–280
model structure, 27–28
performance, 25, 27, 377
Processor Unit (PU) MCM, 25, 26, 28
S/390 vs., 46, 48
security, 33–34
Single Chip Module (SCM), 46
Symmetric MultiProcessors (SMPs), 27,
>58
System Assist Processor (SAP), 28, 41,
>74
trimodel addressing, 34–35
upgrade paths, 373–375
Virtual Image Facility (VIF), 28, 29
z/Architecture, 25, 34–35, 36
z/Architecture
>Virtual Machine/Enterprise System
>>Architecture (VM/ESA), 263–264
>z900 family, 25, 34–35, 36
>z/OS Version 1, Release 1 (OS/390
>>Version 2, Release 10), 238–239,
>>242
>zSeries and S/390 families, 35, 36, 52
Z-Frame, 31
z/OS Version 1, Release 1 (OS/390 Version
>2, Release 10), 238–245
>64-bit architecture support, 238–239,
>>242
>Channel Subsystem Priority Queuing,
>>240
>coexistence, 244, 245
>Dynamic Channel Path Management,
>>240

ease-of-manageability, 240–241
IBM License Manager (ILM), 241,
    362–363
Intelligent Resource Director (IRD),
    239–240
LPAR coexistence, 244, 245
LPAR CPU Management, 239–240
migration considerations, 242–244
msys for Setup, 240–241
OS/390 migration, 242–243
overview, 13–14, 238
Sysplex Distributor, 241, 242
Transmission Control Protocol/Internet
    Protocol (TCP/IP) enhancements,
    241–242
Virtual Internet Protocol Addressing
    (VIPA), 241–242
VM/ESA migration, 243–244
Workload Licensing Charges (WLC), 241
WorkLoad Manager (WLM), 239–240
z/Architecture support, 238–239, 242
z/VM migration, 243–244
centralized support, xv
Central Storage (CS), 35
choosing server configurations, 323
computing power, today's vs. yesterday's,
    xvi
Coupling Facility mode, 35, 52
cryptography, xvi
direct retailing and multimedia, 97
distributed computer communications
    with, 295–296, 297
distributed support, xv
Dynamic Storage Reconfiguration
    (DSR), 35
enterprise multimedia capability, 97–98
ESA/390 Architecture mode, 35
Expanded Storage (ES), 35

Fiber Saver (2029), 72
folder management and multimedia, 97
global interconnected society demands
    and, xv–xvii
Hardware Management Console
    (HMC), 56–57, 58
historical background, xv–xx
information vs. technology, xvii–xviii
insurance claims handling and multime-
    dia, 97–98
Integrated Cluster Bus (ICB) links, 36
Logical PARtition (LPAR) mode, 35
mainframe computers, xv
media inventory and multimedia, 98
motor insurance claims handling and
    multimedia, 97–98
multimedia capability, 97–98
operating modes, 35–36, 52
overview, 10
performance, 377
personal computers (PCs), xv
Power-On-Reset (POR), 35
Power Service and Control Network
    (PSCN), 56
processor controller, 56–57
Remote Support Facility, 56
retailing and multimedia, 97
S/390 servers, xv
scalability demand, xviii, 9
server configurations, choosing, 323
Support Elements (SEs), 56, 57, 58
technology vs. information, xvii–xviii
upgrade paths, 373–375
Web site for, xx
z/Architecture mode, 35, 36, 52
z/VM migration, 243–244
z/VM Version 3, Release 1, 263–264

Reader Feedback Sheet

Your comments and suggestions are very important in shaping future publications. Please email us at *moreinfo@maxpress.com* or photocopy this page, jot down your thoughts, and fax it to (850) 934-9981 or mail it to:

Maximum Press

Attn: Jim Hoskins

605 Silverthorn Road

Gulf Breeze, FL 32561

_____

_____

_____

_____

_____

_____

_____

_____

_____

_____

_____

_____

_____

_____

_____

_____

_____

_____

101 Internet Businesses You Can Start From Home
by Susan Sweeney, C.A.
520 pages
$29.95
ISBN: 1-885068-28-X

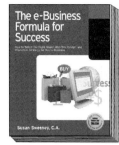

e-Business Formula for Success
by Susan Sweeney, C.A.
360 pages
$34.95
ISBN: 1-885068-60-3

Exploring IBM RS/6000 Computers, Tenth Edition
by Jim Hoskins and Doug Davies
440 pages
$39.95
ISBN: 1-885068-42-5

Exploring IBM @server iSeries and AS/400 Computers, Tenth Edition
by Jim Hoskins and Roger Dimmick
560 pages
$39.95
ISBN: 1-885068-43-3

Exploring IBM S/390 Computers, Seventh Edition
by Jim Hoskins and Bob Frank
432 pages
$59.95
ISBN: 1-885068-70-0

Exploring IBM Network Stations
by Eddie Ho, Dana Lloyd, and Stephanos Heracleous
223 pages
$39.95
ISBN: 1-885068-32-8

Exploring IBM @server xSeries and PCs, Eleventh Edition
by Jim Hoskins and Bill Wilson
432 pages
$39.95
ISBN: 1-885068-39-5

Exploring IBM Technology, Products & Services, Fourth Edition
edited by Jim Hoskins
256 pages
$54.95
ISBN: 1-885068-62-X

To purchase a Maximum Press book, visit your local bookstore
or call 1-800-989-6733 (US/Canada) or 1-850-934-4583 (International)
online ordering available at *www.maxpress.com*